Chicago Public Library

R0401685548

They cleared the lane : the NBA's Black

SOCIAL SCIENCE DIVISION
CHICAGO PUBLIC LIBRARY
STREET

D0665842

DISCARD

SOCIAL SCIENCE DIVISION
CHICAGO PUBLIC LIBRARY
400 SOUTH STATE STREET
CHICAGO, IL 60605

DISCARD

They Cleared the Lane

THE NBA'S BLACK PIONEERS

Ron Thomas

UNIVERSITY OF NEBRASKA PRESS   •   LINCOLN AND LONDON

© 2002 by the
University of Nebraska
Press
All rights reserved
Manufactured in
the United States of
America

First Nebraska
paperback printing:
2004
Library of Congress
Cataloging-in-
Publication Data
Thomas, Ron.
They cleared the
lane: The NBA's
Black pioneers / Ron
Thomas.
p. cm.
Includes bibliograph-
ical references and
index. ISBN 0-8032-
9454-9 (paper: alk.
paper) ISBN 0-8032-
4437-1 (cloth: alk.
paper)
1. Basketball—
United States—
History. 2. African
American basketball
players—History. 3.
National Basketball
Association—History.
I. Title: NBA's Black
pioneers. II. Title.
GV885.7 .T46 2002
796.323'64'08996073—
dc21
2001052234

Portions of this manu-
script have been previously published as "College of
Marin Star Fought beyond
Basketball Court" (July 15,
1996) and "Trailblazing
Black Players" (February 7,
2000) in the *Marin
Independent Journal,* ©
*Marin Independent
Journal,* reprinted with
permission; and as the
series of articles "Basketball's Black Pioneers"
(February 16–18, 1987) in
the *San Francisco
Chronicle,* © *San
Francisco Chronicle,*
reprinted with permis-
sion.

SOCIAL SCIENCE DIVISION
CHICAGO PUBLIC LIBRARY
400 SOUTH STATE STREET
CHICAGO, IL 60605

R040048554B DISCARD

To my father, Laughton F. Thomas, to my wife and my daughter, Iris and Kali, and to my favorite basketball pioneers—Al Attles, Don Barksdale, Pop Gates, Earl Lloyd, John McLendon, and Zelda Spoelstra

Contents

Illustrations

Preface

In twenty-eight years of sportswriting I've read thousands of sports articles, whether it was while checking over my own writing (and enduring next-day paranoia as I compared my story to those written by my peers), or while perusing a newspaper's sports section just for fun. Of them all, the one article that had the greatest impact on my life was a wire service story about Chuck Cooper, an obscure former NBA forward who played for four teams during his six-year professional basketball career.

The *San Francisco Chronicle,* my employer at the time, ran that article in 1978 for one reason only: in 1950 Cooper became the first black player drafted by an NBA team when the Boston Celtics selected him on the second round of the draft. Although I'd been a sports fan all my life and a sportswriter for several years, I'm not sure I had ever before read anything about Cooper beyond his name and historical significance. That day I told my sports editor, Mike Berger, that I wanted to interview Cooper and the other black players who had integrated the NBA.

I assumed that every sports fan knew something about Jackie Robinson breaking baseball's color barrier in 1947 but, like me, most fans knew nothing about whether the NBA's black pioneers were welcomed or scorned by teammates, opponents, and fans; whether they were pursued or shunned by team owners and coaches; or if they felt gratified or frustrated during their pro careers. One thing was certain—whoever they were, their names and histories were virtually unknown.

I added "contact Chuck Cooper" to the "do someday" list I carry around in my brain. In 1982, when I interviewed for a job as *USA Today*'s first NBA reporter, I brought along a wish list of story ideas that I thought would suit a national publication. Writing about the NBA's first black players fit perfectly, but once I secured the job, the story of Cooper and his fellow pioneers didn't make the cut. Contemporary news—such as rookie Dominique Wilkins's rim-bending dunks or Moses Malone helping Julius Erving win his first NBA championship—took precedence.

Scrolling through wire service reports on February 6, 1984, I was stunned to read that Cooper had died the previous day in Pittsburgh at age fifty-seven. My first reaction was regret that I hadn't interviewed him before he died. My second reaction was, "I'd better get started on this story. These players may not be alive much longer." Thus began the sixteen-year journey that culminated in my writing this book. Mostly it was written to satisfy my own curiosity about black players of a half-century ago who joined a league that then had only white players but today has a league roster that is more than 80 percent black. My discovery of how and why that transformation began turned out to be a fascinating exploration of the NBA's evolution that coincided with a struggle in the United States over racial acceptance.

For someone who has enjoyed studying history since I was a child, this book has been the ultimate connect-the-dots pursuit. I believe that if I can understand why event A occurred, then my comprehension of event B can't be far behind and, I hope, neither will the reader's.

A few months after Cooper died I returned to work for the *San Francisco Chronicle* and began researching and conducting interviews for a series of articles about the first two years that black players were in the NBA, 1950 and 1951. I quickly learned that almost no "research" needed to be done because hardly anything had been written about those first six players: Chuck Cooper, Earl Lloyd, Nat "Sweetwater" Clifton, Hank DeZonie, Don Barksdale, and Davage Minor. [A few years later I learned of a seventh player, Bob Wilson.] Constructing that history depended on piecing together the memories of those players with the memories of people who had been associated with them during their college and NBA careers, in addition to the few facts already gathered by the NBA. There weren't many facts to be found, but among those items were a few historical nuggets of gold—such as a copy of both the 1950 league schedule and the original box score (written in longhand) of the first league game in which a black player appeared.

Those two gems of information, provided by the NBA's Terry Lyons, helped settle the main question raised by my eleven-part series of stories that appeared in the *Chronicle* in 1987: Who was the NBA's "first" black player? The answer depends upon the interpretation of the question. If it means, who was the first to be drafted in

1950? the answer is Chuck Cooper. If it means, who was the first to actually play in a game? the answer is Earl Lloyd. If it means, who was the first to sign an NBA contract? the answer is Harold Hunter (who, along with Lloyd, was drafted by the Washington Capitols only to be cut during training camp).

I conducted interviews for the series during numerous road trips while covering the Golden State Warriors from 1984 to 1987. I have a vivid memory of Lloyd, a former six-foot-six, 220-pound power forward, as he entered my hotel room, still physically imposing at fifty-seven in a top coat that warmed him on a Detroit winter day. Lloyd not only recalled numerous events in his basketball career; he had a historian's ability to frame those events in the racial context of the times. He was acutely aware of America's racial hypocrisy, having been raised in segregated Alexandria, Virginia, adjacent to the nation's capital of Washington DC, the supposed beacon of freedom and justice.

Not everything went smoothly, of course. In Chicago I arranged to meet Nat Clifton, a Harlem Globetrotters star before signing with the New York Knicks. By the 1980s he was driving a cab in his hometown while caring for his elderly mother and other family members. Clifton was late for our scheduled interview, then called to cancel for reasons I can't remember. When I returned home we talked on the telephone for about half an hour—informative but frustrating because I sensed that had we met in person we would have talked for a couple of hours. That face-to-face chat never occurred before he died in 1990.

One of the best surprises in my journalism career occurred a couple days before that three-day series was published. I had called John McLendon, a distinguished black college basketball coach who had accompanied Lloyd and Hunter to their Washington Capitols tryout, to double-check some facts. At the time I believed Cooper, Lloyd, and Clifton had been the NBA's only black players in 1950. As we talked, McLendon casually mentioned that there had been a fourth player, Hank DeZonie, whose name I had never heard. After our conversation I searched the NBA *Basketball Encyclopedia* and found the record of DeZonie's NBA career—all five games of it. A brief telephone interview about DeZonie's pioneering effort led to his appearance, by sheer luck, in the series, which caused me to wonder what other facts about the NBA's first black players needed to be unearthed.

The series was published while I was away on a Warriors road trip. I had left San Francisco concerned about how readers would react to it: Would they ignore it because the players involved were relatively unknown? Would I get hostile letters as I had in 1980 when I, a black writer, had had the gall to write a column criticizing white superstar Larry Bird after he had ducked the media during the NCAA Tournament?

The answer came when I returned home to a long list of phone messages and a small stack of readers' letters. Each one praised the series, with some adding personal remembrances about the players or suggesting other related story lines that would have fit with the series. (One of those letters provided the seed of this book's chapter about Cleo Hill.) Controversial columnists usually stir up such reactions; beat writers almost never do. I was gratefully shocked by the response to the series and started thinking about expanding it into a book, and thus began eleven years of futility. I looked for grants that would pay me to take a few months' leave from my job, but scholarly foundations almost never fund sports projects. (When I learned that one foundation turned down my grant request but funded another that explored the spawning habits of salmon, I knew I was in trouble.) Despite the enormous popularity of pro sports, I found that publishers had little interest in producing sports books except for ones about America's pastime, baseball, or superstars' biographies. I worked with two diligent agents; wrote, rewrote, and mailed three sets of proposals; and suffered through the reading of thirty-three rejection letters from commercial and academic presses without securing a publisher.

In 1998 Jules Tygiel, a friend who had authored a popular biography of Jackie Robinson, suggested four academic presses that had begun to publish sports books. I followed Tygiel's suggestions about how to improve my proposal and sent that revision to the four publishers he had named. Three turned it down, but Dan Ross, the director of the University of Nebraska Press, called me after he had read the proposal and bubbled with enthusiasm for my project. I'd been waiting for a Dan Ross for a decade! Armed with the knowledge that my book actually would get published, I began working on it with a purpose and a vague deadline. "Don't rush," Dan said. "This book will be around for a long time. We want you to write the best book you can."

That's what I've done during the longest, most significant adventure of my life. Like learning about DeZonie for the first time, I've encountered many surprising discoveries along the way.

While visiting the Basketball Hall of Fame I found articles about the true first black pro basketball player, Bucky Lew. Leonard Koppett, one of the New York Knicks' original beat writers, recommended that I call one of his peers, Leonard Lewin, who suggested that I call Fred Podesta, who had been the Knicks' longtime business manager. Podesta had a sharp memory and priceless records about the signing of Sweetwater Clifton. It was fortunate for me to get Podesta's name when I did because he died shortly after our interview.

At St. Francis College in Loretta, Pennsylvania, a serene little "postcard" town, I was uplifted by how the memory of Maurice Stokes, whose early death is one of pro sports' saddest tragedies, has been preserved with extraordinary care. In nearby Pittsburgh I was treated like a family member by Chuck Cooper's widow, Irva, and their son, Charles Cooper III, was welcomed warmly at Monk's & Barb's Lounge (the favorite hangout of Stokes's best friend, Ed Fleming), and was nourished by Mrs. Fleming's delicious lima bean soup.

The day I interviewed the NBA's winningest coach, Lenny Wilkens, in Atlanta presented the strangest juxtaposition of pro basketball past and present. Out of curiosity I joined the circle of reporters huddling around the immature guard J. R. Rider after he had returned to the Atlanta Hawks following one of his suspensions. I then interviewed Wilkens, one of only two people inducted into the Basketball Hall of Fame both as a player and as a coach. (John Wooden is the other.) I remember thinking that the matchup of Rider, a prime example of youthful irresponsibility, with Wilkens, reliable as a metronome, would never work . . . one prediction I got right.

Of the many destinations the black basketball pioneers led me to, none was more personally meaningful than West Virginia State College. While writing one of my early proposals, a librarian there, Elizabeth Scobell, and I figured out that my late father, Laughton Thomas, had attended West Virginia State in the 1931–32 school year. As a child I knew he had gone to Howard University and then transferred to another school, but that was all I knew. When I visited the campus in 1999 two archivists found a yearbook that contains a photo of my dad and his Kappa Alpha Phi fraternity brothers. That gave me a deeply emotional connection to the campus as I walked down its pathways, visited its gym, and watched a Yellowjackets football game on a Saturday afternoon, just as my sports-loving father probably had done sixty-eight years earlier.

Considering the sprinkling of black NBA players in the league's embryonic years, any book about the 1950s and early 1960s must be filled in with pivotal white characters. Abe Saperstein, the originator of the Harlem Globetrotters, was a controversial power broker of the times. Team owners Ned Irish and Dan Biasone were racially conflicted—as American society was at the time—as they both fostered the NBA's integration and slowed its progress. There were other white NBA figures—notably Bob Cousy, Dick Schnittker, Bones McKinney, and Walter Brown—who extended friendship, affirmation, or opportunity to black players when it was needed most.

I could not have spent sixteen years researching and writing this book without receiving ideas and support from more people than I could ever name here, but a few contributions were especially valuable. Some were acknowledged in the dedication, but several others deserve special recognition: University at Albany basketball coach Scott Beeten, who convinced me of the importance of the Eastern League; Basketball Hall of Fame librarian-archivist Doug Stark and the NBA's public relations staff, for their research efforts; Zelda Spoelstra, for her unending willingness to contact former NBA players; Dr. David Telfer and numerous staff members at West Virginia State College; sports journalists Leonard Koppett and Jules Tygiel; and Mike Brown, Lowell Cohn, and Cliff Daughtry, close friends who tolerated my sixteen-year obsession with this book.

Two personal mentors must be mentioned here, friends whose contributions were indirect yet essential, both of whom died years ago: Charles Dickerson, my Black Student Union adviser at the University of Rochester, and Charles "C. D." Henry, the former assistant commissioner of the Big Ten. Both gave me insights into the lives and history of black people that helped shape my interests as a journalist. If not for them the article I read about Chuck Cooper twenty-two years ago might not have led to this book.

Trailblazing Black Players

A Chronology

1902   Bucky Lew becomes the first black professional player, getting paid $5.00 to play for Lowell, Massachusetts, in the New England Basketball League.

1923   Bob Douglas originates the New York Renaissance touring team. The team becomes known as the Rens.

1927   Abe Saperstein's Harlem Globetrotters play their first game outside Chicago, in Hinckley, Illinois.

1933   March 27, Original Celtics end New York Rens' eighty-eight-game winning streak.

1935   Hank Williams plays center for the Buffalo Bisons in the Midwest Basketball Conference.

1939   Rookie Pop Gates leads the Rens to the first World Professional Basketball Tournament title in Chicago.

1941   The Globetrotters succeed the Rens as world champs.

1942   The Chicago Studebaker Champions of the National Basketball League NBL formed as first thoroughly integrated professional team (four white, six black players).

1946   Founding of the Basketball Association of America (BAA), later the core of the NBA.

1947   The BAA rejects the Rens' request to be admitted as a franchise.

1948   Playing serious basketball, the Globetrotters defeat the champion Minneapolis Lakers on Ermer Robinson's long shot at the buzzer.

1949   The BAA and the NBL complete their merger, thus forming the NBA.

1950   April 25, Boston drafts Chuck Cooper; Washington drafts Earl Lloyd and Harold Hunter.

1950   May 3, Knicks purchase Sweetwater Clifton's contract from the Globetrotters for $12,500.

1950   October 31, Earl Lloyd becomes the first black NBA player.

1953   Former Marin Junior College star Don Barksdale becomes the first black player in the All-Star Game.

1954   The Warriors, then in Philadelphia, sign their first black player, Jackie Moore.

1955   April 10, Lloyd and Jim Tucker become the first black players on a championship team, the Syracuse Nationals.

1955   November 5, Rochester's six-foot-eight Maurice Stokes debuts with 32 points, 20 rebounds, and 8 assists. He's eventually named Rookie of the Year.

1957   Rookie center Bill Russell's defense carries Boston to its first NBA championship.

1958   March 12, in the season finale, Maurice Stokes, a likely Hall of Famer, falls and hits his head. A coma leaves him partially paralyzed.

1958   K. C. Jones joins Bill Russell in Boston, reuniting a duo that led the University of San Francisco to two NCAA championships.

1958   The Lakers' Elgin Baylor enters the NBA and averages 25 points per game to become the league's first great black scorer.

1960   Philadelphia rookie Wilt Chamberlain wins the 1959–60 MVP award after averaging 38 points, 27 rebounds.

1960   Rookie guard Al Attles makes the Warriors' roster, beginning a forty-year career with the franchise.

1962   March 2, Wilt Chamberlain scores 100 points against New York. For the season, he averages 50.4 points per game.

1962   Cincinnati's Oscar Robertson completes the season averaging a triple-double: 30.8 points, 12.5 rebounds, and 11.4 assists.

1966　　Texas Western, with a predominantly black lineup, upsets all-white Kentucky in the NCAA Final, leading to increased opportunities for black players in college and eventually in the NBA.

1966　　Bill Russell becomes the NBA's first black coach, succeeding Red Auerbach.

1969　　Bill Russell's Celtics beat Wilt Chamberlain's Los Angeles Lakers in the Finals; Russell then retires with eleven championship rings.

1970　　Maurice Stokes suffers a heart attack on March 31 and dies on April 6 at age thirty-six.

1976　　A merger with the ABA brings Julius "Dr. J" Erving to the NBA.

1979　　Rookie Magic Johnson, along with Larry Bird, carries the NBA into national prominence.

1989　　Kareem Abdul-Jabbar, master of the sky hook, retires with a record 38,387 points.

1991　　Michael Jordan leads Chicago to the first of six NBA championships.

2000　　Shaquille O'Neal and Kobe Bryant carry Los Angeles to the NBA title. Has another dynasty begun?

They Cleared the Lane

1

One Step at a Time

Earl Lloyd, a middle-aged educator from Detroit, was walking through Detroit Metro Airport in the early 1980s when he spotted a cluster of tall, trim young men, towering over the other travelers at up to seven feet tall. They weren't difficult to identify as a group of pro basketball players, even if one failed to notice the team insignia that adorned their gym bags. There was something else characteristic of the group: most of the young men were black. Their height, color, age, and lanky appearance all added up to distinguish them as a basketball team, and since Lloyd had been a longtime follower of the National Basketball Association (NBA), he recognized many of their faces.

The temptation to gawk, perhaps even the inclination to search for a piece of paper on which an autograph could be scrawled, probably crossed the minds of many of the other people who noticed the players. Not Lloyd's. His thoughts did not turn to adulation. Instead they turned to a forgotten history that few can appreciate with his depth of understanding.

"It's really funny," Lloyd said. "I was walking through an airport one day and here come the Indiana Pacers, all these young black kids. I just spoke to them—'How you doing?'—and they don't have any idea who I am. Not that they necessarily should know."

The man those players acknowledged with barely more than a nod was the first black athlete to play in an NBA game. Lloyd, who by then was in his fifties, feels no bitterness or resentment that they didn't recognize him. "How would they know who I was?" asked Lloyd, who had a respectable but unspectacular nine-year NBA career. Yet there is an important point to be made: "It's just ironic," Lloyd said, "that here's the past passing by the present and the future and they both know nothing about each other."

Neither those Indiana Pacers nor most sports followers understand that the door to integrating the NBA wasn't burst open by a flood of black players. Instead it was nudged open, inch by inch, by a trickle of players throughout the first twenty years of the league's existence.

That trickle began on October 31, Halloween night, 1950, in Rochester, New York, when six-foot-six Earl Lloyd played his first NBA game. It was, to his recollection, an uneventful evening in terms of what occurred immediately before, during, and after the forty-eight minutes of play between Lloyd's Washington Capitols and the Rochester Royals. Lloyd was listed as a guard in that game, his pro debut, and he played a commendable though not starring role by scoring six points and grabbing a game-high ten rebounds in Rochester's 78–70 victory.

The Northeast had long seen a smattering of black college and professional players, and Lloyd's appearance attracted so little attention the *Rochester Democrat & Chronicle* reporter George Beahon didn't even mention him in the game story. Beahon did mention Lloyd in a second story about a press conference held earlier that day, but the reference amounted to only the following: "The Caps, incidentally, launch their home campaign tonight against the Indianapolis Olympians. Among other rookies, [coach Bones] McKinney has Earl Lloyd, rugged Negro guard, who appears to be a 'find.' He was a draft choice from West Virginia State."[1]

The *Rochester Times-Union*'s Al C. Weber noted only that after Rochester took a 43–29 halftime lead, "Bones McKinney, the Caps' new coach, injected big Earl Lloyd, Negro star of West Virginia State into the lineup and he took most of the rebounds."[2]

Yet Lloyd knows that those forty-eight minutes dramatically changed the face of the NBA, and eventually pro basketball worldwide, forever. When Lloyd stepped onto the court that Halloween night he ended the four-year period of what could be called the original WNBA—the White National Basketball Association. He took the league to a higher level merely by adding brown to its all-white palette of skin color.

The next evening Chuck Cooper, the former Duquesne University star forward who six months earlier had become the first black player drafted by the NBA, debuted with the Boston Celtics in their season opener in Fort Wayne, Indiana. It was a momentous day in Celtics history and not just because Cooper's presence foretold the arrival of future black Boston Hall of Famers Bill Russell, K. C. Jones, and Sam Jones. It also was a turning point for the franchise because head coach Red Auerbach, ballhandling phenomenon Bob Cousy, and high-scoring center "Easy" Ed Macauley participated in their first games as Celtics as well. Over the next twenty years they were directly and indirectly responsible for winning eleven of the Celtics championship banners that hang from the rafters of the FleetCenter in Boston.

On November 4 in a game against the Tri-Cities Blackhawks, Nat "Sweetwater" Clifton took the court for the first time as the New York Knickerbockers' new six-foot-eight center. On May 24 of that year (1950) he had become the first black player with star quality to sign with an NBA team as a result of his previous exploits as a member of the famed black touring basketball teams, the New York Renaissance and the Harlem Globetrotters.

In midseason, on December 3 Hank DeZonie, another former member of the Rens and the Globetrotters, completed the foursome of black NBA groundbreakers when he played for Tri-Cities, a franchise from Davenport, Iowa, and Moline and Rock Island, Illinois. DeZonie's NBA career lasted only five games before he quit in disgust over the off-court racial discrimination he faced. Yet in those pioneering days just getting into five games was beyond what nearly every other black player would achieve.

Fifty years ago the debuts of those four players left a barely perceptible imprint on the NBA, the sports press, and America's sports fans. Clifton and Cooper were valuable but unspectacular additions to their teams. Lloyd played only seven games before he was drafted again—this time by the U.S. Army—to serve during the Korean War. DeZonie collected Tri-Cities paychecks for less than a month.

Besides, Jackie Robinson had initiated the big integration splash—actually an integration tidal wave—when he broke major league baseball's blatant color barrier in 1947. Compared to Robinson the NBA's pioneers didn't cause even a mild ripple on the calmest of lakes, or so it seemed. But the result a half-century later was an astounding change: a league in which by the year 2000 about 80 percent of the players and 90 percent of the stars are black; a twenty-nine-team NBA with franchises in the United States and Canada and thirty-seven players from twenty-five countries outside the United States; a financial bonanza that from 1976 to 2000 saw the players' salaries soar from an average of $130,000 to $3.2 million, the highest among all professional athletes in America; a television attraction that first paid the league $39,000 from the Dumont Television Network for a thirteen-game schedule in 1953–54 but most recently coaxed $2.64 billion out of NBC and the TNT–TBS cable networks for four seasons ending in 2002; and worldwide exposure in which the 2000 All-Star Game was televised in 205 countries in forty-two languages, reaching a global audience of 750 million households.

Lloyd, Cooper, Clifton, and DeZonie, and the sprinkling of other black players who followed them until Bill Russell became the first black NBA head coach in 1966, can proudly point to an exemplary lineage. But they were only the midway point of the play-for-pay black player story, which dates all the way back to Harry "Bucky" Lew in 1902. William Himmelman's comprehensive research found that seventy-three black players participated in predominantly white professional basketball leagues before 1950, including those who played in the Chicago tournament that crowned basketball's acknowledged World Championship team from 1939 to 1948.

"It's a very impressive, long list," said Himmelman of Nostalgia Sports Research, "and having talked to many in the past, I know how proud they were of it and how upset they were that everyone looks at Cooper and Lloyd as the Jackie Robinsons. They were more the Pumpsie Greens, who was the last of the major league baseball players to integrate a team."

It all began with Bucky Lew, whose account of his first game with his hometown Lowell, Massachusetts, team, the Pawtuck-etville Athletic Club in the New England Basketball League, was described in a newspaper article by Gerry Finn that appeared in the *Springfield [Massachusetts] Union* on April 2, 1958. A team representing the town of Marlborough was the opponent when that game was played on November 7, 1902 and Lew was a mere eighteen years old.

"I can almost see the faces of those Marlborough players when I got into that game," said Lew, who was seventy-four when the article was published. "Our Lowell team had been getting players from New York, New Jersey, Pennsylvania, and some of the local papers put the pressure on by demanding that they give this little Negro from around the corner a chance to play. Well, at first the team just ignored the publicity. But a series of injuries forced the manager to take me on for the Marlborough game. I made the sixth player that night and he said all I had to do was sit on the bench for my five bucks pay. There was no such thing as fouling out in those days so he figured he'd be safe all around.

"It just so happens that one of the Lowell players got himself injured and had to leave the game. At first this manager refused to put me in. He let them play us five on four but the fans got real mad and almost started a riot, screaming to let me play. That did it. I went in there and you know . . . all those things you read about Jackie Robinson, the abuse, the name-calling, extra effort to put him down . . . they're all true. I got the same treatment and even worse. Basketball was a rough game then. I took the bumps, the elbows in the gut, knees here and everything else that went with it. But I gave it right back. It was rough but worth it. Once they knew I could take it, I had it made. Some of those same boys who gave the hardest licks turned out to be among my best friends in the years that followed."

Finn wrote that five-foot-eight Lew, who previously had played ball at the Lowell YMCA, completed the season with the Lowell team, then played two years for Haverhill, where he gained a reputation for defense and hitting long-range set shots. Doing the latter was quite a challenge, for the style of basketball that Lew described was antiquated compared to today's game. For instance, there were no bank shots because there was nothing to bank a shot on.

"The finest players in the country were in that league just before it disbanded and I always wound up playing our opponent's best shooter," Lew said. "I like to throw from outside but wasn't much around the basket.

"Of course, we had no backboards in those days and everything had to go in clean. Naturally, there was no rebounding and after a shot there was a brawl to get the ball. There were no out-of-bounds markers. We had a fence around the court with nets hanging from the ceilings. The ball was always in play and you were guarded from the moment you touched it. Hardly had time to breathe, let alone think about what you were going to do with the ball."[3]

Especially if Lew was guarding you. Himmelman, an expert on the first fifty years of pro basketball, said that during Lew's era the forwards were a team's principal scorers. Centers were needed mostly to rebound and take the center jump after every basket, while two other players specialized in "guarding" the opponent's forwards (which is how the position came to be named "guard"). "Generally the teams would groom people to be defensive specialists, and that's what Bucky Lew was," Himmelman said. "They weren't asked to score; they were just asked to shut down opposing forwards. And he was one of the best at that. He was one of the best ten defensive players of that first era, but not one of the best overall players." That distinction was reserved for high scorers such as Ed Wachter, Harry Hough, and Joe Fogerty.

The New England League changed its name to the New England Association and disbanded after the 1905 season. For the next twenty years Lew barnstormed around New England with teams he organized, and in 1926 when he played his final game in St. John's, Vermont, he was forty-two years old.

The majority of pro basketball leagues were located in Massachusetts, New York, Pittsburgh, Philadelphia, and Camden, New Jersey. Most of them played their games after players got off from their daytime jobs and travel was difficult then so teams didn't venture far or often from their home bases. Teams would travel into other areas for a week or two each year, especially if another team had a well-known player. When teams traveled to Massachusetts and played Lew's team, a strange but typical form of racism often occurred. "Teams would go up and play there and nobody ever voiced an objection to playing against him as a black player until they played him and he would shut down their best player," Himmelman said. "Then all of a sudden, they would say we don't want to play against a Negro player. They just used that tactic to get him off the court for the next game. It was like using race as a scapegoat-type excuse."

Between the time of Bucky Lew's first game and 1950, a smattering of black players participated in predominantly white pro leagues. In 1907 Frank "Ditto" Wilson played with the Fort Plain, New York, team in the minor Mohawk Valley League, and in 1935 Hank Williams played center for the Buffalo Bisons in the Midwest Basketball Conference's first season.

The pace of integration was agonizingly slow, however, and few black players had the opportunity to earn a living from pro basketball until Bob Douglas, a resident of New York City who had emigrated from the British West Indies in about 1902, founded the New York Renaissance traveling pro basketball team—the Renaissance Big Five—in 1923. Three years later Abe Saperstein organized the Harlem Globetrotters, another all-black traveling team. For the next three decades one of those two teams was the primary route to a pro basketball career for black players. But the route was extremely narrow because the Rens and Globetrotters carried only about eight players apiece. "The only way blacks had to go, so the ballplayers were tremendous at that time—the sixteen best in the country," said John Isaacs, who played on the Rens from 1936 to 1940 and in the 1942–43 season.

In 1963 the Rens were named to the Basketball Hall of Fame as a team. Only their archrivals, the Original Celtics, and the Buffalo Germans received the same honor. The Rens' selection was well-deserved, for despite traveling and playing throughout America when the harsh effect of segregation was common and often legal, they compiled a 2,318-381 record before the team folded in 1949.

The Rens were named after the Renaissance Casino Ballroom in Harlem, where they played their first game on November 3, 1923, a 28–22 victory over a white team called the Collegiate Five. The ballroom was owned by William Roach, who allowed the dance floor to double as a basketball court to accommodate Douglas's team. It was far from an ideal site for basketball, preceding the era of the beautiful, tailor-made arenas of today's game.

"It was rectangular, but more box-like," said former Rens star Pop Gates, arguably the best player of his day. "They set up a basketball post on each end of the floor. The floor was very slippery and they outlined the sidelines and foul lines. It wasn't a big floor. It was far from being a regular basketball floor. Other than high schools or armories, they had very few places to play at, except the Negro college. It was a well-decorated area—chandeliers, a band-stand. All the big [dance bands] played the Renaissance—Fatha Hines, Duke Ellington, Count Basie, Ella Fitzgerald, Chick Webb's band. They had the dancing before the ball game. People would pay and [dance] prior to the game, at halftime, and after the game."

Dance halls lost their popularity in the late 1920s when the Depression strangled the economy and deprived people of spare cash. According to Susan J. Rayl in her Pennsylvania State dissertation, "The New York Renaissance Professional Black Basketball Team, 1923-1950," lagging attendance convinced Douglas to send his team on the road in 1928 in the Midwest. In 1933 they began barnstorming the South. Beginning in 1931 he had assembled a team so skilled that it was nicknamed the Magnificent Seven because of the excellence of its key players: Charles "Tarzan" Cooper, Clarence "Fat" Jenkins, John "Casey" Holt, James "Pappy" Ricks, Eyre "Bruiser" Saitch, William "Wee Willie" Smith, and Bill Yancey.

The highlight of the Rens' long history was an eighty-eight-game winning streak from January 1, 1933, through a game on March 27, 1933, when they lost to the Original Celtics. From 1932 to 1936 the Rens had a remarkable 497-58 record. "Our basketball heroes were the New York Rens and I used to see them play," Gates said. "I'd sneak in or get 50 cents to watch them play." He also had seen them practice because the Harlem YMCA, where Gates played ball as a youngster, was a practice site for the Rens.

Gates starred at Ben Franklin High School in New York. Because predominantly white colleges almost never recruited black players at the time, he attended black Clark University in Atlanta for a short while before dropping out because of a lack of funds. "Coming from poor parents, and I don't want to condemn the college, but they had a very poor training table, so I more or less stayed hungry all the time," Gates said. "My parents did the best they could—send me $1 a month. You could buy a package of cupcakes and a container of milk. I relished that package of cupcakes and container of milk and made it last the best I could." Gates couldn't tolerate the situation for long and decided to go back to New York. He said that through the kindness of a Mrs. Logan, one of his mother's friends, he was given enough money to return home.

Gates began playing for the Harlem Yankees, who scrimmaged against the Rens to help the Rens' preseason conditioning. The Rens ended up signing Gates in 1938 for a salary of $125 a month, which doesn't sound like much until you compare it to the $17 a month that Gates recalls his father earned doing odd jobs. Thus began a career that spanned eighteen years, capped by Gates's induction into the Hall of Fame in 1988.

At the end of his rookie year Gates was the Rens' leading scorer with 12 points when they won the championship game in the World Professional Basketball Tournament in Chicago. The Rens lost the last World Championship in 1948, 75–71, against the Minneapolis Lakers, soon to be an NBA power. That game hadn't been forgotten by Rens forward George Crowe forty-three years after it occurred. This same George Crowe later had a solid, nine-year career as a major league baseball first baseman and pinch-hitter. "I remember they had us down 18 at the half and we came back," he said in 1991. "We went one point ahead of them and Sonny Woods stole the ball and he gave it to Sweetwater Clifton and Sweetwater threw a pass behind his back and it went out of bounds. He threw that ball away and that cost us the World Championship."

The Rens emphasized passing rather than dribbling on offense "because the ball can travel faster by air than by dribble," Gates said. He wasn't much of an outside shooter, preferring instead to drive to the basket for his points. "I was a running, cutting player," he said. "I was ambidextrous."

The Rens barnstormed throughout the East, Midwest, and South, playing about one hundred games a year and taking on the best teams cities and towns could assemble. In *Art Rust's Illustrated History of the Black Athlete*, Douglas said the Rens traveled about thirty-eight thousand miles a year to games as far away as Iowa, Wyoming, and New Orleans. While the team hit the road Douglas stayed in New York and arranged the bookings. The nation's widespread racial discrimination of course made traveling a hassle; Gates remembered that conditions were especially aggravating in New Jersey, Illinois, Indiana, and Ohio. "You couldn't go in a restaurant," he said. "If you didn't have a Negro area to go to, you had to go to a grocery store and buy food from there. Cookies, you make a sandwich or buy canned whatever—do whatever you could connive to eat." Often they would play in a small town, then drive up to two hundred miles to a larger city where accommodations were easier to come by.

The life was enjoyable as the young players traveled in the team bus nicknamed "The Blue Goose" driven by Tex Burnett. It carried ten people—a club secretary, eight players, and often a trainer—and seniority and stature ruled the seating arrangement. "Tarzan Cooper was a big man on the team," Gates said. "He was sitting at the very front right by the door. He guerrillaed that seat. The rookies, when I came to the Renaissance, I was sitting at the very rear end of the bus. If you were a rookie, 'Go to the rear, rookie.' The club secretary [Eric Illidge] always sat near the front, as did player-coach Fat Jenkins. But Tarzan Cooper, he had the choice seat because he was the tallest, the biggest, the baddest, and strongest and so-called best ballplayer on the team. He was at the front where all the leg room was; he could stretch out. And anything that came into the bus had to go by Tarzan Cooper first before it got to the rear. If my mother or wife or sister sent a big cake out to me, before the cake gets to me it had to go by Tarzan. He had to get his slice first."

Almost anything was a topic of conversation: what players

had done the night before, chatter about upcoming opponents, arguments about who was the best baseball player, trivia questions like which city had the largest population or how many games did Babe Ruth win as a pitcher. "It was a lot of fun, laughing and talking in the bus," Gates said. "Ride the bus from four to eight hours, and if you're not running your mouth, you're sleeping."

Simultaneously, the Harlem Globetrotters slowly began to thrive. Originally the team was named the Savoy Big Five after its home court in the Savoy Ballroom in Chicago. A twenty-three-year-old white promoter named Abe Saperstein began to book games in outlying towns starting with a contest on January 7, 1927, in Hinckley, Illinois.

The team traveled throughout the Midwest and Northwest playing so-called straight basketball, but was able to beat teams so badly that they began to add comedic and ballhandling routines to keep fans entertained while the home team was being overwhelmed on the court. Featuring such stars as Bernie Price, Babe Pressley, and Sonny Boswell, the Globetrotters established themselves as part of basketball's elite when they defeated the defending champion Rens, 37–36, in the quarterfinals of the 1940 World Professional Basketball Tournament, then took the championship with a 2-point victory over the Chicago Bruins. The Trotters lost in the semifinals in both 1942 and 1944.

"When the game was over, we all hung out together," said Isaacs. "No problem. But once we got out on the floor, it was see who's going to come out. You beat us or we beat you."

"This is a fallacy that people have, that the Globetrotters were not good ballplayers," Gates said. "They were excellent ballplayers."

It wasn't until the 1940s that the Trotters' comedy routines became their dominant style of play, yet they proved they still were skillful basketball players when they upset the Basketball Association of America's Minneapolis Lakers in serious basketball 61–59 in 1948 before a sellout crowd of 17,583 in Chicago Stadium, and 49–45 on February 28, 1949, as a crowd of 20,046 at Chicago Stadium watched the wizard-like ballhandling of Marques Haynes. These same Laker teams featured future Hall of Famers George Mikan at center and Jim Pollard at forward, and beginning in the 1948–49 season they won five of the next six NBA championships.

"A lot of recognition should go to Pop Gates, including some who played with the Trotters, including Zack Clayton and Ermer

Robinson," said Haynes, who played with the Trotters from 1946 to 1953 and again from 1972 to 1979, a span of thirty-three years. "All were great talents and proved their abilities against the NBA teams, including the Lakers. We beat them a number of times and, of course, they beat us. During those years we had the best talent in the world when it comes to black players."

Mikan wouldn't argue with that assessment. "There was no monkeying around," he said, referring to the lack of clowning around during their games. "He [Saperstein] had an excellent group of guys. They had Marques Haynes, who could dribble the ball, Goose Tatum, who was quite proficient as a pivot man, Babe Pressley, who guarded me, and a guy named Ermer Robinson who made the shot that beat us before twenty-one thousand at Chicago Stadium. [That was in 1949. Actually Robinson's twenty-footer had beaten the Lakers in their previous game, in 1948.] There was a lot of cheering from both sides. It was quite a day for everyone."

Organized pro basketball leagues as we know them now were still in their infancy, much the same as integrated rosters were. A smattering of leagues were formed in the East and Midwest beginning in the early 1900s of Bucky Lew's day, but nothing that compared to the stability of major league baseball. While college basketball thrived, pro players often competed against each other in small towns and haphazard, short-lived leagues.

By the 1940s two main leagues had survived. The Basketball Association of America (BAA) in the Northeast was created on June 6, 1946, by eleven arena owners, ten of whom owned or operated teams in the National and American hockey leagues. The exception among them was Migiel "Mike" Uline, who owned an arena in Washington DC. The businessmen had first come together to form the Arena Managers Association of America so that they could coordinate scheduling dates for extremely popular ice shows. In 1946 they formed the BAA to fill open arena dates during the hockey off-season.

The National Basketball League NBL was formed in 1937 of thirteen teams in the Northeast and Midwest. It had teams in some big cities but was dominated by small-town teams from places that one would never imagine having an NBA franchise today, like Sheboygan, Wisconsin, and Hammond, Indiana. Because so many players were in military service, the NBL finished the 1942–43 and 1943–44 seasons with only four teams. Nonetheless, several short-lived instances of roster integration occurred. "The war effort brought them together because of player shortages and the disbanding of certain teams because of travel restrictions," Himmelman said. "So as the teams shrunk, players hooked up who hadn't hooked up before."

At this time manufacturing companies often sponsored NBL teams. The 1942–43 season began with five teams, one of which was the Toledo Jim White Chevrolets. To make up for players he had lost because of the war, team owner Sid Goldberg signed five black players: Al Price, Bill Jones and Casey Jones (who were unrelated), Shannie Barnett, and Zane Wast. The team broke up after losing its first four games.

One of the teams, the Chicago Studebaker Champions, was the first thoroughly integrated pro team with its four white players and six black players. The latter all were former Harlem Globetrotters, according to Michael Funke's article "The Chicago Studebakers" that appeared in *Solidarity Magazine* published by the United Auto Workers. In an era of company-sponsored pro teams, the Studebakers were unusual because they were sponsored by a union and wore the UAW logo on their shorts.

Studebaker was a major automaker in Indiana that had built a factory in Chicago to manufacture military airplanes. Its player-workers were exempt from the military draft. A white NBL star, Mike Novak, already was employed by Studebaker. "And it was outside that plant where Roosie Hudson was standing one day in 1942 while another Globetrotter, Duke Cumberland, was inside applying for a job," Funke wrote. "Hudson was invited inside by a company official who recognized him from seeing him play with the Trotters at Studebaker's South Bend, Indiana, plant. Urged to contact some other Trotters, Hudson called Bernie Price from an office phone. Price, in turn, contacted Sonny Boswell. In the meantime, Novak contacted Dick Evans and told him he could get a job at Studebaker and play ball, too. Hillary Brown, another Trotter, got wind of the plants and joined up. Tony Peyton was rooming with Duke Cumberland, and he was the last of the Trotters to join the team. Paul Sokody, who had played NBL ball with Sheboygan, and Johnny Orr [not the one who later coached at Big Ten schools], who'd played college ball, rounded out the team. Everyone, except the security guards Evans and Novak, was a UAW Local 998 member."[4] It's disputed whether three other former Trotters—Babe Pressley, Ted Strong, and Al Johnson—also played for the Studebakers.

Evans, a Chicago native who played college ball at Iowa, said Novak informed him about the team because they had been teammates on the NBL's Chicago Bruins during the previous season. To Evans the fact that there would be black players on the team wasn't important. "He told me who the [former Trotters] were and we knew each other, but I don't recall the emphasis being on integration," Evans said. "It's just that these guys are [at Studebaker] and this is the kind of team that we have. We had a lot of respect for those guys." Evans said he hadn't known any of the black players personally but believes he had seen them play with the Globetrotters several times. Novak was on the Chicago Bruins team that lost the 1940 World Championship to a Trotters team that included Price, Boswell, and Cumberland.

Although having a totally integrated team was a first at least in the pros, Evans said he didn't receive any criticism from friends about having black players as teammates. "They thought it was pretty good to play on a team like that," Evans said. "I never remember anybody saying, 'How can you play with those guys?' because we had a lot of respect for them. And people who saw the games thought it was great. They [the black players] were just like us. Some good guys and some were wise guys. They were just like we were."

Evans said that neither the white nor the black players dominated the team. "We respected those guys and they showed respect for us," Evans said. Funke acknowledges that there was a dispute between Boswell, who supposedly took too many shots, and Novak, who "demanded that Boswell pass the ball to his teammates."[5] Evans said he knew nothing about it, and that may be possible since he played in only nine games. In *Cages to Jump Shots* by Robert W. Peterson, Hudson was quoted as saying their disagreement "had nothing to do with race," and the four players that Funke interviewed, including Evans, all agreed that the integrated team got along well.[6] "I had some good friends [among] the blacks and some I just got along with and some I didn't do nothing with," Evans said. "That's normal with any group of people, a church group or a group out of school."

The team with the UAW logo on their uniforms finished the season last in the league with an 8-15 record. Yet they had functioned in an integrated team environment that the NBA wouldn't see for another twenty years, when during the 1962–63 season both the St. Louis Hawks and the San Francisco Warriors each had six black players on their rosters.

During the 1943–44 season New York Rens star center Wee Willie Smith, by then thirty-two years old, played four games for the Cleveland Chase Brass, and in the 1946–47 season Les Harrison, the owner of the Rochester Royals, took another step forward when he asked Gates and center-forward Dolly King, a former football and basketball standout at Long Island University, to join his team. Harrison needed an infusion of talent when several players, including center John Mahnken, left the Royals and jumped to the BAA. Harrison's teams had previously played exhibition games against the Rens, for whom both Gates and King had played, so he was familiar with the pair.

Like many athletes of his day, Dolly King was a multi-sports star. His basketball coach, the legendary Clair Bee, often recalled that on Thanksgiving Day 1939, King accomplished the awesome feat of playing the full sixty minutes of a football game against Catholic University and then that same night playing an entire forty-minute basketball game at Madison Square Garden. He was the leading scorer in both games.

Despite their prowess as athletes, however, Harrison felt it necessary to assess his players' acceptance of black teammates before bringing new players on board. "We got together with our whole team and said we need players and I've played with them before and I feel we should accept blacks and will you guys go along with it, and they said yes," Harrison said. King signed on October 15, 1946, the first day of training camp. At six-foot-four and 217 pounds he became a valuable reserve frontcourt man for Rochester. The Royals compiled the league's best record at 31-13, but lost the championship series to the Chicago Gears and their six-ten center George Mikan, later the NBA's first superstar.

Harrison said he had encouraged Ben Kerner and Danny Biasone to bring expansion teams into the NBL, but warned them both that he planned to sign some black players. "I said, 'Will you take a chance? We're breaking the color line. We'll have it difficult. Will you accept it?' They said 'yes.'" Kerner's team was the Buffalo Bisons, which, after four subsequent location changes, are now the Atlanta Hawks. Biasone's Syracuse Nationals were the forerunners of the Philadelphia 76ers.

"Then Ben called and said you only need a big man, Dolly King [because Rochester had outstanding guards in Red Holzman,

Bobby Davies, and Al Cervi, all future Hall of Famers]. Why don't you sell me Pop Gates and we'll go through it together?" Harrison said. "I liked that, so I didn't sell him to him. I gave him to him, and they did play that season."

King experienced the usual problems finding restaurants that would serve him. Indiana especially stuck in Harrison's craw. "When we got into Indianapolis, I'll never forget the Claypool Hotel," Harrison said. "They served us in the utility room where the dirty laundry was." Harrison laughed about how when he was inducted into the Hall of Fame in 1979, NBA great Oscar Robertson told him, "Don't worry about the Claypool Hotel. It burned down."

On September 28, 1946, Gates signed his contract with the Buffalo Bisons, a stark example of how much the financial nature of pro sports has changed. At the time Gates was one of pro basketball's elites, a star who had played on two World Championship teams. Yet his contract paid him $3 a day meal money on road trips, $5 a day during training camp, and $1,000 a month during the season.

After compiling a 5-8 record, the Buffalo team moved to the Midwest, where they became the Tri-Cities Blackhawks. Gates, listed as a six-two, 205-pound forward, played in forty-one of their forty-four games and averaged 7.6 points, the third best on the team. Yet the next year the Blackhawks wanted to cut Gates's salary by 50 percent. "These people must be crazy," he thought, so he returned to the Rens.

Gates heard rumors that he and King were dropped from the league because Gates had been involved in several fights during games. "But everybody else was fighting," he said, so those rumors didn't make sense to him. Eventually he was told a much different story. It wasn't until the 1980s that Gates was told that the NBL had wanted to add the Rens as an all-black team to boost attendance, but Eric Illidge, the team's chief money manager, had balked. "Because Eric said, 'I can't get my team. You've got two of my best ballplayers [Gates and King] playing with this league. I want them back with the Renaissance,' " Gates said.

Gates said he never mentioned it to Illidge. But the 1948–49 season lent credence to Gates's suspicions. The Detroit Vagabonds NBL franchise dissolved on December 17, 1948, with a 2-17 record. The franchise was awarded to Dayton, Ohio, and the New York Rens finished out the season as the Dayton Rens, with Gates making history as the first black coach of a professional team. "We really didn't want Dayton, Ohio, as our home court, but the league insisted," Douglas said in Rust's book. "The people in Dayton just refused to attend our games. They would not accept an all-black club.

"Despite a lack of size, a lot of our players being over the hill, a thin bench, and DeZonie's illness, which caused him to miss the last eight games, our club—the only all-black franchise in the history of major league sports—built a competitive 14-26 record over the rest of the season. That season proved to be the last for the Rens."[7]

While the NBL dabbled with integration, the Basketball Association of America remained white. It had a chance to integrate in the fall of 1947, when Douglas asked to have the Rens admitted to the BAA as a franchise. Despite strong support from his close friend, New York Knicks coach Joe Lapchick, Douglas's request was denied.

The NBL had the better players but the BAA was comprised of teams located in larger cities, and the 1948–49 season saw four of the strongest NBL teams—the Minneapolis Lakers, Rochester Royals, Ft. Wayne Pistons, and Indianapolis Krautskys—jump to the BAA. After the defection the NBL added four teams and survived the season, but the NBL was forced to disband and six of its teams were absorbed into the BAA on August 3, 1949. The merged leagues were renamed the National Basketball Association, which began the 1949–50 season with seventeen teams and no black players. Did any of the white players notice?

"We should have," said Fred Scolari, a guard with the Washington Capitols. "The talk always came this way. The Minneapolis Lakers would play the Globetrotters in a series every year, and we would watch the game and then question whether those kids would be good enough to play in the league. I played against a guy in a Denver AAU [Amateur Athletic Union] tournament, a fella named [Ermer] Robinson, a great, great player who eventually played with the Globetrotters because he couldn't come in the league, I guess. I played against him and he was certainly good enough to play. Eventually, Sweetwater Clifton proved it, and you could look around now. But you look back on things and wonder, 'How did that ever happen?' But it did."

2

Jackie's Legacy

For black athletes who integrated sports teams in the late 1940s and early 1950s, Jackie Robinson was like a ghost who rearranged all the furniture and removed all the clutter in the house without leaving an identifying fingerprint. Because his racial breakthrough came in major league baseball, one could argue that he literally had nothing to do with the integration of the NBA. Yet there's no doubt that without Robinson there might not have been any black players wearing NBA uniforms in 1950.

Two other black athletes had dominated the sports scene before Robinson, heavyweight boxing champion Joe Louis and track and field's hero of the 1936 Olympics, Jesse Owens. But their achievements came in individual sports, and both lacked Robinson's willingness to stir the racial pot with candor.

World War II, which ended two years before Robinson's major-league debut, also nudged America toward an integrated society and inspired the Civil Rights movement of the 1950s and 1960s. "Partly, it was because black soldiers came back from the second world war," said Ron Walters, a professor of Afro-American Studies at the University of Maryland. "They had been abroad, imbibed some of that [culture], and some of them had been in places where for the first time they didn't experience racism. He [Robinson] fit right in with new aspirations of a new stage of black life."

Robinson displayed extraordinary ability and charisma after integrating major league baseball in 1947 with the Brooklyn Dodgers, and incomparable courage in the face of opponents' pitches and spikes aimed at his body and several death threats aimed at his psyche. (In *Baseball's Great Experiment* [1983] author Jules Tygiel wrote that Robinson received ten death threats in his first seven seasons.) Those factors made him a heroic figure to black Americans everywhere. Whites, too, were generous (though far from unanimous) with their praise. Robinson's brashness on the baseball field and in the field of racial politics caused him to achieve two things that had been impossible for several centuries: he forced many white people to actually "see" black people for the first time, and he presented a black person that America couldn't help but admire. He helped set in motion the forces that opened the door for the NBA's quartet of racial barrier breakers.

Until Robinson's arrival black people largely existed on the margins of U.S. society. Whites and blacks routinely lived in a world of segregated housing, employment, places of worship, education, and neighborhoods. That separation often was enforced by brutal police, racially biased courts, and gratuitous violence, especially in the South. When blacks and whites mingled, blacks were easily overlooked because they typically worked as maids, railroad porters, janitors, and laborers. "When Ralph Ellison wrote *The Invisible Man*, he wasn't pointing toward discrimination, he was pointing toward invisibility," said historian Howard Zinn, a former professor at Boston University and Spelman College. "Blacks not being in the major leagues didn't occur to the American public until Jackie arrived."

Leonard Koppett, a reporter who covered the New York Knicks from their inception in 1946 until 1973, gave an example of the disconnection between white and black people when he talked about never attending Negro League games as a child. Logistically doing so was a cinch; Yankee Stadium was just one block east of his house. Socially the possibility was as remote to him as walking across the floor of the Grand Canyon. "When I was a kid in the 1930s, the Negro Leagues played in Yankee Stadium and clearly I knew [when] it was happening because every Sunday when the Yankees were away, there would be twenty to twenty-five thousand black people coming to the game, [then] leaving the game," Koppett said. "But with not a word about it in the sports pages I was reading. With no one saying anything about it, it never even occurred to me to go. Eventually I came to feel outraged about what I had been deprived of, as well as what they had been deprived of."

But the nation couldn't ignore Robinson. "When he came, oh wow," Zinn said. "The most important thing he did was to change that invisibility of racial segregation, not just in baseball but in all of society." Robinson's mere presence on the Dodgers roster also formed an impermeable bond with black Americans across the country. They lived thousands of miles from Brooklyn, in an era when television at home was rare and the birth of ESPN video highlights was still three decades away. Yet Robinson had become their neighborhood hero.

"I was ten at the time he was maturing as a famous baseball player and was able to watch him and watch black people's reaction to him," said Walters, a black person raised in Wichita, Kansas. "I can tell you that every time he got up to bat there was a catch in people's throats, and everything stopped: 'Let's see if he can get a hit.' Everybody was tuned into the radio and there was this hush when Jackie stepped to bat. I imagined, 'Are black people all over the country doing this?' And yes, they were. It was a shared reality and that's how powerful his position was. When he got a hit, oh my God, the jubilation. And when he didn't, the whole race was troubled. His exploits were the very stuff of black culture."

Robinson also was a powerful figure when it came to sports business. Not only was he a tremendous attraction in the National League—where attendance jumped from approximately nine million in 1946 to an average of 10,079,000 in his first two seasons—but the Dodgers' quality of play and team camaraderie also prospered with Robinson aboard. He won the first Rookie of the Year Award, won the Most Valuable Player Award in 1949, and during his ten years with Brooklyn the Dodgers played in the World Series six times and won it in 1955. Although some teammates, especially those from the South, stayed aloof from Robinson when he first joined the Dodgers, Tygiel wrote that "Robinson's acceptance by the Dodger players occurred with surprising rapidity. . . . Within six weeks, says [teammate Bobby] Bragan [,] the barriers had fallen. Eating, talking, and playing cards with Robinson seemed natural."[1] If anyone doubted whether a black player would be accepted by his white teammates, one needs only to look at the famous 1948 photograph of Dodgers team captain Pee Wee Reese, a son of the South from Kentucky, standing at second base with his arm around Robinson, defying hecklers among the Boston Braves fans.

Sports reporters working for black newspapers leveraged Robinson's success as they made the argument that pro basketball also should integrate. Sam Lacy, a columnist with the *Baltimore Afro-American* who had chaperoned Robinson through his first few years with the Dodgers, said the Negro Sportswriters Association was pressing for the integration of all professional sports. He and other association members such as Bill Nunn with the *Pittsburgh Courier*, Romeo Daugherty, Bill Clark, Dr. W. Rollo Wilson, and Ed Lawson were ever watchful: "The fact that the baseball experiment

had proved successful, that was the basis for some of my writings,"
Lacy said. "I used that as a sort of lever—that baseball had undertaken it and it was time for basketball. I do remember for a while
there was some opposition, that the fans were closer to the players
and [management] feared some of type of misbehavior. But the
argument was this was a for-pay sport and blacks were supporting
it. I do know the Renaissance were doing very well and were playing
the Original Celtics and the South Philadelphia Hebrew Athletic
Association, and then the Harlem Globetrotters [drew well], and
there was every indication blacks could play and produce and draw
crowds."

Several other factors made the league ripe for integration. Not
only had Robinson integrated baseball, but during the previous
year black players had returned to pro football after a twelve-
year absence. Black players had played in the National Football
League (NFL) from 1920 to 1933, but after white players pressed for
their exclusion, blacks were banned from the league until 1946.
Then the rival All-America Football Conference (AAFC) was formed
in 1946 and announced that it would integrate its rosters. The
Cleveland Browns of the AAFC signed Marion Motley and Bill
Willis, and the NFL responded when former UCLA stars Kenny
Washington and Woody Strode signed with the Los Angeles Rams.
In 1950 the two leagues merged, with Cleveland, San Francisco,
and Baltimore joining the NFL. It certainly didn't hurt that Motley
and Willis were exceptional talents who eventually were named to
the Pro Football Hall of Fame. In addition, a sprinkling of blacks
were playing for high-profile college teams at predominantly white
schools. "What the white world talks of as gradualism is just an
inch at a time, and that's what this first group of [black NBA] players
were entering," Koppett said.

There also was the "who cares?" factor. If the NBA wanted to
integrate, hardly anyone noticed. When Robinson debuted with
Brooklyn it was comparable to an earthquake shaking up the
entire sports world, because major league baseball was king. But
pro basketball was way, way down on the totem pole of sports.
Pro baseball, hockey, and football were far more popular than pro
basketball, and college basketball's popularity almost smothered
all notice of the NBA.

When Koppett started writing for the *New York Herald Tribune*,
his primary assignment was covering baseball's Yankees, Dodgers,
and Giants when the regular beat reporter was gone. In New

York college basketball doubleheaders were the craze, especially since local teams like City College of New York, New York University, Long Island University, and St. John's were among the nation's best. Koppett was the *Herald Tribune*'s third-in-line basketball writer, so he covered the Ivy League and small colleges and wrote feature stories about the doubleheaders.

Then, as Koppett said, in 1946, "Here come the Knicks—perfect assignment for the number three guy. Basketball meant colleges. The NBA is a little thing that got a couple paragraphs and maybe a box score, but when a [former] big college star, like a George Mikan, is playing and that team comes to town, that's a big story. In fact, it was a blow to his prestige that he was playing this cheap pro game, having been an All-American."

The NBA had so little status locally that for many years New York Knicks playoff games either were not played on their Madison Square Garden home court or were played during the day because at night the circus was a much better draw at the Garden. Consequently, if the NBA wanted to bring in black players, who would even bother to object? Abe Saperstein, that's who.

The fact that there were no black players in the Basketball Association of America or its offspring, the NBA, raises the question of whether black players were banned from the league before 1950. "I never looked at it that way," said Danny Biasone, the owner of the Syracuse Nationals, for whom Lloyd eventually played from 1952 to 1958. "In those days, a black player never got the recognition, never got the ink from the newspaper. The white player got all the headlines, but if somebody watched a black player and [the player was] capable, I think they would have signed the black player."

Red Auerbach, who became Chuck Cooper's first coach in the NBA, was sure that a ban never existed. "No. Absolutely not," he said. "They [management] just never thought of it [signing black players]." He nevertheless acknowledges that owners feared the wrath of Globetrotters owner Abe Saperstein, who had helped keep many NBA teams financially afloat by letting the Trotters be the main attraction at doubleheaders that featured at least one game between two NBA teams. "It was just thought that if he [Saperstein] wanted a player, nobody would stand up to him because he wouldn't play in their building. Everybody needed the extra income." Perhaps that doesn't qualify as an outright ban, but it was a mighty strong incentive for the owners in a fledgling league to help keep intact Saperstein's virtual monopoly on black players.

Harvey Pollack has been employed by either the Philadelphia franchise or the NBA since the BAA was formed in 1946. He remembers the days when Eddie Gottlieb, who ran the franchise at the time and who later coached and owned it, was badly strapped for cash and needed to maintain a good relationship with Saperstein in order to survive. The stories that Gottlieb was a tight-fisted negotiator are legend, yet Pollack said the description reflects his circumstances, not his personality. "He wasn't a penny pincher; he didn't have any money," Pollack said. "When the BAA was formed in 1946, they had a salary cap. The salary cap for the whole team was $55,000. The first year he felt so bad that Joe Fulks won the scoring title and led them to a title. Gotty couldn't give him any more money because of the salary cap, so at the end of the year he gave him a new Buick. . . . Basketball wasn't popular. If you averaged five to six thousand people, you were doing great." The Warriors didn't reach the five thousand per-game mark until their eighth season.

Gottlieb had been a schoolteacher and then a sports promoter. According to Pollack, the Homestead Grays of baseball's Negro Leagues was one of Gottlieb's clients. Gottlieb had been the coach–general manager of the Warriors, but was far from rich. When he purchased the team from Walter Annenberg in 1952 he bought it for $25,000, but only $15,000 was his money; two other men chipped in the other $10,000.

He and Saperstein were close friends, and Gottlieb depended upon doubleheaders with the Globetrotters for a revenue boost because attendance was so low. In the 1946–47 season, the team's first, the Warriors averaged only 4,305 fans at thirty home games. During the 1952–53 season that average dropped to 3,346 for seventeen games in Philadelphia. "The Globetrotters were the big attraction," Pollack said. "Whenever you had Globetrotters, you had a sellout. They played first—in your city. When Gotty bought the team in '52, he was very friendly with Saperstein so he arranged to take a lot of his home games out of Philadelphia and play wherever the Globies were playing."

How much did Gottlieb cherish those doubleheaders? NBA records from the early 1950s are so sketchy that the league could not verify it, but Pollack vividly recalled an incident involving a doubleheader at a neutral site during which the Philadelphia

Warriors played the Milwaukee Hawks owned by Ben Kerner. A league rule stated that a maximum of ten players could be placed on a roster, but if a sixth player fouled out he could stay in the game so that each team could keep five players on the court. At that particular game a sixth Warrior did foul out, but rather than keep him on the court Gottlieb brought in a different player who had fouled out earlier and Philadelphia won the game. Kerner protested the outcome, which meant that if he won the protest, the Warriors' victory would be nullified and the game would be replayed.

Ordinarily Gottlieb would have contested the protest to try to keep his team's victory. But Pollack said that in that instance, Gottlieb didn't fight it. Why not? "If [Kerner wins] the protest, we have to play the game over," Pollack recalled Gottlieb saying. "We'll play another game with the Globetrotters and we'll make money." Pollack said that it was one of the few upheld protests in the history of the league, and the game was replayed. "The Warriors played home games in Tulsa, Oklahoma, and Fargo, North Dakota," Pollack said. "That was the only way they could survive. An average of ten games were taken out of Philadelphia, scheduled and played on the road as neutral games."

Since keeping Saperstein happy was crucial to the league's financial health, does Pollack believe there was a ban on black players before 1950? He doesn't know for sure. "There might have been an understanding, but nobody would ever dare put it in writing," he said. In fact, such an unwritten ban existed until New York Knicks owner Ned Irish forced its removal, said Carl Bennett, general manager of the Fort Wayne Pistons and a member of the NBA's Board of Governors from 1948 to 1953. Irish's insistence on opening the NBA rosters to black players was fueled by his desire to sign the center his team desperately needed, Harlem Globetrotters star Sweetwater Clifton. Irish even threatened to pull his team out of the league if he didn't get his way.

Fort Wayne was one NBL team that joined the BAA in 1948 (which then renamed itself the National Basketball Association in 1949). Were black players officially banned then? "I can't answer that truthfully, except I knew [commissioner] Maurice Podoloff would never allow anything that banned any individuals from the league because, even back in those days, you're always making sure you don't get in trouble with the law," Bennett said. "There was nothing to my knowledge like [a rule stating that] the BAA or NBL can't have black players." However, "the understanding was it was not allowed to have the black player."

In a 1949 meeting, held in the NBA offices on the eightieth floor of the Empire State Building, Ned Irish brought the unwritten ban out of hiding when he stated that he wanted to sign Clifton. Irish then left the room while his fellow governors voted on the matter. Bennett said Fort Wayne voted to admit black players because that was the desire of team owner Fred Zollner. "I talked with him: 'It's going to come up. How do you feel?'" Bennett recalled. "He said, 'If they're good enough, they should play.'" However, when the votes were counted, the governors had rejected Irish's request. "He was turned down the first time because the Harlem Globetrotters jammed the arenas when they played their games," Bennett said. "The Board of Governors, I don't think they were against [black players]. I think their biggest concern was the Harlem Globetrotters being the greatest income producer filling these big stadiums. They were afraid that Abe Saperstein, if they took one of his players, he would tell them to jump in the lake, which would cost them hundreds of thousands of dollars."

About six months after Irish was turned down a second meeting was held prior to the 1950 league draft. Owners that wanted to admit black players had been lobbying others that wanted to keep the ban, so perhaps it would have been lifted at the second meeting anyway. But Irish heaped pressure on the owners when he came into that meeting with "firepower," as Bennett put it. "Ned Irish, I give him credit for being the upfront person," Bennett said. "He came into the room and hammered [with his fist] on the table and said, 'Either I get Sweetwater Clifton or we may not stay in the league!' New York was the catalyst for the whole league—he was the big city. . . . How serious Ned Irish was, I don't know. But he was persuasive."

When the vote was taken again it was six to five in favor of allowing the signing of Clifton and the drafting of Cooper and Lloyd. "I think the lobbying was the biggest thing in that period [between meetings]," Bennett said. "Eddie Gottlieb was concerned. He said, 'In the first place, your players will be 75 percent black in five years and you're not going to draw people. You're going to do a disservice to the game.' He was right on one thing but not the other. The NBA draws great crowds. But when we walked out the door, he said, 'You dumb s.o.b. You've ruined professional basketball.'"

A half-century later Bennett is still extremely proud of the NBA's vote that day. "I think, frankly, it was one of the greatest things that we could have done—eliminate this rule that black players could not play. Regardless of how you say it, it's given the community, the country, a little more [momentum] toward where they have to move. . . . I think it's a great thing to allow young [black] men, and now young ladies, to play."

3

Just a Dab of Color

"Boston takes Charles Cooper of Duquesne."[1] With those six words, reportedly spoken by Boston Celtics owner Walter Brown, the National Basketball Association officially integrated on April 25, 1950. That was the date of that year's NBA draft which, unlike the televised extravaganza of today, was held in a closed-door meeting of power brokers at the Bismarck Hotel in Chicago.

The day before, the NBA had reduced the league from seventeen to twelve teams by eliminating five franchises "which 'withdrew' or were 'kicked out,' depending on which version of a closed meeting you listened to."[2] Then, on the twenty-fifth, the dozen remaining teams got their chance to choose from among the year's crop of elite college basketball players.

The thought that a black player, most specifically Chuck Cooper, might be drafted was no secret. On March 18, 1950, sports columnist Joe Bostic of the *New York Amsterdam News*, a black newspaper, wrote that Cooper, "might even make the BAA circuit for being a college man plus the social acceptability of membership on a major college five. . . . He brings much of the same qualifications that Jackie Robinson has for his precedent shattering entry into baseball."[3] But an owner actually had to step up and turn that assumption into reality.

Brown made sure it happened. The Celtics had compiled the league's third-worst record, 22-46, during the 1949–50 season. Because the two worst teams, Waterloo and Denver, had been dropped from the league, the Celtics got the first pick in each round of the 1950 draft. Brown started off the first round by selecting Bowling Green center Charlie Share, then four future Hall of Famers were chosen: Bob Cousy (by the Tri-Cities Blackhawks), Bill Sharman (by Washington, a club that lasted only thirty-five games in 1950 before folding), Paul Arizin (by Philadelphia), and George Yardley (by Fort Wayne). When the second round began it was again Brown's turn to pick first. He dropped his Chuck Cooper bombshell, which, as reported by sportswriter George Sullivan, was followed by a long silence and an exchange between Brown and an unnamed owner: "Walter, don't you know he's a colored boy?" the stunned owner said. "I don't give a damn if he's striped or plaid or polka dot," Brown shot back. "Boston takes Charles Cooper of Duquesne!"[4]

In the ninth round the Washington Capitols chose Earl Lloyd of West Virginia State. "They could have picked me on the forty-fifth round," Lloyd said. "It wouldn't have made any difference. Wasn't anybody else going to pick me." With their next pick Washington chose another black-college star, guard Harold Hunter of North Carolina College, who became the first black player to sign a contract with the NBA though he never played in an NBA game.

Harlem Globetrotters owner Abe Saperstein wasted no time trying to get revenge for the invasion of his black-player monopoly. The day after the draft Saperstein told the *Boston Globe* that he had informed the NBA his team would not play in Boston or Washington again. Brown was deep in debt at the time and definitely could have used the income derived from Globetrotters' appearances in Boston. Yet he boldly held his ground and responded to Saperstein's threat by declaring, "He is out of the Boston Garden now, as far as I'm concerned!"[5]

Cooper felt forever indebted to Brown. "I'm convinced that no NBA team would have made the move on blacks in 1950 if the Celtics hadn't drafted me early, taking me on the second round," he said. "Seven rounds later the Washington Caps took Earl Lloyd, and a couple of months later the New York Knicks bought Sweetwater Clifton's contract from the Harlem Globetrotters. But it was a case of the Caps and Knicks following the Celtics' lead. Walter Brown was the man who put his neck on the line."[6]

Why did he do it? "Walter was the most decent beloved guy you would ever want to know," said Sullivan, the author of *The Picture History of the Boston Celtics*. "He had a temper at times, but after sleeping on it usually apologized the next day. He also could be very stubborn." Brown's stubbornness probably was a primary reason the Celtics still existed in 1950.

They grew into a legend, but at that point the Boston franchise, part of the original BAA, badly needed resuscitation. Sullivan said there was little public interest in pro basketball because the fans' attention was already divided between hockey's Boston Bruins (over which Brown was president) and Holy Cross College (the focus of the city's basketball fervor). The Celtics were an afterthought, if that. Consequently, Brown had fallen $460,000 in debt. To keep the team alive he had mortgaged his house and sold his stock in the highly popular Ice Capades. "He became almost smitten with [the Celtics], as you would for a sickly child," Sullivan said. "That was surprising for a guy, [who] by his own admission, didn't know one end of a basketball from another when he started the team. It was originally to fill dates in the Boston Garden. The Celtics were a joke the first four seasons. They were the doormats of the league and a laughing stock. He wanted to save this frail child."

It helped Brown's financial situation when another New England sportsman, Lou Pieri, joined him as the Celtics' co-owner in 1949. Then Brown abandoned his old pattern of trying to build an NBA franchise by appealing to Boston's provincial thinking. He had been filling Celtics rosters with former New England basketball stars—there were five on the 1949–50 team—and former Holy Cross coach Doggie Julian had coached the Celtics the two previous seasons. Two days after the draft Brown replaced Julian with thirty-two-year-old Red Auerbach, not yet a legend but already able to lead the Washington Capitols to two Eastern Division titles and an appearance in the 1948–49 NBA Finals. Auerbach had coached Tri-Cities for most of the 1949–50 season.

Auerbach claimed he left the Capitols because owner Mike Uline offered him only a one-year contract when Auerbach wanted three years. From the Capitols Auerbach moved on to Duke University as an "advisory coach," which presumably was a holding position until the Blue Devils' head coach, Gerry Gerard, succumbed to cancer. "I was there until the middle of December and felt funny waiting for him to die, so I left Duke and went to Tri-Cities in December," Auerbach said. (Gerard eventually died in 1951 at the age of forty-seven.) Auerbach coached the Blackhawks into the playoffs, but owner Ben Kerner "made trades I didn't like." Mainly he traded center John Mahnken to Boston (ironically), which weakened Tri-Cities in the playoffs. The team was eliminated in the first round by the Anderson (Indiana) Packers; a disgruntled Auerbach went job-hunting again.

Although he barely knew Brown, Auerbach agreed to coach the Celtics for a reported salary of $10,000 a year because "He had a great reputation as a person, plus I liked the area. Walter Brown was a man with no prejudices. When he was in the Garden as president and owner of the Celtics, the women that swept the Garden, he would tip his hat for them and open the door for them. There was no such thing as religious or racial prejudice in his own makeup."

Before the momentous league meetings in Chicago, Auerbach and Brown had discussed what they wanted from the draft. "Everything" could have been their conclusion. During the previous season no Celtics ranked among NBA leaders in points scored, field goal percentage, or free throw percentage, and only one player—Jim Seminoff—ranked among leaders in assists (eighth place). Auerbach and Brown mostly needed big men. Cooper, an All-American player from Duquesne who was an excellent rebounder and defender, fit the Celtics' void perfectly as what we now would call a "power forward."

"I saw him play a lot and to me he was a good player," Auerbach said. "He was an athlete. He was quick. He was a decent shooter. He could run real well, and he was six-six and built real well. And he had a good college record." But the fact that Cooper was black had to be addressed. Did Auerbach and Brown discuss the issue? "Of course," Auerbach said. "I said, 'Walter, the best player we could draft is Chuck Cooper, who is a black athlete.' He said, 'I don't care if he's green. If he could play, draft him.'" Auerbach said Cooper's race was an inconsequential element to him because he was raised in the Williamsburg section of Brooklyn, where black and white kids played together. "I was brought up in New York and we didn't have those kind of prejudices," he said. Auerbach said he and Brown were careful not to "tip our hand and say we're going after Cooper" because had another team known, it might have drafted him ahead of them.

Cooper was absolutely thrilled to be chosen by the Celtics. "He was very, very happy about it," said Patsy Jayne Ware, who was dating Cooper at the time and became his wife in 1951. "Not only happy. I think he was very, very proud that his abilities had been recognized. It certainly was an honor. No other black person had been drafted by an NBA team. He was proud of his achievements and that this had happened for him."

In terms of acquiring big men, the draft had been a bonanza for the Celtics. They not only drafted Cooper and Charlie Share, a six-eleven center from Bowling Green, but also had purchased Easy Ed Macauley from the St. Louis Bombers, one of the teams just dropped from the league. In the 1949–50 season McCauley ranked fifth in scoring with 1,081 points and a 16.1 per-game average, the beginning of a Hall of Fame career. Six years later he was written into NBA lore as the key figure in a trade that brought the great Bill Russell to Boston.

Two days after the draft Auerbach was officially introduced as the Celtics' new coach. He expressed his elation over the team's recent acquisitions: "I think we've got some real ballplayers now," he said.[7] "Macauley is the second-best center in the league to [George] Mikan now and as time goes on I feel he'll be the best. He is unselfish as a team player." At that same press conference Auerbach revealed his intention to abandon Brown's longstanding penchant for college players from the Boston area. To bolster that point Auerbach showed that he wasn't a perfect judge of talent by disparaging Bob Cousy, whose magical passing had led Holy Cross to the 1948 NCAA championship.

It was assumed that the Celtics would take Cousy with their No. 1 pick. Auerbach strongly defended the decision to choose Share instead. He noted the importance of getting a big man and said that at least eleven of the league's twelve teams would have chosen Share. In addition, in comparing Cousy to holdover Boston guard Ed Leede, Auerbach favored the latter: "I'm sure he [Cousy] will make the grade," Auerbach said. "Right now, I don't regard Cousy as good as Leede." In his irascible style he added, "I don't give a darn for sentiment of names. That goes for Cousy or anybody else. A local yokel doesn't bring more than a dozen extra fans into your building. But a winning team does and that's what I aim to have."

Fortunately for Boston, Tri-Cities signed Cousy then promptly traded him to the Chicago Stags for Frank Brian, the league's third-leading scorer the previous season. The Stags almost immediately folded, and in an October 5 dispersal draft the Celtics picked Cousy's name out of a hat and paid $8,500 to purchase his contract. Less than a month later the Celtics' new blood debuted in the season opener, and Boston had broken ground on its path to a remarkable run of eleven championships in the 1950s and 1960s.

In the trio's first season together Cooper was a valuable power forward in what turned out to be the statistically best year of his six-year NBA career. That season he recorded career bests in points scored (615), points per game (9.3), rebounds (562, only 22 fewer than the NBA's tenth-ranked rebounder, Jack Coleman), shots attempted (601), shots made (207), and assists (174). Macauley ranked third in the league in scoring and points per game (1,384 and 20.4, respectively), second in shooting percentage (46.6 percent), ninth in assists (3.8), and ninth in rebounding (9.1). "Local yokel" Cousy ranked ninth in points scored (1,078) and fourth in assists (341), and began to establish himself as perhaps the game's greatest passer. Because McCauley's presence meant they no longer needed a center, Share never played for Boston and spent his rookie year with Waterloo in the short-lived National Professional Basketball League. The next year Boston traded him to Fort Wayne for Bill Sharman, who joined Cousy in forming a Hall of Fame–caliber backcourt.

Auerbach led the Celtics to a 39-30 record that season, just two and a half games behind Philadelphia in the Eastern Division standings. Boston didn't win its first championship until 1957, Russell's rookie season. But the NBA draft week of 1950 was the cornerstone of their dynasty, and breaking the color barrier by selecting Chuck Cooper was a monumental and historic chunk of that cornerstone. Although Lloyd's NBA debut came one day earlier than Cooper's, Lloyd publicly acknowledges Cooper as the NBA's first black player. "Whenever I make a speech, I say I was the first to play," Lloyd said. "[Then] I say I defer to Chuck. . . . He was the first drafted, and I truly believe if he hadn't been drafted, Washington wouldn't have drafted me. How could I not defer to him?"

Before the 1950 draft the Washington Capitols were getting pressure from all sides to integrate. Much of it came as a result of the economic facts of life: the Capitols were suffering from low attendance levels, though Washington's growing black population probably would have come to more games had they had someone of the same color to cheer for.

During most of the 1940s arena and Capitols owner Mike Uline had mainly ignored the benefits he could receive from black patronage, choosing instead to ban black people from all events other than boxing matches held at his arena. The ban prompted the *Washington Tribune,* a black newspaper, to call for a boycott of a physical fitness demonstration held at Uline on May 14, 1943: "Now, Mr. Uline, who makes his living selling ice to many Negroes and whites who cannot afford refrigerators, bars Negroes from his arena when he stages his ice shows," the *Tribune* wrote in its May 8 editorial. "He permits them to attend boxing matches because his cards are mixed, and he wants to make money. He feels he can make money on his ice shows without Negro support, so he bars us from these events altogether."[8]

Eventually, however, Uline needed the financial boost that black attendance could give him. In 1948 he announced that for the first time in the arena's seven-year existence blacks would be allowed to attend all events held there. He officially ended segregation at Uline on January 21, 1948, when he allowed blacks to attend that evening's Washington Caps–St. Louis Bombers game, and the next day the *Washington Post* contained an article about that policy change: "'The trend of the times prompted my decision,' Uline said," reported the *Post*. "He added that poor attendance at Arena-sponsored events also was a major factor. The arena owner stated he has been contemplating a change of policy for over a year, but waited until 'there was no pressure on me' before making a change. He was referring to the pickets who paraded in front of the arena on fight nights urging Negroes not to attend the fights until the arena junked its racial policy."[9]

The article also stated that local black high school and college sports officials were anxious to rent Uline Arena for their events because it seated about seven thousand people, far more than the site they had been consistently selling out, the two thousand–seat capacity Turner Arena. One of the first events to make the switch was the CIAA basketball tournament (which had been held at Turner Arena from 1946 to 1948); it switched to Uline in 1949. Consequently, future Caps draft picks Earl Lloyd and Harold Hunter played their junior- and senior-year tournament games in the Caps' home arena.

Pressure to integrate the NBA also came in the writings of black sports columnists like Sam Lacy (just forty-five miles away writing for the *Baltimore Afro-American*), and from coaches at black colleges in the Southeast. "He [Lacy] wrote about it all the time, and it became conversation that the NBA wasn't that old, but how can they pass up all the talent in black schools," said John McLendon, then the coach at North Carolina College (now called North Carolina Central University) and eventually becoming the first black coach of a pro team. "There wasn't any picketing or protesting in organized fashion, but there were just continuous questions asked by the news media." In addition, "A number of us coaches had tried to get the NBA to look at black players."

Meanwhile, black players weren't necessarily on the same wavelength. Did they talk about playing in the NBA? "No, how do you talk about something that's not available to you?" Lloyd asked. "Most black kids who wanted to play pro basketball, their sole aspiration was to be a Harlem Globetrotter." Others weren't excited by that prospect because they didn't like the comedic aspect of the Globetrotters. They preferred what Pop Gates calls "straight basketball."

Lloyd and one of his West Virginia State teammates, forward Bob Wilson, got to travel with the Globetrotters. But without knowing exactly why, they heeded a warning by West Virginia State coach Mark Cardwell to not commit themselves to the Globetrotters. "Our coach told us, 'Don't sign anything,' without explaining why," Lloyd said.

It wasn't hard for Lloyd to resist the Trotters anyway, because he had been disappointed by the grind. "I didn't like it," he said. "Nice guys, but it was tough—sometimes playing two games in one state [in two cities]. And you go to St. Louis—Abe [Saperstein] stayed at the Chase [the white hotel] and the players stayed at the Jefferson [the black hotel]—and they talk about what a great guy he was." Considering the salary he was offered and the conditions, Lloyd thought being a schoolteacher was more attractive.

Early in 1950 strong indications appeared that the Capitols were ready to sign their first black player. Dick O'Keefe, who played for the Caps from 1947 to 1951, remembers a revealing conversation he had with coach Bones McKinney before the 1950 draft. "Bones McKinney had asked me, 'Dick, what would you think if we had a black guy on our ballclub?'" O'Keefe said. "I said to Bones, 'If he's good, why not?' because I had run a baseball team in the Marine Corps, and a black Marine came up to me and said, 'Can I play on your baseball team?' I said, 'Are you any good?' I always remember his name. It was Richardson. He said, 'Well, I can pitch.' I said, 'Well, come on.' So, with Earl, I said if he's good enough, bring him. And with Bones, who was from Carolina, Bones wanted to win."

Lloyd's West Virginia State team and coach McLendon's North Carolina College squad ended up playing in the 1950 championship game of the CIAA tournament; North Carolina won that March night at Uline Arena. NCC point guard Harold Hunter was named Most Outstanding Player of the tournament, and Lloyd was a standout for West Virginia State. Those two became the players the Caps zeroed in on. "The management and coaches of the Washington Capitols were in the stands," McLendon said, "and shortly after the game they told me 'we will notify you and just might give your players a tryout.' "

One of the Caps' employees who scouted that tournament was John Norlander, a guard who had been a Caps player since the BAA was formed in 1946. He had injured a knee during the 1949–50 season, and while recuperating the team's management had asked him to do some scouting. "We were checking out the best players of the time," Norlander said. "Hunter was very quick, good shooter, good defensive player, handled the ball well. He was pretty much what you would call a point guard today." As for Lloyd, "He could jump. He had long arms. He just had a lot of good mobility for his size at that time. You knew he was going to be a player the first time you saw him."

At the end of March the Caps contacted McLendon and formally invited the players to a tryout at Uline. Hunter said that while he was in college, playing in the NBA "was the farthest thing from my mind." But when McLendon told him about the pending tryout, Hunter was confident about how he would match up against the pros.

"I went in the Army in Texas but was stationed in Utah and the Philippines, and I had plenty of exposure to white performers and a lot of them were major-college players. It was no problem with me equating myself with their talent. In fact, I was player-coach at one time in the Philippines and we had an undefeated team. Finally, somebody managed to beat us. . . . A player is a player, is what I found out. We beat teams when the only college player on my team was me, and I only had one year of college ball. The rest of them came out of high school. But as we played against the officers, most all of them [had] played in college and we ran into one or two of them that had some pro experience, and we still beat them. So I didn't take a back seat to any of them. I figured I was as good as them, better than most."

Tryouts are always stressful, but that one had a load of extra drama connected to it. McLendon recalls that it occurred on April 6. He and Hunter drove up together from North Carolina to DC, then picked up Lloyd at his parents' home in Alexandria, Virginia, a Washington suburb. To get them loosened up before the tryout McLendon drove them to Howard University, a black college located in DC, so they could work out for a short while in the gym. "We ran through a little two-man stuff just to get the ball in their hands, for about a half hour," McLendon said. "We started down to Uline and on the way down the hill, Earl said, 'Wait a minute. I don't know how to switch.' " McLendon immediately understood Lloyd's concern. He knew that Lloyd's college coach didn't let his players switch defensive assignments if their path was blocked by a pick set by an offensive player. Coach Mark Cardwell had always insisted that his players fight through the pick.

"As soon as he said it, I started looking for a playground," McLendon said. "I turned off Georgia Avenue and the first street happened to be a dead end street." They got out of his car to review how to switch on defense, with McLendon pretending to be a third player. Then a passerby walking across campus joined in as a fourth so they could go two-on-two. "We worked for about ten minutes, so Earl could go to the tryout with a degree of confidence."

Hunter also remembers stopping to work on fundamentals before they arrived at Uline Arena, but Lloyd barely recalls it. "He [McLendon] did take us to the tryout and did stop to work on some fine points," Lloyd said. "I can't remember all the details because I was probably scared to death at the time. And in those days, whatever a coach said, you just did it."

At the tryout McLendon and the two players were met by McLendon's assistant coach at NCC, Dr. LeRoy T. Walker. Decades later Walker became one of the most powerful men in sports as the president of the U.S. Olympic Committee. Following that he served as president of the World Special Olympics.

Before the tryout began Walker and McLendon advised the players not to overdo it, just be themselves. "One thing we were saying was this is not the time to do anything different than what got you this invitation," Walker said. "Somebody has seen you with your skills and ability to play basketball. Don't try to do anything different or special or more than you're capable of. Do what got you here. We said to Earl, he had an awful good hook running across the free-throw line. Harold's [forte] was a great crossover dribble without carrying the ball—which [players] do these days and referees rarely call."

Other members of the Capitols were already in Uline Arena when McLendon, Walker, and the two players walked in. "We didn't know what to expect," McLendon said. "You've seen that ad like E. F. Hutton, when they talk everybody freezes. That was what happened when Harold and Earl walked into camp. Twenty-four players froze because it was the first time black players were in a camp. I recall vividly how everyone stopped. . . . Maybe that's where E. F. Hutton got its inspiration."

The Caps players had been told that some black players would be coming for a tryout. "It didn't bother any of us," Norlander said. "It certainly didn't bother me." Black people had lived in his hometown of Virginia, Minnesota. He had had a black teammate at Hamline College. And when Norlander had been in the navy he had been on a team organized by Red Auerbach that played the Washington Bears, an offshoot of the New York Rens.

McLendon said the players received a fair tryout. They went through many three-on-three drills, and he remembers that the combination of Lloyd, Hunter, and Norlander was unbeatable: "It was our regular preseason practice—conditioning, fundamentals," Norlander said. Running the three-on-three drills "was just part of the practice. In fact, it helped me. They were pretty mobile people and I felt that I was fairly mobile."

Hunter recalled, "Earl and I were on the same team against three other guys. One of their pros played with Earl and me. We just played under one basket, and after it was obvious we could hold our own, then they wanted to see if we could shoot free throws. Earl was an excellent shooter, they were very much impressed with his size and his outside shot. Then they wanted to test us to see if we could play man-to-man defense, and they were satisfied with that."

The black players made surprisingly few mistakes. "It was a great tryout," Walker said, in part due to the fact that the white players involved comported themselves well. "I don't know how many players knew that Earl and Harold were going to be there," Walker said. "Some were upstate youngsters and others Southerners, but you didn't get any feeling that there were any hard hits."

Walker said coach Bones McKinney and several other men, whom he assumes were team owners or upper management personnel, watched the tryout from the sidelines. "They were impressed with Lloyd because he handled the ball very well, had good speed, and could put the ball on the floor, which for then was unusual for a big man," Walker said. He recalled that Hunter's speed in the three-on-three drills also caught the Caps' eyes. "Harold had something that's unusual even now," Walker said. "He would create one-on-zero fastbreaks. Because he had speed, he would throw the ball out several feet ahead of him and had the speed to catch it in the middle of the dribble. He would just run by people for lay-ups. They [Caps officials] were absolutely flabbergasted. Mac and I were looking at each other—how skillful these young men were from historically black institutions."

After the workout the coaches and players were beckoned upstairs to the Capitols' office. Both players signed contracts, and because Hunter was one of his players, McLendon remembers having Hunter sign first so he could be the first black player to sign an NBA contract. "I decided I should get something out of this," he said. "Harold was five-eleven, Earl was six-six, so I said, 'Harold, you sign first because you're the shortest.' " So Hunter beat out Lloyd for an historic first "by about ten seconds," as McLendon said.

"They took us to the office and I sat behind a desk and went through the motions of signing," Hunter said. "They told McLendon what they would pay me and they put it on the contract, $4,000, and I signed it. Teachers were starting at $1,000 or $800 a year, so $4,000 was a heck of a salary for me."

When McLendon and Hunter returned to the North Carolina College campus, a public relations man who worked for the school, Earl Ray, interviewed Hunter about the tryout and took a photo of him doing a mock signing of his contract. "The guy, Earl Ray, asked if I had placed any significance to it," Hunter said. "It was a subject that was almost foreign. It was like getting a black astronaut out of a P.E. [physical education] class and saying you're going to the moon. The only thing you looked to as a pro was to go to the Globetrotters, and they only picked a few. There was not much ambition among black players to play professional ball. I hadn't given any thought to it, but McLendon was ahead of us. He personally took me up there. He thought it was a good deal for me, and I signed. That and a dollar will get me a cup of coffee, but it's still a fact of history."

Of course nothing was finalized until the Capitols actually selected them in the draft, making Lloyd their ninth pick and Hunter their eleventh, which is why Hunter's contract is dated April 26, 1950. That day, *Washington Post* reporter Jack Walsh's article stated, "Washington's Caps, who sagged artistically and financially last season, made some momentous draft choices at the NBA meetings in Chicago yesterday: 1. They drafted Ohio State's Dick Schnittker and Southern California's Bill Sharman, two of the Nation's outstanding collegians; 2. They also selected their first Negro basketball players—West Virginia State's Earl Lloyd, who performed for Parker-Gray in Alexandria, and Harold Hunter, captain of North Carolina College, CIAA champion." Later in the article Walsh wrote that Lloyd was "considered a rebound artist and excellent shooter from under the basket. Hunter, at twenty-one, a year younger than Lloyd, is only 5-foot-10." [10]

Four days later sports columnist Shirley Povich again mentioned the new players in the *Post*. (Excuse this mistake on spelling Lloyd's name; it was the thought that counts.) Povich wrote, "[B]efore drafting the two colored players, Merle Lloyd and Harold Hunter, the Caps invited them for tryouts at Uline Arena earlier in the month, and tabled them as 'can't miss.'" [11]

4

A Taste of Sweetwater

Above all else Ned Irish, part-owner and vice president of the New York Knicks, was a businessman. His skills had taken him from a career as a New York sportswriter into new areas of sports promotion and public relations, where his clients included the National Football League. Beginning in 1934 Irish left his deepest imprint in sports promotion when he originated college basketball doubleheaders in Madison Square Garden, which were all the rage until betting scandals tore the heart out of the sport's popularity in the early 1950s.

Business demands also inspired Irish to join in the formation of the Basketball Association of America (BAA) in 1946. Like all but one of the original owners in the league, which eventually formed the core of the NBA, Irish needed to fill dates in his arena. Even with tenants such as the National Hockey League's New York Rangers, college basketball, ice shows, and the circus, some evenings the Garden sat idle. Forming the Knicks franchise was a product of economic logic, not a love of basketball though, as it turned out, in 1946 the Knicks played only seven of their thirty home games in the Garden because other attractions had become so popular. For instance, its twenty-nine college basketball dates (including twenty-one doubleheaders) had filled the Garden to 98 percent capacity. So the Knicks were shuttled off to the 69th Regiment Armory for twenty-three of their home games.

Irish had applied the same business acumen when promoting Harlem Globetrotters games in the late 1940s. To many white Americans at the time, black people were still a pariah to be avoided. Department stores wouldn't hire blacks as cashiers for fear they might miscount or even steal the money, and many hotels wouldn't let blacks eat in their restaurants. A keen businessman like Irish wouldn't assume that black players would be readily accepted, no matter how talented or entertaining they were.

His solution was to test the New York City market by holding

Globetrotters' games in the 69th Regiment Armory in 1946. How did that pan out? "Good enough to warrant bringing them into the Garden the following year," said Freddie Podesta, who became one of Irish's business managers in 1938. "We didn't want to break them in in the Garden. It used to be booked seven nights a week. It was just impossible to get a date. That's why we used the 69th Regiment Armory thirty to forty times a year."

Likewise, the Knicks' purchase of former Globetrotters star Nat "Sweetwater" Clifton on May 3, 1950, didn't come about because Irish's social conscience felt a pressing need to integrate the NBA. Instead, it was the result of a pressing need to find a capable center for the Knicks team and a desire to add a gate attraction for the public. If some positive racial implications were the result that was good, too, but not essential.

The Knicks had been 40-28 during the 1949–50 regular season before Syracuse eliminated them in the playoffs. Even at six-foot-seven-and-a-half inches tall and 235 pounds, and with suction cup–like hands, Clifton wasn't as big as several NBA centers, like six-eleven Don Otten and the great George Mikan. But he was bigger and stronger than anyone else on the Knicks team and, unlike most rookies, he had gained experience playing for the Globetrotters, for the New York Rens, and even as a minor-league baseball player in the Cleveland Indians' farm system.

"I guess what he was looking for basically was a center, and Sweets was a center for the Globetrotters. I don't think he was looking for a black player," said sportswriter Leonard Lewin, who covered the Knicks from the time of their inception until 1975 for the *New York Mirror* and the *New York Post*. "Clifton had gotten a reputation because the Globetrotters had played in those buildings, so they appreciated the black players. Once [other NBA teams] lowered the barriers, the Knicks went after Sweets because he was a major attraction in the Garden. They [the Globetrotters] used to sell out the place. That's why a lot of NBA teams booked them."

There was no denying that Clifton was a proven talent who could compete in the NBA and probably draw fans to the arena. For instance, just four days before the Knicks purchased Clifton from the Globetrotters, the *New York Amsterdam News* reported that he had been the leading scorer during the Trotters' eighteen-game cross-country tour with the College All-Americans. Clifton had led all scorers on the tour with 272 points, and had the highest single-game total of 27 points in Boston.

That article of April 29, 1950, exemplifies the Globetrotters' enormous, worldwide popularity. The tour had concluded with a 77–64 Globetrotters' victory in Washington DC in which the winners had played "straight basketball" until they took a big lead in the fourth quarter. The game had drawn a crowd of 7,398 fans at Uline Arena, "the largest crowd ever to see a basketball game in the nation's capital. . . . The series attracted all-time record crowds in six cities, Cleveland, Indianapolis, Los Angeles, Denver, Cincinnati, and Washington DC." There was no rest in sight, the *Amsterdam News* continued: "The Globetrotters left by transatlantic plane Thursday for Portugal, where they play their first game on May 5. They are also scheduled to play in Switzerland, England, Belgium, France, and Italy, and are tentatively booked for a series of games in North Africa."[1]

The publicity must have been great for Saperstein's financial coffers, but Clifton was itching to leave the team. In a 1985 interview, when asked if his sale to the Knicks came as a surprise, he replied that "It didn't because I didn't want to play with the Trotters because we traveled too much. I wanted to be home more." In addition, "They weren't paying me the money—$500, $600 a month. We didn't have a Washington Generals [the team of designated losers that accompanied the Globetrotters in later years]. We had to win every game and everybody did their best to play against us. They never did pay that much money. They kept you playing all the time."

Clifton's unhappiness fit right in with the Knicks' desire to sign him, and Saperstein was looking for the best possible deal. Clifton had only one year left on his Globetrotters contract, while Saperstein felt pressured by the fact that Cooper and Lloyd had been drafted on April 25. "The thing he was concerned about was he's got a monopoly [on black players] and he's going to lose that monopoly," Podesta said. "Simple as that, and he was also going to lose his bargaining position. Prior to the breakthrough, he could sign a player for whatever he could pay him. He [the player] had no options."

The combination of all of those factors led to negotiations between Saperstein and the Knicks, who were represented by Podesta. Podesta had previously dealt with Saperstein when scheduling Globetrotters' appearances in New York. Negotiations culminated in a luncheon meeting on May 3, 1950, involving Saperstein, Podesta, and NBA Commissioner Maurice Podoloff. "Podoloff knew I had been talking with Abe and he called me and said if I was interested, come down and have lunch with him and Saperstein," Podesta said.

That day, in an Empire State Building restaurant, Sweetwater Clifton's contract was sold to the New York Knicks for $12,500. Immediately after Podesta dictated the following letter to Irish's secretary. She sent it to Irish, who was vacationing in Europe:

May 3, 1950
5:30 P.M.

Dear Ned:

I have just returned from the meeting with Saperstein and Podoloff and we have purchased Sweetwater's contract for $12,500. Abe will assign his contract to us which calls for $1,500 a month. Of the purchase price, Abe told me that he is going to give Clifton $4,000.

The Clifton matter came up because Saperstein was pretty well burned at Boston for drafting Cooper. Podoloff called me and I told him we had made many attempts to purchase Clifton and still wanted him. Abe felt certain that with proper handling and coaching Sweetwater should be the greatest center in the League. The coach seemed very interested in him.

I agreed with Abe that no publicity would be released on the sale until the early part or middle of June. He said he wanted the opportunity to sit down and talk to Clifton, and from our standpoint I think we are in a better bargaining position with the League if we hold off on it for a while.

No doubt you have gone over the draft choices and can see that whole accent of the meeting was on strengthening the bottom ball clubs. Lapchick [coach Joe Lapchick] seems satisfied with his draft choices though I think Scherer [draft pick Herb Scherer] is a big gamble and will certainly require a lot of teaching.

The talk about Chicago now is for the team to be sold and moved into the Amphitheater. In the event that they do not operate I certainly see no reason why Faust [center Larry Foust] should not be assigned to New York.

We were glad to hear from you and hope you will continue to enjoy yourselves.

Sincerely yours,
Fred Podesta[2]

The Knicks wanted to get the biggest publicity splash possible from signing the popular Globetrotter, so Podesta and Saperstein agreed not to publicize it until June. When interviewed in 1999 Podesta said they actually wanted to hold off the announcement until September. "You have to remember, we had to really beg for publicity in those days because college basketball dominated, and hockey," he said. "Between hockey and college basketball and boxing, there's only so much space you can get and professional basketball at the time was just in its infancy. You had to beg to have [sportswriters] go on the road. It was one of the lowest priorities." By September the baseball season was over for most teams, football hadn't yet begun, and training camp for the Knicks was soon to begin.

Roughly a month after Cooper and Lloyd had been drafted, and seventeen days after the Globetrotters' had secretly sold Clifton's contract, *Amsterdam News* columnist Joe Bostic urged black players to pursue pro basketball careers with added vigor since two leagues might be bidding for their services. (After the Denver, Waterloo, and Sheboygan franchises were booted out of the NBA in April, they announced that they would be the nucleus of another league. It was never formed.) Bostic wrote in the May 20 *Amsterdam News*: "Now is the time for Negro basketball players to make a determined move to get into organized court play. . . . The dopes in the NBA who permitted a split played right into their hands. . . . Naturally the new faction will go for anything that looks like a box office stimulant. . . . And name me a single club that the likes of Nat "Sweetwater" Clifton or Marques Haynes wouldn't help? Competition always was the life of trade and it won't be any different in this case. . . . The picture never was brighter for breaking down one more unwritten ban."[3]

The Knicks' effort at secrecy didn't last even a month. Podesta said that when a player of Clifton's magnitude left a well-known team the news was bound to leak out. The Knicks relented and on May 24 officially announced their purchase of Clifton's contract. The next day Sid Friedlander of the *New York Post* wrote that Clifton wasn't surprised that he had been sold to the Knicks, but was surprised by the timing. "Not that the big guy had any objections to playing with the Knicks—on the contrary, he'd been trying to tie in with them for two years," Friedlander wrote.

"But he'd like to get a hunk of that purchase dough, which has been estimated as up in five figures, and he questioned the right of

Abe Saperstein, owner of the Globetrotters, to sell him without his sanction. 'I don't think he had the right to deal me off like that,' Sweetwater declared over the phone. 'I don't know what the price was. He didn't consult me. The deal was a surprise.'

"'I've been trying to go with the Knickerbockers for two years. He wouldn't sell me. I told him I wasn't satisfied and I wasn't going to play for him next season. I had a one-year continuation contract. All I had to do was stay out of basketball for a season and I'd be a free agent and could deal for myself. I didn't cost him much. I think I should get a split.'"[4]

Clifton hoped to negotiate a "split" when Saperstein returned from Europe, and at first thought he had gotten the one he desired. Later, he found that wasn't true. "He told me he sold me for $5,000. So he got $2,500 and he gave me $2,500," Clifton said, as quoted in Charles Salzberg's *From Set Shot to Slam Dunk*. "Being a kid—I wasn't too old then [twenty-seven]—well, I was old enough, but I hadn't had any experience or anything like that—at that time I believed him because I thought everybody was honest. That's the way I was raised, to take a person by their word. But later I came to find out that it was something like $20,000 he got, you understand what I mean? But you know, you got to take the bitter with the sweet. You can't be angry about things like that. If you're not up on things you just have to bounce the way the ball bounces."[5]

Podesta's letter to Ned Irish reveals that Clifton's contract was sold for $12,500, so instead of getting 50 percent of the purchase price his cut was only 20 percent. In 1950 players represented themselves in negotiations with their teams—agents weren't on the scene yet and the NBA Players Association didn't exist to protect players' interests. There probably was no way Clifton could have found out the cost of his contract. On the other hand, Saperstein deserves some credit—he wasn't obligated to share any of the purchase price with Clifton. Doing so probably was his way of maintaining a good relationship with Clifton, who later played for the Globetrotters during NBA off-seasons and twelve years later ended his career playing for Saperstein.

Beyond the money, Clifton was glad to join the Knicks, and New York coach Joe Lapchick felt the same about him: "He knows it's not a pancake league," Lapchick said. "He's tired of the other kind of ball. He wanted to play in New York and he wanted to play with the Knickerbockers. That's good." Lapchick also was enthusiastic about the skills Clifton would bring to his team at the center position, although Clifton was a relatively short one. "He has great arms," Lapchick said. "I think he'll hold his own with any of the big men in our league except maybe the one guy nobody can touch—Mikan. Of course, all that has to be proved. But we scouted him for a long time."[6]

Lapchick coached Clifton until 1956, generally they got along well, and Clifton was extremely popular with his teammates and Knicks fans. But at the time many Americans still angrily resisted integration, and some of them vented their feelings through venomous phone calls to Lapchick's home.

"I was five years old [when Clifton debuted with the Knicks]," said Lapchick's son, Richard, a noted sociologist who specializes in the racial dynamics of sports. "I didn't know what 'nigger' meant. But we lived in a big house in Yonkers, and whenever the phone rang I ran to it upstairs and for several years received what seemed like an enormous number of calls, and it was "nigger lover, nigger lover" for a number of years. I did know a lot of people didn't like my dad. As a five-year-old, even though he was a lovely man, I thought there was something wrong with him." It wasn't until 1967, when Richard was twenty-two years old, that he told his father he had been listening on the phone all those years.

Clifton and Hank DeZonie had both played for the Rens in the late 1940s, and in 1949 DeZonie had played for the New York Harlem Yankees in the semiprofessional American Basketball League (later renamed the Eastern League). There he was voted to the All-Star Team and tied with Pop Gates for second place in the voting for Most Valuable Player. Red Sarachek, Gates's coach when he played for the Scranton (Pennsylvania) Miners, made the connections that resulted in DeZonie becoming the fourth black player to join the NBA in 1950. But because DeZonie played just five games with the Tri-Cities Blackhawks, he's virtually unknown today.

He was no secret to players of his time, though, for the six-foot-six center was well respected by his peers. "I saw him play a number of times," said former Globetrotters star Marques Haynes. "He was a very strong player, very aggressive. He was one who could have played today because his game was so physical. He had the fundamentals down extremely well, as did most in those days."

DeZonie was a modern-day player in a premodern era. He was capable of "playing in the air," as it's called today. "I could get up, I could get UP!" DeZonie said. "I could jump, and all that floating, I did that." But he didn't dunk the ball because "dunking wasn't the thing to do. . . . The main thing was getting the ball, but we never thought of dunking. Even in high school, when a guy looked like he was shooting but was passing to me, I would just shoot the ball. It was never taking the ball and ram it through the basket. That didn't come until guys were six-ten. At that time, guys my height were six-five, six-four, six-three. If you had guys that were six-seven, they were awkward, but now you've got moving big men. I didn't worry about a guy six-ten because they couldn't play."

Another modern aspect of DeZonie's game was his one-handed jump shot instead of the standard two-hand set shot. "If you were shooting with one hand, they want to kick you off the team," he said. "Dribbling with one hand and all of a sudden jump up. What is he doing?" To DeZonie, comparing the deliberate set shot to a jump shot was ludicrous. "It's like loading a flintlock and shooting a machine gun," he said.

Sarachek recommended the idea of signing DeZonie to Ben Kerner, who owned the Tri-Cities Blackhawks and previously had Pop Gates on his team in the NBL. "I met him in New York," Sarachek said. "Kerner was not that type of man [who would reject a player because he was black]. I don't think he minded. He looked for a player, just like I did. It was an opportunity [for DeZonie] to go up, which was better than vagabonding with the Rens. . . . He was a good player, a tough player underneath the boards."

The Blackhawks' roster had been depleted by the departure of several players for the military during the Korean War, so Tri-Cities purchased DeZonie from the Harlem Yankees on December 1, 1950. That day, the *Daily Dispatch* of Moline, Illinois, ran a full-length photo of DeZonie with an accompanying article. No byline is attached to the article and its matter-of-fact style indicates that it probably was a rewrite of a Blackhawks' press release.

> *Hank DeZonie, 26, Negro star of Harlem Yankees, will join the Quad-City Blackhawks this weekend following his purchase from the New York colored basketball club, it was announced today by Ben Kerner, executive director of the quad-city basketball team.*
>
> *The Blackhawks also placed Ed Gayda, rookie from Washington State, on the NBA waiver list.*
>
> *DeZonie, who is 6–5, will operate at a forward spot with the Blackhawks.*
>
> *A graduate of Clark University, Atlanta, where in 1943 he was*

named most valuable man in the Southwestern Athletic conference,
he turned professional in 1944 and played with the New York Wrens
[sic] for three years in the American League.

The newest Blackhawk was No. 2 scorer in the American
circuit last year. He will be the third colored player in the National
Basketball Association. Others are Sweetwater Clifton of the New
York Knickerbockers and Charley Cooper of Boston. [Earl Lloyd
wasn't counted because he already had been drafted into the army.]

DeZonie makes his home in New York and during the summer
was a lifeguard at Coney Island.[7]

The Tri-Cities specifically hoped DeZonie could pick up some
of the scoring lost when six-seven Jack Nickols joined the U.S.
Marines. DeZonie debuted on December 3 against his hometown
team, the New York Knicks, and shot 3-for-13 for a total of 6 points
in Wharton field house, the Blackhawks' arena in Moline. "Hank
DeZonie, new Hawk, played competently, having practiced only
1–1/2 hours with the club," the *Daily Dispatch* reported.

DeZonie scored 4 points in the Hawks' next game against Fort
Wayne. With three seconds left in a tie game DeZonie missed a
shot that could have been the game winner and his chance at
hero status, a Piston going for the rebound was fouled and made a
free throw that resulted in a 77–76 Tri-Cities loss. DeZonie played
sparingly twice against Minneapolis and once against Indianapolis
on December 12.

In five games DeZonie shot just 24 percent from the field (6 for
25), averaged 3.4 points per game, and had eighteen rebounds and
nine assists. "I remember he was pretty good sized, and because
he was black, it was unusual," said a teammate, Mike Todorovich.
"Hank was a nice guy. He didn't play much, and it wasn't a fair
deal because he didn't get much of a chance at all. . . . He was
a character. I can't remember much about his basketball ability
because he didn't last long. I remember very well DeZonie . . . said
'let's go do something together when we get to New York because
Broadway's my beat.'"

The *Daily Dispatch* reported that he was waived on December
14 because star guard Gene Vance had received a thirty-day delay
in reporting to the army. When interviewed more than thirty-five
years later DeZonie said he cut his NBA career short because he
had burned out on basketball and couldn't tolerate his segregated
living conditions in the Tri-Cities. "I was through," he said. "I

wasn't playing. I wasn't interested. Red just thought I could play, and after I got there I was past that stuff. To go in some segregated affair, forget it." DeZonie said that because he couldn't reside with his white teammates, Kerner arranged for him to live with an old woman who chewed tobacco and had a house devoid of radio and television. "This is how it was, I couldn't see it at all," DeZonie said. "Segregated from the rest of the team that was staying at a plush hotel. That would turn you inside out. The thorns of segregation left scars that were unbelievable. These [white] people don't realize what they have done to other people."

So after only five games DeZonie told Kerner that he was quitting. What DeZonie said about his NBA career is no surprise: "It was a miserable experience because all the fun was out of the game. The accommodations, the segregation. I wasn't interested in it."

"No" to the Trotters, "Yes" to the NBA

The day he was drafted by the Boston Celtics—April 25, 1950—was one of the proudest days of Chuck Cooper's life. It was not unexpected; Cooper was an All-American from Duquesne (an East Coast basketball powerhouse), and Celtics scout Art Spector had told him that Boston might draft him. Considering that no black player had ever played in the NBA, however, there was always a chance that all twelve NBA teams would get cold feet and decide to postpone the racial groundbreaking for another year. But that seemed unlikely, especially since newspapers such as the *Chicago Tribune* had mentioned Cooper as a likely high draft pick, along with other stars of the year such as Villanova's Paul Arizin and Notre Dame's Kevin O'Shea.

When Celtics owner Walter Brown boldly announced that he was making Cooper a second-round pick, the breakthrough was official. By being drafted Cooper had joined a very small club of black sports pioneers. He welcomed the challenge but also tried to keep it in perspective. "Actually, I consider it a rather dubious achievement," Cooper told *Pittsburgh Magazine* in 1976. "The Harlem Globetrotters were around long before me. Also a league up in New York state [the Eastern League] produced many great black players, including Dolly King and Pop Gates. So if I was good enough, plenty before me were equally as good."[1]

Nonetheless, Cooper was thrilled to be drafted. "Yes, he was excited and proud to have been the first one," said his closest friend, Harold Brown, who first met Cooper when they were teammates at Westinghouse High in Pittsburgh. "I remember when he called me and said 'I've got something to show you.' There was a little printer's proof of a page [from *Who's Who in Colored America*], and they had his picture and name—"First Black to Sign in the NBA.' This was about a year after he was in the NBA, and he was carrying it around, showing it to people." Cooper was extraordinarily proud to be the first drafted. He was an extremely modest person who rarely talked about his achievements, in sports or otherwise, without being prodded to do so. Carrying that proof page and showing it to his friends was completely out of character.

Cooper was born in 1926 and raised in an era when racial discrimination was commonplace in Pittsburgh, a city that former *Pittsburgh Courier* city editor Frank Bolden described as "too close to West Virginia and the South" to be liberal. Bolden, the black newspaper's entertainment writer, columnist, and war correspondent at different times between 1930 and 1960, described a city thats downtown restaurants wouldn't serve black people and housing was segregated. Bolden came to the city in 1930 to attend the University of Pittsburgh; he lived at the Center Avenue YMCA because no one would rent an apartment to him near the school. Bolden remembers that department stores wouldn't allow black customers to try on clothes, fearing that if the item wasn't purchased it would be unsuitable for white customers later.

Nightlife was segregated, too. When Bolden and his girlfriend went to certain movie theaters, until the mid-1930s they had to sit in the balcony. If they wanted to listen to jazz, their choices were limited. Black and white people both could go to Crawford Grill II, a club owned by the well-known professional gambler Gus Greenlee. But if they wanted to hear famed clarinetist Benny Goodman, blacks couldn't do it at downtown clubs like Lenny Lipman's or the Club Melody.

"The only black employees you had downtown when Chuck was playing were custodians in banks, elevator operators and the bootblacks, Negro women in charge of the ladies' lounge and powder rooms in department stores," Bolden said. "They'd clean up after the white women. But clerks, cashiers, and all that? No, none of that. It came later. And we lost the jobs in hotels as waiters when they decided to put [white] women waitresses in. They came in at a lower scale and blacks lost their jobs. No black bellhops. . . . You had no blacks in the police or fire department. We had two or three, but no blacks in the upper echelon. Every black policeman was a patrolman. No sergeants, no turnkeys [detectives], no inspectors. None of that." Chuck Cooper's father, Charles Sr., had graduated from Virginia Union College and then worked in the Pittsburgh post office.

Bolden said that black people in Pittsburgh weren't pushing very hard to change things until after World War II for fear that doing so could cost them or their relatives their jobs. "It was just like in the South," he said. "Today, they say that's not true. But I went through that. It was true." Cooper's friend, Harold Brown, recalled that when Cooper first started playing basketball he was mentored by older black players such as Coy Allen, the older brother of future baseball major leaguers Richie and Hank Allen. In 1941 Cooper made the varsity team at Westinghouse High as a sophomore, but even then the disenchantment that troubled him in the pros began to appear. For instance, not getting to shoot the ball almost ended his high school career before it even started. A few months into his rookie season with the Celtics, Cooper told the *Pittsburgh Courier's* Bill Nunn Jr., a former teammate at Westinghouse, why he almost quit their high school team.

"One day after I had gone through a rather hectic session of playing defensive ball and being, what I termed, a dummy for the varsity, I suddenly got fed up with the whole thing and walked off the floor," Cooper said.

"I always figured a basketball player was supposed to get an opportunity to shoot the ball some time. But the way it seemed to me I would be an old man before I got a chance to do any shooting. All I heard was 'guard your man, Coop—stick with 'em— keep those feet spread—hands up!' Finally I got fed up. I guess the luckiest day of my life occurred just as I walked off the floor. By the time I reached the dressing room my coach, Ralph R. Zahniser, was waiting for me. He sat down and talked to me like a father. He told me he thought I had a great future in basketball if I would only work at it. He explained to me that the things that looked like a waste of time now would some day pay off. I sat and listened. The more he talked the more ashamed of myself I became for almost quitting. In the end I asked him if he would give me another chance. This time I stuck."[2]

Cooper was a reserve guard that season, averaging 3.6 points in fourteen games, but in the next two seasons he blossomed. Playing center he averaged 12.1 points as a junior and 13.6 as a senior, he led his team to the city championship, and was a unanimous selection to the All-City first team as a senior. Yet he could have scored even more points had he wanted to. "He was a good rebounder," Brown said. "He could score well. He would have scored double what he did if he wasn't so generous. That was his main fault, everyone said. He would give the ball to the man closest to the basket. They used to say, 'Shoot! Shoot!' and he would say, 'Well, the guy had a better shot than I did.' That was all the way to the pros."

In high school Cooper displayed his intolerance of unfair treatment, which became a source of constant frustration in later years. "Nobody pushed him around," Brown said. "He would stand up and fight for his rights."

When he graduated in 1944, colleges in New York were beginning to assemble a collection of extremely talented black players at City College of New York, St. John's University, and Long Island U. The coach at Long Island, the legendary Clair Bee, heavily recruited him, but Cooper decided to attend college elsewhere. Not at Duquesne, however. Although he has repeatedly been referred to as a product of that school's basketball program, the Dukes must share that distinction with West Virginia State College, which produced the NBA's Earl Lloyd and, in 1951, Bob Wilson. West Virginia State was a popular choice for black high school graduates from Pittsburgh, and Bill Nunn Jr., Cooper's teammate, had been one of them. Brown believes Cooper decided to join his close buddy there.

Nunn wrote that as a freshman Cooper averaged almost 20 points per game for the Yellow Jackets during the 1944–45 season, when they compiled a 19-6 record for coach Horace McCarthy. But it was the middle of World War II and Cooper knew he soon would be joining the military so he withdrew from school before the academic year ended. "At the time I entered West Virginia a lot of people told me I was crazy," Cooper told Nunn. "Maybe I was, but to this day I don't regret my decision. Although I was at the school only one semester before I went into the navy, I'll always treasure my days there."

In the service Cooper played on the navy's Fleet City team on the West Coast, where the point guard was future Hall of Famer Dick McGuire. When Cooper was released from the service his basketball skills were again desired by many colleges. "Quite a few schools on the West Coast seemed interested in me," he told Nunn. "But once I got my discharge papers the only thing I could think about was getting home to Pittsburgh. At the time I wasn't thinking much about school. Once I got home, though, and got settled, it didn't take me long to make up my mind. I always have liked being around the 'Burgh, so I guess it was only natural that I should enroll at Duquesne. Besides being one of the best basketball schools in the country, they had a high scholastic rating, too."[3]

Cooper's decision to play in his hometown created "a buzz in the city," Brown said, even though Cooper wasn't the first black basketball player at Duquesne. That distinction belongs to Cumberland Posey back in 1917, although Posey enrolled under a phony name, Charles Cumbert, and his light complexion, wavy hair, and hazel eyes allowed Posey to "pass" for white. No one figured out that he was the son of a black steamboat manufacturer until many years later, when he became well known as a player, manager, and owner of the Homestead Grays of the Negro baseball leagues.

Perhaps because black schools were not yet allowed into the NAIA or the NCAA, the fact that Cooper had already played one year of college ball had no effect upon his eligibility at Duquesne. He played four years there under Chick Davies, with whom he had a great relationship, and Dudey Moore. After Cooper became a starter as a freshman early in the 1946–47 season, he played forward and center and averaged 7.7 points per game. That season Duquesne's administration also demonstrated its strong support for him by canceling games against Tennessee (which refused to compete against a black opponent) and Miami (because interracial athletic contests were illegal in Florida).

"Racism wasn't limited to the South," Cooper told author Art Rust. "We were playing the University of Cincinnati out in the Midwest. There was an out-of-bounds play and they were lining up to guard us. One guy shouted, "I got the nigger!" I walked over to him and said, 'And I got your mother in my jockstrap.' He was shocked. After the game, which as I remember they won, he came over to apologize. I thought I had already said what needed to be said and I told him that. I also said, "If you can take what I said, then I can take a thousand 'niggers.' That was the only time during my college career that I was called 'nigger' to my face."[4]

Cooper played center exclusively his next three seasons, averaging 7.6, 13.5, and 11.5 points, and led Duquesne to berths in two National Invitational Tournaments, at the time the most prestigious college tournament in America. As a senior he was captain of a team that went 23-6 and was ranked sixth nationally. Duquesne achieved an impressive 78-19 record during his career. He left Duquesne as its all-time leading scorer with 990 points and a 10.3 per-game average, and as a senior was named first-team All-America by Converse and *Look Magazine*. In addition he was an honorable mention All-American according to the Helms Foundation, *Sporting News*, and the United Press and Associated Press news services.

Even after leaving Duquesne more honors came his way: in 1950 he played on the collegiate team in the annual All-Star Game between college stars and the NBA champion Minneapolis Lakers. Then the Globetrotters signed him to play for them during an eighteen-game coast-to-coast World Series against the College All-Americans. The college squad included future NBA stars Bob Cousy and Paul Arizin.

The April 8, 1950, *Pittsburgh Courier* reported that Cooper "made his debut as a pro with the Trotters" during their April 2 game in Chicago Stadium, scoring 3 points and rebounding well during a 58–47 win over the All-Americans. The Globetrotters won the series 11-7 in front of a total crowd of 181,364 fans. The tournament's finale, a 77–64 win by the Trotters on April 19, attracted an arena-record crowd of 7,398 to Uline Arena in Washington DC. The Trotters' two centers tied as second-leading scorers with 12 points each. Ironically, within a month both of those centers, Cooper and Sweetwater Clifton, would be acquired by NBA teams and start chipping away at the Globetrotters' virtual monopoly on black players.

It is unclear whether Cooper actually signed with the Globetrotters for the next basketball season or if his agreement with them held for the World Series only. Either way, Cooper had a choice to make after the Celtics drafted him, and *Pittsburgh Press* columnist Roy McHugh wrote that Abe Saperstein tried to entice Cooper, an accomplished singer, by offering him the lead role opposite star Dorothy Dandridge in a movie about the Globetrotters. Instead Cooper chose the NBA, partly because of the symbolism of being its first drafted black player and partly because the salary was slightly better.

Although Saperstein had gone ballistic after the Celtics drafted Cooper—telling the NBA that his team "would never play in Boston again"—on May 4, 1950, he sent a congratulatory telegram to Cooper releasing him from his contract so he could pursue the noble goal of integrating the NBA. The telegram read:

> *Sorry failure telephoning. Thousand and one problems preparatory European leaving. Plan writing fully. Considered carefully circumstances surrounding draft considering opportunity initial colored performer NBA. Agreed if satisfactory to you to relinquish my claims your services to Boston Celtics. Will explain fully if you come over to Europe early June as we discussed. Anything else call my secretary*

*Mrs. Linehan at Chicago. To me you were you are and you always
will be a Harlem Globetrotter. Cordially, Abe Saperstein*[5]

One wonders, however, if the Celtics unintentionally had
given Saperstein a convenient way to get out of the contract.
During his short stint with the Globetrotters Cooper had been
dismayed by some of the players' living conditions and informed
his teammates that they should be treated better. Brown said
Cooper liked the Trotter players, especially Pop Gates, his roommate and coach of the Trotters from 1950 to 1955. Cooper's son,
Charles III, had the same impression: "I grew up when Marques
Haynes [a remarkable dribbler] would be on television a lot with
the Globetrotters, and Dad said, 'But you should have seen Pop
Gates. . . . He was incredible. The ball was just a part of him.'"

However, "What really disturbed me was how the Globetrotters were treated by Saperstein," Cooper once said. "When I was
with the Trotters, they were playing a series of games against the
College All-Stars, who were almost all white. While we all traveled
in the same chartered bus, the hotel accommodations were very
different. Saperstein had one of the few solid moneymakers in the
game at that time. The NBA was even on thin ice at that time, yet
Saperstein had his black players staying in dirty, roach-infested
holes in the wall. I used to point this out to the Globetrotter
players. Not only were the living conditions bad, but there was
a big pay difference between the NBA players and themselves. For
doing that I got the reputation as a troublemaker."[6]

Once Cooper decided to play for Boston, one matter had to be
settled: his salary. Considering Walter Brown's shaky financial status, it is no surprise that he wasn't overly generous. The two sides
eventually reached an impasse, so Haskell Cohen, the NBA's public
relations director, was asked to negotiate the deal. Cohen, a public
relations man who had been involved in picking high school and
college All-America teams since the 1920s, had many Duquesne
connections, was a friend of Red Auerbach's, and also knew Cooper
when he got him a summer job in the Catskill mountains when
Cooper was a teenager. Consequently, NBA commissioner Maurice
Podoloff asked Cohen to intervene. "I signed him in three minutes
[for $7,500]," on June 30. Cohen said he wouldn't term signing a
black player as "risky" for the Celtics, "but it certainly was a big
first and an indication of the times. People were beginning to think
in a more fashionable manner. Cooper was one of the first black

players to go to [a predominantly white] college, and on ability he seemed to make it. It didn't cause that much of a stir because the Knicks signed Clifton about a month later, and then Washington had drafted Lloyd. There were three in the first year [he evidently didn't know about DeZonie] and that took the edge off anyone who wanted to make a stink about it."

6

Frustrated Pioneer

To Frank Bolden, editor at the *Pittsburgh Courier*, Chuck Cooper was the ideal player to initiate a racial breakthrough in pro basketball because he fit Bolden's definition of a pioneer. "He makes a path where there is no path," Bolden said. "He's my type of American Negro. Like Mary Bethune [the educator] and Charles Drew [the doctor who revolutionized blood plasma transfusion during World War II], he made stepping stones out of stumbling blocks. Discrimination and segregation, he overcame that with his ability, and he had to have one hell of an ability for Red Auerbach to draft him."

Cooper also had to have sterling character. "I do remember that Walter Brown was selective," said Ed Leede, a guard on the 1950 Celtics who became one of Cooper's best friends on the team. "He felt he had obtained a player of high personal integrity and felt that was extremely important in introducing a colored player to the team and the public."

The fact that Cooper had been drafted was no guarantee he would make the final roster; he had to earn that honor by his preseason performance. The Celtics obviously were committed to seriously considering black players because Cooper was one of four in training camp in 1950. The others were Isaac "Rabbit" Walthour (a playground legend from New York City), Chuck Harmon (later a major-league infielder), and Hank DeZonie. On October 7, 1950, the *Pittsburgh Courier* published a column by Bill Nunn Jr. that included a letter from Cooper bubbling with enthusiasm about his professional basketball future. The letter read:

> *We started working out last Monday and things have been moving pretty fast ever since. We are going through two workouts daily and it's easily seen that these people mean business. They almost killed all concerned that first week.*

> *There are sixteen or seventeen players here now and we're training*

*right here in the city. Including myself there are four Negroes among
the group trying out. One of the best of this lot is Isaac Walthour, a
bad boy with a real nice set shot. He's fast and deceptive, and hits
in the hole and cuts probably better than anybody here.*

*Harmon, formerly of Toledo, just arrived and I haven't had a chance
to see him in action. Then there's Hank DeZonie from the Rens. I
know you know about him. He's still jumping like mad, too.*

*Among the others are Ed Macauley, Kenny Sailors, Tony Lavelli,
John Mahnken [formerly of the Washington Caps], Andy Duncan
and Sonny Hertzberg, last year's captain. They're all real bad boys
that know basketball inside and out.* [1]

Of the black players mentioned, only Cooper made the regular-season roster. Walthour played point guard; unfortunately, so did future Hall of Famer Bob Cousy. Walthour, who was only twenty-two years old at the time, later played four games for the Milwaukee Hawks in the 1953–54 season. Regarding DeZonie, however, the issue became character rather than performance, a measuring stick that DeZonie resented. "Hank was kind of a problem," Auerbach said. "He came to training camp with his girlfriend and put her up in the hotel. He was one of the flamboyant guys. He wasn't my kind."

DeZonie later heard that the New York Knicks had inquired about him but didn't contact him after he received a bad recommendation from Dolly King, his former teammate on the Rens. "Well, as a young man I was pretty notorious," DeZonie said. "In those days you weren't picked on your ability; you had to be the Pope, you had to be a saint. He said he didn't think I was the right type of person, so that cut me out for the Knicks."

Cooper debuted on November 1 in Boston's season opener against Fort Wayne, scoring 9 points on 3-for-6 shooting and pulling down two rebounds in a 107–84 loss. Three days later a *Courier* article quoted him as saying that outside of a little homesickness, he thought professional basketball was more fun than college ball. In light of later developments, it's ironic that Cooper believed the NBA was going to open up his offensive game. "They don't tie you down, and that's what I like," he said. "In college we were only supposed to take certain shots at certain times. But in this pro game you are supposed to shoot any time from any place. The coach demands that you do it. If you don't you're in for a good bawling out." [2]

Meanwhile, Auerbach was proud of the way his players were responding to their black teammate. Three years earlier even some of Jackie Robinson's teammates resented his presence when he first joined the Brooklyn Dodgers, a reaction that Auerbach partly attributes to the fact that most baseball players had gone directly from high school to the minor leagues, which deprived them of the sophistication that comes with age. A compounding factor was that many major league players were from the Deep South, where discrimination against black people was harshest.

Almost all of the NBA players had attended college, which made them more open-minded, and many had played with and against black players long before coming to the pros. Cooper's presence wasn't a cause for concern or alarm among the white Celtics. "We had a lot of problems, but not from the athletes themselves," Auerbach said. "When Chuck Cooper joined us, some players came to me and said this is a little unusual, but we'd like to room with him. So I changed roommates every three or four weeks. He roomed with Bones McKinney [after the Washington Caps had folded], who was from the South, he roomed with Cousy, he roomed with Sharman. It was no problem. In those days, they wanted to make him feel at home. They wanted to make sure he was part of our group. I think it was very encouraging. I think it showed the possibility of great chemistry. I think it was great."

"I would have to say the response was generally favorable," Leede said. "I think Chuck was taken in quite warmly. There were a few players—I prefer not to mention names—where there might have been the slightest undercurrent of possible resentment. I considered Chuck a good friend, enjoyed his company, and he and I spent a fair amount of time together in Boston. We'd have a beer in the evening and take in a movie. I have fond recollections and heard from him after I had left the Celtics."

Next to his family, the love of Cooper's life was jazz. Birdland, the famous jazz club in New York, was a second home to him, and he was personal friends with singers such as Sarah Vaughn, Carmen McRae, and Harry Belafonte because they sometimes stayed at the same hotels. Cooper's friend, Harold Brown, remembered once walking in New York City with Cooper when they bumped into Belafonte. "Belafonte was saying, 'I heard you came to the theater looking for [a young woman].' Chuck said yeah, and Belafonte said, 'She was asking about you so much it made me jealous—and I don't even like the girl.'"

Whenever he could, Cooper listened to his homeboy from Pittsburgh, pianist Errol Garner. Fortunately Cousy, who became Cooper's lifelong friend, shared his appreciation for music. "We both liked jazz and in New York we'd often go to listen to Errol Garner or George Shearing," Cooper said. "Or he would take me to private clubs in Boston on Sunday when you couldn't get a drink anywhere else. I was lonely, but he made me feel better about things. Cousy is as about as free of the affliction of racism as any white person I've ever known."[3]

Cousy attributed his ease among blacks to his growing up in a New York ghetto with a mixing bowl of nationalities. "I can hate very specifically because I'm very competitive, but I have never been able to understand class hatred," he said. "I can understand rednecks, indigents, or dropouts hating out of insecurity, but out of a higher intellectual plane—racism demonstrated by people bright enough to know better—I don't understand how to hate groups. It's so stupid."

Cooper's rookie season was impressive. "I thought of him as strong physically," Leede said. "He weighed well over 200 pounds, was a good rebounder. I think of him as a small power forward. He did not have tremendous breakaway speed like a lot [of players] today. I can recall his shooting an overhead two-hand set shot which won a game for us and Walter Brown, the owner, came running out of the stands he was so thrilled. He was a tenacious defensive player, and certainly a team ball player. If anything, he would be inclined to pass up a shot more than taking an opening."

For four years the Celtics had been the joke of the league, but when Auerbach, Cousy, high-scoring center Macauley, and Cooper joined the team at the same time, it received an instant injection of talent and leadership. Eight nights after Cooper's NBA debut, the Celtics opened at home as 6,959 fans at the Boston Garden got their first look at their rejuvenated team. After falling behind 19–12 against the defending NBA champion Minneapolis Lakers, the Celtics rallied for a 76–71 victory behind McCauley's 22 points and 19 from Cooper off the bench.

Clif Keane, writing in an article for the *Boston Daily Globe*, raved about the performance of Cooper and another rookie, Bob Donham:

> *It wasn't that Donham and Cooper were spectacular. It was the*
> *great poise the freshmen had that lifted the Celtics out of their*

reckless playing. Donham took charge like a 10-year veteran, and Cooper was springing off the boards taking rebounds away from the Lakers, one of the tallest sets of men in basketball.

The team made a complete about-face with Donham and Cooper in the lineup, and while the game was tied up 10 times with Mikan and the rest of the oldsters constantly yammering at the officials, the rookies still held their poise.

Cooper played the final 34 minutes of the game and Donham went out on fouls, double-teaming on Mikan. Cooper wound up scoring 19 points, while Donham got seven, and led the floor play for several others.

The biggest basket Cooper got came after nine minutes of the last period. The Celtics made a three-point [play]. Cooper took a one-handed set from about 15 feet out and swished the basket. The Celtics held the margin finally to win, 76–71.

In the Celtics dressing room, Cooper, one of the most popular players on the squad, still didn't look as though he had been through a rugged game. "Put it down for me," said the nearby [John] Mahnken. "That Cooper is a great basketball player.[4]

On November 15 Cooper made key plays as the Celtics won their fifth straight game (a surprisingly short franchise record) and moved into first place with the best record in the league at 5-3. "With freshman Charley Cooper in the role of platoon leader, the Celts ran in eight straight points in the late stages after being down, 74–71, with less than three minutes remaining," the *Boston Herald* reported.[5]

Cooper started the rally by making a midcourt steal then being fouled while scoring. The ensuing free throw tied the game at 74. Cooper won a center jump, which allowed Boston to control the ball for a minute before he passed to Donham, who scored. Donham then returned the favor, making an assist on a Cooper basket. Later that year, however, Cooper's reluctance to shoot, or ambivalence about doing so, became an issue. Not that he wasn't scoring—his 9.3 points per game ranked fourth on the team—but Auerbach believed he should be scoring more. Cooper agreed, implied by his comments in a February 3, 1951, article in the *Boston Evening American*. Though he was averaging 9.6 points midway through the season, the night before Cooper had surprised everyone by scoring 19 points, including 13 of the Celtics' first 16 in a victory over Syracuse. Bob Ajemian's entire article focused on why that was so unexpected.

"Like a pendulum, coach Red Auerbach is there to remind him," Ajemian wrote.

> *Still, Charlie Cooper, Celtics' brilliant rookie, won't shoot. Potentially one of the better scorers in pro basketball, Cooper, to the wonderment of many, confines himself to rebounding, passing, general assistance.*
>
> *Last night against Syracuse, he took time off to shoot.*
> *Auerbach feels Cooper can be a high scorer.*
> *"He has all the material," says the Boston coach. "Cooper has one of the longest strides in basketball. You've seen the way he jumps. His shot is good; he has the quick instinct of a top scorer.*
> *"I keep telling him to shoot more. He's coming along slowly. It's a question of getting adjusted, don't forget he's still a first-year man. That adds a mental obstacle."*[6]

Later in the article Cooper admitted feeling conflicted about shooting. "I know I should, Red has told me to try for more," he said. "I guess I'm used to playing possession ball. I never shot much in college. I never had big nights. Now it's a habit with me. Tonight, they were playing me back for a drive. They gave me so much room I thought I'd better shoot."

However, when interviewed for a *Pittsburgh Magazine* article later in 1976, it appears that the Syracuse game had become a tormenting, rather than a cherished memory for him. It appears that Cooper used the Syracuse game to demonstrate that management intentionally prevented him from scoring more: "We were playing Syracuse and their best player, Dolph Schayes, was guarding me," Cooper said. "We wanted to get Schayes into foul trouble, so they started feeding me. Soon, we were leading by 5 and I had 17 of our total 19. Suddenly, Auerbach reverted us to our regular pattern. I scored once the rest of the game."[7]

Over twenty-six years a stark contradiction in Cooper's viewpoint had emerged. Since Cooper has died there is no way to know exactly why. But three explanations seem feasible:

It's possible that on the night of the game, Cooper was perfectly satisfied with how it transpired. But as the years passed he may have come to believe more and more that his scoring potential had been ignored; perhaps he came to reflect on that game from a different perspective.

It's possible that Cooper always believed that Auerbach intentionally had shut down his scoring that night. One can imagine the reporter getting Auerbach's opinion about Cooper's scoring from the coach's postgame comments, then telling Cooper that Auerbach had said he's been urging Cooper to shoot more. Just four months into his professional career, Cooper likely was still feeling his way as the team's first black player and could have been savvy enough not to contradict Auerbach in print.

It's possible that Auerbach went back to the regular offense just out of habit, with no thought of curtailing Cooper's scoring. Considering the many concerns that Cooper must have felt about being treated fairly as a black player fifty years ago, it's possible he was skeptical about anything unusual that happened.

Overall, Cooper's rookie season was a success both for him and the Celtics. The team compiled a 39-30 record, trailing only Philadelphia (40-26) in the Eastern Division standings; New York then swept them in only two games of the opening playoff series. Cooper finished fourth on the team in scoring with 615 points, and second only to Macauley in rebounds, with 562. That season's points, rebounds, and 174 assists were Cooper's career highs.

The next season Cooper was involved in the only fight he said he had in the pros that was triggered by a racial incident. It occurred on February 17, 1952, against the Milwaukee Hawks in Moline, Illinois. By nature Cooper was a gentle man, but he had no qualms about fighting when the need arose. In fact, the NBA was so rugged in those days that fighting skills were a player's key to survival. Cooper had a standing rule about racial slurs—he would give the offender one chance to take it back. If it wasn't taken back then look out.

"One of their players called me a black bastard," Cooper said. "I asked him what he said and he repeated it. So I pushed him in the face as hard as I could. I wanted to fight him but wanted him to throw the first punch. He wouldn't fight—but everyone else did.

"Both benches cleared and everyone started pairing off. [Boston's] Bob Brannum and Mel Hutchins, a couple of muscle guys, squared off. Even the opposing coaches, Auerbach and Doxie Moore, went at it. It was quite a sight, the worst fight I remember. I was thrown out and fined by the league. But when the commissioner, Maurice Podoloff, heard the full story he rescinded the fine. But that kind of name-calling was a rarity.

"There certainly was never any racial problem within the Celtics. Oh, once in a while somebody would get overanxious in letting me know he'd 'grown up with blacks and had been best friends,' the sort of stuff that gets stale after hearing it over again. But their intentions were good and, as I've said, everyone was very supportive."[8]

Especially Cousy, who got a bitter, firsthand taste of what it was like to be black in the South when the Celtics played in Raleigh, North Carolina (probably a preseason game). At first the Celtics were told that Cooper would be banned from the game, but Auerbach threatened not to play. The ban was lifted but Cooper wasn't allowed to stay at the team hotel. "I was just shell-shocked," Cousy said. Rather than find an alternative Cooper decided to take the train back to Boston that evening, and Cousy kept him company.

Cooper's reluctance to stay in Raleigh may have stemmed from some terrifying experiences he had had at black hotels. "I'm not sure where these hotels were, but they would be black hotels in ghetto areas," said Cooper's second wife, Irva, who married him in 1957. "He said there wouldn't be locks on the door and he had to push the furniture around to keep people from coming in his room. He said one night he forgot to do it and somebody busted into his room, and he said he jumped right up in the bed. Chuck was going to kick him. He was going to fight and defend himself."

Immediately taking the train back to Boston allowed him to avoid that kind of traumatic incident. "But when we got to the train station," Cousy said, "we ran into the black-white signs for the men's room. Maybe at that point, I was more embarrassed than poor Coop.

"I remember we had a long wait at the platform. I didn't know what to say. I didn't want to say the wrong thing, and I didn't want to say anything trivial or light because I'm sure he was experiencing emotional trauma. I was just completely embarrassed by the whole thing because I was part of the establishment that did those things."

Although Cooper received little respect from certain segments of society, the fact that he reached the NBA made him a local hero to younger black players in Pittsburgh. Two of Cooper's close friends were Maurice Stokes and Ed Fleming, both seven years his junior, and who later had successful NBA careers. (In fact, Stokes was a potential superstar until a fluke injury ended his NBA career in 1958.) They would watch Cooper play for Duquesne, and Fleming especially tried to copy Cooper's "spread eagle" technique of grabbing a rebound and then extending his arms and legs to protect the ball.

When Cooper played in the NBA Stokes and Fleming were college stars, and Cooper's stories about professional ball inspired them to reach the NBA, too. During the summer all three played ball at Mellon Park, the basketball mecca for the best players in Pittsburgh. That group included Jack Twyman (eventually a six-time NBA All-Star) and Dick Groat (who played one season in the NBA before becoming a major league baseball player). They would gather at the park on the corner of Fifth and Penn, and compete hour after hour. When they got hungry, their case of the munchies was worsened by the tempting scent of fresh baked goods at the Nabisco factory just a few blocks away.

To Fleming, Cooper's generosity was just as important as his basketball prowess. "He always had time to spend with you, talk with you, showing you different things," Fleming said. He and Stokes were into rhythm and blues music, but of course Cooper introduced them to jazz and let them listen to his records. They could borrow his car when they wanted to go out, and since Cooper already was married, they ate at his house, too. What else could two teenage boys ask for? Here was a friend who let them share his basketball, music, car, and food.

After Cooper's rookie season, his scoring decreased each of his next three years with Boston, from 8.2 points per game, to 6.5, to 3.3 during the 1953–54 season. He averaged a plentiful thirty minutes a game during both his second and third years, but only about half that during his last season there.

Cooper still had occasional moments of glory. For instance, one account of a November 20, 1953, game called him "a terror on the boards" during a runaway victory over Fort Wayne.[9] But five weeks later a *Boston Daily Globe* story noted that "Cooper played 16 minutes, which was a new high for him in recent weeks."[10] In March Cooper admitted that he was surprised when his defensive skills earned him a start against New York in a playoff game. Cooper hadn't been in the starting lineup since the previous December 19, and he made the most of the opportunity by holding Boston nemesis Fred Schaus to just one shot in the first quarter, then blanketing Jim Baechtold in the third period of Boston's win.

"Do you remember what I said about Cooper the other day?" Schaus asked a reporter that evening. "I always thought Cooper was a good ball player. But it's awful hard to score and rebound

when you're sitting on that bench the way he has been all year."[11]
That realization must have struck Cooper, too, because the *Pittsburgh Courier* reported that Cooper had asked to be traded. He essentially got his wish on May 15, 1954, when he was sold to the Hawks, who had moved from Tri-Cities to Milwaukee in 1951.

During his year-and-a-half stay with the Hawks, Cooper was subjected to several infuriating situations in the segregated South. The Hawks played an exhibition game in Baton Rouge, Louisiana, where his teammate, Bob Pettit, had been a star at Louisiana State. But Cooper wasn't allowed to play in the game.

"Red Holzman was our coach and asked me if I wanted him to take a stand," Cooper said. "I got angry because I didn't think his offer was sincere—and told him so. I knew they weren't going to cancel with seven thousand people in the stands. So I went out and sat in the front row near the press row. When the teams came out, all the Hawks came over one by one and shook hands in a gesture to the crowd—all except one. Bob Pettit ignored me. Maybe I should be understanding. He was in his hometown and environment. But that's exactly why a gesture by him would have been the biggest gesture of all."[12]

Another episode occurred during an exhibition game in the Carolinas. "We came out of the dressing room at halftime," recalled Mel Hutchins, an NBA player from 1951 to 1958. "Cooper was a starter and he took his jacket off and we had to go in between the crowd, and the small kids had never seen a black without a shirt. They stood back and looked like they wanted to touch his skin to see if it was real. He said, 'Go ahead, go ahead and touch me. The black won't run off.' And the kids just laughed and laughed.

"He felt as an equal, and yet the people wouldn't treat him as one in the South. He says, 'It will change. I know it'll change, but right now I know I have to accept it. I could fight it like some people do, but I have to accept it.'"

Being sold to Milwaukee at first rejuvenated Cooper's career. Playing for Holzman, who later gained fame as the coach of the champion New York Knicks, Cooper began the season by scoring more points than at any time in his entire basketball career. He was averaging 15 points a game in early December, including a spurt in which he scored 23, 27, and 19 points in three consecutive games. By mid-January his average had dropped to 12.5, which still far surpassed his NBA best; Cooper was calling his purchase by Milwaukee the biggest break in his career.

Earl Lloyd of the Washington Capitols became the first black player to appear in an NBA game on October 31, 1950. Courtesy of West Virginia State College, Institute WV.

In 1902 Harry "Bucky" Lew played with the Lowell team in the New England League as the first black professional basketball player. Courtesy of the Center for Lowell History, Lowell MA.

The New York Renaissance compiled a 2,318–381 record from 1923 to 1949. Pictured here in the 1938–39 season are (*left to right*) Wee Willie Smith, Tarzan Cooper, John Isaacs, Pop Gates, Puggy Bell, Eyre Saitch, Zack Clayton, and Fats Jenkins. Photo given to the author by Pop Gates.

IMPORTANT NOTICE TO PLAYERS AND CLUB PRESIDENTS

Every player before signing a contract should carefully scrutinize the same to ascertain whether all of the conditions agreed upon between the Player and Club President have been incorporated therein, and if any have been omitted the player should insist upon having all the terms, conditions, promises and agreements inserted in the contract before he signs the same.

NATIONAL BASKETBALL ASSOCIATION

UNIFORM PLAYER CONTRACT

THIS AGREEMENT made this __26th__ day of __April__, by and between __WASHINGTON CAPITOLS BASKETBALL CLUB__ (hereinafter called the Club), a member of the National Basketball Association, and __HAROLD HUNTER__

of the City, Town of _____ (hereinafter called the Player).

WITNESSETH:—

In consideration of the several and/or mutual promises and/or agreements hereinafter contained, the parties hereto promise and agree as follows:

1. The Club hereby employs the Player as a skilled Basketball Player for the season __1950-51__ which includes the Club's training season and all regular championship games scheduled during such season and includes the playoffs at the close of the schedule season (for which additional compensation is to be received by the player as may be provided by the Association.

2. The Club agrees to pay the Player for rendering services described herein the sum of $ __4,000.00__ in twelve equal semi-monthly payments beginning with the first of said payments on November 15th of the season above described and continuing with such payments on the first and fifteenth of each month until said man is paid in full. Provided however if the Club does not qualify for the playoffs the payments due subsequent to the conclusion of the schedule season shall become due and payable immediately after the conclusion of the schedule season.

...

22. (a) On or before October 1st (or if a Sunday, then the next preceding business day) next following the last playing season covered by this contract, the Club may render to the Player a contract for the term of that season by mailing the same to the Player at his address following his signature hereto, or if none be given, then at his last address of record while in the Club. If prior to the November 1 next succeeding said October 1, the Player and the Club have not agreed upon the terms of such contract, then on or before 10 days after said November 1, the Club shall have the right by written notice to the Player at said address to retain this contract for the period of one year on the same terms, except that the amount payable to the Player shall be such an amount as the Club shall fix in said notice, provided, however, that said amount shall be an amount payable at a rate not less than 75% of the rate stipulated for the preceding year.

(b) The Club's right to renew this contract, as provided in subparagraph (a) of this paragraph 22, and the promise of the Player not to play otherwise than with the Club have been taken into consideration in determining the amount payable under paragraph 2 hereof.

23. This agreement shall be construed to have been made under and shall be governed by the Laws of the State of __D.C.__

24. This Agreement contains the entire agreement between the Parties and there are no oral or written inducements, promises or agreements except as contained herein.

IN WITNESS WHEREOF the Player has hereunto set his hand and seal and the Club has caused this contract to be executed by its duly authorized officer.

WASHINGTON CAPITOLS BASKETBALL CLUB

By _____ President.
__Harold Hunter__ Player.
__506 Hargett St. Durham, N.C.__ Player's Address

WITNESSES:
__J. B. McLendon__
__L. T. Walker__

PLAYERS CONTRACT

AS PRESCRIBED FOR THE

National Basketball Association

The __WASHINGTON CAPITOLS BASKETBALL__
CLUB

Of __WASHINGTON, D. C.__

WITH

__HAROLD HUNTER__

I hereby certify that I have, at this date, received examined and noted of record the within Contract.

Secretary-Treas.
President

Regular Contract:—

Approved ___4/26__ 19 __50__

North Carolina College star Harold Hunter became the first black player to sign an NBA contract, after his tryout with the Washington Capitols. The tryout occurred on August 8, 1950, but the Capitols didn't date the contract until August 26, the day after they drafted him. The other signatures belong to Hunter's college coaches, John McLendon and LeRoy T. Walker. Courtesy of Joanna McLendon.

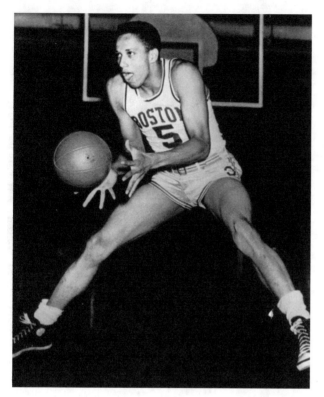

Chuck Cooper's rebounding skills attracted the Boston Celtics, who in 1950 made him the first black player drafted by an NBA team. Courtesy of *The Sporting News* Achives.

Nat "Sweetwater" Clifton stepped into the NBA with a ready-made fan club after starring for the Harlem Globetrotters. His enormous hands were like suction cups handy for rebounding and ballhandling. © Bettman/CORBIS.

Knicks owner Ned Irish threatened to move his team out of New York to force the NBA's board of governors to drop its unspoken ban on black players. Photo courtesy of the author.

Mark Cardwell coached basketball, football, baseball, track, and boxing his first two years at West Virginia State. Despite his preference for football, Cardwell's greatest success was in basketball, where he held a nineteen-year record of 288-68. Courtesy of the West Virginia State College Archives.

Starring for the Oakland Bittners led to Don Barksdale's berth on the 1948 U.S. Olympic team. In 1953 he became the first black player to appear in an NBA All-Star Game. Courtesy of Pamelia Barksdale.

By the time the season ended, however, Cooper's scoring average had fallen to his customary 8.2 after a dispute with management. The Hawks moved to St. Louis after that season. In January of 1956 he was released by the Hawks and then was signed by Fort Wayne, where he completed the season with an average seventeen minutes playing time and 4.5 points. His last professional games were played in the 1956 NBA Finals, which Fort Wayne lost to Philadelphia, four games to one. Cooper next signed with the Harlem Magicians touring team organized by former Globetrotter teammates Marques Haynes and Goose Tatum, then retired after injuring his back in a car accident.

"I think he was glad to stop," said Irva Cooper. "I think it was disappointing because he left the NBA, then he barnstormed with the Harlem Magicians for a year, and by then he was really ready to move on. I think that even though he was the first trailblazer, I don't think he enjoyed that experience. I think it was painful, and nobody likes pain."

By the time Cooper's NBA career ended in frustration, his feelings about his pioneering years had soured considerably. He firmly believed that the early 1950s NBA teams didn't want their black players to be high-scoring stars. "No black superstars were permitted in basketball then," Cooper said. "White management couldn't afford it because they knew white spectators wouldn't put up with it. You had to sort of fit in, if you were going to get in, make your contributions in a subordinate role."[13]

Coincidence or not, Cooper, Earl Lloyd, and Sweetwater Clifton all played subordinate roles for their respective teams beginning in 1950. Each was his team's blue-collar worker—rebounders and defenders who did what now is called "the dirty work" in basketball. The first black player with carte blanche to shoot didn't come along until Elgin Baylor arrived in Minneapolis in 1958. Although NBA coaches and management people dispute it (and there's reason to believe Cooper's reluctance to shoot contributed to it), Cooper always believed that his scoring really wasn't wanted. As a result he didn't shoot as often as he could have and averaged only 6.7 points a game during his career.

Cooper's son, Charles III, had heard his dad talk about the league not being ready for black stars in the 1950s, and that belief influenced the advice Cooper gave his son about basketball. "When I was playing ball, he was very careful not to push me to play," Charles III said. "I always wished he had pushed me more because he had so much to offer, but one thing he never criticized me about was shooting—and I used to like to put it up. . . . He said, 'Shoot the ball. That's one thing I never did. I never shot enough.'"

When the legendary Red Auerbach, Cooper's coach during his first four years playing in the league, was informed about Cooper's no-black-superstars-allowed theory, Auerbach responded, "That's bullshit! The league had nothing to do with it. Once a player was with a team, if I could get a scorer, I don't care if he was green. That [rebounding and defending] was Chuck's game. That's all."

Even Bob Cousy, who remained one of Cooper's closest friends until his death, was surprised that Cooper believed his color limited his scoring opportunities. "It sounds like a cop-out, and the pure fact of the matter is he wasn't a good shooter," Cousy said. "It would disappoint me because he was using blackness as an excuse." In fact, Cooper was only a 34 percent career shooter during a six-year span in which the league average ranged from 35.7 to 38.7 percent. "The early black player had all the skills, except the shooting skills," Cousy added. "The first good black shooter was Elgin Baylor."

Cooper also struggled with the racism he encountered when his teams played games in the South. It almost tormented him to have to acquiesce to it. "Those kinds of things bothered him tremendously because those were social injustices," said his first wife, Patsy Jayne Ware. "He found those very difficult to accept— the concept and principle wherever it was involved, whether he was personally affected or not."

Another problem was his need for work situations in which his opinion was desired, respected, and carried some weight . . . and he liked being well paid. For black players basketball was the antithesis of those. Cooper played in an era in which the coach's opinion was the only opinion that mattered, and he never earned much more playing in the NBA than his initial salary of $7,500. "He made much more money as a businessperson than he ever made in sports," said Maurice Mossy Murphy, former president of Duquesne's alumni association. Murphy wasn't sure of Cooper's maximum NBA salary, but said, "It was under $20,000 because when he made $40,000–$41,000 [as Pittsburgh's director of parks and recreation] he said it was twice as much as he ever made in the NBA."

In Gutkind's *Pittsburgh Magazine* article Cooper strongly expressed his frustration with his professional basketball career.

"People say I look pretty good for 50," he said. "But all the damage done to me is inside. That's where it hurts. [14]

"I realize now I didn't have the temperament for what I had to do. My difficulties were internal, inside of me and inside of the system that prevailed in basketball. Players are supposed to be, if not subservient, then at least subordinate to the whims of management—people don't know and couldn't give a damn about the pressures on a man performing in front of thousands of people each and every night." [15]

After he retired as a player, sports continued to be in Cooper's life mainly as family fun. He spent the rest of his life in public service, and kids in the Frankella Street neighborhood could depend upon his arrival at home around 6 P.M. "He would come home from work, suit and tie on," said Charles III. "He would take his suit jacket off and we would be out there playing football. Right out of the car, somebody would throw him the ball. He'd stay out there maybe a half-hour, forty-five minutes before he'd come into the house. When he pulled up, we'd wonder is this going to be one of the days he throws us a couple, because we were pretty young and we didn't have the arm to go deep."

When Cooper spoke of his NBA days, he often emphasized that as the first black draft pick he was "on a mission" to succeed. Though that mission was sometimes painful, Cooper nevertheless was an NBA fan. His son recalled that when he was young Pittsburgh's television stations didn't carry NBA games and Cooper could barely pull in a weak signal from out of town. "We had a black-and-white, 19-inch TV with rabbit ears, and the only place we could get a shadow was right where that chair is, and I remember me and my dad sitting on the floor watching Bill Russell and Wilt Chamberlain. I'll never forget that. As I recall, he was pulling for the Celtics, of course, and I was pulling for the Lakers."

Cooper, who had a business degree from Duquesne, earned a master's in social work from the University of Minnesota in 1960, then worked with underprivileged neighborhood organizations before becoming Pittsburgh's first black city department head when he was named director of parks and recreation in 1970. That job lasted a mere sixteen months because, true to his independent nature, he resigned when politicians began interfering too much. "He felt like he was a puppet," Irva Cooper said.

Cooper served on Pittsburgh's Board of Education, then worked for the Urban League and a community action group before becoming the urban affairs officer at Pittsburgh National Bank, where he supervised equal opportunity and affirmative action programs until he died. "I don't miss, I have never missed basketball," he said while working for the bank. "I miss the strength, endurance, and agility of my youth, but not the game itself. Right now I'm in a much better position, better than ever before, a position where people recognize me and my accomplishments not because of my color but because of what and who I am. At the bank, they listen to my recommendations and often follow them. It is a better life because I am not subservient to the system; I am part of it."[16]

He devoted his life to making the system more effective for people in need. Irva Cooper always knew her husband was a "sensitive" man who put others' well-being ahead of his own. But she didn't realize how much he had lifted people's lives and spirits until his funeral at Sixth Mt. Zion Baptist Church in the East Liberty neighborhood of Pittsburgh where Cooper had been raised. He died of liver cancer in 1984 at the relatively young age of fifty-seven. "The funeral director said it was the first time that he ever filled two guest books," she said. "They had to put a new one out because people were actually writing on the back of the first one.

"He was a social worker and community developer, and he would go into small towns like McKeesport and work on their project, and they would tell me how much he helped. He would sit right here and eat at night, and he would never mention it. He didn't promote himself. It was, 'What did the kids do? What did you do?' Now, if somebody had made him mad, then I heard about that. But if it was something that he did that was outstanding, I guess he was thinking that that was what he was supposed to do. I never heard an unkind word about him."

Moon Fixer Rises

If someone knows him from his college days at West Virginia State, Earl Lloyd can tell. All the person has to do is utter two telltale words—"Moon Fixer"—which became Lloyd's nickname when he arrived in Institute, West Virginia, in 1946. "When I was a freshman in college, I was the tallest kid on campus and all freshmen have a chore," the six-foot-six Lloyd said. "The upperclassmen wanted to make sure the moon was correct, so that was my job. They called me the Moon Fixer, and it stuck."

He also was agile enough to dribble and sprint downcourt like a much smaller man, was as lanky as a deer, and had coiled springs for legs. Lloyd could jump as high as necessary to retrieve a rebound or challenge a shooter, which attracted the attention of the NBA's Washington Capitols as draft day approached in 1950.

"I would judge Earl as being a very valuable sixth man, because he was six-six, six-seven and he could play a little power forward, a little bit of small forward," said Bill Sharman, his Capitols teammate who later starred with the Boston Celtics. "I don't think he would be a guard, but he was an all-around type of player. Was a good rebounder, good runner, had good speed and you could use him on the fastbreak. I keep thinking of players like John Havlicek and Frank Ramsey, some of the better sixth men in the league."

Lloyd's agility earned him another nickname in the pros, the Big Cat, and his personality and willingness to defend a teammate to the death earned Lloyd the respect of his peers for nine fulfilling seasons with Washington, the Syracuse Nationals, and the Detroit Pistons. "The thing I can truthfully say—and it makes me feel good to say it because you're talking about three years after Jackie Robinson—is the fact that I didn't have one problem with one player overtly," Lloyd said. "I never had a player call me a name with racial [implications]. I'm not saying there weren't some players who had some problems, but they were bright enough to understand that they've got some teammates who might frown on them if they espouse their views on that type of thing. I think the intelligence level of pro basketball at that time was a mite higher than baseball."

It all seemed like such a smooth, natural fit, as if the Lloyd-NBA pairing had been ordained to happen. But a second look at Lloyd's upbringing in a strictly segregated environment in Alexandria, Virginia, reveals that the Moon Fixer's highest leap occurred the night he played in his first NBA game. He had come from an era and an area that offered no windows of opportunity to black people— just narrow slits that only the very lucky squeezed through.

"There are times I'd like to get a baseball bat and run back through history," Lloyd said. "In my age, it was dastardly. Separate but equal; they've got to be kidding. They didn't allow black people to do nothing." Especially in Alexandria, which Lloyd described as being "about eight miles south of Washington, but a thousand miles away, really." Lloyd was born in 1928 and was raised in Alexandria decades before the U.S. Supreme Court's 1954 *Brown vs. Board of Education* decision outlawed the "separate but equal" philosophy that undergirded racial segregation in America. In Alexandria it kept white and black people far apart.

Memories of Alexandria flooded back into Lloyd's mind in 1991 when he returned home from the funeral of his boyhood friend, Oliver "Bubba" Ellis, who became Lloyd's roommate at West Virginia State. "At his wake Wednesday night, fifteen hundred people came by," Lloyd said. "He was a favorite son, mainly because as a young athlete in Alexandria from my time, black folks had nothing to root for. Consequently, they turned to high school athletes. There were no black mailmen. No black cops. No black nothing. As a consequence, we became their champions. Every Friday night we played baseball, basketball, or football. On Friday, the town stopped for us."

Alexandria's black athletes had the spare time and barely enough sports equipment to sharpen their skills. A bat, a ball, and a few gloves were sufficient, and Lloyd became an accomplished high school pitcher. "I was six-four, 185 pounds and growing, and could throw the ball through the wall. Just didn't know where it was going," he said with a laugh. He must have had genuine potential, however, because in the 1950s he turned down an offer to play for a Pittsburgh Pirates minor-league baseball team.

For a game of basketball an entire neighborhood could share one ball and play games on dirt courts. On Friday nights the teenage athletes were rewarded with the attention of admiring adults. "As a youngster you really love playing, but you're not really aware of the social ramifications," Lloyd said. "It was just support. We didn't see ourselves as messiahs." How could they? Given their surroundings, it was hard enough just to see themselves as self-respecting human beings. Lloyd's neighborhood was "dirt poor," and when he ventured beyond it, everything else reminded him of that fact.

"Here's a black kid who came through a segregated system—I never sat next to a white person until I was twenty-two years old," Lloyd said. That breakthrough occurred when he participated in unofficial games between West Virginia's top college players in 1950. "It's amazing," Lloyd continued. "It's hard to fathom, but it really was a way of life. And I come through an era where not only do they tell you you're inferior, but they treated you inferior. . . . You tend to buy into that. You might not espouse it—'Yeah, I'm inferior'—but burning deeply you kind of buy that. Who is there to tell you that you're not?

"My high school [Parker-Gray] is as big as this room and they're talking about separate but equal, and I go to George Washington High [for white kids] and it's like a college. They let you know in their own way that you're not as good as they are. We used to play football in the municipal stadium, which the city owned. You go to George Washington, they had carpet [meaning grass] that thick on the field. You look at the lights; it looked like broad daylight. They uniform sixty people with all-new uniforms, and we're sewing our [equipment] up. It's obvious! When I hear 'separate but equal,' that's a rib-tickler for me. I fall on the floor laughing. Separate, no question. But equal, that's bull, unless you've got a different yardstick than mine."

Although feeling inferior crept into Lloyd's psyche, his family and high school coach instilled in him certain values and personal habits that combated the message society was giving him. "In my hometown, I could have started a role model agency: two older brothers, my Mom and Dad, my teachers and your coaches," he said. "You just knew what was expected of you. If we had a curfew, the whole town knew it. . . . We've lost that compelling urge to take care of each other, and I think integration forced us to do that. We don't have that now. People live four houses apart and don't know each other."

Lloyd's father, Theodore, worked in a coal yard, at the time a pretty good job for a black male. But, "He was a weekend alcoholic," said Lloyd, who attributes that to the depressing situation they lived in. If balloting were held for sainthood, Lloyd definitely would vote for his mother, Daisy Lloyd. "My mother was the biggest influence in my whole life," he said. "She was a true matriarch. Her thing was, 'I don't care where you are, soap and water doesn't cost much.' She felt if you were dirty or unkempt, it was an embarrassment to her because that was her responsibility."

The importance of Lloyd's attire, hygiene, and punctuality was a theme he returned to again and again during interviews over several years. Throughout his childhood and NBA career, impeccable personal appearance was considered essential for black people who wanted to get ahead and be respected; exhibiting anything less corroborated the stereotype of the slovenly black. "You always know what they say about us: that we're late, shiftless, stink, and steal," Lloyd said. His mother wasn't the only one to preach the cleanliness-is-next-to-Godliness message. Lloyd's high school coach, Lewis Johnson, and his college coach, Mark Cardwell, gave him the same advice.

"When I was in Syracuse, sometimes someone would say, 'Man, why do you always wear a shirt and tie?'" Lloyd said. "I explained we go to some places that have got those signs 'We deserve the right not to serve folks who are boisterous or not properly attired.' That sign is not for you. That sign is for me. My philosophy is if you got a problem with me, tell me; I'm not going to give you a club to use on me. If they put me out of some restaurant, it's not because I'm boisterous, it's not because I'm not properly attired. They're putting me out because they saw black folks. That was the kind of teaching I had from my coaches."

There are no limits to the high regard Lloyd had for coach Johnson, not only because of the way Johnson comported himself—"Never raised his voice, never cursed, but he was the man," Lloyd said—but also because of the respect coaches commanded in those days. "If he stood there for two hours and never said a word, it was quiet for two hours," Lloyd said. "Challenge him? That's unheard of. When the man told you do it, you did it or hung your suit up. No going home saying, 'Coach is mistreating me.' We felt like the man was a genius and the man never told me anything wrong." Including where to go to college. Coach Johnson suggested his own alma mater, West Virginia State, the only endorsement Lloyd and his mother needed. It turned out to be the ideal place for Lloyd. Since coaches Johnson and Cardwell had been teammates there, Lloyd played under the same basketball philosophy for eight consecutive years. The college was located in the small town of Institute, just minutes outside the boundaries of Charleston (the state capital). Geographically the relationship mirrored that of his hometown of Alexandria to Washington DC. And the college exuded the caring atmosphere Lloyd had experienced while growing up. "It was like a big family affair," Lloyd said. "You had your teachers' phone numbers. If you need some help, you call them at home."

Lloyd had landed there during the birth of the coming powerhouse of black college basketball. "My college coach came to my school to recruit and he had one returning player, and this is a place I could go as a freshman and play," Lloyd said. "I was green as corn but thrown in the breech, you've got to play. Most of the guys I played with were army veterans, so I learned from them and the coach."

Coach Cardwell had taken over West Virginia State's team in 1945 and began to assemble an almost unbeatable squad in the Colored Intercollegiate Athletic Association (now the Central Intercollegiate Athletic Association) which produced several significant sports figures. Lloyd and forward Bob Wilson became two of the first seven black NBA players. Guard Bill Nunn Jr., a team captain, became a prominent sports columnist with the *Pittsburgh Courier*, then switched to scouting for the National Football League's Pittsburgh Steelers. Nunn was instrumental in bringing to the Steelers their future stars John Stallworth, Mean Joe Greene, Donnie Shell, Lynn Swann, and Ernie Holmes. West Virginia State's reserve Joe Gilliam eventually became head football coach at both Tennessee State and Jackson State. More than two hundred of Gilliam's players signed NFL contracts.

During Lloyd's career, the Yellow Jackets went 80-14, and the 1947–48 team was the first to go unbeaten throughout the CIAA regular season and postseason tournament, which determined the black intercollegiate champion. The next season the Yellow Jackets extended their winning streak to thirty-two regular-season games before it was broken, and repeated as black intercollegiate champs. Lloyd made the CIAA all-conference and all-tournament teams in 1948, 1949, and 1950; he was fortunate that although he was the tallest player on the team, he played facing the basket in a double-post offense instead of playing center with his back to the basket.

That increased Lloyd's attractiveness to the Washington Capitols because at six-six he would have been too short to play center in the pros.

The CIAA tournament had been played in Washington DC since its inception in 1946, which gave the Capitols ample opportunity to watch Lloyd and North Carolina College's Harold Hunter develop as players before drafting them in 1950. Lloyd brought skills to training camp that the Caps badly needed coming off a 32-36 season, and he and Hunter received positive reactions from their teammates. "I didn't have any problems," Hunter said. "I put that with management. We had a general manager [Bob Foster] and [coach] Bones McKinney, and they called players in before [rookie] camp started. They said for the first time in history in pro basketball teams are integrated. We want to put this on the table. If you have any problems with having black players on the team, I don't think anyone would hold anything against you if you leave." No one did. "A lot of those guys had played in colleges with black people, and you can go anywhere in the South and see white and black kids playing together. You just didn't see it on state-supported teams," Hunter said.

That left one old obstacle Lloyd had to overcome: his feelings of inferiority. In this case they didn't stem from being black, but rather from being in the presence of so many stars from major college basketball powers. "When you see a guy like Dick Schnittker [from Ohio State], the guy was College Player of the Year in college basketball," Lloyd said. "He's ostensibly above everybody in college, more so me, because I'm playing at one of those little black schools. Lord knows, you're inferior." And there were more, including Southern Cal All-American Bill Sharman, UCLA's Alan Sawyer, Warren Cottier from North Carolina State, and Tommy O'Keefe from Georgetown. "I was kind of awestruck," Lloyd said, though those feelings didn't even last a week. "After about three or four days of scrimmaging a bulb lights up, and it's a great revelation what the bulb is saying: 'These guys, they're no better than you are,' " Lloyd said. "Then the rest was history. You just went on and took care of business."

Lloyd was living at home with his parents and didn't have a car, so Sharman would pick him up to ride to practice together. "At that time, I didn't even realize the NBA didn't have other black players," said Sharman, a native of southern California. "I was very surprised, and stupid I guess, but on the West Coast we didn't have an NBA team." Sharman had played against and with black players in high school and college. "I guess at that time things were a little tougher for black people on the East Coast. It just kind of shocked me."

Meanwhile, Hunter appreciated the support he received from Schnittker. The Capitols had been a slow, plodding team, and Hunter, a five-foot-nine whirlwind, believes he was drafted because McKinney foresaw the day when the game would be played at a faster pace. During training camp Hunter found he could sprint down the court while many of his teammates "would float down the court." But, in a subtle way Schnittker assured Hunter that it was okay for him to maintain his playing style.

"We were all told it was best not to get in cliques because you never knew who your teammates would be," Hunter said. "Everyone was winging it, although we all knew who the coaches were leaning toward. In the locker room one day, the veterans were kidding me: 'Hunter, you go too fast. You've got to slow down that ball for the old veterans.' Schnittker was sitting across from me: 'Go as fast as you want, Hunter. When you get there, I'll be there.' He didn't say much, but that said everything."

Schnittker, a six-five guard-forward, pointed out that some veterans were "set-up people" who liked a slow pace, but he considered himself "a runner" who felt complemented by Lloyd's and Hunter's style of play. "Here's some guys who can run with me," Schnittker said. "They probably got some heat because some older guys weren't in shape, but Bones handled it well by saying run as hard as you can and if you get tired wave to me and I'll take you out for five minutes."

Hunter said he didn't make the roster because of uncertainty about the status of six-foot-eleven center Don Otten. When it appeared that Otten wouldn't be joining the team, management began scrambling for as many tall players as it could get; Hunter got cut in the process. Otten eventually played for Washington and two other NBA teams that season. Hunter might have been cut anyway because there was concern that at five-nine, an opposing guard could post up Hunter too easily near the basket.

Hunter played in the semipro Eastern League, then tried out the next season with the Baltimore Bullets. In 1950 they had released two black players during training camp, George Washington from Morgan State and Lenny Rhodes from Toledo University. Unfortunately for Hunter, in 1951 two black players had a lock on Baltimore roster spots, guard Davage Minor and his best friend, Don Barksdale, a high-priced acquisition whom Minor had helped lure from the Amateur Athletic Association on the West Coast. Hunter believes he had no serious chance of sticking with Baltimore because some teams were reluctant to have black and white players room together on the road. As the third black player, who would have roomed with him? After one more season in the Eastern League Hunter turned down an offer from the Globetrotters and began a teaching and coaching career. He went on to succeed John McLendon at Tennessee State.

Hunter feels no resentment about missing out on an NBA career. "It's like looking at a beautiful woman who's very famous and being mad because you don't have her," Hunter said. "If you ain't got it, what you going to worry about? . . . I took, and still do take satisfaction that I must have been ahead of the pack to be given that consideration. I couldn't control the situation that caused Don Otten to get signed by another team, nor could I control the friendship that existed between Don Barksdale and Dave Minor. I knew [Baltimore management] had a problem with three blacks— can't put three blacks in one room or give him a room all by himself and let it be obvious that nobody's going to stay with this black person." Hunter surmised that if he had been an inch or two taller, or white, or had Baltimore had a more progressive management, he might have become an NBA player. But perhaps most important to him, "I proved to myself that I had the ability to stay."

Lloyd immediately became a fixture with the Capitols. He started the first game he played in the NBA on October 31, 1950, Halloween night. That loss to the Rochester Royals in Rochester, New York, was uneventful, and as a result he has almost no memory of it. But the significance to him of stepping onto the court that night cannot be overestimated: "For me to come from that kind of [segregated] background," Lloyd said with disbelief in his voice, "go to a small black school and be the second black guy ever drafted to go to the pros, and to go to a training camp and start the season. When they call the starting lineup and you run out there, that's . . . that's . . ." Lloyd struggled to describe his feelings. "That's not important to a lot of people, but considering the situation, that's real important," he finally said.

The only other memorable event that night occurred after the game, which went into the books as an eight-point loss. "All I can remember is Bones called us all to his room, and I came from a school where we might have lost 10, 12 games in four years. I said, 'Oh no, we're going to catch hell.' We walked in his room and Bones is sitting there. He had a tub full of beer and pop, so I was kind of shocked. I said, 'Damn, what do you do if you win?' But he had a young bunch of kids—we must have had five rookies. I think he was taking some pains to say, 'This is your first game. We've got 81 more to go so don't even worry about it.' I had a lot of respect for Bones. He was a wild man, but [his philosophy was] if I've got to deal with you one-on-one, I'll deal with you on your merits. The guy was good to me."

Although Lloyd is rather casual when speaking about his career debut, the next game of the season—the Caps' home opener on November 1 against the Indianapolis Olympians—was one of the highlights of his life. Only 1,625 fans attended Washington's 100–84 victory at Uline Arena; the *Washington Afro-American* estimated the small "colored turnout" at 10 percent, including Lloyd's parents. He scored 8 points, and the *Washington Post* credited him and rookies Schnittker, Sharman, and Sawyer with helping turn a close game into an easy win. "I'll never forget," Lloyd said. "My mother's from the country in Virginia and is very, very bright—a lot of mother wit. She and my father were at the game, and I'm the only black dude on the whole floor. It's the opening home game and they introduce all the players. There's only one black player in the whole building, and that's me. Two little kids are in front of them, and you know how kids are writing each guy's number down. The announcer calls me out—I'm number 18—and they say, 'Well, we know him!' Well, my mother can't question that.

"There's two white dudes behind her, and one of them asked the other guy: 'You think this nigger can play any basketball?' My mother turned around and looked them right in the eye and said, 'Trust me, the nigger can play.' Some people said, 'Why didn't you get upset?' She said, 'Well, they had to be ignorant because in 1950 there were no tokens.' If they have a black player starting on a team in 1950 the one thing you know about him is that he can play. At least he can play better than the guys on the bench."

Lloyd's sixth game, on November 12 in Fort Wayne, Indiana, also left him with a distinct memory. It was there that McKinney displayed uncommon loyalty to his rookie. The hotel the Caps were staying in allowed Lloyd to sleep there but wouldn't let him eat in its restaurant, which didn't bother Lloyd considering Fort Wayne's proximity to the Mason-Dixon Line. "Hell, I was shocked

that they let me sleep!" he said. "I was halfway home." Lloyd
had settled in with his room-service meal when "Bones McKinney
came up to my room and said, 'Let's sit down and have dinner,'"
Lloyd said. "I could appreciate that because he was letting me know
'you're part of this team, regardless.' I said, 'Bones, the important
thing is that I know how you feel. No need for both of us having a
funky meal. Now you go downstairs and enjoy yourself.' But I let
him know I appreciated that. I never forgot that."

Before he was drafted into the army for the Korean War, Lloyd
played only seven games with Washington, averaging 7 points
and 7 rebounds, and shooting 45.7 percent. Today that shooting
percentage wouldn't be worth mentioning, but players' accuracy
in 1950 was much worse than it is today. Lloyd's percentage must
have appeared remarkable because had he continued at that pace
he would have finished fourth in the NBA in that statistical category. (As it turned out, Lloyd never shot better than 37.4 percent
throughout the remainder of his career.) He had quickly established his worth as a player, and at his last game with Washington
on November 14, his family and friends held a generous going-
away ceremony for Lloyd at halftime.

The *Afro-American* reported that William Pitts, principal of
Parker-Gray High (Lloyd's alma mater), presented him with a military dressing case, gold tie clasp with engraved initials, and a box
of linen writing paper. Uline Arena manager Jack Riley gave Lloyd
a large portrait of himself in a Caps uniform and presented a copy
to Parker-Gray High. McKinney presented Lloyd with a scroll.

"In my hometown, I'm a favorite son, and they came on en
masse," Lloyd said. "You take a guy like Dick Schnittker, he's a
first-class person and I'm sure he's heard stories about black folks
and how they don't come together. My whole hometown turned
out. They wanted to show appreciation of their own. The Caps
gave me a large picture, and I think a watch. It was touching."

McKinney, only thirty-one, had played for Washington the
previous four seasons as a scrawny six-six, 187-pound frontcourt
player (hence the nickname "Bones"). He picked himself as Lloyd's
replacement on the roster. The *Washington Post* reported that
McKinney wanted to fill "the yawning gap" caused by Lloyd's
entrance into the army.[1] "It's a sad memory I have of Earl when
he was going in the service, leaving us," Schnittker said. "That was
my biggest disappointment."

The team struggled with a league-worst 10-25 record and lagging attendance when Mike Uline folded the Washington franchise in January, 1950. Lloyd missed the rest of that season and all of the next, then resumed his career with the Syracuse Nationals, who had acquired him in a dispersal draft after the Capitols folded. Once again Lloyd had gotten lucky. He was comfortable in the small city of about 220,000 and felt fortunate that he had been easily accepted by the team's management and players, all of whom were white, of course. "You're a product of segregation," Lloyd said. "You have to get past your cynicism, because it's easy to be cynical. Plus, you've got to trust people. I can't pinpoint one thing, but I just walked into a situation for me, particularly at that time, as ideal as you could get. Outstanding owner [Danny Biasone], good coach [Al Cervi] and good people."

In the 1950s, however, it wouldn't have been wise for a black person to drop his or her guard completely. When Lloyd dropped by to see Biasone at the bowling alley he owned, Lloyd would never mingle with bowlers on the ground floor. Instead, to avoid any chance of a racial confrontation, he immediately would go upstairs to Biasone's office. "In the '50s, you were in a place and no one [else black] was in there," Lloyd explained. "That's delicate. With teammates I had no problems, but you're a black kid from a little Southern town, and you're not used to mingling with white folks. You're very cautious. You might walk into a white lady and you have to be careful."

For the next six years with Syracuse, as well as two with Detroit after that, Lloyd was a mobile power forward who specialized in defense, rebounding, and, Lloyd believed, being called for unwarranted fouls. "He tried many times to change the number on his jersey because he felt by habit the refs would call '11' even if the foul wasn't on him," recalled teammate Dolph Schayes.

"I owe Earl a lot of thanks," said Cervi, his coach for four full seasons. "He's an unsung star. Anybody can score. Lloyd was an excellent defensive player; that was No. 1 on my roster. . . . Lloyd and [center Red Rocha] were the backbone of the team. They were the hidden factor. They got their double figures [in scoring], made their foul shots, played team play."

And Lloyd had no "backdown" in him during an era in which professional basketball was much rougher than it is today. The pace was much slower because there was no twenty-four-second clock, a dunk seldom was seen, driving the lane to the basket was considered hazardous to one's health, and fights between players were commonplace. "We had a saying, 'Nobody comes through the middle without a ticket,' and I don't recall having sold any tickets," Lloyd said. "It was tough. I don't think anybody tried to hurt anybody, but there were certain things you discouraged. Running down the middle for lay-ups, it was a given that when you ran down the middle you took your own risk. Nobody said, 'Don't go,' but there was a little risk involved."

When playing opposite the high-scoring Dolph Schayes, a future Hall of Famer, Lloyd's job was to defend the opponent's frontcourt scoring threat. His worst assignment was guarding Minneapolis Lakers center George Mikan, a legend in his day at a dominating six-foot-ten, 245 pounds. "Playing Mikan was like playing a truck," Lloyd said. "You knew you'd get your brains beat out."

It wasn't an easy matchup for Mikan, either. "I had to really work hard," he said. "Earl tried to outrun me and tried to get me to the outside so he could shoot set shots. Take a look at the game today. They always try to get the center out of the center. You have guys like Luc Longley shooting seventeen-, eighteen-footers."

Lloyd's old teammate Schnittker, who ended up with the Lakers after the Capitols folded, almost felt sorry for Lloyd as he tried to contend with Mikan. "George took time to set up inside and Earl would steal the ball and George would take a swipe at him," Schnittker said. "He could jump higher and he would block George's shot, and George was very irritated by that. He really frustrated George, but eventually Earl would get so many fouls because George was protected so much [by the referees]. After George hit him with one of his elbows, Earl would still be lying on the floor and say, 'Who me?'"

"I used to use every trick in the book to draw the fouls," Mikan said, "and he was unlucky he got caught. I'd fake to the left, go to the right. Fake to the right, go to the left. I could shoot with both hands, and I scored a lot of my points from offensive rebounding." Lloyd understood why the task of guarding Mikan fell to him, especially since Syracuse didn't have a legitimate center until Johnny Kerr joined the Nationals in 1954. But there were times when dealing with Mikan exhausted Lloyd's patience.

Harold Brown, Chuck Cooper's friend from their high school days in Pittsburgh, recalled one time while he was visiting Cooper at a hotel and Lloyd dropped by. "This was at the end of one of the seasons, and Earl was pissed about conditions [in Syracuse],"

Brown said. "He was saying he was going to ask for a raise, damn it, because he has to take all those big people—Mikan knocking him in the head with elbows. He wanted some more money."

Lloyd got his licks in by setting rock-hard picks against defenders who harassed Syracuse ballhandlers. "I guess Earl was my protector," said George King, a Syracuse guard from 1951 to 1956. "The game was a little different. People could get a little mean tripping and gouging. When we started playing, that was before fines for fighting, so there were fights all the time. I was a little guy, five-eleven-and-a-half, and not very big, and I needed somebody to help me. The Cat was always available and he would say, 'Run them over to me and I'll take care of them.'"

"I watch guys being pressured in the backcourt," Lloyd said, "but if you set a bone-chilling pick, he doesn't have to work that hard because the [defender] is looking over his shoulder. You just took care of your own." Especially if a fight broke out. "I just know it seemed like in a fight I always wanted to get my back up against his back," Kerr said. "Earl was the type you would like to be in a foxhole with." Particularly when playing Boston, which always seemed to have a big bruiser such as 215-pound Bob Brannum or 230-pound "Jungle Jim" Loscutoff. "Many a time Earl was the only black in the building, and he had the courage to stop a fight or help a teammate. He never held back," said forward Ed Conlin.

Lloyd was loyal to his teammates because they were loyal to him, and they genuinely liked him. Being accepted was especially important in the 1950s because a team truly was like family since players spent so much time together. Geographically the league was compact, extending no further west than Minneapolis or south than St. Louis, but travel took much longer than today because of long train rides or bumpy airplane rides on the likes of the DC-3. "Didn't make for much more than sitting there and hoping not to throw up your last dinner," Schayes said. Mohawk Airlines flying out of Syracuse didn't have jets so, "It took you forever to get to Fort Wayne," Conlin said.

Players passed the time with card games and bull sessions, and Lloyd was just one of the group. "He's always upbeat," Conlin said. "And, he's funny. His nickname is Earl the Squirrel. We used to accuse Bob Hopkins [another player] and Earl of telling tall tales, and of course his voice would go up a register and he'd say, 'If I'm lying, I'm flying.'"

Race was the litmus test to Lloyd, and his teammates passed

it again and again. There was nothing they could do about exhibition games in some Southern cities that had segregated hotels, which forced Lloyd to stay at a black hotel or with a black family. "Now you say why schedule a game where I couldn't play, but in 1952 it wasn't as sensitive as it is now," Lloyd said. But white players had a choice to make in NBA cities such as St. Louis and Fort Wayne, which essentially were cities of the South where Lloyd often was turned away from segregated restaurants. "As long as the people you're with are in your corner, you can handle it," Lloyd said. "But if you walk into a restaurant, [are refused service] and they keep eating, you've got a problem. Any place where I would not be served, my teammates wouldn't eat. You appreciate it."

Lloyd no longer was the team's only black player after Jim Tucker from Duquesne joined Syracuse in 1954. "Someone who was one of your own," Lloyd said. Tucker said Lloyd was like a big brother to him; coming from the small, segregated town of Paris, Kentucky, Tucker needed a mentor to help him negotiate a more integrated environment. "Being young and wanting to hang out in the bars, he would remind me I had an image to uphold and a game to play, and whether it was tonight or tomorrow night, I should be ready," Tucker said. Lloyd also passed along his coaches' emphasis on dressing properly. If the team was headed to a function that required a tie, Lloyd would let Tucker know, and Tucker didn't doubt Lloyd's advice. "He was one of the best dressers I had ever seen and a very classy individual," Tucker said. "And coming from Paris, you don't have the social graces you should have."

In 1955 they became the first black players to play on a championship team when Syracuse edged Fort Wayne, 92–91, in the seventh game of the NBA Finals. It was the first season in which the twenty-four-second clock was used to speed up the game, and the average score soared from 79.5 ppg. to 93.1. Beating Fort Wayne made the victory that much sweeter because the Pistons' crowd was so rough on black players. "You hear them call you nigger, pork chop, Satchel Paige, and all those names," Tucker said. "It only made me want to play a little harder."

The next season the Nationals lost the Eastern Division finals to Philadelphia, which went on to defeat Ft. Wayne again in the championship round. However, that 1956 off-season was memorable because it included a ten-country tour abroad by the Syracuse team. The tour included stops in Iceland, Germany, Iran, Egypt, Spain, and France, and for once in their careers Lloyd and Tucker were the stars of the show because they were black. "That probably was the biggest thing, that we were black and something other than the Globetrotters," Tucker said. "They dearly loved the Globetrotters and anyone who was black and could bounce a ball. . . . It was a different role. I enjoyed it. It was a little embarrassing because I wasn't [usually] the star. I'd see my name in print, TUKER."

"It was extremely interesting and exciting, and Earl and I were treated differently than any time in our lives. We were the guys interviewed at the airport that people wanted to talk to. In Egypt, our guide told me he didn't want to take me where he was taking the white players because they were going to spend a lot of money, so he would drop them off and come back and take me to an out-of-the-way bar and I'd spend $10. I was still too young; I took a camera and didn't take a picture. I was just so awed that I know I enjoyed it, but I didn't appreciate it."

After six years with Syracuse Lloyd and Dick Farley were sold on June 10, 1958, to Detroit, where the Fort Wayne franchise had moved. Two years later Lloyd felt he was being outpaced by younger players and retired at the age of thirty-two. Lloyd had been a Pistons assistant coach and television announcer before he was named the team's head coach on November 3, 1971, immediately after the abrupt resignation of Butch van Breda Kolff ten games into the season. Lloyd thus became the fourth black NBA head coach in history, behind Boston's Bill Russell. Lloyd coached Detroit to a 20-50 record that season, then was fired in October, 1972, at 2-5. He worked as a Pistons scout, in personnel relations in the auto industry, as an educator, and finally for former NBA star Dave Bing's steel company before retiring in 1999.

Looking back on his career, how does Lloyd feel about being the first black player to participate in an NBA game? "I don't play it up or down," he said. "Out of the CIAA, there were a lot of guys that could have made it and I'm a firm believer in timing. We played in a conference tournament where there was a pro team and they scouted me, unbeknownst to me. Here I am an Alexandria boy, and I was in the right place at the right time. I just hope I conducted myself where I made it easier for others, and I think I did."

8

West Virginia State
Spawned the Pioneers

It is strange, though not a coincidence, that three of the NBA's first ten black players had basketball roots at West Virginia State College—a small school located in the small town of Institute, eight miles west of Charleston, West Virginia. It had only 1,270 students when two players—one who began his college career there (Chuck Cooper) and another who built his basketball reputation there (Earl Lloyd)—helped integrate the NBA in 1950. By the 1951–52 season, when Bob Wilson, the high-scoring center on Lloyd's college teams, played his sole NBA season with the Milwaukee Hawks, West Virginia State's enrollment had fallen to 999.

It is strange, but not unexpected, because strange events have become commonplace at the land-grant college along the banks of the Kanawha River. It's safe to posit that no other college in America sits on land that once was owned by President George Washington and eventually was sold to the state of West Virginia by black descendants of a white slave owner, Samuel I. Cabell. The school officially opened to students in 1892. It is also safe to assume that no other American college operated as an all-black school for the first sixty-two years of its existence, then integrated so quickly and thoroughly that more than 50 percent of its students were white within just six years of the 1954 *Brown vs. Board of Education* Supreme Court decision.

It was a remarkable transition welcomed by both the institution and the white students living nearby. The college's enrollment had doubled within three years after the end of World War II when many former soldiers could attend school on the GI Bill. But from a peak of 1,785 students in the 1947–48 school year, by 1953 the enrollment had fallen to 837 as the numbers of matriculating war veterans dwindled. *Brown vs. Board of Education* was a blessing: it outlawed segregated public education and in essence legalized the enrollment of white students who had been barred from attending West Virginia State.

For many years a sprinkling of white students had taken classes at West Virginia State under the cover of secrecy. Occasionally, when asked if his school had white students, school president John W. Davis would always reply, "Well, I haven't seen any." The need for that subterfuge ended with the monumental Supreme Court decision, and 399 white students flocked to West Virginia State for the next school year for three reasons: (1) Unlike political leaders at several other Southern states, almost immediately after the *Brown vs. Board of Education* decision was announced, Governor William Marland emphatically stated that West Virginia would obey the new law. (2) West Virginia State was a highly respected institution whose faculty once included Dr. Carter G. Woodson, the founder of the Black History Month concept, and Dr. Percy Julian, an innovator in the research of arthritis and glaucoma. Honored guests of the school included Eleanor Roosevelt. (3) As a state school, its $25 per semester tuition was considerably less than at nearby private colleges.

In West Virginia State's third year as an integrated school enrollment had risen to 2,223; by the year 2000 it was educating approximately 4,900 students, about 85 percent of them white, 12 percent black, and 3 percent from other ethnic groups.

It has been a surprisingly smooth melding of races and cultures at the school, although it's not a melting pot. Whites tend to be commuter students who mostly attend classes during the day and drive home, while black students usually are from other areas of the country, live in the dormitories, and are more involved in campus activities. Consequently, visitors to the campus might think they're at a predominantly white school during the daytime and a black college at night. West Virginia State has always had a black school president, and many of its top academic administrators and the majority of its student government officers continue to be African-American.

To Andrew Aheart, a math professor there since 1948, integration "probably helped us more than hurt us, but there were certain things we lost." He said that when it was a black college the atmosphere was more like a "family unit," reflected in the fact that black graduates during the 1940s through 1960s comprise the majority of attendance at alumni functions today. On the other hand, he believes integration has given West Virginia State "a wider view and more contacts. White students don't just graduate in isolation; they have jobs, they become presidents of companies. That was helpful, but we lost some of the closeness we had."

The results of a half-century of transitions at West Virginia State have not been perfect, yet few educational institutions could have withstood them without being torn asunder at some point in their histories. That never happened at West Virginia State, which is why a 1966 article in the *Saturday Review* called it, "A Living Laboratory of Human Relations." (It is strange, too, that during the course of researching this book, the author discovered that his father, Laughton F. Thomas, attended West Virginia State in 1931. Unfortunately, he never graduated because he ran out of money during the Depression and couldn't afford to return to school.)

Despite all of the changes that have occurred at the college, the basketball tradition remains. Fleming Hall, built in 1942 and the home court for Cooper, Lloyd, and Wilson, still hosts West Virginia State games. It is obsolete in many ways, and the program's record has slumped in recent years. Yet the gym's mere existence, along with a maize-and-yellow overhanging banner, pay homage to the undefeated 1948 team of which Lloyd and Wilson were members. It is hoped that under new coach Bryan Poore the twenty-first-century Fleming Hall will once again become the intimidating, 1,850-seat setting it once was. "Don't be losing in the pit," Lloyd warned senior forward Brian Smart on a visit to the campus in 1998.

The establishment of West Virginia State as a basketball power from 1945 to 1950 was largely due to one man: coach Mark Cardwell. Known as "Foxy" from his days as a clever, Negro All-American halfback at West Virginia State, and as the "Gentleman Coach" and "Miracle Man of the Mountains" due to his coaching prowess, Cardwell quietly commanded respect throughout the black basketball world.

After compiling an outstanding record at segregated Kelly-Miller High in Clarksburg, West Virginia, Cardwell returned to his alma mater in 1945 as a coach and faculty member. The previous season Chuck Cooper had excelled as a freshman center under coach Horace McCarthy, then went into the navy. At the age of forty-four Cardwell became West Virginia State's "coach" at a time when the term was all-encompassing. His first two years there he coached basketball, football, baseball, track, and boxing.

Football was Cardwell's first love, which isn't surprising considering his career as a prep player in Columbus, Ohio, the site of football-crazed Ohio State University. Although his West Virginia State football teams never won a conference title, he was considered a tactical genius during a coaching career that lasted until 1959. Yet baseball was the setting for an anecdote that exemplifies Cardwell's most outstanding trait—his extraordinary composure.

"This always stuck in my mind," said Joseph Peters, who played on Cardwell's baseball team in the late 1940s. "I came up in a small coal field and every time we would lose we had some type of excuse—got bad calls from officials or it was a slippery field. In my senior year in baseball, I had gone the whole season without striking out. We were playing Wilberforce and on a 3-2 pitch the umpire called me out on a pitch over my head. I just went after the umpire. Coach walked to the plate and said, 'Pete, what's the problem?' I said, 'This umpire called a strike over my head.' Coach said, 'Pete, if it was close enough to call, it was close enough to swing at. Just sit down.' On the bench, coach came over and said it wasn't important enough to get upset about. For a while it just really upset me because I felt I wasn't being supported by my coach. But in the ninth inning I came up and hit a home run and coach said, 'You've forgotten about that strike, haven't you?' It always stuck with me. After that, I always felt it's just sports. You enjoy it while you're participating in it, but it's not worth getting upset about."

In basketball Cardwell had his greatest success—a nineteen-year record of 288-68, including 80-14 during Earl Lloyd's four years as a Yellow Jacket. If Cardwell had been white, or if black college teams had captured the white-owned media's interests, then he might be known today as the first John Wooden. Cardwell's children, Betty Spencer and Mark Cardwell Jr., recalled that just like Wooden at UCLA, Cardwell retained an unruffled demeanor during even the most intense games.

"He sat on the bench with that leg crossed," Betty said.

"His arm folded," added Mark Jr.

"He said you ought to coach in practice," Betty said, "and don't walk up and down the sidelines yelling and coaching the whole time you're playing ball."

"And you recruit players that have a head on their shoulders," said Mark Jr., who was going to try out for his father's team when Cardwell unexpectedly died of a heart attack in 1964. "He used to tell me all the time don't blame a player for a physical mistake because everybody makes physical mistakes. You blame a player

---

with my mother, or we'd be sitting in the car while he would go in the house and spend an hour." Once a player arrived on campus, the Cardwells took care of him in ways that created a family atmosphere and kept many players in school even though they were short on funds. "Many a tuition was $5 or $10 short, and he would reach in his pocket and pay it," said Mark Jr. "Gosh, he would be so illegal now," Betty said with a chuckle. "When I think about all those players that ate at our house, day in and day out."

"I can remember many a time on Saturday, Daddy cooking bacon and pancakes for the team," Mark Jr. recalled. "Especially the first two weeks of practice before school starts, my mother would fix huge pots of green beans because the cafeteria wasn't open and the [cook] wouldn't feed them. Mama would pack sandwiches for trips. Things were different back then."

Racially West Virginia wasn't nearly as harsh as many Southern states because it had a very small black population, which whites didn't feel threatened by. His children had an idyllic childhood in Institute due to that and the fact that Cardwell was an older man whose career and financial status were secure. "It was like the sun shined every day," Mark Jr. said. If there were recreational facilities that banned black children, the Cardwells didn't mind because they could use campus facilities such as the swimming pool. There were several whites-only movie theaters in Charleston but there also were two black theaters. "And when State lost a game, it was like a big black cloud," Mark Jr. reminded his sister. "People used to walk around sad. Remember when Mr. Byrd used to announce the score at the Saturday night movies? That was almost as important as the movie—to hear him say how badly State beat somebody. When State got beat, you couldn't enjoy the movie."

But when Cardwell's teams traveled elsewhere in the Deep South, he was responsible for making sure his players were protected from the harm that racism could deal out. Just like at other black schools at the time, road trips required careful planning so neither a coach nor his players would find themselves in an embarrassing or dangerous situation. For instance, along the way it was important to know which service stations would sell gas to black customers and, of those, which stations would let black people use the restroom. Coach Cardwell addressed those potential problems when they traveled by bus by using one particular Greyhound driver, Fred Watson. "Dad always requested him, and they were very good friends," Betty said. "He used to come down to our house. He was more like a [protector] on the bus. He knew just where to take them and where there would be trouble. He was a white man, because Greyhound didn't have black drivers at that time. They only had black janitors."

There also was the matter of feeding his players. The sandwiches that the Cardwells made themselves and food prepared by the college cafeteria sometimes sufficed, but there also was the need to stop and buy food along the way. For many years there was a black-owned restaurant in Culpepper, West Virginia, at which the team frequently ate, but that relationship ended in the early 1960s because Cardwell was just as protective of his white players as he was of his black players.

By then West Virginia State's student body was more than 50 percent white and the team was well integrated. "He went in there in 1962 or '63 with two or three white players," Mark Jr. said, "and the black guy that ran the place for years and years said, 'Coach, we've had some trouble around here and I don't want those white boys eating here.' And Daddy just took the whole team out of there and left. Then the guy tried to say, "I'll pack you sandwiches." And Daddy said, "That's okay. That's okay." After eating there for years, he never went back.

"My daddy took his white players in every place. If they couldn't go, then the rest of the team couldn't go. And he would not let the white players room together—always mixed them up." During segregation, when the West Virginia State team arrived at its destination, to avoid the hassle of finding a hotel that would accommodate black guests (and undoubtedly to save money as well), the players and assistant coach would sleep on the opposing campus. Meanwhile, Cardwell would stay at the opposing coach's house. When the opponent came to West Virginia State, the roles were reversed.

Considering all the survival skills needed by black teams at the time, one can see why the Yellow Jackets' groundbreaking trips to San Francisco in 1949 and 1950 were the highlight of many players' college careers. It must have been a relief to get away from the South's stifling atmosphere for at least a couple of weeks.

The trips resulted from the Yellow Jackets' 23-0 record in the 1947–48 season, the only undefeated record in all of college basketball that season. That caught the eye of Frank "Bow Tie" Walsh, the colorful basketball promoter at San Francisco's Cow

Palace. Walsh, who died in 1973, was a born promoter. "He could sell a refrigerator in the North Pole," his widow, Margaret M. Walsh, said. Though the Cow Palace was built for livestock shows, Walsh one day walked in and saw great possibilities for it as a major basketball arena, a rarity on the West Coast at the time. He staged the first intercollegiate basketball games there in 1947, and soon was importing the best teams from across the nation.

For Walsh, organizing tournaments was a labor of love. Mrs. Walsh said the Cow Palace only paid him for the three months that basketball was played there, but arranging the events was a year-round chore. Her secretary's salary supported the family, she wrote her husband's correspondence late at night, and she made the colorful bow ties that became Walsh's trademark. "He never got enough credit," said famed coach Pete Newell, whose University of San Francisco teams appeared in Walsh's events. "He brought to the Bay Area some of the greatest teams and greatest coaches. He brought City College of New York, Long Island with Clair Bee, and Indiana State when John Wooden was coaching there. . . . Frank was a wonderful guy. He never made a dime out of it."

Promoters are always looking for a new attraction to lure fans to an arena, which drew Walsh to West Virginia State. Because of his friendship with Abe Saperstein, Walsh was very conscious of black college basketball. He knew that Madison Square Garden had refused to invite black schools to the National Invitational Tournament (NIT), college basketball's most prestigious tournament at the time. Walsh decided to fill that void by inviting the best black college team in the nation—West Virginia State College—to play against several of the premier West Coast teams. "It sounds like something my dad would do," said his daughter, Loretta Bresh, who now lives north of San Francisco. "He was not just a very creative person, but he truly saw no boundaries. His vision was to connect the world through sports."

It is hard to grasp today just how forward thinking Walsh was until one realizes that his invitation to West Virginia State was unprecedented. The Yellow Jackets' 1949 trip generated a letter of congratulations from West Virginia governor Okey L. Patterson, because it's believed they were the first black-college basketball team to compete on the West Coast and the first to participate in an interracial tournament. Certainly they were the first to play against major basketball programs from predominantly white schools.

The letter was reprinted in full in Charleston's major daily, the

Charleston Gazette. It concluded, "All power and success to you on your western trip. We know that, win or lose, you will be good sports for your college and for our state."[1]

"I still run into guys today and they say, 'Were you on the team that went to California?'" said Frank Enty, a player on the team who succeeded Cardwell as head coach. "With the coverage of black newspapers that had national distribution, it made headlines." Walsh's idealistic efforts also provided important experiences for the players involved.

Lloyd said the trips enriched his life because, "Here's a young black kid who grew up in the cradle of segregation in Virginia. You get to a small black college in the hills of West Virginia and you never compete against white guys. And when you're raised in the cradle of segregation, it's very easy to think you're inferior because you've been treated inferior all your life. My parents emphasized you're as good as anybody, but when you get on the bus you go to the back. To go to California, it was a great shock. I could see from freshman year to senior year, I had grown tremendously. That was the icing on the cake."

The trips were cultural and athletic revelations. To prepare the players for socializing in a white environment, Wilson's gym teacher told them the people they would encounter in the West wouldn't be dancing the jitterbug, which was popular among black people, but instead would be doing the Lindy Hop. So the Yellow Jackets were given lessons in that dance step. "Our first trip, we were entertained by the YWCA in San Francisco," Wilson said. "It happened to be all white people who showed up to introduce us to their city. . . . When we went to the first reception they danced, and I'm sure some were surprised we could do all those dances. That was a very warm welcome."

The players even got to feel rich, at least for a few minutes. "We went to the state treasury in Sacramento and they let us hold a lot of bonds," Lloyd recalled with a laugh. "A guy said, 'You've got $1 million in your hands.' I couldn't count that high."

Walsh didn't have a big expense budget at the Cow Palace, so when he brought teams cross-country he would arrange other games along the way to help meet team expenses. On those trips the Yellow Jackets played in Colorado, Iowa, Nevada, and Southern California before or after their games in the Bay Area.

In 1949 they brought a thirty-two-game winning streak into the Cow Palace and generated the publicity Walsh had hoped for. The day the Yellow Jackets played their initial game against St. Mary's, the February 11 *San Francisco Chronicle*'s headline read "West Virginia Five Encounters Gaels." The article noted the game would be "a 'first' in inter-racial relations here," and featured a large photo of Earl Lloyd, the "Moon Fixer." Theirs was the featured second game, even though the opener pitted Bradley against University of San Francisco (which later that season won the NIT). Tickets ranged from 50 cents for children to $1.50 general admission to $2.50 for the expensive box seats.

That night, with a crowd of 5,216—one considerably larger than the Cow Palace average of 4,398 for twenty-two doubleheaders that season—West Virginia State lost, 66–52, to a St. Mary's team that featured future NBA player Frankie Kudelka. The Gaels jumped out to a 12-point lead in the first half and never were threatened, as Kudelka scored 22 points to offset Lloyd's 16. The Yellow Jackets bounced back the next night with a foul-plagued 57–44 win over Santa Clara in which Wilson scored 23 points and Lloyd 15 before 1,852 fans. Ironically, just two days before that game Santa Clara had announced that football star Melvin Lewis had enrolled as the school's first Negro student in the almost–one hundred years of its existence.

The Yellow Jackets had adjusted quickly to a different style of basketball. "They just played rougher," Lloyd said fifty-one years later. "St. Mary's prepared us for Santa Clara. We figured if that was the way it was, you've got to step up. In our conference, we were a big team. We were a slow-down type of team; St. Mary's and Santa Clara were up and down the floor. . . . Our thing was slow it down, keep it close, bang the boards and wear people down. They had some people that were big and fast and were not about to be worn down."

West Virginia State was 1-3 on the road trip (also losing to Loyola of Los Angeles and the University of Nevada), but an article in the May 1950 issue of *Color Magazine* noted the greater significance of their trip: "The important thing was not so much a matter of who won the games, but that the famous 'Yellow Jackets' were facing white opponents and showing the world that Negroes and whites can compete against each other in good fellowship. West Virginia's team, national Negro basketball champs for 1947, 1948, and 1949, and only undefeated college team in the nation for 1948, demonstrated to other white and colored schools that the world of sports and its many spectators are primarily interested in skillful performances and not in the color of the players. These great teams further helped to prove that athletics are a big help to all races in their fight to remove color lines that bar human progress."[2]

West Virginia State again accepted Walsh's invitation to bring a team in 1950. The Yellow Jackets beat Loras College (in Iowa) to become 13-1, then lost its Cow Palace opener to San Jose State 52–50. One highlight of the trip was meeting California Governor Earl Warren, who four years later became chief justice of the Supreme Court that handed down *Brown vs. Board of Education*. Warren had asked coach Cardwell for a special favor: would his team add a game against inmates at nearby San Quentin prison? On February 6, 1950, the team traveled across the Golden Gate Bridge and got a tour of the prison before the game. The prison left a deep impression on Lloyd at a time when legitimate employment opportunities were very limited for African-American college graduates. Mostly they could only teach or work in the post office.

"At that time, I didn't know what I wanted to be," Lloyd said. "To think of pro basketball, I had no predecessors. But San Quentin left a profound effect on me. Not that I had any inclination toward being a crook, but I learned what I *didn't* want to be. You take a young black guy into maximum security prison, it scared the hell out of me. We saw the jute mill where they made burlap bags. It was dank, and it was dusty and guys who didn't get executed probably died from black lung disease. It looked like there wasn't much rehabilitation going on. They just housed people."

The game was held on a makeshift court in the prison dining hall. The inmates were rugged but the game nevertheless had its humorous moments. One time an inmate got ready to take a foul shot when Walsh called out, "Take your time! You've got plenty of it!"

"I think they put in some stands," Lloyd said, "and the strangest thing about it was the prison population rooted for us. Maybe they thought if we won, they would leave with us." The Yellow Jackets won 65–37, then lost the next night 78–68 to the Blue and Gold American Athletic Union team that starred former UCLA standout Don Barksdale, the best player on the West Coast. Five years later he became the first African-American to play in an NBA All-Star game. In the West Virginia–UCLA game Barksdale scored 23 points while Lloyd scored 21 (a significant achievement). "He was by far the best I ever played against [in college]," Lloyd said. "Barks could do it all. Playing against Barks was a defining moment for me because I felt I fared well. That's when I felt I had a little talent. That shows you how much I respect him." Two months later Lloyd was drafted by the NBA's Washington Capitols, and six months after that he was making basketball history.

West Virginia State holds a unique place in basketball history. "People ask what is it about West Virginia State," Lloyd said. "It's hard to explain it. First of all, we were isolated and they had a lot of campus activities. It was the perfect place for me. It was a genuine love affair between the team and the students. Nobody spoiled you, but they genuinely loved you. There was something about it that was special. I had the right coach at the right time, right place at the right time, met the right people at the right time."

The Gentlest Giant

When Nathaniel "Sweetwater" Clifton signed with the New York Knicks in 1950, he entered the NBA under completely different circumstances than Chuck Cooper or Earl Lloyd had known. The latter two were scrambling to join an NBA roster and weren't thinking about making their names instantly recognizable. Clifton, although technically a rookie with the Knicks, had already accomplished those goals before he played his first league game on November 4, 1950, at Tri-Cities.

Clifton was already twenty-four, twenty-six, or twenty-eight years old. (He liked to maintain some mystery about his age, although the NBA *Encyclopedia* lists his birthdate as October 13, 1922, which would have made him 28.) His two seasons with the Harlem Globetrotters had given him international exposure in Europe, Asia, and South America, and his nickname—derived from his love of soda pop—gave him instant recognition. Therefore, six-foot-seven-and-a-half, 235-pound Clifton was the first black gate attraction in NBA history.

"I heard it was hard for some of the (black) players," said Ernie Vandeweghe, Clifton's roommate on Knicks' road trips. "Remember, the Globies were a very good team. They put on showtime, but they were very good players. And having been a Trotter and having played in some of the cities, he carried with him a little popularity that possibly made it a little easier for him. We always kidded him that he had his own cheering section. I felt fans were very supportive, especially New York fans." Clifton said that he was so popular, "They [even] loved me in St. Louis at Kiel Auditorium" at a time when St. Louis was one city many black players of that era despised because of the racist slurs they heard from fans. Clifton softened even the hard hearts of St. Louis.

From the time he was a teenager Clifton had a trio of assets that made him a crowd pleaser: exceptional size, a flair for entertainment, and a personality as sweet as his nickname. He had extraordinary height—growing to six-foot-six (which was considered giant-sized in those days) by the time he was a high school senior—and unbelievably large hands that measured ten inches from the tip of his thumb to the tip of his baby finger and required size 13 gloves. His hands helped him hold a basketball, palm down, with the ease of most people when gripping a tennis ball. He could hold a basketball in one hand and wind up like a pitcher getting ready to fire a strike to home plate. Globetrotters owner Abe Saperstein claimed that Clifton "can do more tricks with a basketball than a monkey can do with a peanut."[1]

Clifton, who died in 1990, also was a superior athlete who enjoyed sharing the spotlight with teammates. In January of 1942 he became the talk of Chicago's prep sports when his two stunning performances led Du Sable High School to its second consecutive city championship. In the semifinal game against Austin, a 78–27 rout, Clifton scored a phenomenal 45 points, nearly double the tournament record of 24.

"The 19-year-old Clifton is without a peer as a ball handler," the *Chicago Daily News* reported the next day.

> *He shoots with either hand or both. His height makes him a terrific rebounder and practically impossible to guard under the basket. But his long suit is a fancy brand of blind passes and the ability to palm the basketball with either of his hamlike hands.*
>
> *Yet he has a fault and it is a strange one. The big boy, although blessed with capabilities of always scoring at a high rate each game, doesn't shoot enough. Or at least he didn't before last night's walkaway.*
>
> *"Sweetwater" has an explanation for his actions. As long as he keeps feeding that ball to teammates Morris and Randolph, excellent shots both, Du Sable functions in smooth style, he explains. . . . Where did he learn all those fancy ball-handling tactics? Well, his cousin plays with the Harlem Globe Trotters, a crack Negro professional team, and big Nat likes to scrimmage with the boys once in a while."[2]

In the championship game Clifton, who had been playing basketball only three years, scored 25 more points against Marshall, prompting *Daily News* columnist Lyall Smith to ponder whether Clifton or forward Dwight Eddleman (from the town of Centralia) was the greatest high school player in Illinois history. (Smith chose

Eddleman, who eventually played four NBA seasons and appeared in two All-Star games).

During high school Sweetwater let go of his real name, Clifton Nathaniel, in exchange for Nathaniel Clifton. "The media changed my name when I started doing good in high school," Clifton said. "They said Nathaniel [as a last name] was too long to put in the paper. I never changed it back. As long as I have it right when I pay my taxes, I'm okay."[3]

Clifton seemed to be loved by everyone who knew him. "This was an extraordinary man," said Fred Podesta, the Knicks' executive who negotiated Clifton's sale to the team. "There was nothing you could dislike [about him]. If there was any time the words sartorial splendor could be applied. . . . I never saw him without a suit and trousers. He always dressed perfectly. Very pleasant, but I think if Sweetwater would be around today he would probably be a multimillionaire [from commercial endorsements]. Everybody liked him."

After high school Clifton played one season at Xavier University, a black college in New Orleans, before being drafted into the army in 1944. Three years later he was discharged, played for a semiprofessional team in Dayton, Ohio, then turned professional with the New York Rens. He signed with the Globetrotters in July 1948 for a reported $10,000 per year, which Abe Saperstein claimed was the highest salary ever paid a black player.

Soon after that Clifton, a legendary slugger in Chicago's local softball leagues, began a professional baseball career that conceivably could have put him in the major leagues. Bill Veeck, the publicity conscious owner of the Cleveland Indians, saw Clifton playing with the Globetrotters one evening and told Saperstein, who doubled as an Indians scout, that someone with Clifton's speed, size, and reflexes could be a good baseball player. Clifton had only played basketball and softball until then, so the Indians gave him two weeks of workouts before sending him to the minor leagues. He starred at first base on three minor-league teams, the last in 1950 at Double-A Wilkes-Barre, where he batted .304 with 27 doubles, 7 triples, 9 home runs, and 86 RBIs. "There's no question in my mind he could have played in the majors," Veeck told the *Chicago Tribune*.[4] But Saperstein became concerned about losing Clifton to baseball, so he took Clifton on a European basketball tour. Clifton never played professional baseball again.

Tired of all the travel and upset about feeling underpaid,

Clifton told Saperstein that 1950 would be his last season with the Globetrotters. Clifton's demands motivated Saperstein to sell Clifton's contract to the Knicks. However, Saperstein and Clifton remained friends, and during NBA off-seasons Clifton often returned to the Globetrotters, who played the looser style of ball he enjoyed.

The NBA Clifton joined had a totally different atmosphere than today's league. "The outstanding characteristic of the life was intimacy," said Leonard Koppett, a former Knicks beat writer for the *Herald Tribune* and the *New York Post*. "There were eight teams, the whole population was eighty players. You played a lot of doubleheaders, and any time you played a doubleheader you had half the league in the arena. And the intensity of hometown rivalry was much more wild than nowadays. People in Syracuse hated anyone in a Boston or New York uniform, and were fiercely loyal to anyone in their own uniform." That was a plus for black players during home games, but a minus on the road because, "People who hated them [for being on the opposing team] hated them even more because they were black."

It also was a time when the relationship between the media and the players was more casual and, to a degree, more trusting than it is today. "Socially and psychologically, we were in the same business and same social cast," Koppett said. "We were the same social class, made similar incomes. Yeah, the star players made more than I did, but not that much more that their life was different. When they had to go somewhere at home or to a restaurant, they went either in their own car or on a bus, the same as I did. They didn't have a seven-mile long limo pull up with two flunkies to take them wherever they wanted to go."

The demarcation line between them wasn't completely blurred, however. Players knew that there were some things they couldn't say in front of a writer, and the writer understood that. Koppett said they could nevertheless still talk about which movie they saw the night before, and the sport of basketball was a constant topic of conversation among the players and between players and writers.

However, there were virtually no black sportswriters nationwide except for those at black publications and a handful (at most) at white-owned newspapers. Consequently, at major newspapers the images of early black NBA players were crafted almost exclusively by white writers, and Koppett believes that that situation skewed the coverage in stereotypical ways. For instance, just like Earl Lloyd, Clifton was fastidious about his personal appearance and hygiene. "He shouldn't offend anybody," Koppett said. "On the one hand, it's a personality trait, but it's also a devastating example of the constantly on-guard life. That's what whites were oblivious to."

In retrospect Koppett believes a compliment that the press frequently bestowed upon Clifton actually was an unconsciously condescending remark: "What a fine gentleman he is," Koppett recalled hearing frequently. "And we said that a hell of a lot about a lot of black players, as if that's something to be surprised at, as if that's something to call attention to. What you're really saying is, 'He's not like the others.'" It never dawned on Koppett to ask Clifton what it was like to be one of the first black NBA pioneers, to ask about any special pressures or responsibilities he may have been feeling. "I don't think so, because we would feel it wasn't right to focus on that—because the goodhearted thing is integration: 'You're just like everyone else.' So why sit down and ask why you're different?"

Into this setting stepped Sweetwater Clifton, who from 1950 to 1957 thoroughly enjoyed his Knicks teammates as much as they enjoyed him. "Around Chicago and in the army, I was used to playing with white players, and I could get along," he said in 1985. "I figured everybody had to make a living and nobody gave me any dirt. They were a great bunch of guys. Wasn't anybody I disliked or had any trouble with. I still hear from the guys, and I played with Dicky and Al McGuire, and Vandeweghe was great. We called him the Doc."

"Our team was very close," said Vandeweghe, who simultaneously played for the Knicks and attended medical school. "Never two or three [together], always ten or eleven. Card games or church on Sunday, Sweets was always along with the group. He was definitely part of the team."

"A terrible card player," Vince Boryla said with a chuckle. "Sweets was nice to play cards with. Paid all of his bills, a little late sometimes, but paid all his bills. Out of every pot we would cut out money and for breakfast get sweet rolls, coffee, sandwiches, coke, and beer. You'd be surprised how many games we won over a card table, just talking about games and attitudes."

Clifton's free spending ways—he had a weakness for new cars—sometimes got him into amusing situations. "He spent money like there was no tomorrow," Podesta said. "One day, he came in and wanted to buy a present for his wife, and I believed him. You wouldn't make up something like that. So I gave him some money and he came back the next day and needed more money. He had bought her the most expensive lingerie you could find. He said, 'If you don't believe me, I'll have her come in with me.' " Podesta decided to take Clifton's word for it.

The only snag in this tightly knit team occurred when the Knicks traveled to cities in the South, such as Baltimore. Those trips could have turned into the usual awkward situation for black players, where negotiations were undertaken to find out if he could sleep and eat at the team hotel. Clifton bypassed that hassle altogether by choosing to stay at hotels that the Globetrotters had frequented. "I knew somebody in every town I played in," Clifton said. "They used to come around and get me. I really liked entertainment, to go to clubs. Coach Lapchick was a good guy. He wouldn't try to hold me with the team. He knew I didn't smoke or drink. That's why he gave me my freedom, so I never had any problem."

His teammates didn't like these separations, but were helpless to prevent them. "It bothered us a great deal, but at that time you understood it," Vandeweghe said. "I understood that was a problem the hotel had, not a problem I had."

As a player Clifton was a legitimate force: extremely long arms, ran well, good leaper, athletic. He had the entire package to be an excellent power forward. Unfortunately, among the undersized Knicks he had to play center. "I was a rebounder and scored some and played some defense," Clifton said. "I mostly guarded the tough guys on the other team. My idea was to try to have a winning team. We used to win about every year until Boston got Bill Russell. We never had a tall man."

The Knicks reached the NBA Finals during all three of Clifton's first three years, losing to Rochester his rookie season and then to George Mikan's Minneapolis Lakers twice. Clifton was just too short to effectively defend the gigantic Mikan. "He was a fantastic player," six-ten-and-a-half Mikan said about Clifton. "He wasn't quite as tall as me, but he had great big hands. He could handle that ball. He was quite proficient shooting set shots, and I had to go out there after him." Mikan first played against Clifton in a Catholic Youth Organization tournament in 1941 or 1942, when Mikan was a college freshman at DePaul. "He was a sweet guy,"

Mikan said. "When games were over, we would go out together and do the town together."

Did Clifton try to use his strength against Mikan? "They all did," Mikan replied. "I always thought they were attracted to me like a bee to the honey and always tried to use two or three men. But we got along all right."

It is often said that the Knicks would have won a couple titles if Long Island University star Sherman White hadn't gotten convicted in the college basketball gambling scandal of 1951. Because the NBA was so desperate for gate attractions in the 1950s, teams could make "territorial" picks in the draft that would give them the rights to local college heroes. It is assumed that in 1951 the Knicks would have selected White, a fiercely competitive and high-leaping six-foot-eight center who led the nation in scoring in 1951 at 27.7 points per game. Had he been matched with Clifton and Harry "the Horse" Gallatin, another tenacious rebounder, the Knicks would have been close to unbeatable. When White no longer was an option, the Knicks tried to sign Globetrotters star Willie Gardner. Gardner actually did sign in 1957, but a heart ailment prevented him from ever joining the team.

At first Clifton didn't play up to expectations because he wasn't aggressive enough, which really aggravated coach Joe Lapchick. In a 1954 column by the *New York Times*'s revered Red Smith, Lapchick said that in Clifton's rookie season "he was the mildest, inoffensive fellow you ever saw. On a train out of Indianapolis one night I had to tell him he was doing a bad job under the boards, letting them take rebounds away from him."[5] That all changed the next season when, acting completely out of character, Clifton decked Boston's Bob Harris with a one-two punch that would have made Joe Louis proud. It was the first and last time an NBA player assailed Clifton with a racial slur.

The story of Clifton's KO is one that Lapchick and Knicks players love to tell, and, befitting a story that has grown into lore, each has a slightly different version. Vince Boryla, a forward on the team, recalled that the fight began with a midcourt confrontation. Vandeweghe said it started when he and Al McGuire [who coached Marquette to the 1977 NCAA title] double-teamed Harris, who "pushed Al into me and the two of us went sprawling. Sweets stepped in and said 'don't hit my friend.'"

Clifton's recollection was entirely different, but just as colorful. "Bob was from Oklahoma and I don't think he appreciated the way I would play," he began. Clifton explained that he was handling the ball with one hand and Harris, evidently feeling he was being shown up, started arguing with him about it. Then both Vandeweghe and Clifton agree that Harris uttered the magic word: nigger. "He told me that, and said where I come from black guys don't do like that," Clifton said. And the fight was on. "I got lucky and knocked him down. Ever since then, I got a lot of respect from the guys."

Ah, Clifton was just being modest. Joe Lapchick gives a more detailed blow-by-blow description: "They squared off, and when they did, the whole Boston bench jumped up and started out on the floor. Well, Sweets let go and I give you my word, in the ring or out of it I never saw a prettier left hook and right cross. He spread [Harris] like apple butter, out cold. There was a screech of tires and a smell of burning rubber. Everybody who'd come off the Boston bench slammed on the brakes when Sweets landed that left and that right. They wheeled around and sat down. I was delighted. For once, Sweets was showing them he was in business. Also I'm a fight fan, and I can get a lot of pleasure out of a couple of punches like that."

Later, still fascinated by those hellacious punches, Lapchick asked Clifton if he had ever been a boxer. "'Not as a pro,' he told me, 'but when I was growin' up I lived in the neighborhood with that Bobby Satterfield. I used to whup him every day before breakfast.'" In 1950 "that" Bobby Satterfield was the fourth-ranked light heavyweight boxer in the world.[6]

Clifton's lack of assertiveness also could be seen in his reluctance to shoot during his first season. Vandeweghe recalled that in Clifton's first practice with the Knicks, he blocked a bunch of shots and passed the ball well, but never took a shot. "He did not play well for a while," Vandeweghe said. "When he first joined he played with his back to the basket. He'd pass the ball or give it to the cutter. He never made any attempt to score, and one of the secrets of the NBA is to keep your man busy. Although he passed beautifully, he was not effective enough. It took him about a year to become a force."

Clifton was merely feeling his way. "When I came to the NBA, I didn't give the impression I was trying to take over the team," he said. "I was doing a lot of passing, playing defense, and rebounding. We had guys who were pretty good scorers. When I was with the Trotters I had a lot more freedom because they know how I play. Here, I was a stranger so I kind of worked myself in. I would never try to take over."

Clifton said he regretted that the Knicks never had a good black ballplayer who understood his Globetrotters style of play. "And that kinda held me back, 'cause you can't do something with the other guys because they played the straight way," he said in *From Set Shot to Slam Dunk*. "I felt like I was sacrificing myself for some guy and I don't think other guys would have done that. I'll put it this way: at that time they weren't making any black stars. You already had to be made. It was frustrating but here's the way I played it: I played the way the guys wanted me to play."[7]

There were two other reasons for Clifton's reticence on offense: the impact of being a racial pioneer, and Lapchick's conservative coaching style. "In other words, being the first in something, you don't want to do anything that'll mess it up for somebody else," he said. "Maybe if I'd have screwed up some way there wouldn't be any blacks in the NBA today. There was pressure on me, but the thing that made it okay was that the fans, especially the kids, really liked me. I really appreciated that. I think that maybe that was the biggest thrill I had.

"The only thing is, I'm sorry today that I couldn't have done much more. I could have if I'd had someone behind me, pushing me in the right direction. What I had was Joe Lapchick. He was a good coach but he didn't have the imagination, you know. He wasn't really up to what the modern-day game was. He had that old-fashioned style that the Celtics [the Original Celtics of the 1920s] had earlier."[8]

Lapchick's son, Richard, has no doubt that Lapchick told Clifton not to use some of his fancy Globetrotter moves. However, Richard believes his father's reasons were much different than Clifton suspected. He said that his father and Bob Douglas, owner of the New York Rens, had been very close friends. Through that association Joe Lapchick learned that the Rens didn't respect the Trotters' comedic routines, believing their trick maneuvers reinforced negative stereotypes about black people. Consequently, Lapchick wouldn't want a black player on his team to use them. "I know my father was really sensitive to the Globetrotter image, and having been educated by Bobby Douglas didn't want that clowning to go on," Richard Lapchick said. "But that was also my father's conservative style of coaching. I went to St. John's when he was coaching there, and he also didn't want behind-the-back dribbling or fancy passes, whether you were black or white."

Although Clifton may have felt like he was playing in a straitjacket, he became a very effective player for New York. As a rookie he averaged 8.6 points and 7.6 rebounds, then the next season increased it to 10.6 points and 11.8 rebounds. By the second month of that season Joe Lapchick called Clifton "the most improved player in the National Basketball Association."

"With the Globetrotters, Clifton was just a part of the comedy act aimed at entertaining the fans," Lapchick said. "He knew practically nothing about the scientific side of the sport. His jump from the Trotters to the Knicks was comparable to a sandlot baseball player moving directly to the majors."[9]

His best scoring year came in his fifth season, when he averaged 13.1 points, and played in the 1957 All-Star game during his last season with the Knicks. As a reserve Clifton played extremely well in twenty-three minutes, scoring 8 points and grabbing 11 rebounds, which tied two other players for the second-highest total in the game. After that season he was traded to Detroit, where he played his last NBA season as a reserve. Throughout his career he was a formidable rebounder who ranked in the league's top 10 in both the 1951–52 season (11.8 per game) and 1952–53 season (10.9).

"He was very athletic and if he got his hands on the ball, no one could get it from him," said Leonard Lewin, who covered the Knicks for the *Herald Tribune* and the *New York Post*. "He was tremendous under the boards. He used to rebound with guys who towered over him. If you took his hands and put them on Patrick Ewing's body, you would have one of the greatest centers of all time." Most of all he was a winner. In eight seasons, his teams missed the playoffs only once.

Disappointed in his lack of playing time with Detroit, Clifton retired from the NBA and joined the Harlem Magicians team operated by former Globetrotters stars Marques Haynes and Goose Tatum. After several seasons with that team he returned to Abe Saperstein's teams, playing for the Trotters and the Chicago Majors in the short-lived American Basketball League. Clifton retired in the mid-1960s after a knee injury.

It bothered Clifton that players of his era were not included in the players' pension plan, and he would have loved to have played in today's high-salary days. "Other than that, I had a good life," he said. "The playing was fine. I don't think I would change very much of it."

After leaving basketball Clifton drove a taxi cab in Chicago. It wasn't a fancy job, but it satisfied Clifton's desire for independence—his mother had suffered a stroke and driving a cab allowed him to check in on her during his workday. On August 31, 1990, Clifton suffered a fatal heart attack as his cab pulled away from Chicago's Union Station. He died doing something in which he took great pride. "I might not be, but I think I'm the best cab driver out there," he once said. "The way I look at it, if you're gonna be something, be good at it." [10]

10

Barksdale, a Man of Many Firsts

One of my idols was A. Philip Randolph, who was the first guy to form a black union, the porters association. Once in a while my Dad used to take me to meetings, and I'd listen to these guys. . . . I listened to how tough it was. I made up my mind that if I wanted to do something, I was going to try to do it all the way, no matter the obstacles. All you can do is try your best. And I never knew what it was to say, "You can't do this" or "It can't be done." I figured some day it's going to be done.

Don Barksdale, the first black NBA All-Star

Among the first wave of black NBA players, and possibly among all of the league's early players regardless of color, the label "Renaissance Man" belonged to one person: Don Barksdale. The hurdles he encountered were high, yet he refused to let them prevent him from achieving lofty goals.

Barksdale's talents and interests were so diverse that he could not be pigeon-holed. How many other professional basketball players majored in art in college and were accomplished portrait painters? Throughout his life he had a penchant for crossing paths with famous people. The entrepreneurial spirit was in his blood, and because he was determined to succeed at everything he pursued Barksdale spent his life enmeshed in the role of black pioneer.

"There are about 14 firsts in my life," he said. Among them were being the first black beer distributor in the San Francisco Bay Area; first black television show host in the Bay Area ["Sepia Revue" on KRON-TV in 1949]; first black consensus All-American in college basketball [1947]; first black member of a U.S. Olympic basketball team [1948]; and first black player in an NBA All-Star Game.

Basketball was the linchpin. After establishing himself as the best basketball player on the West Coast while starring for UCLA and in the highly competitive Amateur Athletic Union, he was signed by the Baltimore Bullets in 1951 as one of the NBA's highest paid players. Bullets management began subjecting him to callous treatment just months after his signing. He overcame that and in 1953 played in the All-Star Game, a game that included twelve future basketball Hall of Famers.

On the court Barksdale was the epitome of speed, grace, and Olympic-caliber leaping ability that was the envy of his peers. "If there was anybody I loved when I was young, Joe DiMaggio and Don Barksdale were my heroes," said George Yardley, who grew up on the West Coast before becoming a six-time NBA All-Star. "I admired him tremendously. He was at the top of the ladder when I was playing."

Barksdale, six-foot-six, mostly played center although he had trouble keeping his weight above 200 pounds, so his success was based on quickness. Here's how he described himself as a player in 1991: "Fast, and I had the quick dribble and jump. You never stood and jumped in the air and shot. . . . Half the time I had to play center. I'd get the ball in the center and fake, go left and then fade away and take a jump shot. And if I got on the side, I had a very fast first step that I could almost go around anybody. If I got the ball in the corner, I could fake like Chris Mullin and go.

"The biggest problem I always had was my hands were not big. I couldn't even palm the ball. Had I been able to palm the ball, I would have been [a terror]. I had to use stickum and everything else. I wish that ball was a little smaller. And then I was a good rebounder, excellent rebounder. I was able to jump pretty high."

Barksdale believes he could have jumped even higher on today's resilient court surfaces. "Most of the floors we played on were like playing on concrete," he said.

Barksdale was so talented that he is one of the few players from the 1950s who could probably excel in today's fleet game. That's what Tex Winter believes, and no one is better equipped to make that evaluation. Winter played for the University of Southern California when the Trojans lost twice to UCLA in the 1946–47 season that stamped Barksdale as an All-American., then went on to a brilliant college and pro coaching career. He is one of the few players to bridge the gap between Barksdale's era and today. In the early 1990s, as a Chicago Bulls assistant coach, he was the architect of the "triangle offense" that helped Michael Jordan's teams win six NBA titles under head coach Phil Jackson. In the year 2000 Winter rejoined Jackson as a Los Angeles Lakers assistant where he taught the offense to today's superstars Shaquille O'Neal and Kobe Bryant.

Winter's memories of Barksdale are accompanied by more than half a century of perspective and hands-on contact with the game. "Barksdale had the kind of physical prowess that he could play pro ball today," Winter said in 2000. "No question in my mind. He was a great player. He wasn't a great shooter, but he could score because of his athletic abilities. Could block shots, could run like a deer. I never knew what happened to him in pro ball.

"He was a phenom to us. It was really the first experience I had playing against that caliber of black athlete—and I did play against Jackie Robinson, also." Winter wouldn't necessarily say Barksdale was the superior athlete between the two, but Barksdale was the superior basketball player even though Robinson also had been All-Conference at UCLA.

Barksdale's four-year career as a black NBA pioneer, distinguished as it was, is only a part of the achievements that made his life exceptional. Growing up in Berkeley, California, during the 1920s and 1930s, he was strongly influenced by the budding black labor movement spearheaded by A. Philip Randolph, who headed up the Brotherhood of Sleeping Car Porters that represented baggage handlers on trains. Largely through Randolph's efforts, in 1937 the Brotherhood secured a contract with the Pullman Company, the first contract between a company and a black union. Don's father was a member of that union (as was the father of future U.S. Congressman Ron Dellums); Barksdale attended Pullman porters meetings with his father and there developed a determination to explore and succeed that continued throughout his life.

That determination was never more visible than on March 16, 1993, when more than four hundred friends and admirers of Barksdale gathered at Kimball's East nightclub in Emeryville, California, to pay tribute to him eight days after he had died of cancer. It was a standing room only crowd that included former Boston Celtics stars Bob Cousy and Tom Heinsohn. A succession of distinguished speakers took the stage and presented a wide range of images of the man being honored.

Scotty Stirling, long-time NBA executive and scout, tried to encapsulate Barksdale's greatness on the court by relating that Bill Russell once said Barksdale "was Scottie Pippen before there was a Scottie Pippen."

Bill Walsh, who gained fame as the coach of the San Francisco 49ers pro football team, recalled being a teenager in his car listening to Barksdale's deep, mellow voice as a disc jockey on KDIA radio station out of Oakland. "His voice used to help me fall in love with my date," Walsh said. "I'd try the deep voice, but all I got was the steamed-up windows and the dead battery."

San Francisco sportscaster Gary Radnich, who specializes in a hip, off-the-cuff approach to sports that offends many traditionalists, appreciated Barksdale's flair for entertainment that stemmed from his love of music and led to his ownership of Oakland nightclubs for almost thirty years. Before white club owners welcomed black entertainers such as Lou Rawls and Moms Mabley, Barksdale's clubs gave them a platform where their talents could be displayed. "Style, you can't buy," Radnich said about Barksdale. "About the first six months I was here, there was an article saying 'won't make it six months.' Don called me up, didn't know me, and said, 'Hey man, I know exactly what you're doing. You are one crazy white boy. You just keep on pushing.'" In closing his remarks Radnich scanned the packed-in crowd, then said, "And I know if Don was here, he'd look around and say, 'Hey, man, I sold the place out.'"

But it was Barksdale's generosity and concern for youngsters that was the dominant theme of the tribute. "The measure of a man," longtime NBA figure Al Attles noted that evening, "is the difference he made in other people's lives."

Barksdale measured as tall as they come. While hospitalized in 1982 Barksdale had read an article about parents having to pay up to $85 to have their child participate in prep sports in the Bay Area, so he formed an organization called Save High School Sports to provide additional financial support to school districts. From 1983 until his death, Barksdale's Celebrity Waiter luncheons—imagine having Hall of Famer Nate Thurmond hand-deliver your ham and cheese sandwich—charity golf outings, and other events raised more than $1 million to help keep local prep sports alive.

"Nobody could work a room better than Don Barksdale," recalled Andy Dolich, the former marketing director of baseball's Oakland Athletics. "He was the Pied Piper of preserving precious programs. He never waited for somebody else to do it. He could take your money and leave you laughing and you wouldn't even feel the bruises. He was the ultimate Robin from the 'Hood. He made the rich feel richer."

It's ironic that despite all of his achievements, Barksdale couldn't even make the basketball team at Berkeley High School because of one of the few unenviable "firsts" in his life.

Barksdale's best friend, Em Chapman, who also is black, was a better player at the time and made Berkeley High's roster. Every year Barksdale wasn't deemed good enough. "They used to cut us alphabetically, and I was the first man cut three years in a row at Berkeley High," Barksdale said. "Em made the team, but the coach, Jack Eadie, said, 'One black is enough.'" So Barksdale developed his game at San Pablo Park near Berkeley. "We'd go there at 9:30 in the morning and our folks were lucky to see us at 6:30 at night," Barksdale said. "We'd run home for lunch and have a track meet trying to get back so we could play some more. That went on five, six hours a day."

In addition, Barksdale persevered under the tutelage of Dutch Rudquist, who coached an amateur team at the park. "No matter if you were playing in practice, you had to play your butt off," Barksdale said. "And if not he'd call you Bonehead and say, 'Come here and sit down, and when you're ready to play we'll put you in.' So I learned to play against older guys and tougher guys."

At San Pablo Park Barksdale competed against superb athletes such as future major league baseball player Billy Martin, Lionel Wilson (who pitched in the Negro Leagues and eventually became mayor of Oakland), and Johnny Allen, arguably the Bay Area's best black athlete in the 1930s. When Barksdale first started playing in the park, he and Johnny Otis, the musician who later discovered the great blues singer Etta James, regularly were the last players chosen for pick-up teams. "They'd flip a coin and say, 'Oh, you've got to have Johnny today,' or 'You've got to have Barks,'" Barksdale said. "Two years later of playing every day, all of a sudden I was playing against the big boys and I was outscoring all of them."

His efforts paid off one day when a San Pablo Park team beat a junior college team in an exhibition event held prior to a University of California–Berkeley basketball game. A coach at Marin Junior College (now College of Marin), located just north of San Francisco, was impressed and asked Barksdale and Chapman if they would be interested in playing for him. "Hell, I hadn't an offer from even high school, so I said, 'Oh yeah, I'd be interested.'" Barksdale said. He also was interested because two of their black friends, Johnny Allen and Walter Loving, previously had played for Marin. "It was one of the few schools that would even think about bringing in a black player," Barksdale said.

Barksdale immediately became a starting center in 1941 under coach Scoop Carlsen, then switched to guard in 1942 for new coach Dutch Clymer. With Barksdale as Marin's leading scorer and rebounder, he and Chapman carried Marin to the 1942 Northern California Junior College Conference championship with a perfect 13-0 conference record and a 21-1 mark overall. Barksdale led Marin in scoring with 12.8 points per game, Chapman followed at 10.5. Barksdale also competed in track and field for the school, setting the national junior college high jump record at 6 feet, 3 inches, winning the Northern California JC high jump and broad jump championship, and coming in fourth in the 100-yard dash.

After Barksdale's two years at Marin, UCLA coach Wilbur Johns offered him a basketball scholarship, probably the easiest recruiting coup Johns ever pulled off since UCLA was Barksdale's first choice, hands down. As a teenager Barksdale had met Jackie Robinson and Kenny Washington when as star football players at UCLA they had come to Berkeley to play the University of California. From then on, Robinson, the future baseball legend, and Washington, who helped re-integrate professional football in 1946, were Barksdale's idols. For Barksdale becoming a Bruin was a dream fulfilled.

Barksdale received his junior college degree in January, 1943; when he arrived at UCLA the basketball season was half over. Nevertheless the Bruins wanted him to begin playing right away, and Barksdale immediately was cloaked in hero's status when he scored a game-high 18 points to end UCLA's eleven-year, forty-two-game losing streak against Southern California.

Barksdale played only five games that season and averaged 16 points before he went into the army, eventually being sent to Camp Lee in Petersburg, Virginia (which, decades later, was the birthplace of NBA great Moses Malone). Barksdale was in all-black Company I of the Quartermaster Corps, where "blacks were either cooking food or cleaning up dumps." Barksdale wanted to get transferred to Camp Ross in California, where he had been offered a position in Special Services as a player-coach of a military team.

Getting there was the hard part, but it led to Barksdale's introduction to one of the great legal figures of the twentieth century. A friend suggested that Barksdale ask a black attorney in the U.S. Justice Department to help him get a transfer, so

Barksdale hitch-hiked 136 miles to Washington DC and met with the attorney. "He knew what a black kid in college was going through in the Quartermaster Corps," Barksdale said, "and he told me frankly, 'I cannot promise you anything, Don, but I'll try.' And damned if he didn't do it. That was a changeover, too, for me. I could have gone overseas and got killed. As it was, I came back to California and I was able to play basketball and hone my skills. So when I came out of the army, I went back to UCLA and I was ready."

Who was the attorney to whom Barksdale felt so indebted? The esteemed Thurgood Marshall, who in 1954 headed the team of attorneys that won the landmark *Brown vs. Board of Education* decision that banned racially segregated schools. In 1967 Marshall became the first black U.S. Supreme Court Justice.

Playing again for coach Johns—Barksdale called him "one of the sweetest guys in the world"—Barksdale was a unanimous All-Pacific Coast Conference selection for the 1946–47 season and became the first black consensus All-American basketball player. Then his career got sidetracked by the NBA's silent ban on black players.

During Barksdale's senior year Jackie Robinson had signed with the Brooklyn Dodgers, which at first was an inspiration for black athletes everywhere. "We thought it was the greatest thing in the world," Barksdale said. "All the black athletes across the country thought it would mean immediate opening of the doors, but it didn't. It still went along very slowly."

Instead of getting the kinds of offers his talent warranted from teams in the Basketball Association of America (the precursor of the NBA), Barksdale saw white college stars being courted while he was totally ignored. Barksdale signed with the Oakland Bittners of the American Basketball League, which was affiliated with the Amateur Athletic Union. At the time the AAU was considered a slight step down, if that, from the NBA, though in terms of exposure AAU ball was as big or bigger than the NBA because it had teams across the country (the NBA was based largely in the East).

Winter said that when he coached Kansas State from 1953 to 1968, he urged most of his players to move on to AAU ball instead of the NBA because the AAU provided a better long-range future: AAU teams were affiliated with companies that would employ and train players in a profession. "Even to this day, I had a couple players who went to the Phillips Oilers who now have very good franchises with Phillips Petroleum," Winter said.

Once again Barksdale was a pioneer as the first black player signed by an ABL team, then he set an ABL scoring record as a rookie with 386 points in twenty-three games. That season Barksdale also became the first black athlete to appear in a sports event against white players held in the state of Oklahoma, a portent of both good and dreadful things to come.

In January of 1948 the Bittners played four games against the Phillips 66ers, the dominant AAU team, in Bartlesville and Oklahoma City, Oklahoma. Oklahoma was home territory for the 66ers, and in the first game of the series Phillips matched up its star center Bob Kurland (a giant of the time at seven feet tall) against the much quicker Barksdale. That night Kurland was honored as the outstanding athlete in Oklahoma, but Barksdale outscored him 17–5 in a 45–41 upset victory for the Bittners.

"Don completely outplayed Kurland from start to finish, and then the civil war started," Laddie Gale, the Bittners' coach, told the *Oakland Tribune*.

"The next night, Kurland was taken off of Barksdale and R. C. [Butcher] Pitts was assigned to cover him. And believe me, that's all that Pitts did. Don stayed in there and took it, along with the rest of our squad.

"By the time the series ended in Oklahoma City Saturday night I felt like a man driving sheep to the slaughter. I don't want to infer that the officiating beat us, but I do want to infer that the officiating worked only one way so far as the rough stuff was concerned.

"In one game, if I recall correctly, Phillips got thirty free throws to our sixteen, and they were fouling our boys all over the court. Barksdale took the brunt of it, and not once did he let a peep out of him or complain.

"Each night the crowd gave him a tremendous hand. But I'm not kidding myself. I know what the crowd would have done had Don raised a finger in retaliation."[1]

It wasn't long before Barksdale got a bitter taste of Southern "hospitality" when he defied a death threat he received in Kentucky while playing for the 1948 U.S. Olympic team. As the time approached for the 1948 U.S. Olympic Trials, Barksdale had a difficult decision to make. As the 1944 winner of the National AAU hop, skip, and jump competition (now known as the triple jump), Barksdale had a good chance of qualifying for the U.S. team on the track and field squad. Yet he also had been invited to the basketball team's tryouts, where competition was expected to be much stiffer. The choice was up to him, and consistent with Barksdale's business instincts, he chose the path that presented the opportunity for more financial and long-term gain: he chose basketball.

"Why are you trying to make the Olympic basketball team when you hold the record in the hop, skip, and jump?" asked Jack Robinson, a basketball star from Baylor. "He looked at me and said, 'You can't be a pro in hop, skip, and jump. Watch it. When I make the team the rest of my life it will be 'ex-Olympic cager.' He was smart as could be, and I used to read the papers and it always said, 'Don Barksdale, ex-Olympic cager.' He was right."

Barksdale eventually made the Olympic team that won the gold medal in London, but he felt as isolated as the black spot in the middle of a target: the first black basketball player on a U.S. Olympic team; the only Northerner on a practice squad based in Bartlesville, Oklahoma; the lone black player to appear in three pre-Olympic exhibition games in the South; and the survivor of a death threat in Lexington, Kentucky.

The Olympic tryouts were held in a tournament in New York's Madison Square Garden on March 27–31, 1948. The tournament included three AAU teams and one YMCA team in the independent bracket, and four college teams in another bracket. The winners of the brackets (the AAU's Phillips 66 team and the University of Kentucky) each received five slots on the fourteen-man Olympic team, while four at-large players completed the squad.

Barksdale, who had been playing with the AAU's Oakland Bittners, was given an at-large berth from the independent bracket, but not without heavy lobbying by Fred Maggiora, a member of the Olympic Basketball Committee and a politician in Oakland, which was adjacent to Barksdale's hometown. About eight years later Maggiora told Barksdale that some committee members' responses to the idea of having a black Olympian was "Hell no, that will never happen." But Maggiora wouldn't let the committee bypass Barksdale.

"This guy fought, fought, and fought," Barksdale said, "and I think finally the coach of Phillips 66 [Omar Browning] had said, 'That son of a bitch is the best basketball player in the country outside of Bob Kurland, so I don't know how we can turn him down.' So they picked me, but Maggiora said he went through holy hell for it—closed-door meetings and begging."

The other at-large players chosen were Vince Boryla, Ray

Lumpp, and Robinson. Barksdale played forward, and Robinson said his lanky physique resembled future NBA star Julius Erving. Players didn't dunk in games back then, but "Barksdale could do everything at the rim and above it that they can do now," Robinson said.

The Olympic team was split into two training units: head coach Browning's Phillips 66 players were in Bartlesville; associate coach Adolph Rupp worked his Kentucky players in Lexington. Each unit added two at-large players and three alternates. Then the squads played three exhibition games against each other to raise funds to be able to attend the Olympic games.

Barksdale joined the Phillips 66 squad well-prepared for his four-week indoctrination into the Olympic team: prepared not by the many years he had spent developing his basketball skills, but by his three-year stint in the army at Camp Lee in Virginia. The racism he had encountered there provided the coping skills he needed to survive his Olympic experience.

Bartlesville, Oklahoma, was a small but rich town, headquarters for the Phillips Petroleum Company yet today. Typical of the situation in the South, Barksdale lived away from his teammates, staying with a black family in town, and didn't participate in team meals. At first his teammates created more problems for him than solace. "There was hostility," Barksdale said. "I heard a couple of things like, 'Separate the men from the boys,' and, just out of earshot, 'Don't worry, if he comes by me I'll get him.'"

Barksdale responded in practice with actions, not words. That's the form of revenge he had learned at Camp Lee. "You never let it beat you," Barksdale said. "You just gave as much as you could without opening your mouth. Never say anything."

Barksdale fought back with a trusty weapon, his sharp elbows. As he reminisced about Bartlesville in 1991, he patted his right elbow with his left hand, just like a policeman might pat his most dependable pistol. If done the right way, Barksdale said with a don't-mess-with-me tone in his voice, a quick jab in the chest could break an antagonist's ribs. "You give back what you take, but you don't make noise about it," he said. "If a guy hit you or elbowed you, next time you go by, elbow him right back. Don't say a word and if he says something to you, just say, 'Oh, I'm sorry,' and go about your business. If you open your mouth, you start a confrontation. All of them are against you; not just one." But while

Barksdale struck back in silence, "Under my breath I was saying, 'Mess around like that and I'll hit you. I'll kill you.'"

Forty-eight years later Robinson and another teammate, R. C. Pitts, were surprised to hear that Barksdale had detected some resistance from his teammates. To them elbows, bumps, and bruises were just part of the game, and Barksdale had been easily accepted by his teammates. But Pitts, a native of Oxford, Mississippi, understood why Barksdale would have been on guard. "I can understand how that thought [could have crossed] Don's mind, and I think it would have crossed mine, too, but he handled it so smoothly that we never had that impression," Pitts said. "It had to bother him, but he never showed it."

By the time the Olympics ended Barksdale certainly felt comfortable with his teammates, and vice versa. "At Phillips, all the guys had to go to work at 8 o'clock," Robinson said. "When they would get off work we would practice at 5 P.M., so Don and I had all that time on our hands and so there was no way we weren't going to get acquainted. In Bartlesville we wanted to go to [movies] and the sign said 'Blacks in Balcony.' I couldn't change the show or the town, so I just went to the balcony with Barksdale."

When the Phillips and Kentucky squads played three exhibition games in the South to raise funds for the Olympics, Barksdale's teammates backed him up several times. Sometimes the incidents he encountered took on a humorous twist. On June 30 the squads played their first exhibition game in Tulsa, Oklahoma, where Barksdale was allowed to stay with the team in the town's ritziest hotel, the Mayo. "The owner said it was all right for him to stay as long as he was with one of the players so people would know he's not just wandering around the hotel," said George Durham, the team's public relations director.

One day Barksdale's roommate, Shorty Carpenter, was going with Barksdale to get a haircut. Durham happened to be talking to coach Browning and hotel owner Burch Mayo when an offended white woman addressed Mayo. "I'll have you know there was a black man in the hotel," Durham recalled her saying. "Burch Mayo said, 'Oh no, that's a Pakistani.' And she said, 'Oh, that's fine.'"

Two days later the teams had a rematch in Kansas City, Mo., and on July 9 the exhibition finale was played on the University of Kentucky's home turf in Lexington. Before the teams arrived Robinson was involved in a troubling conversation about Barksdale with Louis Wilke (chairman of the U.S. Olympic Basketball

Committee), coach Browning, and several players. "They said, 'We've got problems. What are we going to do? Rupp said we can't bring that so-and-so into the state,'" Robinson said. "Someone said, 'If he doesn't go, we don't play.' Everybody blinked. I said, 'Just give the tickets back.' I figured at thirty-two [actually four-teen] thousand tickets, Rupp wasn't going to give that up."

A compromise was reached. Barksdale could play the game but couldn't stay with his teammates in a Lexington hotel. Instead he would be housed with a prominent black family and provided a Cadillac with a driver. The accommodations were fine, but Robin-son said, "Of course, he was hurt. He said, 'You've just got a room, don't you? Well, I've got a mansion.'"

In Lexington Barksdale encountered racism at its worst—and may have been fortunate to live to tell about it. The easiest way to describe Lexington of the 1940s would be to draw a line down the middle of a piece of canvas, then paint one half completely black and one half completely white. There wasn't the vicious racism one found in some other Southern cities—no lynchings or Ku Klux Klan activity—but it was rigidly segregated. "Lexington used to be a terrible town for blacks," said lifelong resident John Will Brown.

White-owned hotels were off limits to blacks, so black visitors stayed with private families or in black-owned boarding houses. Black people were banned from white-owned restaurants, but they could enjoy a delicious meal at several black restaurants in town such as the Hurricane or the Derby. The bus station and train station on Main Street were both segregated, with black and white waiting rooms, bathrooms, and water fountains. The races also were separated on the trains, even if just by a piece of string or a length of cord. There were no integrated concerts—whites had theirs, and blacks brought in their own stars. Duke Ellington, Cab Calloway, Redd Foxx, and Moms Mabley performed in dance halls or at the Lyric Theater at Third and DeWeese Streets.

DeWeese Street, with its taverns, restaurants, and clubs, was the black social center of Lexington. If a black person wanted to see a movie there were two choices: the white-owned Ben Ali, the Strand, the State, or the Opera House theaters, which let black people sit in the balcony; or the Lyric, the only theater in town where blacks could sit anywhere they chose. Lexington's public schools were rigidly segregated, based on the Day Law passed in 1903 that prohibited integrated schools. "Everybody understood where they were supposed to go," said former high school coach S. T. Roach. "I don't think there was that much tension."

Lexington also had its racial quirks. For instance, black people were allowed to vote, a freedom many black Southerners didn't have for another twenty years. Although trains and buses throughout the state had segregated seating, public transportation within the city had mixed seating. Surprisingly, Lexington had two black policemen. Of course, they couldn't arrest white people.

Black attendance at sporting events reflected the common racial customs of the time. Some events allowed blacks, but only if they watched from their own section of the arena. Although whites revered coach Rupp, blacks detested him. "It was known that Rupp didn't want black players," Roach said. He recalled that when Texas Western, with its five black starters, whipped Kentucky in the 1966 NCAA Finals, "blacks all around the Commonwealth rose up and cheered because Rupp had gotten beat."

This was the racial environment Barksdale entered when Browning's and Rupp's squads played in Lexington. Barksdale stayed at the home of a black physician, Dr. J. R. Dalton, and the night before the game the black community gave him a star's welcome. "They had a big softball game and they introduced me . . . it was like I was a national hero," he said. "They had advertised I was going to be there and they had a band there playing."

After the game John Will Brown drove Barksdale to American Legion Post 132 on Georgetown Street, a social gathering place where war veterans could have a few drinks and reminisce. Was it a black legion post? "Back then, it better be all black," Brown said with a laugh. Brown remembered being very impressed by Barksdale's understanding of Lexington's racial climate. "He was very suave," Brown said. "He knew what the situation was. He knew what the mental handicaps were, and the guy adjusted."

That same evening Barksdale received a phone call at the home of his hosts. The voice on the other end delivered a cryptic message: "If you play in that game tomorrow night, you're going to get shot." Except for the family he was staying with, Barksdale didn't tell anyone about the call because he didn't know how serious it was. "It could have been any idiot calling," he said. Yet, he considered not playing in the game, being held on a portable court set down on an outdoor athletic field called Stoll Field. "But I said, how is this son of a bitch going to shoot me on the damn outdoor basketball court, and I knew then that we were going to leave [Lexington] right after the game." Nonetheless, "Yeah, I was nervous. I was scared."

Long before media hype became in vogue, that night's Olympic exhibition game was hyped to the max. The *Lexington Leader* called it the "basketball battle of the century." About two thousand fans showed up just to watch the Phillips 66 team practice. The game was to be broadcast over four different Lexington radio stations and a crowd of approximately fourteen thousand was expected. "This will be the largest crowd ever to see a basketball game in Kentucky, the largest ever to see one in the South, and also the largest ever to see an outdoor, night cage attraction anywhere in the nation or the world."[2]

When he arrived at the game site Barksdale looked around for the black people he had met the previous evening. At first he didn't see any. Then he saw his black cheering section, all herded together in the end zone.

It was a close game, and in the first half a timeout was called. Thus began a few minutes of terror that Barksdale called "the bottle incident." He was on the court with teammates Jesse "Cab" Renich, Gordon "Shorty" Carpenter, R. C. Pitts, and a fourth player Barksdale couldn't remember. All of them understood the racial code that said that black and white people never drank from the same glass in the South, but when the timeout was called, the trainer ran out to the players with a quart bottle of water for them to share and a bucket to spit in. Barksdale remembers every detail of what happened next.

While recalling the incident, Barksdale pantomimed one of the players picking up the water bottle, pouring in a mouthful, swishing it around, and spitting into the bucket. Then the bottle was handed to Renich, who also took a swig of water. He spit into the bucket. Then he passed the bottle to Barksdale, the moment he had been dreading. "I didn't have time to think," Barksdale said. "As it was passing around, I said, 'What do I do when it gets to me?' I started to turn around and walk away, and then I said that just doesn't make sense. When it got to me, a hush fell over that stadium that was the scariest thing I've ever been through."

Just a few minutes before that fourteen thousand people had been screaming and yelling like a normal crowd at a sports event. Suddenly the stadium had become as still as a cemetery. "It was quiet, man," said Barksdale, lowering his voice to a whisper. Barksdale heard a low-pitched rumble coming from the stands, caused by the indiscernible mix of white fans talking to each other and black fans talking to each other. "You could see them leaning over to each other talking quietly, but you heard a 'Hmmmmmmmmm,'" Barksdale recalled. "And I said, 'Oh, shit, what am I going to do with that bottle?'

"I took the bottle, and I never will forget, Shorty Carpenter was next to me." Then Barksdale made a split-second decision: he would not be intimidated. "I took a drink, spit in the thing and handed it to Shorty and prayed. And Shorty took it and stood there for a second—not a second—and took the bottle, [drank and] spit, and it broke the silence. And all of a sudden, people got back to normal. But for one-half of a minute there, it was like kicking a field goal with one second to go with everybody praying."

If Carpenter, a native of Ash Flat, Arkansas—"which is about as redneck as you can get," Durham said—hadn't taken that drink, if he had tossed that bottle away, Barksdale feels it could have been "personally devastating." But Carpenter didn't give in, and when he took that drink, the black section of the stands let out an audible sigh of relief. "Then we went back and played the rest of the game," Barksdale said, "and all the black people afterward said, 'How did you have nerve enough to do that, man?' They couldn't believe that I did it because, right there, they had water fountains for colored and white."

Barksdale also knew he had taken a big risk. He leaned forward toward this interviewer and spoke with an ominous tone. "If a black man went to a white fountain, they put his ass in jail," he said. "Segregation was segregation all down the line. If you went out with a white woman, they'd kill you. There's many a black kid dead for doing nothing because some ass just said, 'I'll kill a nigger,' and they didn't go to jail for it. No, I wasn't scared about getting arrested. I was scared I was going to be killed. I was scared to death."

Despite that frightening incident Barksdale played his best game on the exhibition tour. He scored 12 of his 13 points as Phillips overcame a five-point halftime deficit to win 56–50, thus humiliating Rupp in front of Kentucky Gov. Happy Chandler. "Donald was grabbing rebounds like mad and starting the fast-break," Durham said.

Robinson, a point guard, said the team never discussed it, but because of the discriminatory treatment Barksdale had received in Lexington, players "just kind of fed him" the ball. "The coach never said a word," Robinson said. "Nobody said a word and he was just great. So when the spotlight was on us [after the game] they gave us a present and they gave him a great applause. In the dressing room he said, 'I want to thank you for what you did tonight, Jack.' I said, 'I didn't do anything.' He just said, 'You know what you did,' and turned around and just walked off."

Barksdale and his teammates didn't talk about the "bottle incident" immediately after it occurred, but he said sometime during their Olympic journey, R. C. Pitts, a Mississippian, told him, "Don, that was dangerous what you did, but I'm proud of you."

Barksdale was just as proud of Carpenter, who by drinking from that bottle had risked being alienated from his white Southern friends. "He was a big, rough farm guy," Barksdale said. "I don't even know how it came up, but somewhere along the line I ended up telling Shorty, 'Thanks for not throwing that bottle away.' And he said, 'Never a doubt, Barks,' and laughed."

As Barksdale described the Lexington game and all the events involved in it, the emotion in his voice and his reenactment of what had happened transported the listener almost a half-century back in time. Those events didn't haunt Barksdale every day, but they weren't just another memory, either. "It's a funny thing, those kinds of things don't last long," he said. "You're scared, but the game chases it out of your head and then you don't think about it again until later on. It gets way back, somewhere back in your mind, but you don't think about it any more. Later on, you say, 'Wait a minute.' When it comes back to you, then you get scared all over again."

Barksdale's Long Haul
to the All-Star Game

After Don Barksdale returned from the 1948 Olympics he received a letter from Ben Kerner, owner of the NBA's Tri-Cities Blackhawks, saying that Barksdale was a great player and apologizing "for the league's unwritten law of no blacks," as Barksdale recalled it. He returned to AAU ball and at the same time operated a beer distributorship selling Blue and Gold beer. (His marketing man was Ernie Nevers, the legendary football star from Stanford.) That combination of athlete-businessman eventually gave Barksdale the leverage needed to squeeze a lucrative contract out of the Baltimore Bullets.

Barksdale said that in 1949 or 1950 he turned down an offer from the New York Knicks because their financial terms were too low. In 1951, a year after the NBA's color barrier had been broken, Baltimore signed Davage "Dave" Minor, Barksdale's close friend and teammate at UCLA and on the Oakland Bittners' squad. Next, the Bullets pursued Barksdale.

"When they contacted Don and myself, I decided to leave amateur basketball," Minor said. "Don decided he did not want to turn pro." After joining the Bullets Minor wrote to Barksdale that he was being treated fairly and that Baltimore wanted to keep them together. "I was shocked when Don turned pro," Minor recalled.

"They started calling my mother and father, and sent letters to me asking would I be interested in playing," Barksdale said. "By then, I had built up my beer business where we were selling ten thousand cases a month, so I was making a little money. So I wasn't as easy to deal with as I would have been in 1948. I'd have jumped at $5,000 [then]. Now it was a matter of economics. When they made an offer, I turned the first one down. They came back with a better offer, a combination radio-basketball job, and it totaled up to $20,850."

In addition to playing ball, the proposal was for Barksdale to host a postgame television show and be a disc jockey for KPIM radio every night for an hour. Barksdale believed that at the time George Mikan was the highest paid NBA player (at about $25,000) and estimated that the Bullets' offer placed him among the league's top ten salaries. He took the deal, which Bullets officials said made him the highest paid athlete in Baltimore sports history. (The *Baltimore Sun* regularly referred to Barksdale's contract as a two-year deal at $17,000 per year. That's $3,850 less per year than Barksdale named, a discrepancy that may have arisen if he was including income from his broadcasting work.)

Barksdale had finally made the NBA as a twenty-eight-year-old rookie, but from his first day as a Bullet the pressures on him were enormous. After signing, Barksdale and a friend, Ishmael Evans, began a cross-country drive from the West Coast to Baltimore. Transmission trouble caused Barksdale's car to break down in Cleveland, so he rode a train the rest of the way, finally arriving in Baltimore on October 16, 1951.

The trip had taken a week (normal for a coast-to-coast trip) but the *Baltimore Sun* reported that Bullets officials believed Barksdale had left the West Coast four days before he actually had. When he was "several days late" in arriving, they became concerned enough to ask the state police to watch for him. Did the police ever bother him? "No they didn't," Barksdale told the *Sun* the day he arrived. "The first time I heard they were after me was when I got here. Shucks, there was nothing to worry about. My mother knew where I was."[1]

Barksdale hadn't been able to reach the Bullets, but two days before he arrived his mother informed team officials of Barksdale's actual departure date, which relieved their anxiety. Nonetheless, when he arrived he had missed some training camp and his new teammates were getting ready to leave for Bangor, Maine, where they were to play the second contest (an exhibition against Boston) in a five-game road trip. When Barksdale arrived in Baltimore he was taken to a gymnasium where he ran for about two hours, then took the team flight to Maine.

"We played against Boston that night, and I must have played three-fourths or almost the whole game," Barksdale said. "I did extremely well, but that night at about 3 o'clock in the morning, my ankles were big from driving across the country, working out, and then playing a full game. The next night they were going to play again and they insisted I play. So my start-off was playing on ankles that were swollen up [to] twice the [normal] size. Through the whole exhibition season I never had a chance to rest them. The season opened and they had taped me so tight I couldn't even feel my feet. That's how I opened in Baltimore."

Barksdale believed the Bullets insisted that he play hurt "because they had advertised they signed this black cat. It's Baltimore, which is considered the South. So the South finally signed a black man and he's going to play whether he could walk or crawl." It's also important to remember that this occurred long before teams had trainers and long before sports medicine had become a medical specialty. By today's standards the medical care athletes received then would be considered quite crude.

It was an ominous beginning of an extremely stressful season for Barksdale, who averaged a disappointing 12.6 points and 9.7 rebounds per game. His ankles never completely healed, so he played the entire season in pain. "In fact, my ankles never did get completely together again in my life," he said. "I have troubles right now" (1985, when Barksdale was sixty-two years old).

The team was terrible, finishing with a 20-46 record, the second-worst in the NBA. It lacked a legitimate center, which meant that Barksdale had to play the position even though, at a lanky six-foot-six and 195 pounds, on the professional level meant he was strictly suited for the forward position. Worst of all, Baltimore's management was extremely impatient with its new star despite his ankle problems, playing him out of position, his poor supporting cast, and the fact that he was making the transition from amateur to professional ball. Fred Scolari, the team's player-coach, acknowledged that all those factors, plus Barksdale's superstar status, led to unreasonable expectations. Unfortunately, he didn't turn out to be the franchise's "Moses," as the *Baltimore Sun* sometimes referred to him. "His game was to run and shoot, so consequently we didn't win," Scolari said. "A lot of blame was placed on him; a lot of blame was placed on me. As far as I'm concerned, Don did his best. I really believe that on the right team at the right time, Don Barksdale would have been a great, great player in pro ball."

Because of his injuries Barksdale got off to a very slow start, averaging only 6 points in his first four games. Then on December 22, just twenty-three games into the season, Bullets management turned nasty when it placed Barksdale on the inactive list for undisclosed reasons. They quickly changed his status to an indefinite suspension, possible at the time because no players union existed to protest the move and no agent could have negotiated on his behalf. "After a brilliant amateur career, Barksdale has been somewhat of a pro disappointment," the *Associated Press* reported. "Early in the season he complained of sore feet and played very little. In all, he has averaged only ten points a game."[2]

Several days later the Associated Press reported that, "It was rumored that he broke training rules."[3] At least that's what Bullets management wanted the public to believe. Instead, Barksdale said management merely invented a way to implement vindictive cost-cutting measures at his expense. "They kept talking about how much money they were losing, so they were looking for a way to mess with me because I was making more money than the other guys, and there was a slight bit of jealousy among two other players I was playing with," Barksdale said.

Management set him up after Baltimore played Philadelphia on Tuesday, December 18, in New York City. "Buddy Young [an early black pro football player who at the time was playing for the New York Yankees NFL team] and I went out after the game and I got back about 2 A.M.," Barksdale said. A team official was waiting in the hotel lobby and accused him of breaking curfew. "We didn't even play the next day," Barksdale continued. "He went back to Baltimore and said I broke up the curfew, which didn't exist. He was looking for a way to bust my contract. I went to their office and said 'I can see you're not making money. You don't have to go through all this crap if you want to cut my salary.' They fined me $5,000 for being late that night [which was a hefty 24 percent of his season salary, according to Barksdale's figure]. I said, 'Okay, you got it, but I'll never play for you again.'" In saying that Barksdale meant that he would play out his contract but wouldn't re-sign with Baltimore.

"The Bullets today suddenly lifted the suspension of Don Barksdale and announced the Negro star will be seen in action tonight when the club plays Philadelphia in the windup of a National Basketball Association double-header at the Coliseum," the *Baltimore Sun* reported on December 26." The announcement was made after a two-hour meeting involving Bullets officials, Barksdale, and the club's attorney, Robert Goldman.

> *All sides, however, maintained tacit silence regarding the exact nature of Barksdale's offense in New York eight days ago that led to his suspension. Financial disciplinary action also was levied against the West Coast Negro, but whether this was in the form of*

> *a contractual readjustment or a simple fine club spokesmen refused to say. Nor would they reveal the amount of the penalty.*
>
> *Rumor had it that the club would attempt to force Don to accept a new contract at a lower figure than the reported $17,000 per annum for two years he signed for or, failing that, to take a big bite out of his stipend in the way of a fine.*
>
> *Business Manager Bob Elmer said the club was delighted that the matter had been straightened out and said he felt sure Don could help considerably in the drive for a playoff berth.*[4]

By then the Bullets were 9-16 and the season quickly became a lost cause. In other ways, however, it was a good experience for Barksdale. People in Baltimore "were just unbelievably nice," he said. "In other parts of the league I ran into very little trouble. In fact, almost none. Once in a while you'd run into a ballplayer that would come up with, 'Now we're going to separate the men from the boys,' or if you were going down the sideline, you might get knocked up in the stands once or twice. Your answer to that was the next time you come down you try to run over the top of him. You couldn't let anybody intimidate you."

Barksdale found it "comical" that even though no more than eight black players were in the league at the time, it seemed like they always ended up guarding each other in a game. "Every time we played against Boston, Chuck Cooper watched me and I had to watch him," Barksdale said. "Play Syracuse, I watch Earl Lloyd and he watched me. I never figured that one out, and we used to laugh about it because we'd get together afterward and talk about it."

Barksdale formed several strong friendships with white players. He, like so many other black players in those pioneering days, considered Boston star Bob Cousy a close friend. "Cousy and I were real tight," Barksdale said. "Cousy's just a real down-to-earth cat."

Barksdale also became buddies with Mel Hutchins, another white player who regularly befriended black players. But on the court they were rivals. "Barksdale was tough. A good shooter," Hutchins said. Hutchins, who played in four All-Star games, was an outstanding defensive player and used both that and his strength to his advantage. "Barksdale was a little frail and you could bounce Barksdale a little bit," Hutchins said. "He didn't like anyone hitting him. Barksdale was a shooter and knew that's what he was in there for. You would hit him and he would say, 'What did you do that for?' Well, that's part of the game." After they retired they joked about it. Hutchins said he asked Barksdale, "Why didn't you hit me?" and Barksdale replied, "Because I felt you would hit me back."

Off the court they were fond of each other. "We exchanged suits a few times because we were the same size [six-six, 200 pounds]," Hutchins said. "He got his tailor-made; mine was off the rack. Everything [for Barksdale] had to be perfect."

Barksdale's second season was a huge improvement over his rookie year. He reported to training camp on time and in excellent shape, then played near the level that had made him such an extraordinary player on the West Coast. Barksdale averaged 13.8 points (ranking fourteenth in the NBA in points per game) and 9.2 rebounds, shot 39 percent from the field (compared to the previous season's 34 percent), and was chosen to play in the 1953 All-Star Game in Fort Wayne, only the third ever held. "I was extremely happy I was chosen because the coaches chose you," Barksdale said during the 1993 All-Star Weekend, a month before he died. "All we [the NBA's black players] would say when we got together was 'I'm glad one of us made that sucker.' If any one of us got on there [the team] they were lucky, because it was tough. Sweetwater should have been scoring twice what he [usually] scored, if he could have had the ball enough. I should have been scoring 8 or 9 more points a game."

Barksdale played eleven minutes for the East in the All-Star Game, which was eventually won by the West squad, 79–75. He missed his only shot, made one of 3 free throws, took down 3 rebounds, and had 2 assists. Nothing special in the box score, but nonetheless memorable for the first black NBA All-Star. "Only I didn't touch the ball much, and you can't score if you don't have the ball," Barksdale said. "That happens. I didn't play long. At least I got in the game. No big thing. And this is no bitterness. I was lucky to be chosen to play."

Despite their horrible 16-54 record, the Bullets still had a superior record to Philadelphia's and stumbled into the last Eastern Division playoff berth. They were swept by New York 2-0 in the best-of-three division semifinals. Since signing another contract with Baltimore was out of the question, on August 27, 1953, Barksdale was traded to the Celtics for an undisclosed amount of cash in addition to six-foot-four Fran Mahoney (who had played six games with Boston the previous season) and three rookies, Vernon Stokes, Herman Hedderick, and Jim Doherty. Only Mahoney and

Hedderick ever played again in the NBA, and for a total of only seven games.

In Boston Barksdale played a diminished role, partly because of recurring ankle problems and the cortisone shots he needed to be able to play. He averaged 7.3 points in the 1953–54 season and 10.5 the next season, after which he retired at age thirty-two. But he could not have chosen a more enjoyable way to end his playing career. "I got to Boston, and I consider that probably the best years of my basketball life because of my teammates, Red Auerbach and Walter Brown," Barksdale said. "Walter Brown had to be one of the great people in sports. He was the first owner I ran into that you could sit down and have a conversation with. During the end of a game, he'd be sitting over by the bench and he'd sit and chat and invite you to his office any time you want to come."

During Barksdale's two-year stay the Celtics were 42-30 and 36-36, reaching the Eastern Division playoff finals before losing to Syracuse both years. The Celtics were the highest-scoring team in the league at the time but had no dominant center. They were soft on defense and couldn't compete with the league's heavyweights—which all changed when Bill Russell joined them in 1956. Barksdale is proud to say he played a role in the dynasty that resulted.

Russell was starring for the University of San Francisco in 1956 when Barksdale, who had returned to the Bay Area, influenced him to reject an offer from the Harlem Globetrotters and sign with Boston instead. "I asked Bill and his father to name me somebody on the Harlem Globetrotters outside of the center [Meadowlark Lemon] and the guy who has the ball," Barksdale said. "They couldn't do it. I was telling them that in the NBA, at least the box scores would get out. People know you all across the country and you're in town more than once. But the Trotters are in town once a year and you're gone."

Barksdale also raved about Russell to Auerbach and Brown. "Bill was getting married, and Walter Brown flew out here," Barksdale said. "I picked him up at the airport and he and I went to Bill's wedding and Bill met Walter. From that point on, I think Bill ended up going to Boston."

Teammates' Jealousy Kills Cleo Hill's Career

Overall the integration of the NBA went relatively smoothly in the 1950s and early 1960s. Black players encountered some blatantly racist acts that even ignited a few fights, and frustrations about their roles on teams and hassles about accommodations in the South continued. But the situation in the NBA didn't come close to the racial slurs, high spikes, beanballs, and threatened boycotts that Jackie Robinson endured; and no NBA players had to face the physical intimidation (and sometimes pain) that white National Football League players inflicted on black opponents in the late 1940s and early 1950s. Football's violent nature made black players an easy target for whites who despised them. Whatever the reasons, the NBA had been a more than tolerable experience for its black players.

Yet not enough worthy black players got the opportunity to play in the NBA, and today many are convinced that racial discrimination—often a very subtle form of it—suppressed their numbers.

The total number of black players increased steadily, so that in the 1954–55 season the nine black players on rosters comprised 9 percent of the league and just five years later those figures had increased to twenty-four and 24 percent. Yet nearby there was a stark contrast that begs for an explanation. In the heart of the New York–to–Philadelphia corridor lay the minor-league Eastern Basketball League (EBL), overflowing with black players with big-time credentials. These weren't former small-college players or even black-college players who had received little publicity before. Rather, many had been standouts in the college scene at Big Ten or Big Five schools, or in New York City when the Big Apple still was a mecca of collegiate excellence.

The EBL was a haven for a dozen or so players—both black and white—implicated in gambling scandals of the early 1950s and subsequently banned from the NBA. Among the white players were high-scoring center Bill Spivey from Kentucky, and Jack Molinas, one of the NBA's top rookies in 1953 until he was booted out of the league for betting on its games. Among the banned black players were Ed Warner and Floyd Layne from City College of New York and, most prominent of them all, Sherman White from Long Island University. (Their attorney, LeRoy Watkins, stated that they would not agree to be interviewed for this book, and Warner refused directly.)

The fact that Sherman White, a six-foot-nine, multitalented forward had denied himself a chance to play in the NBA is considered one of the tragedies in basketball history. What made White special to a junior high schooler named Al Attles in Newark, New Jersey, was that White was a two-time All-American who "had played in the big time. I remember my mother had bought me a maroon radio, an Emerson. It had a crescent-shaped antenna that you pulled out of the back. I used to sit it on my table next to my bed and I would listen to the LIU Blackbirds." Years later as an NBA player, Attles played with White in the famed Rucker tournament held in New York during the summer. "He was just such a competitor," Attles said. "A very no-nonsense guy when he played."

In 1996 the NBA selected its top fifty players of all time. If White had played in the league, "He's in the top fifty," said Ray Scott, who played several seasons in the Eastern League before he began an eleven-year professional career with Detroit in 1961. "Any team you put Julius Erving on and Connie Hawkins, White has to go on. Sherman was very well grounded in fundamentals and had a great understanding of the game, but his will to win was like Bill Russell's. He didn't like mistakes: taking a bad shot, not covering your man. He did not abide that at all. . . . . He would stare at you and give you the look."

Even excluding the banned black players, a large disparity existed between the percentage of blacks on NBA rosters and the percentage playing in the Eastern League, which occasionally acted as a feeder system to the NBA. The Eastern League eventually expanded into the current Continental Basketball League.

The Allentown (Pennsylvania) Jets operated in the Eastern League from 1958 until 1980. John Kimock, one of the part-owners of the team, estimates that about 70 percent of its players were black. For instance, six of the nine players on Allentown's championship team in the 1962–63 season were black, including former

NBA players Andy Johnson and Boo Ellis, and Hank Whitney, Roman Turman, Gene Hudgins, and Walt Simon, who played six solid seasons in the ABA. That same season, 39 percent of NBA players were black. "There was no discrimination as far as [Eastern League] club owners were concerned," Kimock said. "Everybody wanted to win a championship. I think if you went with a solid white team, it would have finished last."

How could the disparity in numbers be explained? Black players of that era would offer a one-word answer: quota. As far as they were concerned, though unspoken and unwritten it was nevertheless impossible to overlook. In the 1950s and early 1960s their numbers were limited by an implied quota system throughout the NBA, although no team owner or league official would be foolish enough to publicly admit it at the time. They believed that some teams were reluctant to add "a little pepper," as Guy Rodgers, one of the NBA's best guards, called it. Oh, maybe a dash of it here and there, but not a generous sprinkling. "You had a lot of players who were Caucasian who were mighty good, and they certainly deserved to stay," Rodgers said. "But there were black players who, if they hadn't had that quota, they should have stayed also."

"There was a quota—[of] sometimes two or three, and the highest was four," said Ray Scott said, who played in the NBA from 1961 to 1970. "You had hard-core owners who were trying to market to the public. It was where they saw their public, and they didn't look at the black community. But the players were so good in college and getting better and better, and they were missing out on a gold mine."

The quota concept seems plausible considering the fact that the league began with a secret ban on black players to placate Harlem Globetrotters owner Abe Saperstein (who wanted "first dibs" on any talented black player that came along). Since Saperstein let his team participate in doubleheaders that featured the Trotters game as the main gate attraction and an NBA game as the secondary event, NBA owners were glad to accommodate Saperstein until New York Knicks owner Ned Irish forced the league to integrate in 1950.

Irish's bold stance opened the rosters to four black players in 1950, but it's difficult to believe that at the time any institution would have instantly switched from a "no blacks allowed" stance to "everybody's welcome." Those types of transitions take time, and race relations throughout America were still crude and cruel.

As the NBA edged slowly toward unqualified integration, many deserving players were cut from rosters, were not drafted, or were not invited for tryouts because owners feared having too much color on a team would offend their predominantly white audience.

During the 1962–63 season a conversation between Syracuse forward Joe Roberts and team owner Dan Biasone verified what Roberts had sensed all along: for business reasons owners kept a lid on the amount of "pepper" on their rosters. Despite being only six-six, the previous season Roberts had been one of the most productive rebounders in the league, averaging an impressive 8 rebounds in just twenty-one minutes playing time per game. He logically expected to get even more playing time in 1962–63, but Syracuse drafted Bradley All-American forward Chet Walker and Roberts's court time suddenly shrank to almost nothing. Walker eventually became one of the best scoring forwards in history, so there's no denying his talent, but he and Roberts had different strengths and Roberts believes there was no reason both could not have played, if it hadn't been for the quota system. "It was just a matter of too many brothers on the team," Roberts said. "Chet Walker came up and four was too many."

One evening before a game at Madison Square Garden, Roberts voiced his frustration about lack of playing time directly to Biasone and got a stunningly frank response. "I said I want to play," Roberts said. "He said, 'Look at the audience, Joe. What do you see?' I said 'people.' He said, 'White people. Until I see seats white, black, white, black, this [meaning mostly white players] is what you'll see on the team.'" Despite the situation, Roberts genuinely liked Biasone. "He was a good man, but that was the way it was," Roberts said. "He wasn't prejudiced." He was just a white businessman trying to make money in a prejudiced society, and he lacked the fortitude to take a stand against certain norms.

Alex Hannum, who was Roberts's head coach at Syracuse, was surprised to hear about Roberts's conversation with Biasone. Hannum had played in the NBA from 1949 to 1957, and his coaching career in the NBA spanned the years of 1957 to 1971. Hannum said Biasone never talked to him about the number of black players Hannum could have on the team. "No," Hannum said. "It was never an issue in my mind or in my conversations with any team I played with or coached."

At Syracuse Hannum and Biasone jointly decided which players made the team, and, in terms of the racial makeup of the team,

"He didn't care," Hannum said. "I can't remember any instance of Danny influencing it one way or the other. We were just interested in who could win games for us." Or course, it's possible that Biasone was conscious of the racial mix on the roster without ever voicing that concern to Hannum.

The existence of a quota was confirmed by Fuzzy Levane, who coached the Milwaukee Hawks from 1952 to 1954, the New York Knicks from 1958 to 1960, and St. Louis for sixty games in the 1961–62 season. When interviewed in 2000 he was eighty and still scouting for the Knicks. Levane is one of the few people alive still employed in the NBA who was around in 1949 when the NBL and the BAA merged to form the current league. Back then, Levane was playing for Rochester.

Although Levane said that he personally didn't base roster cuts on a quota, an understood limit on the number of black players teams kept existed because owners were afraid of offending white fans. "Three was unwritten with every team, unless the guy was so good," Levane said. "Like with Boston—Bill Russell and the Joneses. These guys [who were cut] were fringe players." Why would management be concerned about having more than three? "Fans," said Levane, who explained that at the time very few black people attended games. "Boston sort of broke it when they came up with Russell and Sam Jones. They won world championships, so other teams, they brought them [black players] in, too, because they wanted to win games and found out that was more important than having a quota."

During the first fifteen years of NBA integration, how restrictive was the quota? The feeling was that the magic number varied from owner to owner, from franchise to franchise. From 1950 to 1955 only two teams—the 1952–53 Baltimore Bullets and 1954–55 Syracuse Nationals—had more than one black player on their rosters, and both of those topped out at two. The 1955–56 season saw a small step up to three on Ned Irish's Knicks—with Sweetwater Clifton, Ray Felix, and Walter Dukes—and on the roster of the Rochester Royals owned by ~~brothers Les and~~ Jack Harrison. That season the Royals added Maurice Stokes, Ed Fleming, and Dick Ricketts; the next season Rochester became the first team to have four blacks at one time when first-round draft pick Sihugo Green made the roster.

Except for the expansion Chicago Bulls in 1961–62, the unwritten maximum of four continued for the next five years, reflected in the recollections of black players of that era. Al Attles, an NBA institution himself after spending forty years with the Warriors franchise in Philadelphia and later in the San Francisco Bay Area as a player, coach, and front-office executive, felt the effects of the quota system firsthand as a rookie in 1960.

That year the Warriors had made Attles their fifth-round draft pick after he had starred for a small black college, North Carolina A&T. He had never thought of pursuing a professional career and would have gone directly into teaching school, but Wilt Chamberlain's close friend and Attles's college teammate, Vince Miller, called Attles and told him he was good enough to make the Warriors' roster. "So I said, 'Vince, I'll tell you what. I'll go up for a week and then come back home.'" Once he got to training camp Attles competed as hard as he could and eventually made the cut. He thought his main competition was a white player named Pickles Kennedy, which he later learned was a noble but naive assumption.

The year before, the Warriors' black players had been Wilt Chamberlain, Guy Rodgers, Andy Johnson, and Woody Sauldsberry—the maximum allowed under the quota of four at the time. All four returned to training camp in 1960, and Attles remembers being the only black newcomer. Adding him made five—one above the limit—although the idea of a quota didn't occur to Attles until he had a conversation with a black redcap at the Philadelphia airport. "When I got to Philadelphia, for some reason we got friendly," Attles said. "We were talking one day and he said he told Woody Sauldsberry, who had been the Rookie of the Year two years before, that he was going to get traded. Woody said, 'Why?' And the redcap said [it was] because they've got this guy from A&T coming up."

That "guy from A&T" was Attles, and it's probably no coincidence that after he made the team, Sauldsberry was traded to St. Louis. "I wasn't aware of all this, but what you found out later was you didn't compete against everybody," Attles said. "You just competed against those blacks because you were competing for one of four spots versus one of twelve spots." In his case the competition was squeezed even tighter because Chamberlain and Rodgers were stars of the team. "So whatever number of blacks were trying out, you basically were trying out for two spots," Attles said. "Then my roommate was Andy Johnson, so really there was only one spot. I got lucky enough to get that one spot, and you really don't think about it very much because you're looking at your situation. But then when you look at the league, you say, 'Uh oh, this [quota system] is across the league.' "

As time went on race-based roster trimming lessened, although in the mid-1960s it existed at least in the minds of some NBA coaches. Bill King, the Golden State Warriors' broadcaster in 1962, recalled that when he started announcing NBA games it was rare for a team's tenth, eleventh, or twelfth man to be black, and a general "understanding" held that if a white player and a black player were contending for an end-of-the-bench spot, the white player would get it if they had equal ability. He recalled the negative reaction he heard from some coaches when Red Auerbach used five black starters for the first time: Sam and K. C. Jones, Bill Russell, Satch Sanders, and Willie Naulls. "I believe it was 1965 when Auerbach first started five blacks," King said. "I heard 'Did you hear what Auerbach did last night?' That was the only time I can remember when there was conversation about that sort of thing. Coaches mostly, but I can't remember which one, [saying]: 'Jesus, what the hell is Red thinking about?' "

Black players of the time believe the quota was a major reason black players trickled into the league at a controlled pace, but other factors must be considered too. From 1950 to 1965 the league had eight to ten teams each with a roster of from ten to twelve players. So, at most only 96 to 120 NBA jobs were available at any one time across the country, as opposed to today's twenty-nine teams and 331 jobs. Far fewer black players attended predominantly white colleges in those days, and virtually none at white schools in the South until after Texas Western's almost all-black team upset Kentucky in the 1966 NCAA championship. In addition, instead of today's sophisticated techniques, scouting in the 1950s and 1960s was conducted largely by word of mouth, with coaches relying on friends in the game for tips and advice. For instance, scouting reports from former Celtics Don Barksdale and Fred Scolari helped convince Red Auerbach to trade for Bill Russell in 1956; Scolari also recommended K. C. Jones, and Bones McKinney, who had played for Auerbach in Washington, tipped him off to fellow North Carolinian Sam Jones.

Add all those factors and the result is a separate Eastern League filled with black players, many of whom were talented enough to be NBA players. It is generally agreed among black players of the time that four of those players—Cleo Hill, Hal Lear, Wally Choice, and Dick Gaines—should have been in the NBA. Maybe

they would not have been stars or even starters, but they were
talented enough to be in the NBA. Instead they were denied the
chance to play in basketball's highest level, and the fans were
denied the opportunity to see them perform.

Of the many black players who should have been but weren't in the
NBA, Cleo Hill is spoken of in almost Jordan-esque terms. Highly
praised as an innovator, Hill stretched the game to accommodate
his plethora of scoring talents. While other Eastern Leaguers may
have been starters in the NBA had they been given the chance, Hill
most likely would have become a star. Yet the six-foot-one guard
who preceded Earl "the Pearl" Monroe at Winston Salem played
only the 1961–62 season with the St. Louis Hawks before getting released. Unfortunately, he got mashed in a power struggle between
coach Paul Seymour and the Hawks' Big 3 frontcourt comprised
of Bob Pettit, Clyde Lovellette, and Cliff Hagan, and never got
another taste of NBA play. (It continues to be a sensitive subject, at
least for Pettit and Hagan. Through an NBA employee they refused
a request to be interviewed.) Ultimately no one profited. Seymour
was fired after only fourteen games, the Hawks had a miserable 29-
51 season, and Hill was relegated to playing in the Eastern League
and coaching at Essex Community College in New Jersey (where
he nevertheless had an outstanding record).

"Cleo undoubtedly was one of the best and most colorful basketball players we had on the American scene, and the American
public was deprived of his true value," said his famous college
coach, Clarence "Big House" Gaines. He should know, since Gaines
coached Hill at his peak, when he was averaging 23.2 points per
game during four seasons at Winston-Salem Teachers College (now
Winston-Salem State), and breaking Sam Jones's CIAA record by
scoring 2,503 points during his career. As a senior Hill's 26.7 ppg.
had carried Winston-Salem to a 26-5 record and the CIAA title. He
wowed crowds with his assortment of shots. All Hill had to do was
use the tools at his disposal, and he had a bigger tool box than
almost anyone else.

"Right-hand jumper, right-hand hook, left-hand hook, and
his most outstanding shot was a two-hand set shot," Gaines said.
"St. Louis was having trouble with outside shooting and that's
what they wanted him for, but you're talking about a six-foot-one
kid who was playing above the rim. When you think about an
artist, you think of someone who has mastered the fundamental

skills and their creativity puts him on another level. He was a true artist. People always want to compare him with Earl Monroe. They were very different. Earl was very spectacular. Cleo is probably the most scientific player I ever worked with."

A lot of words are used to describe great athletes, and though "scientific" usually isn't one of them, it fits Hill because of the way he incorporated so many skills into his game. Like a highly creative chemist, he mixed a little of this and a little of that to make a wonderful concoction. Growing up in Newark, New Jersey (where Attles was a high school rival), Hill followed the norm and learned to shoot the one-hand and two-hand set shots and the hook shot, then added different moves along the way. Players from New York usually weren't good outside shooters, so from them he picked up tips on how to drive to the basket. He began playing high school ball as a forward, but Sherman White, who left his unmistakable imprint on players throughout the Northeast, told Hill he would have to play guard in college and always let him play that position when they were teammates during the summer. Hill once saw Tennessee State player Jim Satterwhite block an opponent's shot by pinning it against the backboard, and added that arrow to his quiver, too. Hill had everything that he needed to be a great NBA player—except the right team situation.

"Cleo Hill was one of the most versatile players I have ever seen—could jump out the gym, could shoot every shot," Rodgers said. "He went to St. Louis and I don't think some of his teammates or the ownership or [the fans of] St. Louis [were] ready for a player of his ilk. He was unbelievable and he could do everything Michael Jordan could do today. He was just a marvelous, marvelous athlete."

Marty Blake, who has been involved in the NBA since 1954 and was general manager of St. Louis at the time, made Hill the NBA's initial first-round draft pick from a black college. The Hawks had lost to Boston in the NBA Finals the year before, repeatedly hurt by their lack of outside shooting from the backcourt. Blake brought Hill to St. Louis, where, after a very encouraging start, Hill became the victim of bad timing. During the previous season the Hawks' point guard role had been shared between veteran Johnny McCarthy and rookie Lenny Wilkens (who was a masterful floor leader). During Hill's lone season Wilkens was in the army and played only twenty games. Because McCarthy was a poor shooter, coach Paul Seymour wasn't comfortable using him as a starter, though neither of the other two returning guards, Al Ferrari and Fred LaCour, was a smooth playmaker. Seymour threw Hill into the mix as a potential point guard even though scoring was his strong suit; it was a very uncomfortable fit.

Jerry Gross, who teamed with Buddy Blattner to form half of the Hawks' radio announcing team, said that Hill didn't display the ballhandling skills or exude the confidence that Monroe and Oscar Robertson had as rookies. "Cleo never had that," Gross said. "He was a skittish, scared-looking rookie. Maybe in college it was different, but this was a different world and different lifestyle and he was scrambling to be accepted."

The other strategic problem was the Hawks' playing style. Using three frontcourt scorers and having no Wilkens to lead the fastbreak, St. Louis played at a slower, more conservative pace that didn't suit Hill's skills. "Cleo was a terrific player," Blake said. "The only problem was he was quick and we weren't."

The problems went deeper than that. Pettit, Hagan, and Lovellette were coming off a season during which they had averaged 27.9, 22.1, and 22.0 points per game, respectively, so naturally they were the focal point of the team's offense when Hill arrived as a rookie after signing a one-year, no-cut contract for $7,500. The Hawks' need for more outside scoring was obvious to everyone involved, but achieving that balance was not easy, especially in an era when salaries were based on box score totals. "During that time, you didn't hear people talk about 'I've got to get that championship ring,'" Hill said. "During that time, it was personal effort, your points, your stats."

Hill and Seymour established an immediate rapport. During rookie camp the former NBA backcourt man enjoyed working out with the rookies and one day scored on Hill several times. The next day Hill asked for a second chance, and while playing one-on-one he dunked on Seymour and at the same time whacked the coach in the jaw. "I broke his tooth accidentally and he said, 'You can't quit now,'" so they kept playing. At other times they had shooting contests, or other guards were asked to stay after practice so Hill could sharpen his defensive skills. On the first day of veterans' training camp Seymour gave Hill some useful tips about moving without the ball so it would be easier for him to catch passes from teammates.

Theirs was an unusual bond, especially since Hill really hadn't accomplished anything up to then. "Paul is more than a coach, he is a friend," Hill told the *Winston-Salem Journal* during the Hawks' preseason. "I guess that's because we have so much in common." They were about the same height, both were guards, and both had tremendous two-hand set shots. The difference between the two, however, is revealed in Seymour's comment in the same article: "Hell, I wish I'd had his speed when I was a player. And you won't have to worry about his scoring. Hell, he can do anything he wants. You just gotta harness him a little. He wastes so much. When he gets rid of those unnecessary movements and [his] tendency to shoot too quick, he'll make it big."[1]

The Hawks played a nine-game series of preseason games against a Philadelphia Warriors team that included Wilt Chamberlain and the excellent backcourt of Rodgers and Attles. In the Hawks' preseason opener Hill shot 7 for 13 and scored 16 points. The next night Seymour's allegiance to Hill was shown when the coach thought the Warriors' Ed Conlin had committed a flagrant foul against the rookie guard. Seymour became so incensed that he charged Conlin and was ejected from the game. Then came one of the highlights of Hill's season when the Hawks played an exhibition game before seven thousand fans in Winston-Salem and, boosted by his own cheering section from his alma mater, scored 21 points in a Hawks victory. Pettit led both teams with 30 points, Hagan scored 11, and Lovellette 10. It should have been an encouraging night, but Coach Gaines could foresee problems ahead. "I said, 'Paul, this kid is going to get you in trouble,' because those older players resented the kid because he cut down their averages."

Hill remembered no personal animosity emanating from the "Big 3," although some could have been expected since two of them were from the Deep South (Pettit hailing from Louisiana and Hagan from Kentucky). Lovellette had grown up in Terre Haute, Indiana, with black schoolmates and friends. "I describe Pettit as a Southern gentleman," Hill said. "And Lovellette was a happy-go-lucky guy. He just wanted to shoot. Hagan was kind of stoic. He wouldn't joke much. They never said anything to me that said, 'These guys are tough on me.'"

Hill continued to excel during the preseason, averaging 15 points a game, and started in the season opener against the Cincinnati Royals. The Hawks lost, but Hill scored 26 points on 9 of 15 shooting from the field and 8 for 8 free throws. "Hill, drawing roars from the large crowd with his spectacular leaps while driving for shots or snaring rebounds, topped the Hawks in the [first] half with 15 points," reported the *Post-Dispatch*.[2] The Hawks then lost their second game, one in which Hill shot only 2 for 8 but added 12 free throws and 8 rebounds in New York. Already the seeds of dissension had begun to sprout. At halftime Seymour berated Lovellette for asking to come out of the game simply because he wasn't getting the ball. Lovellette scored 20 points after intermission, and after the game Seymour reiterated to the team the need to get the ball to the Big 3. He also placed some fault on them. No lineup changes in the frontline would be made, he said. "However, the front liners have got to start moving the ball. If they don't, I'll pull out whoever is not passing the ball, whether it's Pettit, Lovellette or Hagan."[3]

Hill was as inconsistent as the wind—as were all the St. Louis guards. Seymour kept searching for the right backcourt combination, which meant that Hill repeatedly was in and out of the starting lineup. In one stretch he scored 4, 12, and 1 points, followed by not getting into a game against New York. Then on November 7 Hill busted out with 20 points and 12 rebounds in forty-three minutes against the Los Angeles Lakers. On the twelfth against Cincinnati, Hill played a team-high thirty-eight minutes and totaled 16 points on 6 for 9 shooting, 5 rebounds, and three assists during a 136–126 loss. There was no reason to think Hill wasn't headed for a productive rookie season. But by the time it ended, unresolvable conflict had developed between Seymour and the Big 3, Seymour was fired, and Hill had lost his playing time and confidence in his shot.

Wilkens was still in the army, but the Hawks had flown him in to see the season opener in which Hill scored 26 points. He watched the game dressed in his second lieutenant's uniform and came away highly impressed with Hill. "I went back after that figuring he definitely was going to be playing," Wilkens said. "Then I began hearing all kinds of stories." Several weeks passed. "Finally when I got a chance to come in one weekend, they weren't playing him and I kept hearing stories that he wouldn't pass the ball or that some of the veterans didn't like his game," Wilkens said. "These were some of the stories that were in the papers—that Cleo wouldn't play any defense or that he shot the ball every time or that he was kooky. I met him and he was none of those things, but he was an offensive player so you shouldn't expect him to be doing a point guard's role."

Seymour believed that Hill's outside shooting would force defenses to stretch in order to cover him, thereby opening up the inside. Hill didn't want to stir up any problems and was reluctant to shoot too often, but Seymour wouldn't tolerate such reticence. "Seymour wanted me to shoot more and I said I don't think they want me to shoot. He said, 'If you don't shoot, you sit,' " Hill said. But Seymour's strategy wouldn't work if the Big 3 didn't pass the ball to Hill when he was open, and, for whatever reason, they didn't. Seymour eventually got frustrated to the point that he resorted to threatening his star players if they didn't pass to Hill more often.

"I remember distinctly the confrontation between Seymour and the players," Gross said. "He called timeout, I think in Detroit, and said, 'I'm tired of this. The next guy who doesn't throw Cleo the ball, there's going to be a $100 fine.' They looked at him like, 'Are you out of your mind?' As it happened, the ball went in and never went out even though one of the Big 3 was being double-teamed. Paul called time out and said, 'The next guy who doesn't pass him the ball, I'm going to punch him in the mouth.' And that did not endear him to Pettit, Hagan, and Lovellette."

Hill didn't recall that incident, but he did remember a similar occasion when St. Louis played in Madison Square Garden, where it was presumed Hill, hailing from New Jersey, surely would have had friends and family in the crowd. "They knew that the Garden was close to where I was from and they were passing me up," Hill said. At halftime, "Seymour said the next guy who is passing me up, you get fined $100. I guess they knew if we lost enough, they'll get a new coach. When he said that, that perked things up. When we came out [for the second half], they overpassed and I didn't want to shoot that much. There's a little on you if you take the shot, then you miss."

Why wouldn't the Big 3 be glad to pass to him, especially since his effectiveness eventually would increase theirs? "When people say it was black and white, that wasn't it," Hill said. "It was the points. You hear announcers say you need three players who can score. I never heard anyone say you need four who can score."

Gross also said race wasn't a factor, because the previous season he had seen the Big 3 get along well with black players on the team and the same occurred in seasons that followed. In addition, Hill wasn't the only rookie outside shooter they ignored. "They did the same with the little white kid [James Darrow] from Bowling

Green, who was five-eleven but never got the ball back." Darrow lasted only five games that season.

Gross believes Hill's problems were caused by all of the publicity about him before he had played many games. His beliefs were based on a conversation Gross had with Lovellette and Hagan on an Elektra airplane as the team flew to a game. "It shocked me one day on the back of the Elektra when the comment was 'he's got to earn his ink,'" Gross said. He said that comment was made by Lovellette, and Gross challenged him on it. "Clyde got along with everybody," Gross said. "He got along with the blacks and whites. He was the friendliest of the Big 3. But they had this pride thing that the kid has to earn his publicity [over time]. I just told him and Hagan, 'I don't understand how you can feel that way. You guys just admitted you need outside shooting and admit the kid can do it.' And that was the answer Lovellette gave me. And I looked at Hagan and he just smiled." Gross added that he never had a similar conversation with Pettit, so he doesn't know if Pettit shared his teammates' chagrin at Hill's publicity.

Lovellette didn't recall much about Hill as a player. "I can't remember," he said during an interview in 2000. "I don't think he was treated very well, but I'm not sure. He had talent. To me, he was a nice guy off the court and on the court. He played hard—a good defensive player. I can't remember what happened to Cleo." That may sound evasive, but in all fairness to Lovellette, thirty-eight years had passed and he played only forty games that season before a torn Achilles ended it, which meant that he was Hill's teammate for just half a season.

Lovellette also didn't remember Seymour's threatening time-out in Detroit or the conversation with Gross on the airplane. Did he feel Hill was getting too much ink too soon? "I feel that way as far as the rookies coming into the NBA now," he said. "I think you ought to prove yourself before you get that amount of money. If that was the comment I made as far as Cleo is concerned, I can't remember it. I can't remember saying anything like that to Gross or anybody else. If they have that recollection, that's fine."

Lovellette admitted, however, that passing to a teammate—any teammate—was something he did infrequently once he got within scoring range. It was a trait he developed at Kansas University, where coach Phog Allen had told Lovellette that if he got the ball within ten feet of the basket, he had a better chance of scoring than someone taking a 20-footer. "I know I didn't have a lot of assists," Lovellette said. "When it came in to me, unless I was really covered up it [the shot] went up. Bob and Cliff had more assists than me." Lovellette said he also could have been accused of not passing to former Hawks guards Slater Martin and Jack McMahon, who were white. About Hill, Lovellette said, "It wasn't because of the color of his skin that I would not work with him. I don't think there was a racially prejudiced player on the team—at least it never came out."

Everything came to a head on November 16, when Seymour told Gross he had been misquoted in a newspaper article that stated he was willing to trade any of the Hawks' top players, including Pettit, a St. Louis sports icon. Because owner Ben Kerner was close to the Hawks' stars, Seymour figured the comment could get him fired. "Well, did you say that?" Gross said he asked Seymour. "We have to make a trade," Seymour told him, "but I didn't include Pettit." Then Seymour added, "I'm out of here. I'm through." In fact, Kerner was upset because he believed Seymour had tried to horn in on management's authority to make deals. "No Hawks' players are on the market until they are put there by this office," Kerner told the *Post-Dispatch*.[4] The next day, November 17, he fired Seymour with a 5-9 record. Firing coaches was nothing new for Kerner, a team owner who had employed sixteen coaches—including interims—in just thirteen seasons.

"Seymour had his ideas, especially concerning rookie Cleo Hill—and he's entitled to them—but I couldn't run a smooth club with the bad feeling between team and coach," Kerner said. Seymour blamed his firing on his determination to use Hill as a starter, and believed that Pettit, Hagan, and Lovellette had undermined his attempts to get scoring from the backcourt through Hill. "They didn't help the kid, but went against him," Seymour told the *Globe Democrat*. "That's my only gripe, the way they boycotted the kid. One of my front line said, 'Why should he start: I had to sit on the bench a year before I got a chance.'" "And I was stunned," the coach continued, "when one of the big men said to me that the kid was getting too much publicity. What do they want, all the money and the publicity, too? It takes the heart out of you when your own team players won't help you. Well, they won the battle and the war." Seymour went on to say that Kerner had told him to take Hill out of the starting lineup, so he held him out for two games and then started him again because "the team still needs more than three men in order to win consistently. But I wouldn't treat a dog the way they treated him."[5]

In an article in the *Winston-Salem Journal*, Seymour and Hill both ticked off specific ways they were undermined by the Big 3. Hill believed that "They played harder when other backcourt men were in there," and Seymour added, "They wouldn't rebound when Clee shot. And they wouldn't go down fast if he was leading the fast break. When he'd take that hook [a unique Hill creation], they make faces like 'What the hell kind of a shot is that?' But it's okay for them to take 40-foot capers."

"Man, I can't play my natural game with those guys making facial expressions and groaning," Hill said. "Once I made a pass and the crowd gave me an ovation. When we came back on defense, they looked at me and said, 'Can't you give up the ball without a show?'"[6]

St. Louis Post-Dispatch columnist Bob Broeg chided Kerner for being influenced by players' insurrection and empathized with Hill. "Although Kerner envisions himself as the man in the middle, the most unfortunate figure in this sad situation is Cleo Hill, the quick, acrobatic rookie the coach figured had the best chance to be the out-scorer the Hawks needed," he wrote. "Perhaps Seymour was stubborn, but who better than a basketball technician, himself a former backline star[,] would know a diamond in the roundball rough when he saw one?

"Sure, the kid is a bit of a showboat or, as they'd say in baseball, a 'hot dog,' but there's more than a little salami in one of the Unmentionables—er, pardon, Unmatchables. And if Cleo has a lot to learn about defense, the rookie has far more excuse than two of the big three."[7]

Quoted in an article in *Sports View Magazine*, Pettit denied that any players tried to undermine Hill: "As I recall, he was a player with a lot of talent. I really don't recall any of the controversy. I don't think any of the players cared how many points a rookie scored. I don't remember any resentment of any kind on the part of a veteran. The players were looking for any rookie to come in and make a contribution."[8]

Pettit, the team captain, was named to replace Seymour until an interim coach could be found. Pettit coached one game (a victory over Cincinnati), then Fuzzy Levane, a former Hawks coach who had been directing a team in the Eastern League, was named interim replacement. Levane and Hill agree that Levane gave the rookie a fair chance to play, but two problems got in the way. "He wasn't what I needed," Levane said. "I needed a point guard." And, because of all the controversy regarding Hill, he had lost faith in his own offense. Even when he scored 14 points in a win over Syracuse on November 26, Levane could see that Hill was pressing. "Cleo was so anxious to get rid of the ball, fearing he'd be accused of taking too many shots, that he was hurting us the other way," Levane said. "I finally called a time-out and told him that if I had confidence to put him in the game, he'd have to have enough confidence to do things. He was playing scared pool."

"I had all those shots and I was losing confidence in all of them except the drive," Hill recently explained. "That's natural. I didn't have a place to practice. When Seymour was there, I was starting and playing and the shot was going down. But when they benched me, I didn't have a chance to shoot." Hill explained that Kiel Auditorium had only two baskets, so he couldn't work on his own shooting while other players were involved in practice. Once practice ended, the trainer immediately closed down the gym.

By mid-season Hill wasn't playing much. In January he was disillusioned to the point that he told the *Winston-Salem Journal* that he planned to quit basketball after the season and become a schoolteacher. The season ended as a certified disaster for the Hawks: a 29-51 record, twenty-five games behind Western Division champion Los Angeles and the second-worst defense in the league. In addition, the roster had changed as often as a traffic signal as eighteen different players wore St. Louis uniforms. Hill's statistics were mediocre, at best. While playing in fifty-eight of eighty games, he averaged eighteen minutes, 5.5 points, 3.1 rebounds, and 2.0 assists, and shot 34.6 percent from the floor. Not very encouraging. But his performance can be evaluated in another way. While playing for Seymour, who had utmost confidence in him, Hill played in thirteen of fourteen games, he averaged 28 minutes, 10.8 points, 5.5 rebounds, and 2.3 assists, and he shot 36 percent from the floor. After Seymour was fired Hill's production plummeted to playing in forty-four of sixty-six games, averaging fifteen minutes, 4.1 points, 2.4 rebounds, and 1.9 assists, and shooting 34 percent from the floor.

It had been a rough introduction to the NBA, although Hill did get his teaching degree during the off-season and he returned to the Hawks for workouts before their 1962 training camp began. At that point Hill felt optimistic, because over the summer he had practiced diligently and regained confidence in his shot. A new coach, former NBA star Harry Gallatin, had been hired by Kerner after compiling a 79-35 record at Southern Illinois–Carbondale. Unfortunately, with the return of Wilkens from the army and the addition of draft picks Chico Vaughn from Southern Illinois and John Barnhill from Tennessee State, the backcourt was packed with candidates.

Hill got almost no time to prove his worth because on September 11, 1962, the day before training camp officially opened, Gallatin cut him from the squad. Considering the uproar that had surrounded him the previous season, it is strange that Hill's release was barely mentioned in St. Louis newspapers. The *Post-Dispatch* didn't write about it at all; the *Globe-Democrat* mentioned his release in one paragraph of an article about numerous roster changes. Gallatin's main goal that year was to strengthen the Hawks' defense, and he considered Hill part of the problem rather than part of the solution. "He was kind of overshadowed here. I can't remember that much about him," Gallatin said in a 2000 interview. "I think he had a lot of publicity when he came but he didn't make a big impression on me. . . . Cleo was not a great defensive player." Hill also was at a disadvantage because Vaughn had played for Gallatin in college and Barnhill, who played college ball for John McLendon, had played against Southern Illinois. "So I probably was impressed more with those two than with Cleo Hill," Gallatin said.

The way Hill was released hurt him almost more than getting cut. He recalled that Gallatin, who had retired as a player just four years before, participated in a team practice the day Hill was released, and Hill remembers blocking one of the six-foot-six Gallatin's hook shots that day. "He didn't know I grew up watching him play," Hill said, alluding to Gallatin's long career with the New York Knicks. "That fake to the right and swing left, I knew that from TV." Hill said that he showered after practice, then learned from the following conversation that he was cut from the team. "He [Gallatin] said, 'How good are you at teaching?' I said, 'I think I'm pretty good.' He said, 'Well, we're going to let you teach,' and that was the end of my game."

Gallatin doesn't remember how he cut Hill. "It might have had a lot of significance to Cleo but as far as I was concerned, I guess he didn't fit in my plans," said Gallatin. Contrary to Hill's belief, Gallatin said Kerner had nothing to do with his decision. Gallatin eventually kept Vaughn, Barnhill, and a total of six black players—at that time an all-time high for an NBA team. With Wilkens directing the revamped St. Louis team, the Hawks bounced back to a 48-32 record and stretched the Lakers to seven games in the Western Division playoff finals. "I would have loved to have played with that team," Hill said. "They came up the court fast."

After Hill was cut Seymour told him that three teams were interested in signing him. When no one contacted him, Hill said Seymour called again about a month later and told him, "I think Ben Kerner is more powerful than I thought," implying that Kerner had talked other teams into not giving Hill another chance. Hill didn't call the teams himself: "I didn't know how to contact them." It was an era when players didn't have agents to do that type of telephone legwork for them. Hill played for a short while with the Philadelphia Tapers in the new American Basketball League before returning to St. Louis, and then went to Newark to work as a substitute teacher. In New Jersey in 1963 he began a five-year Eastern League career and continued his emotionally painful withdrawal from the NBA.

"While I was in St. Louis I didn't watch them [the Hawks], and when I got back to Newark I didn't have time to watch them because I was playing Saturday and Sunday," Hill said. "The only time [I watched them] was in the playoffs when the teams were the Celtics and 76ers. I was trying to get over that because it would bring back memories. Everybody I met would say, 'why did people do that to you?' " Hill would reply, "I don't know," instead of telling them the real reason he believes he was let go. "I would hate to say my coach was like a big brother to me," Hill said. "I wouldn't want them to think I was only on the team because the coach liked me."

Hill never soured on basketball, however. He eventually became head coach and athletic director at Essex Community College in New Jersey, compiling an outstanding 489-128 record. Just as he had done as a player, Hill adopted tactics used by coaches he admired. Yes, Gallatin had ended his professional career, but Hill liked his approach to the game so Hill used some of the fundamentals and conditioning drills Gallatin used. From Temple coach John Chaney, an old backcourt rival from Eastern League days, Hill adopted the match-up zone defense. And, just like Hill was as a player, his teams were extremely versatile. Essex set a national scoring record in 1974 by burying Englewood Cliffs College, 210-67, but also once won a game 8-4.

Today Hill looks back on his one NBA season with no resentment. He appreciates the fact that Blake made him a first-round draft pick when it was "unheard of" to select a black-college player that high, and Hill said the no-cut contract he signed with St. Louis helped him establish a firm financial footing. "I was angry before, but you can't walk around being angry the rest of your life," he said. "But I look at it this way. You have so many guys who don't get a chance to play."

13

Eastern League Provides
Haven for NBA Rejects

Eastern League fans were well aware of the scoring exploits of the Pettit–Hagan–Lovellette trio—the first to average a cumulative 70 points per game in the NBA—and proud they had their own trio to surpass them. From 1957 to 1961 the Easton-Phillipsburg Madisons had a devastating threesome of their own in outside marksman Hal Lear, do-everything guard Dick "Chink" Gaines (who could muscle down the lane with anyone), and the master of moves Wally Choice (also a terror on the offensive boards). Forward Jay Norman, Lear's teammate at Temple, set the picks and was a defensive specialist, while center Jim Ratcliffe, the only white fixture on the team, grabbed the rebounds. None of the three scorers even pretended to be a point guard. (Ray Scott noted that none of them liked to make the inbounds pass "because they knew they would never get the ball back.") As Choice said: "We were compatible. We never bitched and complained about anything. We just ran the hell out of everybody. If you played us, you better be in shape. We uniquely complemented each other. None of us needed the ball that long. All three could score, and score rapidly."

They won the 1959–60 Eastern League championship and compiled a 67-45 record during their four seasons together and there's no reason to think they would not have played more team-oriented ball in the NBA had they had gotten the chance. They had excelled at the highest levels of college ball, and Stan Novak, an Eastern League coach from 1950 to 1980, has no doubts about their place in today's NBA: "I would say all of those guys could have played today because the numbers have progressed to twenty-nine teams and there's more of a chance that anybody could play." Novak, a longtime NBA scout, helped assemble the Detroit Pistons team that won two championships with Isiah Thomas.

The Easton-Phillipsburgh stars played a total of only three NBA games—all of them played by Lear. Were Lear, Choice, and Gaines good enough to make an NBA roster in the late 1950s and early

1960s? Novak, who said he never heard anyone affiliated with the NBA mention a quota, couldn't give a definitive answer. "I think they should have been given a better opportunity to play," he said. "They were all great players in our league. It guess it doesn't make them feel any better, but today they could play anywhere in [the NBA]." Collectively they represent the myriad of reasons the numbers of NBA black pioneers were so low.

Hal Lear

He was six feet tall, 165 pounds—in terms of size and quickness Lear compares himself to current Portland guard Damon Stoudamire—and he was such a terrific shooter that in his hometown of Philadelphia he was heralded as "King Lear." He preceded Wilt Chamberlain at Overbrook High, then as a senior at Temple University was teamed with Guy Rodgers to make a stellar, all-left-handed backcourt that reached the NCAA Final Four in 1956. Rodgers handled the ball then Lear shot it. In 1956 he set the then-NCAA Tournament record by scoring 48 points in a third-place game against Southern Methodist, a scoring touch that allowed him to average 40 points for Easton in the 1960–61 season.

"What made him a great shooter was a gift from God and a lot of practice," Rodgers said. "He may have had the sweetest touch this side of heaven."

"He was as good a shooter as you could find," Novak said. "He was a sweet shooter. He just had the proper form. He stroked the ball and he could shoot from medium and long distance[s]. And he was a lefty, which made it harder to guard him."

As usual, during the 1956 draft Philadelphia owner Eddie Gottlieb opted for the potential gate attraction and made Lear, the local Temple star, his first-round draft pick. "They gave me a call and offered me such a paltry sum of money that it took all summer to agree on $3,000," Lear said. That was pretty typical of the ridiculously small NBA salaries in those days. One black player was already on the team—reserve forward Jackie Moore from LaSalle—and Lear believed the "quota" was one per team. Making the NBA was an ambition of his because he loved the game. He certainly was going to try, even though the Warriors were the defending NBA champions under coach George Senesky.

In 1956 they returned a solid backcourt of Tom Gola, ballhandlers Jack George and George Dempsey, reserve Larry Hennessy, and Larry Costello, back from military service. In addition, early in training camp a *Philadelphia Inquirer* article detailed several difficult adjustments Lear had to make in the NBA:

> *Seldom taking his favorite corner jumper because that spot on the court was occupied by forwards; playing man-to-man defense, usually against taller guards, instead of Temple's zone defense; and becoming mainly a passer in Philadelphia's offense instead of being his team's primary scorer.*
>
> *With it all, Lear has shown good scoring punch in the intrasquad drills. He has been hitting as well as anyone on the team, and also shooting as much. It's questionable once the exhibition grind gets into full motion that he will have as many opportunities to shoot. The job of the Warriors backcourt men essentially is to feed the big guys, and [the guards'] scoring is secondary.*[1]

There was another factor involved that Lear believed had a negative impact on his chances of making the roster: "I didn't feel welcomed," Lear recalled in 2000. "Several things happened. I guess this is how sports went in those days. Jackie and I were cronies, so I did have a friend. But [veteran Warriors] wanted Larry Hennessy to make the team, so they made him look good and beat up on me, and coach let it happen. In practice you could hack a guy to death and he'd never take a shot."

It turned out that Hennessy and Lear both made the eleven-man opening-night roster, then both were cut in mid-November, just before rosters were trimmed to ten. Bob Armstrong, a six-eight reserve frontcourt player, got the open roster spot. Lear had been cut after playing just three games and scoring 4 points in fourteen minutes of action. "Lack of height and a good outside shot hampered him," the *Inquirer* stated.[2] Lear said the explanations he received for being released amounted to double talk. "Senesky told me Gottlieb thought I wasn't ready, and Gottlieb told me Senesky felt I wasn't ready," Lear said.

Was the quota a factor in their decision, or was it favoritism toward Hennessy? "Certainly both," Lear said. He and Moore had concluded that the chances that two black players would make the roster "were probably slim," Lear said. On the other hand, "Larry Hennessy had a good outside shot but he was pretty slow. I think I had a little more potential than Larry did, but it probably was a little bit of both." Lear refused to let getting cut erode his confidence because he believed that in 1956, "Willie Naulls [a black UCLA star] and I should have made the Olympic team and didn't because of the number of blacks they were taking. I was very disappointed about that and said I'm not going to let anybody's judgment affect me again. So I went to the Eastern League and American Basketball League and did better financially than many players in the NBA."

Three weeks after Philadelphia released Lear, St. Louis announced it had acquired him. But an hour before he was to report to the Hawks, the part-owner and coach of the Easton-Phillipsburg Madisons, Chick Craig, reminded Lear that he had already signed a contract with the Eastern Basketball League team. "Craig also pointed out that his . . . team had a game in Wilkes-Barre the following Sunday for which several thousand tickets already had been sold, since it was to be Lear's first appearance in that city. Lear had to honor his contract. Lear notified [St. Louis coach Red Holzman and owner Ben Kerner] and the Hawks decided not to pick him up. The game in Wilkes-Barre drew about 1,000 people despite a heavy snowstorm. Lear responded with 51 points."[3]

It was simply a case of bad timing. Lear speculated at the time that if St. Louis would have called a week later, the Madisons probably would have let him out of his contract. Instead, less than two months later Lear was the talk of the Eastern League as he averaged 37 points per game. It was the beginning of his fulfilling and lucrative eleven-year Eastern League career.

Lear said that the year after he was cut by Philadelphia the New York Knicks invited him to training camp. But their financial offer fell far short of what Lear already was earning: "They said, 'This is the NBA,' I said, 'Nonetheless, if I'm going to put myself out, I want a two-year contract at X amount of money. If you can't do that, then sayonara." Some Eastern Leaguers were NBA players recovering from injuries, players who had been cut from NBA rosters or who were keeping in shape while stationed at a nearby military base. Most, like Lear, had fulltime jobs and augmented that money with what they earned playing basketball on the weekends. He was a management trainee for the city of Philadelphia, earning $3,000 to $4,000 per year and $200 a weekend playing in the Eastern League (and occasionally for a team in Philly called the Harlem Comedy Team, a takeoff on the Globetrotters). "I made $10,000 playing basketball and another $3,000 at the job when others were making $3,000 for playing [NBA] basketball," Lear said. "I wasn't going to give up $13,000 for $3,000."

Lear said he doesn't regret that decision "because I don't think it [getting cut] was any measure of how good I was or wasn't." In pickup games and tournaments during the summer, as well as various preseason or postseason games pitting Eastern League against NBA teams, Lear got to judge himself using other NBA players as the standard. In addition, he played for three teams in the short-lived American Basketball League during the 1961–62 season, averaging 13 points per game. The ABL was filled with former NBA players and coaches, but Lear didn't see it as a proving ground for his talents "because I played against pros all along. I never felt that I couldn't play. All the guys knew I could play, and when I played with them, I was treated with respect. I was asked to do the same thing: Would you please score 30 points?'"

Also, missing out on the NBA didn't cost Lear the huge salaries of today and gave him time to build a different career. He was a city employee for seven years and by the age of thirty had become an executive. In the late 1960s Lear was employed by Dr. Leon Sullivan, an advocate of progressive ideas about urban employment; after that Lear served as an administrator at Albert Einstein Medical School in the Bronx for more than twenty-five years before retiring to Arizona.

Lear stopped playing in the Eastern League in 1967, when he was thirty-two, although even at the age of sixty-five Lear still shoots around in the gym, just for fun. He works out at the same fitness club as former NBA players Eddie Johnson and Sedale Threatt, and ex-Globetrotters showman Meadowlark Lemon. He enjoys taking cruises and lives in a big house on a golf course. He resides in the same development as NBA stars Jason Kidd and Charles Barkley, "but not in $3 million houses like them," Lear said.

Does Lear hold any bitterness toward the NBA? "No, because I think life worked out well for me," he said. "I felt anything I had to prove, I did, and I wasn't penalized economically."

Dick Gaines

Growing up in Brooklyn Dick Gaines learned how to play basketball and baseball among extremely talented athletes, including future Basketball Hall of Famer Lenny Wilkens, and Tommy Davis, who became a baseball star with the Los Angeles Dodgers. Gaines favored baseball at first, which was a natural inclination since

Jackie Robinson was his idol, but Gaines eventually leaned toward basketball as he grew into a rugged, fearless guard.

In 1953 he was named New York City's most outstanding high school player, then starred for Seton Hall under famed coach Honey Russell. In his three varsity seasons there Gaines helped Seton Hall reach the NIT championship twice, and he graduated in 1957 as Seton Hall's fifth-leading scorer at 19.6 points per game. He was only six-one, but his leaping ability and burly 215 pounds also allowed him to average 7.6 rebounds.

"I was always going toward the basket," Gaines said. "I tried to get as close as I could and if that couldn't do it, I would pull up and shoot the jump shot. I used to love to get there with the big guys."

The Syracuse Nationals drafted him in 1957 after compiling the second-best record in the league (38-34) and getting swept by Boston in the Eastern Division finals during Bill Russell's rookie year. The Nats had talented young guards in Larry Costello and Al Bianchi, but player-coach Paul Seymour and Bob Harrison both were over thirty so Gaines thought his youth would be an asset to the team. "When I was at Syracuse, I knew I had the skills and Paul Seymour said so, too," Gaines said. "He said he didn't know if they could take another rookie on, but they already had the two blacks. They had Earl Lloyd and Bobby Hopkins."

Gaines loved the rough style of NBA ball. For instance, he fondly remembered banging against six-seven veteran Alex Hannum in an exhibition game. "Alex Hannum was a hatchet guy and I must have upset him because I hit him," Gaines said. "That was nothing. He did tell me, 'Rookie, next time you're going to get it.' I said, 'I'll be right back.'" Gaines believes he played well during the exhibition season, especially during games in Paducah and Benton, Kentucky. But in Baltimore he was told he would be released. Gaines had an inkling the release was coming because he was already getting less playing time. His response: "I was kind of happy. I didn't want to play there because I had gotten the word New York would pick me up. But that never happened." Later he heard rumors that he was "difficult to get along with," but he doesn't know the origin or reason for those rumors.

Sherman White asked Gaines to play for the Hazleton team in the Eastern League in a game against Easton. Hazelton then offered Gaines sixty dollars a game to play, but Easton topped it and Gaines became the EBL's top rookie during the 1957–58 season.

Syracuse, which had been 41-31 that season, invited him back to training camp in 1958, and Gaines was cut again. Was race a factor? "It was hard to tell," Gaines said. "In the Eastern League you only played weekends, and when I went to camp I wasn't in the best of shape. I had gained a little weight. The second time they didn't look at you as long to give you time to get in shape. They give you a week and a half and then you're gone, and they extended [the invitation] to me because I was one of their top choices the year before. It depends on what they're looking for. They were going to sign Hal Greer [a great shooter], and they had Larry Costello. They had Al Bianchi."

Cutting Gaines could not have been an easy decision because Dolph Schayes, the greatest player in Syracuse history, remembers him as an "excellent" player. "He was good, posted up and he was strong, but our strength was the backcourt," Schayes said. Today a player of Gaines's caliber surely would get a tryout with another team. But in the 1950s few second chances were given. "There were only eight teams," Schayes said. "There was a lot of talent, not many jobs."

Gaines, a resident of Montclair, New Jersey, then began a long career as a physical education teacher; he returned to the Eastern League, where he frequently made the All-League team. He loved playing in the Rucker League and in summer tournaments where he could drive the lane against NBA players, including Wilt Chamberlain. One of his biggest thrills occurred after a game between NBA players and Eastern League All-Stars, probably in 1962. Dick McGuire, one of the slickest passers ever, was playing for the NBA team, and Gaines recalled that afterward McGuire came into the locker room and said, "Gaines, you're the toughest guy I ever played against in my life." "That was a heck of a compliment coming from Tricky Dick, a guy I idolized as a kid. That was when the guards were getting bigger and the smaller guards couldn't handle guards with jumping ability who could dunk. . . . That was a heck of a compliment, but it didn't do any good."

Gaines didn't get any other NBA tryouts, and by the time he was drafted by the Pittsburgh Condors in the American Basketball Association, he was over thirty, was well established in his school district, and didn't want to give up his job for a league with an uncertain future. He turned down the Condors' offer and kept playing in the Eastern League until 1967 when, at thirty-one, he found it difficult to stay in shape.

Gaines has lingering bitterness about not making an NBA

roster. "Oh yeah," he said, "because you knew you're better than guys that were there." Consequently he's rarely attended an NBA game. "I've been, in person, to two pro games in my life," he said in 1999. "It's been hard for me. I can go now, but I just don't bother. It was very hard to go watch a pro team."

Wally Choice

Wally Choice hasn't strayed far from his roots in Montclair, New Jersey. He was born one block from Glenfield Park, grew up one block on the other side of the park, honed his basketball skills in the park, and for the last thirty years has been running a basketball camp for kids there. As a youngster, just like Al Attles, Choice was greatly influenced by the black college stars in the New York City area who later were banned from professional ball. He watched their games on television, and claims to have picked up most of his basketball watching and trying to mimic guys like Sherman White and Ed Warner.

After being named a high school All-State player in New Jersey, Choice went to Indiana University in 1952, just one year after the graduation of the Hoosiers' Bill Garrett, the first black basketball player in Big Ten history. As a freshman Choice wasn't eligible to play for Indiana when it won the 1953 NCAA title, but he did play on its conference championship team the next year. As a senior he led Indiana in scoring, at 21 points per game, and by shooting 51 percent from the floor. He was the first black captain of Indiana's basketball team. It was, as he put it, a "fruitful" collegiate career.

At about six-five, 220 pounds he wasn't an exceptionally big forward, but he was exceptionally versatile. "I'm about Elgin Baylor's size and I use him as an example because he is African-American and put an end to the myth that you had to be six-nine to be a good forward," Choice said. "I was inspired by seeing someone like that. [Scouts] want to believe everyone has to be six-seven or above, and then you get Michael Jordan and players who are exceptional, and most of them are average-sized basketball players. They have flexibility because of size, speed, and jumping. . . . It didn't matter if many forwards were six-nine. It mattered to my advantage because I was quicker than they were."

Choice challenged defenders with a variety of shots. "Most players had one shot," Lear said. "He could shoot jump shots, he could shoot hook shots, shot a one-hand set, and could drive to the basket." If the proof is in the statistics, Choice's talent is undeniable. In the last three seasons of his EBL career, he averaged 27.4, 41.3, and 34.1 points per game.

If Choice had to give his professional basketball career a grade, he probably would give it an "incomplete." He was signed by the St. Louis Hawks in 1956 but never went to their training camp. He then played in the Amateur Athletic Union while serving in the army before the Knicks gave him a tryout in 1958.

Choice felt he had a terrific training camp with the Knicks, but he didn't make the final roster. Fuzzy Levane said he released Choice because veterans Richie Guerin, Carl Braun, and Ron Sobie all played his same position, and Levane preferred to keep Brendan McCann, a good passer, over Choice. "He [McCann] was the last backcourt man but he had a quality Ned [owner Ned Irish] and I liked—a backcourt man who could feed." Levane said a quota on black players had nothing to do with Choice being cut. However, Levane said Irish did impose a limit on the number of black players the roster could have at that time. "Three was [the maximum], as far as Irish was concerned," Levane said. Indeed, in Levane's two seasons as New York's coach, the Knicks had two black players on the final roster during the 1958–59 season (Ray Felix and Willie Naull) and three the next (Naulls, Johnny Green, and Cal Ramsey). Levane said that if an exception was to be made, "the fourth guy had to be one of the first seven [players on the roster] and you would keep him. But if he was going to be tenth, eleventh man . . ."

Choice never got another NBA tryout despite a stellar career in the Eastern League. "Wally Choice was an Elgin Baylor–type of player," Gaines, his longtime teammate, said. "He could go inside, outside, had a million moves in the pivot. One of the greatest offensive rebounders I ever saw." And, like so many Eastern Leaguers, he relished playing in the Rucker League and Philadelphia's Baker League, where he competed against Chamberlain, Connie Hawkins, and Julius Erving. "There were NBA players that wouldn't play in that league because they didn't have the temperament to compete at that level," Choice said. "This is in-your-face basketball. . . . No one cared about your reputation as an NBA ballplayer. That was the proving ground. A lot of guys realized how good they were in those leagues."

Choice stopped playing in the Eastern League in 1964, not for negative reasons but because "It was just time I got on with my life." He bought a building and a drug store in his neighborhood, and now is involved in housing development and owns a service center in a local mall. "I have no axes to grind," he said.

Choice's viewpoint on never playing in the NBA could be summed up in the adage, "You can't miss what you never had." In his playing days he watched NBA games and projected himself as a player. "What would I do or how would I do as an NBA player?" he said he wondered. "I really felt I wouldn't have had any problem at all functioning at a top level in the NBA. I never had sour grapes or felt I was being cheated, because I never got into the league long enough or deep enough to come up with the fact I was or was not good enough to play. I remember conversations with Lear and Dick. I don't think any of us felt we couldn't have done very well as NBA players."

John McLendon, Naismith's Protégé

Deserving players were not the only black talent underrepresented in the early days of an integrated NBA. While players were making gradual but steady inroads onto team rosters, black coaches were left out entirely for fifteen years. It took the combination of two racial barrier breakers from Boston—Red Auerbach and Bill Russell—to produce the first black coach in NBA history in 1966; the instant success that followed proved that Russell was up to the task. In fact, the first three black coaches in the NBA—Russell, Lenny Wilkens, and Al Attles—all eventually won championships. But one coach who surely deserved to coach in the NBA, John B. McLendon, was left behind, and he might have been the best of them all. Not only did he have an outstanding record as a college coach, a sterling reputation for communicating with players, and the distinction of being the first black coach of an integrated professional team, but McLendon also was the last living coaching protégé of basketball's inventor, Dr. James Naismith. No one's basketball roots reach deeper than that.

When McLendon died at eighty-four on October 8, 1999, the honors he received had begun to catch up to his achievements and included being inducted into the Basketball Hall of Fame in 1978 and earning the respect of the international basketball community. Yet even among avid basketball fans, McLendon's name usually goes unrecognized because the majority of his coaching was done at black schools from 1940 to 1969, when his teams were largely overlooked by white fans and the majority press. They, instead, tracked the careers of white coaches such as Kentucky's Adolph Rupp and Oklahoma State's Hank Iba, neither of which had to battle the overt and covert racial discrimination McLendon faced. The sports world wasn't ready yet to appoint McLendon to a high-profile college or NBA coaching job, which in the end turned out all right because McLendon simply found other ways to flourish by becoming:

- one of the earliest proponents of fastbreak basketball;

- one of the 1946 founders of the Central Intercollegiate Athletic Association tournament for historically black colleges, the third-largest basketball tournament in America behind the Atlantic Coast Conference and the Big East tourneys;

- a strong advocate for the integration of the NCAA and NAIA postseason tournaments. The NAIA relented in 1953; historically black schools couldn't play in the NCAAs until 1970;

- the first coach of any color to win three consecutive national championships (the NAIA Tournament from 1957–59 with Tennessee A&I, now named Tennessee State);

- head coach of the Cleveland Pipers in 1961 in the American Basketball League, making him the first black person to lead a team of black and white professional players;

- the first coach to resign because he couldn't tolerate the interference of a team owner (George Steinbrenner);

- the first black coach to write a book on basketball: *Fast Break Basketball, Fine Points and Fundamentals*;

- the first black coach at a predominantly white college, Cleveland State, in 1966;

- the holder of an exceptional 496-179 college coaching record;

- one of the key contributors to North Carolina coach Dean Smith's trademark four-corners offense;

- an internationally known proponent of basketball through his work as a member of the U.S. Olympic Committee, a U.S. Olympics coach, a representative for Converse basketball shoes, and a widely traveled public speaker.

"I did all I could do in the time frame I was in," McLendon said. "Sure, I would have liked to coach at Michigan or University of Iowa, where I got my master's, or University of Kansas. If I was coming along now, I might get a chance to do that. But, you can always be disappointed.

"I do think I should have been given a chance to coach in the NBA, but they just weren't ready for it. When I first started applying for it, I got some of the best letters of refusal you ever saw. But I got the opportunity with Cleveland State."

Those who played for McLendon understand how great a coach he was. His best-known player, Dick Barnett, starred for McLendon at Tennessee State and for the Cleveland Pipers before a fourteen-year career as an NBA guard. A fixture on the New York Knicks' two championship teams, Barnett said that of the coaches who influenced him, "McLendon and [Knicks coach] Red Holzman probably had the most impact in terms of their style. They were very similar in terms of preparation and discipline."

Naismith invented basketball in 1891 while a professor at Springfield (Massachusetts) College. He had been asked to devise a wintertime activity for male students. McLendon was born in 1915 and grew up in Hiawatha, Kansas, and was ten years old when he first saw the game being played at a local junior high school. He immediately became fascinated by it and decided to become a physical training teacher and basketball coach. He failed to earn a spot on school teams for six years, then finally made a junior college roster at Jarvis Christian College. That's when McLendon first realized the value of fastbreak basketball. The team went 17-0 and McLendon once scored 20 points in his best game. "All I did was streak to the ball," he said. "I made 20 points on the fastbreak because I outran everybody. I was thinking this fastbreak is a pretty easy way to score points."

McLendon had wanted to attend college in Springfield, Massachusetts, because that's where Naismith had invented the game. But when his father learned that Naismith had become a professor at Kansas University, just forty miles down the road from his home, he convinced McLendon to attend school there, where, in 1933, he would be one of the school's very few black students. His father didn't mind McLendon's ambition to be a coach, "but my mother didn't like it because she planned for me to be a doctor. She tolerated it. She did make me adopt a strong program of abstinence, never drank coffee or tea or alcoholic drinks, and she wouldn't give me a pillow to sleep on because she said coaches had to have straight shoulders."

One could say that at Kansas McLendon "adopted" Naismith, even though the professor already was in his seventies. "When I walked in his office and I told him I was his new advisee, he said, 'Who told you that?' " McLendon recalled. "I said, 'My father.' And he said, 'Come on in. Fathers are always right.' "

McLendon was a student in Naismith's courses in physical education, anatomy, and kinesiology, and also helped him navigate the racial barbed wire of the times. "When I was sent to UK, it was the first time I ever had a white teacher," McLendon said. "The first class he assigned me to was Economics 101 and I was back in about ten minutes because the man opened the class with an ethnic joke. I got up and left and told Dr. Naismith I couldn't take that class. He said, 'By all means,' and he commented from time to time that some people were ignorant and don't let that stop you."

Basketball bonded them together. Naismith was a stickler for fair-mindedness when it came to how a coach related to his players. "Anything that can't be applied to the best player, don't apply," Naismith told McLendon. Naismith also believed in supporting individuality among players as long as it wasn't a detriment to the team. McLendon followed suit. Sure, Barnett shot his unorthodox "Fall back, baby" jumper in which he tucked his legs under his body. But it went in, so "McLendon never tampered with that," Barnett said.

The most important basketball tenet Naismith passed on was his belief in what we now call fastbreak basketball, which he expressed one day while he and McLendon were watching a group of kids, maybe eight to ten years old, playing ball. "There wasn't an adult present, and he said stop and watch this game and see what you can see," McLendon said. "He was watching the movement of the ball and I said, 'All the players chase the ball wherever it goes.' He said, 'That's the way the ultimate game is supposed to be played.' " When McLendon asked for further explanation, Naismith replied, "When you have the ball, from that point you attack the basket. When the other team has the ball, from that point you attack them."

In 1936 McLendon became the first black graduate of Kansas's physical education program, and five years later became head coach at North Carolina College (now N.C. Central) in the Central Intercollegiate Athletic Association. From 1940 to 1954 his fastbreaking teams led the CIAA in scoring ten times, and when he moved on to Tennessee State, McLendon's teams continued to run opponents off the floor.

Preseason conditioning at Tennessee State consisted of grueling runs to build endurance. "We would get on the track, take one lap, go off the track and down towards the farm," said John Barnhill, who played in the NBA and the ABA from 1962 to 1972. "We'd go downhill going and have to come back up that hill. He gave us a certain amount of time to get up there and back, and if you didn't, you couldn't be on his team."

In 1946 McLendon introduced his delay offense, which he called "two-in-a-corner," and North Carolina College used it to defeat Virginia Union in triple overtime to win the first CIAA championship. "I wanted to get the big guys that couldn't dribble or pass out of the game," McLendon said. "I couldn't take them out, so I put them in the corner." A dozen years later it proved to be the key to Tennessee State's victory in the NAIA tournament championship game, and in 1970 McLendon explained his delay offense at a coaches clinic in Colorado.

McLendon said that North Carolina's Dean Smith attended that seminar and asked McLendon to expound upon it after his talk. They spent a couple hours discussing it, which became a basis for the famed delay offense Smith later used to protect a lead. "They called it four corners," McLendon joked. "I always say they took my two corners and made it a victim of inflation." (In Smith's autobiography, *A Coach's Life: Dean Smith,* he names McLendon as one of several coaches who applied a delay game similar to his.)

Besides the usual coaching duties, McLendon had the added responsibility (or burden) of protecting his players from the South's sometimes harsh racial discrimination. It took planning and often guile to keep them out of harm's way. Rather than risk being rejected by restaurants that only served white customers, McLendon had school cafeteria workers prepare boxed lunches for his players before they left on road trips. "When I was at Hampton, I don't think I ever took my team to a segregated eating place," he said. When travel routes were laid out, McLendon had to make sure they included gas stations that accepted black customers and allowed them to use the bathrooms. "Sometimes they didn't want you to get anything but gas," McLendon said. "Many times, you just weren't welcome."

"I was aware of segregation in the South," Barnett, an Indiana native, said, "but I wasn't aware of the machinations he had to go through to make sure we were shielded from overt segregation."

Despite his earnest efforts, at times McLendon and his players were subjected to the same race-based rejection that was common to black people in the 1940s and 1950s. Then, as Naismith had suggested to McLendon years before, McLendon tried to keep his players focused on their goals rather than on the ignorance of others. "We had little ways," McLendon said. "We would say, 'I wonder what these people are going to do next.' We tried to make them a butt of the joke and imitate them. Young people can adjust. We always put people that treated us like that in a lower class. They were showing how ignorant they were and how mean they were. You had to have some kind of rationale to have fellas keep focused on other things than being constantly put down, and had to do the same for yourself."

After winning three consecutive NAIA titles for Tennessee State, McLendon could have gone on and coached there forever. In 1960, however, Ed Sweeney, the owner of the Cleveland Pipers, asked McLendon to coach his team after watching Tennessee State play in several tournaments. The Pipers then were in the amateur National Industrial Basketball League (NIBL), which was filled with company teams such as Phillips 66 Petroleum Company, Caterpillar Tractor, and the New York Tuck Tapers (the team Lenny Wilkens could have played for had he turned down the St. Louis Hawks). Sweeney, the owner of a Cleveland plumbing company, was attempting a bold move in a league of white college stars. Not only did he want to hire McLendon, he also assumed that some Tennessee State stars would come along with him.

"I was the general manager and there were three daily newspapers [at the time]—the *Press*, the *News*, and the *Plain Dealer*," said Mike Cleary, now executive director of the National Association of College Directors of Athletics. "We went out with the sports editors, plus the NBC and ABC affiliates, and said, 'We're thinking of hiring a black coach. What do you think?' They said, 'You're nuts. Cleveland's not ready.' That made Ed even more [eager to] say 'we're hiring him.'"

McLendon accepted the job because he had been "one of the people yelling the loudest" about the lack of black head professional coaches, and being a member of the NIBL was the accepted step between college and professional ball. Both white and black followers of basketball wondered if white players would respond to a black coach. "I thought it was an interesting challenge," McLendon said.

The Pipers jumped into integration full bore, with a black coach, six black players (including Tennessee State stars Barnhill, Ben Warley, and Ron Hamilton), and seven white players. "We didn't do John any favors," Cleary said. "Of the white players, all of them were from below the Mason-Dixon line." Yet, "We did not have one moment of racial conflict on this team. In fairness, if there was any knock on John, it was he was so easy on the white players."

One of the white players was Gene Tormohlen, a former University of Tennessee star who in 1959 had been drafted by Syracuse in the second round. Tormohlen, who later played six years in the NBA and who now is the top scout for the Los Angeles Lakers, believed that he needed to "fine-tune my game" a little before trying out for an NBA team, so he accepted McLendon's and Cleary's offer to play for Cleveland. The team arranged for him to get a job in recreation, and in return he played for the Pipers.

"When I first met with Johnny I didn't know what to expect, but he was an offensive coach," Tormohlen said. "He believed in what the Lakers did when Kareem [Abdul-Jabbar] and Magic [Johnson] were there. The training camp the first year, we worked out three times a day, and his workouts weren't easy. He had everybody in shape because that was his philosophy: 'We're going to run the ball.'"

Although the Pipers were relatively inexperienced, they compiled the league's best record, 24-10. McLendon's running game produced four of the league's top seven scorers. Then the Pipers won the week-long AAU national tournament in Denver, upset the phenomenal 1960 Olympic team that included Jerry West and Oscar Robertson in an exhibition game, and swept eight games during a three-week tour of Russia. The experience of McLendon leading an integrated team had been an unqualified success.

"He was a quiet, mild-mannered human being," Tormohlen said. "I'm sure he got upset with us, but if you get beat Saturday and go to church on Sunday, he said you were okay. No yelling or screaming. He would call me over and say, 'Gene, you're not getting rebounds like you did in college, and I want to know why.'

"This is something I don't know that I can say for any other coach in America. Everyone liked him—even if you didn't play. He was your friend. Johnny was someone everybody loved. Being in pro basketball for thirty years, I've never heard anyone say anything bad about Johnny McLendon."

After the season Sweeney's financial problems caused him to sell the team to Steinbrenner, the son of a wealthy shipbuilder. Steinbrenner quickly had the team enter the new American Basketball League that had been founded by Harlem Globetrotters owner Abe Saperstein in response to the NBA rebuffing his efforts to own his first West Coast franchise. (Bob Short was instead allowed to move the Minneapolis Lakers to Los Angeles in 1960.) Cleary said Cleveland joined the ABL because Saperstein "was willing to give us seven or eight doubleheaders with the Globetrotters, which assured a full house." Saperstein also jazzed up the league by conceiving the 3-point basket, now an NBA fixture. "Abe bought a fight bell for every franchise and every time a guy hit a 3-pointer, we rang the bell," Cleary said. "It really caught on. It was corny, but it was good." Since McLendon continued as the Pipers' coach, he became the first black coach of an integrated professional team. [Pop Gates had been the first African-American professional coach with the NBL's Dayton Rens in the 1948–49 season, but his players were his teammates from the all-black New York Rens.]

As the owner of the New York Yankees baseball team since 1973, Steinbrenner has developed a reputation for firing managers or interfering so much that they resign. "He was exactly the same then as he is now," McLendon said in 1992.

The makeup of the team had changed somewhat from the year before. Tormohlen was traded to Kansas City and the Pipers lured Barnett from the NBA's Syracuse Nationals. Did Steinbrenner interfere with the team roster? "Oh, yes, of course," McLendon said. "That's typical. One time he took one of my players and sold him at halftime to the team we were playing." That player, Grady McCollum, was coveted by Red Rocha, who coached the team from Hawaii. "Red wanted Grady on his team and Steinbrenner decided this was a time to make a little cash. . . . We were in the room at halftime and I asked him not to come in the locker room at halftime. I said I like to keep that between myself and my team, and he agreed to that. But on this occasion, he came to the dressing [room] and got my eye and said he wanted to see Grady. "I said, 'See what George wants,' and Grady came back in tears and said, 'He sold me to Hawaii.' All the players were upset. We beat them real good and I told Grady he didn't have to play against his teammates. I told him we'll take them to court."

The Pipers were one of the ABL's best teams in the first half of the season, losing the midseason playoffs to Kansas City by only one game. McLendon resigned on January 30, 1962, with a 26-27 record after losing seven of the previous nine games. From news reports in the *Cleveland Plain Dealer* it's apparent that he actually had stepped down because he had taken his players' side in a dispute with Steinbrenner and the team's other owners.

Earlier in January several unnamed players had publicly objected to their pay being late and "threatened a rebellion," a *Plain Dealer* article said. "Steinbrenner asked the players to refute this story." At the urging of one of the Pipers players, Jack Adams, a rebuttal was signed by the players. Then McLendon came out on the side of the players and said he was considering resigning. "McLendon, whose statement to the newspapers accused Steinbrenner of pressuring the players into signing their statement, said he deliberated a long time before making his charge. 'I don't like to hurt basketball,' declared the coach. 'If today's talks are satisfactory in terms of the future then there is the possibility I'll be staying.'"

McLendon and Steinbrenner had met for several hours, and Steinbrenner was quoted saying, "I'm hoping that John decides to stay. It was an enlightening afternoon."[1] McLendon resigned, and Bill Sharman, the former Boston Celtics great, immediately was named to replace him. The turmoil hadn't stopped, though, because the next day Steinbrenner sold the Pipers for about $175,000 to Ralph Wilson, who already owned the Buffalo Bills football team. A few days later McLendon was named vice president of the Pipers, who went 19-11 under Sharman and went on to win the league championship. Cleary said Steinbrenner really irritated McLendon, remembering that, "He was tough on John, and John wasn't used to handling a Steinbrenner-like personality." But McLendon said, "I never let him get to me. He was quite annoying, but in the back of his mind he wanted his team to win. But he just had ways to upset the team. He wanted to make friends with the players but that [McCollum] incident gave them the distance [from Steinbrenner] and I don't think he overcame it."

Meanwhile, McLendon worked for the state department for six months, returned to Tennessee State as an assistant coach to help his successor and former player Harold Hunter, was head coach at Kentucky State for three years, then was hired by Cleveland State's president, Dr. Harold Enarson, as the first black coach at a predominantly white college.

After three seasons there, McLendon accepted an offer in 1969 to coach the Denver Rockets in the American Basketball Association, the forerunners of today's Denver Nuggets. While there he had the distinction of being the first professional coach of Spencer Haywood, who as a nineteen-year-old had led the United States to an Olympic gold medal in 1968 after several big-name stars such as Kareem Abdul-Jabbar had decided not to participate in the Olympic games. Haywood decided not to return to the University of Detroit and instead signed with Denver, since he already had a good relationship with McLendon (who had been an assistant coach on the Olympic team). A year later Haywood revolutionized professional basketball by winning a legal battle that forced the NBA to let him play for Seattle even though his college class had not yet graduated. Haywood thus became the first "hardship" case that was allowed, which paved the way for college stars such as Magic Johnson and Isiah Thomas to turn professional early and led to the existence of "early entries" in the current NBA draft.

McLendon implemented his usual fast-paced offense and grueling preseason conditioning drills. Because of the thin air in Denver, it is an especially tough place to play fastbreak ball. Which only gave McLendon more reason to tout the fastbreak, because he figured visiting opponents would be left gasping for air. Haywood said that he, guard Floyd Theard [who played for McLendon at Cleveland State], center Lonnie Lynn [a staunch McLendon ally], and veteran center Byron Beck all supported McLendon's methods, which included running around Green Lake in Denver. Otherwise, however, the team largely objected to his training regimen, and first-round draft pick Bob Presley, a seven-foot center, was so out of shape that McLendon cut him and instead retained Lynn as a backup center-forward.

"Coach always encouraged me," Lynn said. "I've got a few trophies sitting around my house, have a scrapbook with some electrifying write-ups. But the greatest compliment I ever got was when John McLendon chose me to be on his team. That showed me that I could play. That means everything in the world to me."

Unfortunately, many Rockets didn't share his loyalty. Haywood believes it was difficult for some players—both white and black—to take directions from a black coach, and McLendon's conditioning drills irritated them. "The style was a running style and pressing defense," Haywood said. "You have to be in tremendous shape and have to put your body through rigorous training to do that, and most people don't know how to do that. That's when you separate men from the boys, and a lot of boys stepped up, both white and black." Then Haywood imitated the whining he used to hear from his teammates: "Oh, I got blisters on my feet. He's running us too hard. How can I make it around this big lake?"

McLendon said he was confronted with two major problems in Denver that prevented him from getting the players he wanted. He had been told that none of the players had no-cut contracts, "But when I announced we were to be the Celtics of the West, the two starting guards [Lonnie Wright and Larry Jones] said running was for horses and automobiles," McLendon said. "I tried to cut them and then found they had no-cut contracts."

The other restriction was that the owners had decided to keep the roster exactly racially balanced at six black players and six white ones. The situation prevented him from bringing in former Tennessee State star John Barnhill, who is black, and guard Larry Brown, who is white and who led the ABA in assists that season. McLendon said the team's Chairman of the Board Bill Ringsby never directly told him about the six-and-six policy. "All they did was avoid the imbalance," McLendon said. "I had a chance to get Larry Brown but they just said, 'We don't have the money.' This was never written down, but you finally get the message. I never even confronted them with it."

The Rockets' schedule was another high hurdle to climb, because Denver opened the season playing an absurd twenty-one of its first twenty-eight games on the road. Out of that mess McLendon managed only a 9-19 record, and years later he cracked that if Haywood, who averaged 30 points per game that season, hadn't been playing for him, "I would have been 0-28."

The Rockets fired McLendon on December 9, 1969, and replaced him with thirty-five-year-old Joe Belmont, a former ABA referee who had directed the team's marketing and scouting activities. Belmont's only previous coaching experience had been leading Duke University's freshman team in 1957. Belmont moved Beck from forward to center and did the reverse with Haywood. Lynn and Theard were released, and the Rockets took off on the way to a 42-14 record under Belmont. They even won the Western Division with an overall 51-33 record.

On the surface that reversal of fortune makes McLendon look bad in comparison. But Haywood and Lynn take a different perspective—that Belmont merely benefited from McLendon's conditioning program and a highly favorable part of the schedule that had Denver playing fourteen of its next nineteen games at home. "He [McLendon] did all the training, he put the team together," Haywood said. "It was such a strong influence on the team that you could take a referee and make him a coach, and become the second-best team in the league. That's ridiculous." Belmont lasted only thirteen games the next season, eventually leaving with a 3-10 record.

Getting fired turned out to be a blessing for John McLendon. "I was spoiled by the Industrial League experience," McLendon said. "That was the best; college is next. I'm really not cut out for professional coaching. You don't have enough control over your team and I depend on the player-coach relationship, and this type of relationship is practically destroyed. They might be sold, and now with the free-agent system, you don't have enough control over who you have."

A few days after McLendon was fired Converse shoes vice president Grady Lewis offered McLendon a position as the company's representative, telling him "Whatever is good for basketball, and good for Converse, you do—and do it anywhere around the world." McLendon thoroughly enjoyed being Converse's roving ambassador for twenty years. He eventually retired from Converse, but never retired from basketball. "It's just a great game," he said. "You had to be highly keyed up and at the same time perfectly relaxed."

Until he died in 1999 at age eighty-four, McLendon was a fixture at the CIAA tournament he helped create and taught a class at Cleveland State titled "The History of Sports and the Role of Minorities in Its Development." His sharp recall of events made him an essential resource for reporters interested in basketball history, and he conveyed that history himself by writing several articles, including a major piece about his relationship with Naismith for the *New York Times* in 1996.

There aren't enough words to describe what the game of basketball gave to John McLendon, and there aren't enough to describe what he gave back.

The Coming of the Superstars

The black NBA players of the early 1950s were carefully selected for their skills on the court and their deportment off of it, and most didn't botch the opportunities that came their way. Not only did they give maximum effort when they played, they were well aware of the fact that their reputations as solid citizens would ease the way for black players who hoped to follow them into professional ball. The Chuck Coopers, Earl Lloyds, and Bob Wilsons of those early years did not falter as they cleared the lane in the NBA for black players of the future.

Unlike baseball, however, in which black stars such as Jackie Robinson, Larry Doby, Monte Irvin, and Roy Campanella first cracked the color barrier, none of the NBA's black pioneers were extraordinarily talented. It may be that the nature of baseball—more of a one-on-one game of pitcher versus batter—gave individuals more of an opportunity to stand out. In contrast, basketball in the 1950s demanded a team-oriented approach, and not passing to a black teammate easily could limit his scoring. Or maybe the absence of early black stars merely reflects their athletic skill. Don Barksdale had been a superstar talent in the 1940s, but World War II and the NBA's unwritten ban on black players until 1950 consumed his best years as a player. He and the popular Sweetwater Clifton played in one NBA All-Star Game apiece, yet neither of them left a lasting imprint on the professional game.

That kind of achievement was left to the superstars of basketball, and the NBA's black superstars began to enter the league in a trickle in the mid-1950s. They were the players who significantly changed and popularized the game by bringing their unique skills, styles, and personalities to the court, and when fans watch the NBA of the twenty-first century, unbeknownst to many of them they also are watching the legacy of its first black stars. There would be no Alonzo Mourning if there hadn't been a Bill Russell, who made interior defense and shot-blocking a science as the defensive anchor of eleven NBA championship teams. There would be no Vince Carter soaring in for a reverse dunk had there not been an Elgin Baylor, who bobbed his head with a distinctive nervous tick then levitated in the lane for shots and rebounds. There would not have been a six-foot-nine Magic Johnson leading the Los Angeles Lakers' "Showtime" in the 1980s and 1990s had there not been another tall playmaker named Oscar Robertson after whom Johnson could pattern his game. Today's Lamar Odom, the six-ten Los Angeles Clippers star, developed much of his versatility by emulating Johnson, which makes Odom a second-generation descendant of Robertson's. However, there probably never will be another Wilt Chamberlain—a player whose incredible size, agility, and force of will allowed him to *average* 50 points a game during an entire season.

Not only did these pioneers change the way professional basketball was played and remembered, their status and outspokenness helped knock down racial barriers encountered by all black players. Less-talented players certainly felt insulted by racist practices in the South, felt boxed in by the unspoken quota that limited their numbers, and felt frustrated by their lack of coaching and front-office opportunities. But there was little or nothing they could do to change such things until black players with superstar status arrived and asserted themselves.

Earl Lloyd had dealt with racial incidents in the early 1950s, before *Brown vs. Board of Education* was handed down, and back then he never considered sitting out a game to protest them. "You never thought about that," he said. "I came through an era where that was a way of life for me. Russell came through an era where the law had said, 'You can't do this.' But in 1952, there was no law. Plus, when you do that kind of thing you'd better have some stature. When Russell does that kind of thing, people [accept] that. But if I do that . . ."

For instance, on January 16, 1959, Baylor, the NBA's first great black scorer, refused to play in a regular-season game in Charleston, West Virginia, after he and two black teammates, Boo Ellis and Ed Fleming, were denied rooms at the Daniel Boone hotel and couldn't find a restaurant that would serve them. Baylor sat out the game, and the Lakers lost to Cincinnati.

Baylor did so not to make a political statement but as a matter of individual principle, and every time a star player took such a stance it helped chip away at discrimination. "When you do something you hope something good will come out of it, that people will recognize it and be conscious of what's going on in this country," Baylor said. "If it serves its purpose, great. . . . At the time when you're being embarrassed or humiliated, you're not thinking 'I have to do this for everybody else.' You're just thinking about what's happening to you.

"It was just an unfortunate incident. We didn't think it would happen because we were assured we would all stay together. The owner, Bob Short, had a letter that made it perfectly clear we would eat together and stay together, because that was brought up before we went there. In fact, for any of the [other] Southern cities [where we were scheduled to play]. The owner, Short, was upset about it and I was upset and a lot of people were upset. But it did change things."

The next year Baylor flew back to Charleston with teammate Hot Rod Hundley, a former University of West Virginia star, to play in an annual game pitting professionals against college players. "I met with people in the NAACP [National Association for the Advancement of Colored People] and there were a lot of changes," Baylor said. "I don't know if it was because of me or if they were already in motion. I was well received when I was introduced and it went great. I had fun."

On October 17, 1961, Russell, who singlehandedly revolutionized the center position, and all the other black players on the Boston Celtics and St. Louis Hawks teams, refused to play an exhibition game in Lexington, Kentucky, after the restaurant at the Phoenix Hotel refused to serve several of them. The Celtics involved were Russell, Al Butler, Sam Jones, K. C. Jones, and Tom Sanders; the Hawks were Cleo Hill and Woody Sauldsberry.

Normally Celtics owner Walter Brown didn't schedule games where his black players had to contend with discriminatory conditions, but this exhibition game was being played to honor two former University of Kentucky stars, Boston's Frank Ramsey and St. Louis's Cliff Hagan. Brown had been assured the Phoenix Hotel where the Celtics were staying would serve meals to the black players even though other restaurants wouldn't. When Sam Jones and Satch Sanders went to the hotel restaurant a waitress refused to serve them. They informed their black teammates, which eventually resulted in a meeting with Auerbach. While that took place, K. C. Jones watched another example of segregation unfold.

"Russell's telling the story and Satch and Sam are sitting

there," K. C. recalled. "I look out the window and I see this black player from St. Louis walk across the street [toward a restaurant]. I say, 'Sam, watch this.' In about a minute, he's coming back across the street. We were all hurt [about being refused] but it was very visible with Sam. Red said, 'Wouldn't it be better if you played here and let it be known to the press after the game?' Bill said, 'No, I think it would be best if we go home.' Red said all right, and I think Red took us to the airport."

Throughout the turbulent Civil Rights era and the social upheaval during the Vietnam War, Russell continued to speak out against racism. In fact, one time he spoke out so boldly that a Boston newspaper refused to print what he had said. "My paper was an afternoon newspaper, which gave me great latitude on my deadline," said George Sullivan, who covered the Celtics for the *Boston Herald Traveler* through the 1960s. "I often was the last guy out of the locker room and that was Russell's style, too, and we shared many a cab. One day after practice he said 'Boston is the most racist city in the United States.' I wasn't sure if he was talking on the record, so I said, 'Say that again and I'll write it. And Russ said, 'Your paper hasn't got the guts to run that story!' "

Around that time an incendiary politician in South Boston, Louise Day Hicks, was stirring up violent protests against school busing in her community, which was one of the reasons Russell called Boston the most racist city in the nation. "I wrote the story," Sullivan said. "My sports editor almost had cardiac arrest: 'What a story!' He rushed to the managing editor, who said the same. Then I was told the publisher said, 'It is a great story. George deserves a bonus, but it would further inflame the town.' "

So the story was "killed," meaning the *Globe* refused to print it. "When I walked to the locker room the next day, Bill held up the newspaper and said, 'I've been reading this back and forth. I can't find the story,' " Sullivan recalled. "Russell cackles when he laughs, and he really cackled that time. He had me. So I said, 'For once in your life, you're right.' "

In some circles Russell's boldness brought him great respect. But it also made him the lightning rod for racists, to the degree that once during a break-in of his suburban Boston home, invaders trashed his house, destroyed many of his trophies, and defecated in his bed.

The players that follow carried superstar status on their shoulders. Upon them rode the fortunes of NBA players—both black and white—of years to come, because they and white superstars such as Jumping Joe Fulks, George Mikan, and Bob Cousy set the standard for greatness. Taken in the chronological order in which they entered the NBA, the following black pioneers were the first to carry the superstar label.

Maurice Stokes (1955–58)

If a fluke brain injury hadn't ended his career after three seasons and eventually led to the end of his life when he was only thirty-six, Maurice Stokes might be considered the NBA's ultimate superstar. A six-seven forward-center, he carried about 260 pounds filled with power, finesse, and creativity—a combination seldom seen since his career tragically ended during the 1958 playoffs.

Stokes was an All-American at unbelievably small St. Francis College in the beautiful countryside of Loretta, Pennsylvania; St. Francis had only 658 students when he led the Red flash to the NIT Final Four in 1955. He loved the school so much that in his will Stokes asked to be buried on campus. Stokes is the only person interred there who was not a Franciscan priest. When the Rochester Royals (the long ago forerunner of the Sacramento Kings franchise) made him their first pick of the 1955 draft, the typical complaint against black players was that they weren't highly skilled on offense. This sounds unfathomable today, but until Stokes joined the league no prolific scorers could be found among the black NBA players who had preceded him. The player to fit that description closest was Don Barksdale, and his highest scoring average was only 13.8 points.

However, Chuck Cooper, who had mentored Stokes in Pittsburgh, knew that the NBA was on his horizon and believed that when Stokes arrived, the image of black players would change. Harold Brown, Cooper's best friend, recalled black players' seemingly limited offensive skills being the topic of conversation among several white players in the early 1950s. "Chuck would be arguing with them about how good [black players] were," Brown said. "When Mo came out of college, Chuck told them ahead of time 'this is a man who's going to show you how it's done.'"

Indeed he did, in every aspect of play from 1955 to 1958. In his first NBA game on November 5, 1955, Stokes produced 32 points, 20 rebounds, and 8 assists, totals that weren't an aberration. The numbers simply typified his extraordinary skill in every aspect of the game. Considering Stokes's size, only the Hall of Fame's six-five Oscar Robertson and six-nine Magic Johnson compare. "Maurice had pretty much the same characteristics as Oscar," said Jack Twyman, who played basketball in Pittsburgh's Mellon Park with Stokes and was his and Robertson's NBA teammate. "Big, strong, six-eight, played at 260 to 270 pounds, very agile. He was a guy who could rebound at one end and dribble through three or four guys and lay it in at the other end. Very quick. A good shooter." If Stokes had had a normal career, there's no doubt in Twyman's mind that he would have been a Hall of Famer. "In fact, I'm not so darn sure he shouldn't be in the Hall of Fame anyway," Twyman said. "No question, he should have been one of the top players in the game. He was Magic before Magic. He could play pivot, forward, bring a ball down as a guard. He was all over the court."

Ed Fleming knew Stokes's game and Stokes the person better than anyone. They were best friends from the time they were grade schoolers living a block from each other in Pittsburgh. He, Stokes, and Twyman all played two years with the Rochester Royals before Fleming was traded to Minneapolis, where Baylor was his teammate.

"If you were playing with Maurice and he got the rebound, your best move would be to take off and go because he didn't need you to help him bring the ball down," Fleming said. Plus, Stokes had all the shots—a two-hand set shot he first learned by watching Sweetwater Clifton on television, the jumper, the drive, and exceptional timing on the offensive boards.

Unlike many great offensive players who seem allergic to playing defense, Stokes was a force there, too. "You couldn't manhandle him and at that time in the pros, there wasn't anyone around that could match him in size and quickness and finesse," Fleming said. "I can remember a reporter asking me on the plane, since I had played with Baylor and Stokes, which was better. My response was that I thought Maurice could stop Elgin but Elgin couldn't stop Maurice."

Stokes, whose team moved from Rochester to Cincinnati after his second season, was selected to play in the All-Star Game all three of his NBA seasons, during which he averaged 16.4 points, 17.3 rebounds, and 5.3 assists. During each of his seasons he ranked among the league's top three in rebounds and among its top nine in assists, a feat of versatility that even Oscar Robertson never matched.

On March 12, 1958, Cincinnati was to play its season finale in Minneapolis in a matchup between teams that were tied for the last playoff berth. Prior to the game three old friends from Pittsburgh, the Lakers' Fleming and Cincinnati's Stokes and Dick Ricketts, got together for a meal. No one could have known it at the time, but a conversation they had foreshadowed Stokes's fate. "We went out to eat in Minneapolis together," Fleming said. "Maurice was walking with his head tilted back a bit and I said. 'What's wrong with you?' He said he had a cyst or boil on his neck. I looked and said, 'Are you supposed to be playing with that?' He probably should not have been playing, and I recall he got hit on it that night. They beat us, and the next night they went to Detroit, and he got it hit again."

In the Minneapolis game Stokes accidentally was knocked down and his head smacked the floor. After resting for a while he finished that game, and three nights later gave a subpar, 12-point, 10-rebound performance in the playoff opener in Detroit. What followed constitutes one of the worst tragedies in professional sports history. A few hours later, during the team's flight back to Cincinnati, Stokes vomited repeatedly, suffered convulsions, and came close to dying, which prompted teammate Richie Regan to informally baptize him during the flight. He was paralyzed for the next twelve years until he died of a heart attack on April 6, 1970, in Cincinnati.

In the last three years of his life, Stokes painstakingly typed out his unpublished autobiography from his bed in Good Samaritan Hospital in Cincinnati. Here's how he described what transpired after his last NBA game: "When we got back to the hotel, we went across the street to have some beer before we went to the airport. Although I had not played well, I never had any idea that there was something wrong. But when we arrived at the airport, I began to feel sick and weak. I remember some of the ballplayers saying, 'Try and make it back to Cincinnati.' About 10 minutes before we were to board, I told Dick Ricketts that I felt like I was going to die. When we were in the air for about 10 minutes, I could not get my breath. The airline stewardess gave me some oxygen, which saved my life. Also, at that time I began to perspire profusely. While we were in the air, they called ahead for an ambulance to be at the airport. I don't remember getting into the ambulance. At that time I would regain consciousness for a while and then I would black out."[1]

Fleming was living at the Talmadge Hotel in Minneapolis and had gone out for the evening. When he returned to his room that night several messages from his parents and Ricketts were waiting, and through calls to them he learned that Stokes was seriously ill. By then it was late Saturday night or Sunday morning, and on Monday morning Fleming drove to Covington, Kentucky, to see his stricken friend in St. Elizabeth's Hospital near the Cincinnati airport.

"When I got there, Maurice was packed in ice, in and out of consciousness," Fleming said. "I just couldn't stay in the room. He started to cry, and I had to go in the hall. It was very emotional for me. His body was in ice and he had a temperature of 104. He was in bad shape.

"I knew he had gotten sick, and I had thought he would be okay. I can remember going out in the hall at St. Elizabeth's Hospital. There was a statue of the Blessed Virgin Mary, and if I hadn't held onto that, I would have passed out."

Stokes was in a coma for six weeks. The fall in the Minneapolis game had caused a swelling in the membrane around his brain, a condition called post-traumatic encephalopathy. For the rest of his life Stokes was a living contradiction. His mental acuity was fine—he was an avid reader, a reflective thinker, had a high appreciation of nature's beauty, and retained a sharp sense of humor. Physically, however, Stokes endured years of grueling therapy just to be able to slowly walk along parallel bars with braces on his arms. He gained limited use of his hands to make ceramics and use an electric typewriter, and could mouth words comprehensible only to those who visited him often.

Throughout that time Twyman was his lifeblood, after voluntarily becoming Stokes's legal guardian. Twyman handled his legal and financial affairs, and helped arrange fundraisers to pay Stokes's enormous medical bills. One of Twyman's creations was a benefit game between NBA players held annually at Kutsher's Country Club in the Catskill Mountains. Even after Stokes died the benefit raised money for indigent former NBA players until its finale in 1999. In a time when America was torn by racial strife, the relationship between Twyman, who is white, and Stokes was a beacon of inspiration.

"Jack did everything, and I have nothing but the greatest admiration for his taking care of Maurice as his brother," Fleming said. "When you say I am my brother's keeper, there was no better example than that." Stokes was so appreciative that in his will he left half of his estate to St. Francis College in honor of Twyman, "without whose prolonged and arduous work no estate would be available for me to give."

In return Stokes was the best example of courage that Twyman ever saw. "By far, his most outstanding characteristic was that in twelve years, I have never seen him have a down day," Twyman said. "I never failed to see him vote in any election—local, state, or national. I have never seen him not want to help someone who came to visit him. I have never seen him not have a smile on his face. So you can imagine the impact that he had on people like his nurses, on me or on people who came to visit."

One of those visitors was future star forward Chet Walker. Growing up in Benton Harbor, Michigan, Walker had watched a few of Stokes's games on a "little bitty black and white TV" and had been greatly impressed by Stokes's versatility, especially for his size. "In a way, I patterned myself after him," Walker said. "I liked to drive across the middle and hang, the way he did. And he had this nice fade-away jumper on the baseline I used to shoot a lot."

Walker, who used those moves to become an All-American at Bradley and a seven-time NBA All-Star, had "the privilege" of visiting Stokes in the hospital as a rookie during the 1962–63 season. Walker's coach, Alex Hannum, had played with Stokes and brought Walker to the hospital in Cincinnati to meet his idol. "Even though he couldn't speak, he recognized me and knew who I was," Walker said. "I was very surprised. I was just out of college and I was young and immature and sometimes as a young player, you don't realize how you affect other people. I was a college All-American but didn't realize a man of Maurice's status would be impressed by me."

Even though Stokes was virtually paralyzed he was a source of strength for his former teammate, Jack McMahon. "When I was coaching Cincinnati, whenever I'd get down I'd go see Maurice and he was the greatest tonic anyone in the world could have," McMahon said. "Here's a guy who everything in the world went bad for. You talk about superstars. Everybody around him was better from being around him. . . . Every time he'd see me he'd get such a laugh around his face because I had put on weight and he remembered me as a 180-pound basketball player. So each year I'm getting fatter. One time I saw him in the Catskills and I knew every time I saw him he was going to laugh. He said to me, 'It's amazing how far the human skin can stretch.' I love that guy. He's among the all-time great persons."

Bill Russell (1956–69)

Beginning in 1950 when coach Red Auerbach joined the Boston Celtics, he began to assemble a team of championship caliber. In five quick seasons shrewd player acquisition had brought his team a wealth of offensive players—Cousy, Bill Sharman, Frank Ramsay, and Ed Macauley—that led the NBA in scoring and made the playoffs every year. But they could never get to the NBA Finals because they had one glaring fault. "We had everything but the ball," Auerbach said. "We had shooters, quickness. We had smarts. We had everything but on the crucial plays in the game, coming March and April, we couldn't get the ball. Our center was Ed Macauley, who soaking wet was 185 pounds."

As a result, on April 29, 1956, the Celtics executed the second-most significant trade in sports history, behind only Babe Ruth's acquisition by the New York Yankees. The Celtics traded Macauley and the draft rights to Cliff Hagan to St. Louis for the draft rights to Bill Russell, the six-ten center whose shot-blocking and rebounding had led the University of San Francisco to consecutive NCAA titles. The fact that Boston had given up two future members of the Basketball Hall of Fame is inconsequential. That trade will forever be considered a landslide in the Celtics' favor because with Russell they won eleven of the next thirteen NBA championships, a feat that one can safely predict will never be equaled in any major sport.

There had been excellent, even great, defensive players before Russell, but he raised defense to a higher dimension. He made it a weapon. "Russell was a brilliant guy, and he made shot-blocking an art . . . as he did rebounding," Auerbach said. "He was the greatest rebounder in the game, ever, far and away." With him guarding the basket the Celtics became unstoppable, and Russell's almost maniacal will to win gave them an intangible that can't be quantified. Without him the Celtics probably could have made up the 15 points per game he contributed, but they never could have replaced the 22.5 rebounds per game he snatched, the innumerable shots whose direction he reversed (blocked shot statistics weren't kept until 1973), the extra possessions Boston got because Russell just tapped shots away so he or a teammate could retrieve the rebound, or the psychological damage he inflicted on opponents.

Perhaps John Kundla, who coached George Mikan and the Minneapolis Lakers to five NBA championships, came closest to describing Russell's impact after he had carried Boston to a 3-0 lead in the 1959 NBA Finals (despite averaging only 7 points in those games). "He's the guy who has whipped us badly psychologically," Kundla said. "A man has it bother him when his opponent scores points. But he feels that sooner or later the guy will miss and he will start scoring. But Russell has our club worrying every second. It's getting so every one of the five men on the court thinks Russell is covering him on every play. I never sensed that a defensive player could mean so much to the game until Russell appeared."[2]

Russell could intimidate an entire team because he was so quick and had so much range that opponents must have felt he had the wingspan of a condor. He might tip away your lay-up, then next time down the court block your 15-footer. "He made shooters shoot so quick, take bad shots, arch the ball a little higher, and he'd scare them," Sharman said.

Russell's mastery of defense stemmed from his intellectual approach to the game, an astute analysis of basketball that began with his USF and Boston teammate, K. C. Jones. Like a baby handling an object for the first time, as curious college players they looked at the game of basketball from every angle and developed unique theories on defense that eventually became the bedrock of the Celtics' dynasty. From 1958 to 1967 they were the "Mr. Inside" and "Mr. Outside" of Boston's defense, with Jones regularly defending outstanding guards such as Oscar Robertson and Jerry West.

To Russell the key to producing an excellent defense is understanding that it's not easily detected. "In basketball, there are subtle skills and there are obvious skills," Russell said. "The obvious skills are ones they keep stats on—assists, rebounds, steals, blocks, points, field goal percentage, free-throw percentage. Then there are subtle skills. Good defense—they don't chart that." What about statistics compiled for blocked shots? "Blocking shots is the last line of defense," he said. "Everything else has failed."

One of Russell's basic tenets was that there were "soft" points and "hard" points during a game. The soft points were ones he accepted that a foe invariably would score, but the hard points— perhaps a power forward averaging 8 points gets 18 instead— probably will decide the game. "Those are bonuses," Russell said. If he minimized them the Celtics usually won.

Another Russell philosophy is that although a basketball play invariably is finished by a vertical move, the game actually is dominated by horizontal moves. "If you add up the shots and rebounds, made and missed, you've taken up about three minutes of a forty-eight-minute game," he said. "What happens to the other forty-five? All we see is the end result. It's like seeing a balloon and not seeing people putting the air in it."

Russell kept copious mental notes about opponents' offensive habits, which in some ways were easier to assemble than in today's era of videotape and a twenty-nine-team league. Only eight or nine teams were in the league during Russell's first ten seasons, which meant Boston played at least ten games against each opponent during the regular season. Because there were many doubleheaders, Russell could watch two other teams play before or after the Celtics played their own games. Consequently, Celtics' opponents were an intimate enemy, and Russell knew their moves well enough to often dictate what an offensive player would do with the ball.

"I would decide what kind of shot he was going to take, not him," Russell said. "You're right-handed and you like to shoot the jump shot after taking one dribble. The first thing I do is approach you on the right side and make you go left, which is the least comfortable of the two ways for you. When you go left, you don't stop after taking a single dribble. You might take two dribbles, or you might go all the way [to the basket]. I make you go left and then I play you to do what you normally do."

Even when Russell made a fundamental mistake, his recovery skills could shock an opponent. Clyde Lovellette, one of the most potent scoring big men of the 1950s, experienced that recovery one time after he was convinced he had beaten Russell. "His first step was as quick as I've seen, as quick as the fastest runner you could think of," said Lovellette, who was a burly six-nine center-forward. "I remember one time very clearly in Boston. I caught the ball at the top of the circle. I gave a fake and zoom, he goes in the air. I figure I can take a couple bounces and be at the basket. You have to remember—he was in the air when I started my drive. He came down and blocked my shot, and I must have been ten feet from him when I started down the floor."

"Well, I don't remember that specific play," Russell said about forty years later, "but I know why that happened. I used to practice landing." He would land in a flex position, pivot on one leg to change direction, then spring off that leg. "And that first step is about eight feet [long]," Russell said.

His greatest challenge was defending the enormously talented Wilt Chamberlain, a Goliath of his day at seven-foot-one, 275 pounds (three inches and 55 pounds bigger than Russell), who had the athletic skills of a decathlete.

"There were players you couldn't outsmart," Russell said. "Wilt was one. He was really smart, which created all kinds of problems—big, strong, fast, great ability, and smart. That's a load." Russell deduced that he couldn't challenge Chamberlain vertically, but that Chamberlain's weakness (to use the term very loosely) was his lateral movement, "and the nights that I got him to play lateral more than vertical, we [won] the game," Russell said. "No matter what it looks like or how many points he got, it doesn't make any difference." No one shut Wilt down, so Russell's goal was to keep him significantly below his season average and to limit him to soft points. "Now, if he gets 60 of them, I'm hurting," Russell joked.

Sometimes their one-on-one matchup evolved into a mental chess match that Russell especially loved to engage in against the greatest players. It wasn't planned; it just happened, and sometimes Wilt was the protagonist. "You couldn't do the same thing to him two nights in a row," Russell said. "He had this fade-away jump shot. He would fade away and shoot the shot, then I got to the point that I could get to it. I could block three or four out of ten. And so he made an adjustment. He rubbed his shoulder against me and then would go up, and then my hand would come to here [Wilt's wrist] and not to the ball. So that went on two or three games, and then I noticed what he was doing. So when I'd get up to him I'd turn so he couldn't rub me." And Russell, who was sitting in a chair while explaining this, made the subtlest turn away from his interviewer, maybe a two-inch adjustment.

Although Russell and Chamberlain were good friends off the court, there also was pride involved in their relationship. For instance, in 1965 after Chamberlain became the first NBA player to sign for a $100,000 salary, Russell asked for a raise. He wasn't greedy about it; he just requested and received $100,001.

An overlooked yet critically important aspect of Russell's skills was his uncanny passing ability. He prided himself on being the Celtics' second-best passer (Cousy, of course, was the best), averaged 4.3 assists during his career, and few NBA followers recall that Russell ranked among the league's top 10 in assists for four different seasons. The timing of his passing was impeccable. "It's not just throwing the pass; it's getting it into your rhythm to shoot it," said Jack McMahon, who played and coached against Russell.

Just like with defense, Russell took special pleasure in understanding the subtleties of passing. "Most of our plays went through me so I had to be a good passer, and I knew how to run the plays from all five starters for us with the timing, the rhythm, the nuances," he said. That was important because if a teammate was having trouble running a play, Russell knew how to help him. "Like feeding the post," Russell said. "Not many guys are good at that. The pivot can help you by giving you the proper and big target. If I feel the man [defender] right here [behind his right ribcage] then I put the target out here [left hand extended]. That's easier for you. The pass doesn't have to be 100 percent accurate."

By understanding the subtleties of the game, having the physical ability to execute them, and possessing an unquenchable thirst for victory, Russell became the player who left the deepest imprint on professional basketball, regardless of era or color. "If I had to pick a ball club, I'd start with him and go from there," Lovellette said, surely reflecting a common opinion within the NBA.

Elgin Baylor (1958–71)

If one had to characterize the major difference between the NBA of the 1950s and the league in the year 2000, the concept of "playing in the air" must be considered the demarcation line. In the 1950s a ballhandler would dribble down the middle of the court and dish off a crisp bounce pass to a teammate for a lay-up. In 2000 that same fastbreak often is finished off with a lob pass over the rim that's turned into a powerful slam dunk by a player who seems to defy gravity.

The latter conjures up images of dunking masters such as Julius Erving, Dominique Wilkins, Michael Jordan, and Vince Carter, but the "Wright brother" for their later flights actually was Elgin Baylor, a Lakers phenomenon from 1958 (in Minneapolis) until his retirement in 1971 (in Los Angeles). Over a fourteen-season period, the six-foot-five forward averaged 27.4 points per game though he played on extremely painful knees during the last half of his career. He denies that he could helicopter over the court while defenders succumbed to the pull of gravity, but sometimes impressions are just as important as fact.

"Without warning Elgin Baylor would rise in the air and actually hover for what seemed like forever," *San Francisco Examiner* columnist Wells Twombly wrote after Baylor retired on November 4, 1971. "There was no escaping the obvious. Here was an athlete who practiced levitation. He did not have to return to the ground if he didn't want to. There was no logical way for the manner in which he behaved. Elg would leap into the smog-kissed atmosphere and he would hang there, suspended. He didn't have to go down if he didn't want to."[3]

Could Baylor actually hang in the air longer than other mortals?

"Yes, no question about it," said Chick Hearn, who in the year 2000 had broadcast Lakers games for forty years. "He got up high but he stayed up. The other guy went up with him but Elgin wouldn't shoot until the guy came down. For many years I thought he was the greatest player who ever lived, and at times I still do. He was doing things in the sixties that people are getting credit for in the nineties. Dr. J with his hanging moves and spins, Elgin was doing that in the sixties. He was a tremendous athlete. The best ability I've ever seen in terms of hanging in the air."

Which was a trait that Baylor denies is based on fact. Was there something different about him? "No, because I just think if two people are going to jump up in the air, maybe one guy might jump higher than the other guy but I don't see anyone staying up any longer than the other guy," Baylor said. "The difference is, you know when you're going to jump, the defensive guy doesn't. If the offensive guy hesitates on his drive when he goes to go up, the defensive guy is going to commit himself before the guy is off the ground. So naturally I'm [seemingly] going to be up longer than the defensive guy." Baylor considered it crucial to get the defender to jump before he did "because the guy doesn't know when I'm going to shoot. I would shoot on the way down, also. The guy makes a good defensive play and I see I can't get the shot off, I'm going to shoot it going down."

According to the basic tenets of basketball, a shooter should release the ball at the peak of his leap. But Baylor and a few other NBA stars to come—such as Michael Jordan and Mitch Richmond—had the extraordinary strength, balance, and coordination to shoot accurately while in their descent. Consequently, it looked like they were hanging in the air, and they badly messed up their defenders' timing.

During the Lakers-Celtics classic battles in the 1960s, Baylor often was guarded by Tom "Satch" Sanders, one of the finest defenders of his day, with Russell backing him up as a safety net. Yet many of Baylor's best games were played against Boston,

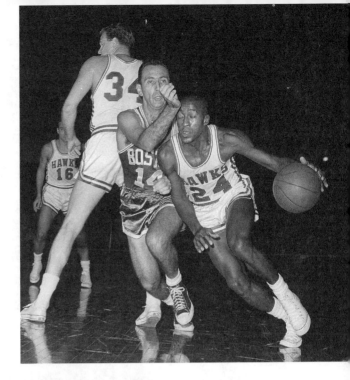

St. Louis Hawks rookie Cleo
Hill drives around Boston's
Bob Cousy in 1961. ©
Bettmann/CORBIS.

Elgin Baylor denied that he
could hang in the air longer
than humanly possible, but
Cincinnati defender Wayne
Embry probably disagreed
with him. Photo by Malcolm
W. Emmons.

Temple's rare left-handed backcourt of Guy Rodgers (*left*) and Hal Lear (*right*) was one of the best in college basketball history. While Rodgers became an NBA star, Lear's NBA career lasted only three games before he was released by Philadelphia and joined the Eastern League. Courtesy of Temple University.

Coach John McLendon stands in front of a portrait of his mentor, Dr. James Naismith, who invented the game of basketball. Taken at the Basketball Hall of Fame, of which both McLendon and Naismith are members. Courtesy, AP/Wide World Photos.

Maurice Stokes outreaches Boston's Tom Heinsohn for a rebound, 1958. Stokes was the NBA's first triple-threat big man because of his scoring, rebounding, and passing skills. Courtesy, AP/Wide World Photos.

Maurice Stokes underwent years of agonizing physical therapy after suffering a brain injury that hospitalized him for the last twelve years of his life. Courtesy, Kevin Grace.

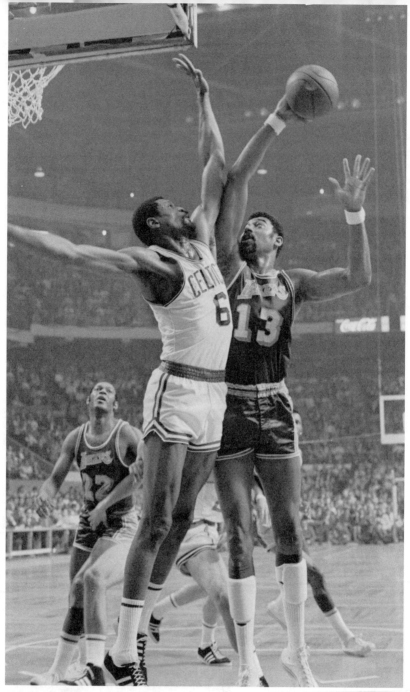

The battle between Bill Russell (*left*) and Wilt Chamberlain was the longest-running, epic struggle in NBA history. © Bettmann/CORBIS.

Al Attles originally agreed to become Golden State's head coach on an interim, thirty-game basis. He ended up coaching 1,075 games and winning the 1975 title. © NBA Entertainment. Photo by Mitchell B. Reibel.

Earl Lloyd, whose forte was defense, closes in on Philadelphia's Nelson Bobb, 1953. © Bettmann/CORBIS.

Toronto Raptors coach Lenny Wilkens has won more games than anyone in NBA history. © AFP/CORBIS.

No wonder Boston Celtics coach K. C. Jones was smiling in September 1983. His superstar, Larry Bird, had just signed a seven-year contract with Jones's mentor, team president Red Auerbach. © Bettmann/CORBIS.

including once scoring an NBA Finals record 61 points against them in 1962. Sanders said Baylor stayed in the air so long that it was bewildering because when trying to block Baylor's shot, Sanders timed his jump expecting to meet the ball at a certain point. If Baylor decided to shoot on the way down, it caused a bunch of problems. First of all, Baylor might make the basket. "He's arching his shot so he will clear your hand, and if the accuracy is still there you're in a world of trouble," Sanders said. If Baylor missed, he had an automatic advantage while going for the offensive rebound. When he shot, Sanders was at the peak of his leap while Baylor was already descending, so Baylor's feet hit the court first and he could crash the boards. "This makes him doubly dangerous," Sanders said. The other problem was inherent with guarding a superstar. Occasionally someone would block Baylor's shot, but over the course of a game, "outstanding scorers can put up many more shots than you can ever block," Sanders said.

Baylor also distracted defenders with the strange habit of nodding his head to the left—Hot Rod Hundley once said it looked like a sergeant checking his stripes—before making his move. "It was just a nervous habit," Baylor said. "I would just move my head, and the only time I would do it was when I played basketball. I was perfectly normal. There wasn't anything wrong with me.

"It started in college, and I did it so often that everyone would make comments on it and I wasn't aware of it until I looked at film. I didn't know why I was doing it. Finally, they decided it might be nerve damage so I had to take some tests at Georgetown and they gave me a thorough examination and found there wasn't anything wrong. You do things when you're under pressure. The doctor was obviously a sports enthusiast because he was telling me about baseball players that did it, football players, golfers had little idiosyncrasies that they would do under pressure. He said, 'Hey, nothing wrong. You're perfectly normal. Don't worry about it.' So I didn't, because I only did it when I played basketball, so I think it was just a nervous habit."

The head nod just contributed to Baylor's amazing repertoire of shots, and so did Baylor's instincts for the basket. "You could blindfold me and I could drive to the basket and I would hit the rim and maybe make the shot, because I just knew where the basket was at all times," Baylor said. "I didn't even have to look for the basket." Add up all those factors and you understand why Hearn believed that, "Trying to guard him was such an uncertain proposition."

Perhaps Baylor's most distinctive trait was that he was a tremendous scorer with a conscience. While being praised for the spectacular shots he did make, Baylor took great pride in bad shots he didn't take. "If I saw I didn't have the shot I would just pass the ball off," he said. He wasn't just a generous passer, or a very good one. "No," said Sanders. "He was an extraordinary passer. The rule for us whenever we played him, which is why those of us who were guarding him took such a whipping, was you never doubled him. One, because he was going to get his points no matter what; and two, his passing was uncanny. He didn't just pass because he was doubled; he passed to the person in best position to score. Many players who are doubled swing the ball around the perimeter and hope someone else will pass to the player who can score. But Baylor had the ability to pass to the right person. In Boston the rule was 'No help. We won't double-team.' Which allowed him to victimize me."

Baylor's other trademark was his tenacious rebounding. Although he was only six-five he was incredibly strong, his hands clutched a ball like a vise, and he had great timing on the boards. And after he took down a defensive rebound he was an adept ballhandler on the fastbreak. "When you start picking forwards for an all-time team, you've got to take Elgin first," Earl Lloyd said. "That's saying something, because I love Julius Erving. Doc can do it, but Doc doesn't have Elgin's strength. He's an axe. Rip those boards down and handle the ball on the break. . . . The man was just unbelievable."

The bane of Baylor's career was severe knee problems that began in the 1963–64 season, his sixth. After games he often could hardly walk, it was difficult to ride in a cab or a plane, and he frequently got injections from doctors to dull the pain. Near the end of the next season Baylor went up for a jump shot and simultaneously tore his left patellar tendon and split his kneecap. Surgery and ensuing treatment by famed sports physician Bob Kerlan lessened the pain during the remainder of Baylor's career. Unbelievably, though his knees never fully recovered, he still averaged more than 24 points per game four more times.

Perhaps the finest example of Baylor's commitment to his team occurred when he retired after playing only nine games of the 1971–72 season. The Lakers were a powerhouse, and Baylor, coming off a torn Achilles, could have hung on hoping he would finally play on a title-winning team after losing to Boston in the NBA

Finals seven times. Instead, Baylor voluntarily retired in November so that younger forwards Jim McMillian and Keith Erickson could get more playing time. "I figured in a sense I was depriving them, and I knew the coach wanted to develop them," Baylor said. "And by retiring it made it a lot easier for myself, too, because I don't know how much I would have played."

"I could understand," said Bill Sharman, former Boston Celtic great who coached that team. "He had a great career. I felt the same when I left the Boston Celtics—and I wasn't even injured. I felt I could play two or three more years, but Red Auerbach had Sam Jones coming on strong so I didn't feel after a good ten years that I wanted to play half as much. But I was hoping that Elgin would still be with us. It was definitely his idea to retire, not mine."

In Baylor's absence McMillian had an outstanding season, averaging 19 points per game, the Lakers set a record by winning thirty-three consecutive games, their 69-13 record remains an all-time best, and they crushed New York in the NBA Finals, 4-1. "That's the kind of unselfish player he was," Hearn said about Baylor's last sacrifice for his team. "He could have played, but not up to the form he had. He didn't want to disparage the great memories all of us had of him."

Guy Rodgers (1958–70)

During Wilt Chamberlain's first three years in the NBA, two debates raged among basketball fans in Boston and Philadelphia. The loudest and most captivating debate involved the merits of the two centers warring in the pivot—Philadelphia's Wilt Chamberlain and Boston's Bill Russell. The other was a secondary debate: Who was the better playmaker, Philadelphia's Guy Rodgers or Boston's Bob Cousy?

Because of Cousy's charisma and ability, the fact that the topic was even deemed worthy of discussion was a tribute to Rodgers's marvelous playmaking skills. "I have always said to every sportswriter who asked me that the best ballhandler I ever saw was Guy Rodgers, bar none," said his former teammate Tom Gola, a Basketball Hall of Famer. "I never saw anyone take the ball from Guy Rodgers. He was quick, kept the ball low."

"The key to a great playmaker [today they are called point guards]," said Al Attles, Rodgers's longtime backcourt mate with the Warriors, "is the ability to take the ball against pressure wherever he wanted to take it. Guy could take it anywhere."

Rodgers was a six-foot, 185-pound, two-time All-American at Temple University. He played in the NCAA Final Four twice, averaging 19.6 points as a collegian to become Temple's all-time leading scorer, then in a twelve-year professional career played in four NBA All-Star Games and recorded 6,917 assists, many of them on dazzling passes. His contribution to the game often gets overlooked. However, to those in the Philadelphia area who grew up watching Rodgers perform at Northeast High School, at Temple University—where he and Hal Lear formed one of the best collegiate backcourts ever—and then with the Warriors, Rodgers remains the king of ballhandlers.

Scott Beeten, now the head coach at University at Albany, grew up in Allentown, Pennsylvania, and said he "got hooked" on basketball from watching Rodgers's games at Temple. Then he closely followed Rodgers's professional career. Few could deliver a pass to a teammate or play keep-away with a defender as well as Rodgers did.

"The person he would be most compared to was Bob Cousy," Beeten said. "Not taking anything away from Bob Cousy, who was certainly a great player and a prototype, but Guy was a little more spectacular and never quite played with the same [caliber of teammates] that Cousy had."

Rodgers wouldn't engage in comparing himself with Cousy. "I never thought about it," he said. He did acknowledge that Cousy was just one problem the Celtics presented when Boston played Philadelphia. "I played against a very fine Bob Cousy, but I also had to have as much stamina to face those other guys on the team. My difficulty was with a Bill Sharman and Sam Jones, because Sharman ran forever and took you through so many screens, and Sam Jones had the backboard shot and he was taller."

Beeten is one of the leaders in an effort to get Rodgers, who died on February 19, 2001, elected to the Basketball Hall of Fame. There's no doubt in Beeten's mind that Rodgers deserves to be there, but Beeten believes bad timing resulted in his being overlooked. Certainly the Celtics' regular appearances in the NBA Finals limited Rodgers's public exposure, but there were other factors, too.

First, Rodgers played when the NBA had much less television coverage. "If Guy was playing right now, his team would have been one of the highlights on SportsCenter every night, and they'd be showing one of the non-dunks," Beeten said.

Beeten also believes Rodgers's chances of being a Hall of Famer were diminished by the Warriors' franchise move to San Francisco in 1962 after Rodgers had played four NBA seasons. "Had he stayed in Philadelphia for his entire career, I have no doubts he would be recognized as one of the greats of all time," Beeten said. "Philadelphia is a great basketball city with a tremendous basketball tradition." Beeten believes that Rodgers helped put Philadelphia on the basketball map because his play at Temple popularized the storied basketball rivalry called the Big 5: Temple, LaSalle, Villanova, Pennsylvania, and St. Joseph's.

When the Warriors moved west Rodgers was pulled out of the basketball limelight. It was hard for even his biggest fans to follow his career because with the three-hour time difference, stories and box scores of West Coast games sometimes arrived too late for East Coast newspapers to print them. Rodgers never played on a championship team and played three of his last four seasons for expansion teams in Chicago and Milwaukee, so his days in the league's spotlight were limited.

All of those factors combined to deny Rodgers some of the recognition he deserves, although nothing can deny his talent or his understanding of the playmaker's role. That knowledge was the product of many lessons Rodgers learned from older players on the training playgrounds of Philadelphia. "There was just an array of ballhandlers to learn from," he said. "Now, I think the street basketball is mostly talking talk and shooting one another down, rather than learning the fundamentals of the game."

He was schooled by Victor Harris, a summer league coach who was "one of the top ballhandlers I've ever seen," said John Chaney, who eventually became the winningest coach in Temple's history, and by local players who reached the NBA a few years before Rodgers, such as Gola, Paul Arizin, Ernie Beck, and Jackie Moore. Of course, Wilt Chamberlain was there, too. Long before the Civil Rights movement arrived, black and white players competed against each other all over the city. Sometimes all of the players were black, sometimes there was mixed competition, and sometimes Rodgers was the only black player on the court. Most important, though, was that "You could play against some of the top players in the game," he said. "Oh, and there were so many players. It was like a Who's Who of Basketball in Philadelphia."

Rodgers had an inspirational high school coach named Ike Wooley, an Irishman who put his players through so many drills that Rodgers dreamt about them. One drill led Rodgers to develop one of his pet moves—the behind-the-back pass. "I used to get bored with the drills and I would play around and do different things," Rodgers said. "We used to dribble in and out of chairs and work on your first step for quickness, and I would get to the chair and instead of going in and out, left hand, right hand, I would do stutter steps. By accident, to prevent knocking myself out on those chairs, I would go behind my back left-handed or right-handed. Also, he [Wooley] had told me the secret to the game of basketball was the knowledge. Once, he told me you can play a long time if you're a playmaker and can create for others to score. He was a wonderful person."

As Rodgers made a reputation for himself in high school ball, he also received guidance from Harlem Globetrotters stars Goose Tatum and Marques Haynes. Haynes believes himself to be the first Globetrotter with a college degree. There had been talk of Rodgers skipping college and going directly from Northeast High to the Trotters. "They said 'this is not the life for you and you should get an education,'" Rodgers said. His mother, Alfrieda, concurred, but she also knew that many colleges didn't accept black students. After she wrote to some schools and received replies that her son was unwelcome, Haynes and Tatum talked up Rodgers's skills to several coaches they respected and he subsequently received some scholarship offers. But his mother wanted him to stay in Philadelphia, and when she died a month before he began college he chose Temple out of respect for her wishes.

There he hooked up with Lear to form a devastating combination in a rare all-lefty backcourt. "The entire game just seemed to revolve around him," Beeten said about Rodgers. "Even when he was playing with Hal Lear, Hal was the superior shooter and one of the best scorers I've ever seen, but Guy was the hub of the wheel. He scored and passed and ran the fastbreak when it was just starting to evolve. He had quickness, was the most powerful guard I've ever seen, and just a fantastic passer.

"He could pass as well off the dribble as anybody I've ever seen. He knew when to run. He knew when to stop. He was so strong to the basket and drew so much attention that the around-the-back pass was a regular part of his game. I used to see him set up the defender and fire the ball past the guy's ear. I thought it was almost humiliating. It just froze defensive players. The guy would be trying to get his hands up and by the time he did, Guy's teammate would be scoring inside."

The Philadelphia Warriors made Rodgers their territorial first-round draft pick in 1958, and a year later Chamberlain joined the team and Rodgers became the starting point guard. That was both a blessing—because the seven-foot-one Chamberlain was such an easy and willing target for passes—and a challenge—because Rodgers couldn't concentrate so much on him that the talents of Paul Arizin, one of the highest-scoring guards in the league, and Gola, a fine all-around player, got overlooked.

"With Arizin, who was a superb athlete, I would do my best to make sure he got off to a fast start," Rodgers said. "Arizin was important to our offense and you wanted to get him going, and then milk him. Gola, I tried to put the ball on him for lay-ups on the fastbreak. It was important to give it to the guy who was good on closing [on the basket], and he was always one of the guys that would fill a lane. As a point guard, if you don't hit those guys and give them the opportunity to make a lay-up or two, ballplayers would stop running. Why run if you don't get the ball? I didn't want anyone to stop running because I made my living putting the ball on people, so I made everyone as happy as I could because that made my job easier."

To Rodgers those decisions were just a small part of the technique he needed to do his job correctly. "There is so much involved—floor position, controlling the tempo, and there are split-second decisions that have to be made," he said. "It's not like a chess game where you have time, and no coach can come out on the floor and position his players. A point guard is an extension of his coach."

Rodgers had to be aware of the game clock and the 24-second clock. He kept track of who was in foul trouble on both teams; he might want to attack an opponent in foul trouble, but wouldn't pass to a foul-plagued teammate if Rodgers felt his teammate might pick up a charging foul. A tenacious rebounder would be rewarded with a few passes. An injured teammate might get set up for an easy score and receive help from Rodgers on defense. Orchestrating the fastbreak, that was an art.

"A fastbreak starts with the best damn defense you can play," Rodgers said. "You play as good as possible to make them lose the ball or miss a shot. You need guys that can rebound and give the proper outlet pass. It's like preparing a meal or dessert; you have to have the proper ingredients. When you take off, it's from that outlet pass and you're attempting to cause an advantage. I chose to do it the fundamental and easy way first, but when you're playing against superb athletes that really play defense, sometimes they cause you to do things that are a little more complex. They might cause you to dribble behind your back or pass behind your back, and you have a split-second reaction."

"Guy Rodgers was an incredibly quick basketball player who was the best passing guard in the league," said former NBA guard Jim Barnett, who played from 1966 to 1977. "Great on the fastbreak. Passed off the dribble. Would fake behind his back and take the shot himself. He was ahead of his time. On the two-on-one with Wilt, he would use a backboard pass. They both would be coming in from a 45-degree angle, and Guy would bounce the ball off the backboard and Wilt would dunk it coming in. It was impossible to stop." When Barnett, who announces Golden State Warriors games, sees today's Jason Kidd, it's like going back in time. "That's the kind of speed Guy Rodgers had, and quickness with the ball," Barnett said.

The San Francisco Warriors traded Rodgers to Chicago after the 1965–66 season, and in Chicago he had his best statistical season as the floor leader of the expansion Bulls. He recorded career highs of 18 points and 11.2 assists per game, and led the league in total assists with 908. They won thirty-three games and made the playoffs, commendable achievements for an expansion team. He retired in 1970 after two seasons with the expansion Milwaukee Bucks, who at least gave him the pleasure of feeding passes to a rookie who would become the NBA's all-time leading scorer, Kareem Abdul-Jabbar.

Considering his thorough knowledge of the game, one would have thought that Rodgers would become a coach, but he restricted his coaching to participating in basketball clinics. "I always wanted to get my gray hair at a natural time," he said. "I think all that would have happened in my thirties and forties if I would have gotten involved in coaching."

Wilt Chamberlain (1959–73)

Statistics alone reveal Wilt Chamberlain's greatness, if one merely mentioned the 100 points he scored in an NBA game, the 50.4

points per game he *averaged* for the entire 1961–62 season, the 22.9 rebounds he averaged during his NBA career, the fact that he probably will forever be the only seven-footer to lead the NBA in assists, the season he played more than forty-eight minutes per game, and perhaps the most famous non-statistic in sports history: in fourteen seasons Chamberlain never fouled out of a game.

A fiction writer could ascribe those feats of wonder to a basketball superhero and at some point his editor would say, "Stop. You've gone too far. This is fiction, but it's also got to be believable." Yet those are the footprints seven-foot-one, 275-pound Chamberlain laid down in the NBA from 1959 to 1973, and it is safe to assume that no one will ever completely fill them.

To talk of Chamberlain's basketball accomplishments denies a full appreciation of his athletic legacy, however, for he also was an outstanding track athlete who, had he chosen to, probably could have been an Olympic decathlete. After basketball he became a champion volleyball player. "I think that my legacy should be that I gave credence that you could be big, bigger than most, and still have athletic ability," Chamberlain said.[4]

Because he was the epitome of the individualist, both on and off the court, his personality was a lightning rod for the clamoring public and media. As the saying goes, after God made Wilt he broke the mold. "He was a guy who was changing the whole image of professional basketball and the big man in professional basketball," said Tommy Hawkins, who was both Wilt's opponent and teammate during a ten-year professional career. "Everybody knew Wilt Chamberlain. Wilt was as popular internationally as Muhammad Ali. He shared that type of spotlight."

In doing so he was a groundbreaker for black athletes because of the way he orchestrated and controlled his personal life. "He marched to his own drumbeat," Hawkins said. "He was the Big Dipper. He was Wilt Chamberlain. He was afforded a respect and social awe that very few people in life ever had. Wilt had a Swedish maid. Wilt owned buildings and night clubs. Wilt was a Renaissance man. There had been Joe DiMaggio, who married Marilyn Monroe. There had been Babe Ruth and Ted Williams. But basketball did not enjoy the position that baseball did at that time, and it was people like Wilt, Mikan, Elgin, Russell, Bob Cousy, and Oscar Robertson who brought the sport to its forefront. And Wilt did it not only as a great basketball player, but as a great individualist. Wilt, before he was twenty-one, was making more money than chief executives of major corporations."

In so many ways the sports world revolved around Chamberlain's axis, beginning in the days when he was a teenager. "You could see it when we were in seventh grade," said junior high and high school teammate Jimmy Sadler. "He would be great not because he was tall, but because he could do so many things. Back then pretty much everyone who was tall was awkward too. Not Wilt. He was graceful. He could easily run the floor. And he had great coordination. By ninth grade—and I remember this distinctly—I was thinking, 'He could play in the pros *now*.' "[5]

At Overbrook High School in Philadelphia he was the city's shot put and high-jump champion, and he also ran cross country. Yet those achievements were dwarfed by what he did on the basketball court. His 2,206 points still stand as the city's prep record; he once scored 90 points in a game—including 60 in one ten-minute span—and led his team to two city titles and a 56-3 record. In 1955 his team won the city championship by defeating West Philadelphia, which starred future NBA forward Ray Scott. "I was a junior and he was a senior, and our record was 17-3," Scott said. "And you can guess what all those losses came from. Because of Wilt's size and strength, he probably was more dominant there than in any time in his career."

To secure him as a hometown gate attraction, Philadelphia Warriors owner Eddie Gottlieb thought up the concept of the "territorial draft pick" and snookered the rest of the league into adopting it. Then Gottlieb used that rule to draft Chamberlain in 1955 before he had played even one college game. It didn't matter that Gottlieb had to wait four more years until Chamberlain was eligible to actually play in the NBA. He was going to be worth the delay.

When he entered the University of Kansas freshmen weren't allowed to play varsity ball, but Chamberlain quickly proved he could exceed all expectations of him. In his freshman debut he scored 50 points against the Kansas varsity before fifteen thousand stunned fans; a year later in his varsity debut he dropped in a still-existing Kansas record 52 points and grabbed 31 rebounds against Northwestern. As a junior he tied for first in the high jump in the Big 8 track and field championships by clearing six feet-six-and-three-fourths inches. And in basketball, surrounded by North Carolina defenders, his Kansas team lost in triple overtime in the

1958 NCAA championship game, one of the most famous college contests ever played. Then he spent one season with the Harlem Globetrotters before the Warriors' draft rights became effective.

Once again Chamberlain merely shrugged off the adjustment to a higher level of play. In his first appearance against the New York Knicks he scored 43 points and grabbed 28 rebounds, leaving an indelible impression on Red Holzman, who later coached the Knicks to two NBA titles. Comparing him to the overpowering Chamberlain of later years, Holzman wrote, "He was more agile then. He was quicker. He was leaner. A sapling who was to grow into a redwood as the years went on. He was a shooter that night, not the scorer he became by using his strength going to the basket. He hit 20-foot jumpers facing the basket."[6]

The onslaught continued as he overwhelmed defenders to average a then-NBA record 37.6 points per game and 27 rebounds. He had arrived, and the rest of the league was scrambling to catch up. "He came into the NBA and was 'The Man' as a rookie," Hawkins said. "So he was always at the pinnacle of what was happening. He was the guiding star when he got there because even though you had the Celtics and Bill Russell, no one had seen anything like him."

In Chamberlain's third season he surpassed the inconceivable when he averaged 50.4 points per game, scoring 40 percent of his team's points. Guy Rodgers was the Warriors' point guard that season, one in which Chamberlain's leaping ability, speed, and strength were on full display. "Wilt was extraordinary because if one of my passes went awry, he could go get it," Rodgers said. "He could jump out of the gym. Sometimes I would make passes and that sucker would go arm pit over the rim to get it. Wilt had to be one of the greatest athletes I have ever seen in my life. Not many years ago they had the slam-dunk contests and Michael Jordan and Doc Erving would go 94 feet from the basket and run to the free-throw line and dunk it. Wilt, when he was in college, could just rock back and take one step and dunk the ball for his free throw." Rodgers once saw Chamberlain fly exceptionally high to block a shot and catch the ball in one hand, but the play was negated when the referee called it goaltending. "I went to the referee and said, 'How could you call that goaltending?'" Rodgers said. "And he said to me, 'Guy, what I saw is not humanly possible.'"

"When I jumped I felt like a bird," Chamberlain said. "I felt like

I was flying. It's tough to call it a superhuman feeling, but *damn*, it was exhilarating."[7]

His airborne flights necessitated the changing of three NBA rules: Taking a running leap from the foul line to dunk a free throw is banned; an inbounds pass can no longer be tossed over the backboard so a teammate can catch and dunk it; and an offensive player can no longer catch a teammate's shot and guide it into the basket. In the strictest sense of the term—the rule book—Chamberlain truly changed the game.

Chamberlain, who was fast enough to be a quarter-miler in high school, still had speed that amazed Rodgers. "There have been a lot of fast athletes that played basketball, and I put Al Attles at the top of the set," Rodgers said, referring to his backcourt mate. "They used to call him the Jersey Jet. There were times he and Wilt could beat me running ninety-four feet." Chamberlain, who prided himself on being one of the first players to make weightlifting an integral part of his training, also built up his strength and endurance as an avid track and field performer. He had to, just to withstand the rigors of taking 39 shots and playing forty-eight-and-a-half minutes per game that season. (An NBA game lasts only forty-eight minutes, but ten of Philadelphia's games went into overtime.) "You ask anybody who has scored 50 points how they felt after they did it. They'll tell you, 'Exhausted,'" Hawkins said.

In his autobiography Chamberlain said he even astonished himself with his strength once when he stopped Boston's K. C. Jones from driving to the basket. Jones was only six-foot-one but he weighed a solid 200 pounds and was tough enough to almost make the roster of professional football's Los Angeles Rams (though he had never played college football). As Jones described it, he was going "100 miles per hour" toward the basket when Chamberlain scooped him up out of the air with one arm. "I've got him beat, and he stepped over, got me around the waist and didn't move," Jones said. "I had no momentum. I did not move, and my head was there and my feet were back there. I got two foul shots out of it, but I was shaking at the line."

Put all those physical attributes together with Chamberlain's Goliath-like size and one had an unstoppable point producer who reached his pinnacle on March 2, 1962, when he scored 100 points against the New York Knicks. That night he shot 36-for-63 from the floor and overcame the glaring weakness in his game—foul shooting—to make an NBA-record 28 of 32 free throws. Ironically, the greatest individual feat probably in basketball history was witnessed by only 4,124 fans because it occurred during a neutral-site game in Hershey, Pennsylvania. "I spent twelve years in his armpits, and I always carried that 100-point game on my shoulders," said Darrall Imhoff, the Knicks' rookie center. "After I got my third foul, I said to one of the officials, Willy Smith, 'Why don't you just give him 100 points and we'll all go home?' Well, we did."[8]

The Warriors moved to San Francisco after that season, and a year later six-foot-eleven Nate Thurmond was drafted by the Warriors. Being schooled by Chamberlain in their practice sessions was one of the reasons Thurmond eventually became a Hall of Fame center and is today considered one of the game's best defenders ever. Chamberlain not only outweighed 235-pound Thurmond by 40 pounds, he also had a full package of bewildering shots. There was his fade-away jump shot, "leaning back with that big frame and he could kiss the ball off the boards so pretty, it was hard to block," Thurmond said. Then there was his fingerroll lay-up, when Chamberlain got his defender out of position then would reach his hand over the rim and roll the ball off his fingertips into the basket. "And he could certainly slam it on you from any mistake you made position-wise," Thurmond said.

Chamberlain's dominance is even more impressive when one considers his limitations. Chamberlain almost always positioned himself on the left side of the basket, which made him somewhat predictable. Although he was a superb athlete, Thurmond said he didn't have the forward-like ballhandling and outside shooting skills of Hakeem Olajuwon, Patrick Ewing, or David Robinson of the 1990s. Chamberlain didn't use his strength to intimidate, however. "He didn't want to hurt anybody," Thurmond said. "He was very gentle out there."

Chamberlain's salary demands and Thurmond's development caused the Warriors to trade him back to the new Philadelphia team, the 76ers, in 1965. It was there in 1967 that Chamberlain finally achieved the ultimate when he played on a championship team for the first time since his high school days. Throughout his NBA career in Philly he had been stymied by psychologically deflating defeats to Boston in the playoffs. Boston fans constantly derided Chamberlain for coming up short against his nemesis, Bill Russell; Chamberlain's defenders argued that Wilt's supporting cast of players wasn't as strong as Russell's. But that wasn't so in

1967, when Philadelphia won the title with a team that was voted the best in NBA history.

Surrounded by forwards Chet Walker and Luke Jackson, guards Hal Greer, Wali Jones, and Larry Costello, and sixth man Billy Cunningham, Chamberlain was freed to explore all of his talents instead of being simply a points machine. He established then-career lows of 24.1 points and 14 shots per game, but set then-career highs by shooting 68.3 percent from the field and averaging 7.8 assists. The Sixers compiled a 68-13 record, downed Boston in five games in the Eastern Conference finals, and buried San Francisco (the team that had traded Chamberlain away) 4-2 in the NBA finals.

"He became more of a team player," Walker said. "He told me one time that the owners [in San Francisco and during his previous stint in Philadelphia] had insisted that he go out every night and try to score 50 points. That was box office; they could promote that—'Come see Wilt score 50.' And he said they were not interested if the team won or lost. But when he came to Philadelphia, before he got there we had a wonderful team. He just blended in and became a passer. . . . I heard he was selfish but it proved just the opposite. He enjoyed it tremendously. We had to encourage him to shoot because he was obsessed with getting 10 assists a game. . . . He proved that he could be the team player that Bill Russell had been over the years."

That pattern continued when Chamberlain was traded to Los Angeles in 1968 after demanding a three-year deal totaling $1 million. In Los Angeles he suffered one of his most frustrating losses to Boston when coach Butch van Breda Kolff benched him in the closing minutes of Game 7 of the 1969 NBA Finals, which the Lakers lost to Boston in Russell's last game as player-coach. Chamberlain had one more season of triumph coming his way, however, because the 1971–72 Lakers redefined the phrase "winning streak" when they won thirty-three games in a row.

Once again Chamberlain was playing on a team that allowed him to practice his special, giant-sized form of versatility. Then thirty-five and surrounded by pinpoint shooters Jerry West, Gail Goodrich, and Jim McMillian, Chamberlain's scoring was needed even less than in 1967. Instead, coach Bill Sharman, former star of the Boston Celtics, asked Chamberlain to play defense a little further from the basket than usual, like Bill Russell had done.

"Before, I thought Wilt was such a great jumper and rebounder that we would dominate everything under the boards," Sharman said, "but I thought he was capable of going out a little further and scaring shooters, and could still hustle back and get rebounds." That year Chamberlain made the NBA All-Defensive first team for the first time in his career, he led the league in rebounding for the tenth time, and anchored a team that had a 69-13 record and whipped New York 4-1 in the Finals.

"He got better as he got older," Thurmond said. "When I first came in, it was all about, 'Can I get 50, 60 points?' His rebound numbers were always good, but his offensive rebounding became better later, his passing became better later, and his shot-blocking became better later. When they won thirty-three in a row nothing, absolutely nothing, came through the hole. When that streak got rolling, Wilt didn't want that to stop!"

Chamberlain played one more year, shooting a single-season record 72.7 percent from the field—that's sinking 426 of 586 shots—then retired. It would be futile to list all of his records here, but in the NBA Register it takes fourteen lines of type to list his regular-season records; Michael Jordan, the consensus greatest player of the post-Wilt era, requires only seven lines.

After retirement Chamberlain was never far from the spotlight. He once challenged Muhammad Ali to a championship heavyweight boxing fight. The bout never occurred because they couldn't agree on a contract, but Chamberlain, whose self-confidence had no ceiling, wrote in his autobiography, "If pushed to answer the question of who would have won, I think I would have. Ali may have been in over his head—and I wasn't the only one who thought this way."[9] In that same book Chamberlain caused an uproar by claiming he had made love to 20,000 women, a boast for which he deeply apologized. "I regret the context in which people chose to take it," he said. "It's like saying you saw Casablanca a thousand times. You mean you saw it a lot. I used 20,000 as a figure of speech. If I had been bragging, I'd have mentioned some names."[10] Chamberlain remained in the public consciousness, never tiring of reminding sportswriters of his extraordinary basketball talent. "Every artist wants his due for his painting—especially if it's the *Mona Lisa*," he explained.[11]

Chamberlain also was extremely kind-hearted, so much so that his former coach, Alex Hannum, called him "one of the most misunderstood sports characters in this world." He was a faithful player in the annual Maurice Stokes fundraising game, which after Stokes's death donated money to needy former NBA players. Even in 1999, twenty-six years after Chamberlain's retirement, he flew cross-country to attend the last Stokes game. But that was nothing compared to the effort he put into getting to the game in 1970. Here's how it was described in the 1993 Stokes Game program:

> *He had boarded a flight that was to take him to New York, but the plane was hijacked over Denver. It finally touched down in Chicago and Wilt immediately rented another plane to take him to New York City. From there he took a private plane to Monticello, but just as the plane approached Sullivan County Airport the runway lights went out. The pilot wanted to return home, but Wilt wanted to play in the game so badly he told the pilot to set the plane down in an open field. From there he was able to rent a car, and pulled in just as the game ended. He spent a few hours socializing and signing autographs, and then left for the West Coast again, this time utilizing slightly more conventional methods to get there.* [12]

Wilt remained devoted to his parents, dedicating his autobiography to "my mother and father, who were the two greatest teachers in my life." [13] Perturbed by the lack of athletic opportunities that were available to his sisters when they were children, Chamberlain later helped finance women's track teams. In 1996 Chamberlain opened his heart to the ailing sixteen-year-old granddaughter of former teammate Paul Arizin. (She was suffering from brain cancer that eventually killed her.) At the All-Star Game in which the NBA's 50 greatest players were honored, she asked to be introduced to Chamberlain. "Wilt took her hand and, with her in a wheelchair, took her around to meet the other players and to get all of their autographs," Arizin said. "She even got Bill Russell's, and he didn't give it out to anyone. Wilt was the only man in the world who could have done that for her. So when you remember Wilt Chamberlain, look beyond the statistics to the human being." [14]

Chamberlain died on October 12, 1999, of congestive heart failure. A testament to his near mythical status was that so many of his friends responded with incredulity, as if they believed he was immortal. "It's just a devastating thing, man," said Philadelphia basketball figure Sonny Hill. "I couldn't believe it. I still can't believe it." [15] Both Philadelphia newspapers crafted large special sections devoted to his memory. Memorial services were held for him in his native Philadelphia and his adopted home of Los Angeles, each attended by a long list of sports dignitaries who loved and revered the Dipper. "We've lost a giant of a man in every sense of the word," NBA Commissioner David Stern said. "The shadow of accomplishment he cast over our game is unlikely ever to be matched."[16]

Oscar Robertson (1960–74)

In today's NBA the mark of an extraordinary performance is the "triple-double" when a player reaches double figures in points, rebounds, and assists. After almost any game it instantly captures headlines. The term was invented for Magic Johnson, the six-foot-nine engine who pushed the Los Angeles Lakers to five NBA championships in the 1980s and compiled 138 triple-doubles in his thirteen-year career. But the statistic was invented by Oscar Robertson, who compiled 178 triple-doubles in his career. Not only did he *average* a triple-double during the 1962–63 season, he also averaged a triple-double for his first *five years* in the league.

That is not a typo; that is a phenomenon. After being the first three-time College Player of the Year at the University of Cincinnati from 1958 to 1960, as a rookie Robertson immediately shook up the NBA in 1960 by averaging 30.5 points, 10.1 rebounds, and 9.7 assists. It was an incomprehensible entrance into the league because no backcourt man in NBA history had ever scored at that rate. But it was just the beginning. The next season, the six-five, 225-pound-plus, do-everything guard reached triple-double heaven by averaging 30.8 points, 12.5 rebounds, and 11.4 assists. The fact that he maintained that excellence over five years—averaging 30.3 points, 10.6 assists, and 10.4 rebounds during 384 games—is the greatest testament to his plethora of skills.

"The years I had him, his stats were 10, 10, 10, 10," said Jack McMahon, who coached the Royals from 1963 to 1967. "He'd have 10 baskets, 10 assists, 10 rebounds, 10 free throws. He'd get 30 points, 10 rebounds, 10 assists, and the amazing part about it was he could pick the quarter he would get what he needed."

Robertson was known for passing off to teammates early in the game, then taking over later when his leadership was needed most. "That's even better, because everybody was involved," McMahon said. "But if he had 10 points at halftime and I'm sitting in the locker room, as the coach I'm thinking, 'Well, I've got 20 from Oscar in the second half.' You could bank on it." Robertson could be consistent because he mastered every element of the game. He was big and strong enough that few defenders could deter him. Even if one could defend him, Robertson never would admit it to himself. He couldn't even conceive of it.

"You've got to be able to say, 'No one can do the things that I can do with a basketball. I can play with anybody,'" he said. "You've always got to have this. You can't go out in any contest and say, 'I don't know if I can do it. This guy, maybe he'll beat us, or maybe I can't do this with this team.' I didn't think that anybody could outplay me on the court. Nobody."[17]

Jack Twyman, a high-scoring Hall of Fame forward on Robertson's teams, draws a telling distinction between "the Big O" and other terrific guards like Bob Cousy, Jerry West, Hal Greer, and Guy Rodgers. Those four were opportunistic players who took advantage of situations as they developed, Twyman said. Yet Robertson's size and strength could dictate the flow of the game. Exceptionally strong guards like K. C. Jones or Al Attles—"He'd touch you and you'd be black and blue," Twyman said—had a chance of slowing him down. But the average-sized guard had little chance, which resulted in Robertson consistently being double- and triple-teamed.

"He had great ball control and court presence," Twyman said, "and if double- or triple-teamed, he was aware of the fact somebody was open. Oscar could get him the ball—and a lot of times that was me."

Efficiency was Robertson's trademark. Like Utah's John Stockton in the 1990s, Robertson almost never resorted to fancy moves like dribbling or passing behind his back. Why waste the motion when the tried-and-true would work? "For all the times I saw Oscar play, I only saw him dribble behind his back once," Attles said.

Chet Walker was an outstanding small forward from 1962 to 1975 who usually didn't guard Robertson, though occasionally he drew that difficult assignment because his coach wanted a bigger defender on Robertson and Walker was six-foot-seven, 220 pounds. "It was extremely exhausting because Oscar was not a one-dimensional player," Walker said. "He presented the whole package to you. There was nothing that was predictable—great shooter, strong, played inside, played outside. When you guarded Oscar, you had to be aware of every part of the game. He was a fine defensive player—wasn't that quick but he was so smart. Once in a while he did something fancy, but he was almost the perfect ballplayer. His game was so simple that it became complex."

Robertson's devotion to perfection gave him a reputation for sometimes being too demanding of his teammates. Was it well deserved? "I never had that recollection," Twyman said. "I don't think Oscar was any tougher than I was. I have no recollection [of] Oscar ever being unfair to anybody. We all wanted to win and do what it took."

However, Tommy Hawkins, who played four seasons with the Royals, said: "Oscar saw the whole floor at all times, and because he had that complete notion of what was supposed to be going on, he could be a little intolerant sometimes. He wanted to get it done and if you weren't doing it, he would tell the coach to 'put someone in who can get the job done.'" Playing on the same team with Robertson was difficult for highly sensitive players. "He was very competitive and wanted to win and could not stand people who were not making contributions," Hawkins said. "He was intolerant of teammates who were not pulling their fair share of the load. Nothing personal, but it was about consistent performance. That was the way he played and that was the way he thought the team would have the most success—focus and dedicated effort. When he walked in the locker room, the ball boys knew their job was to get him a basketball. He would go to the dressing area and start squeezing that ball. He would start rubbing it and fondling it, and as he dressed, the ball was always at his foot. As he put on his shoes, he would always take time to touch it. Everybody wants the feel of the basketball, but Oscar was even more devoted to it than anybody I ever saw."

Robertson had an unusual shooting style that made it extremely difficult to block his jump shot. He would jump slightly backward to distance himself from the defender, his elbow was pointed straight ahead, his right wrist was cocked back, and he cradled the ball above and behind his head like a waiter balancing a platter held high. "He would get his elbow up, and the closer you got to him the closer his elbow got to your face," Attles said. "Only thing you could do was hit his elbow or get your face knocked off."

He was greedy for lay-ups, which is why Robertson was notorious for maneuvering closer and closer to the basket for shots as a game went along. "He would pass up a wide-open 16-footer and he would allow you time to recover, then take another dribble or two to 12 feet and shoot it right in your face," recalled former NBA guard Jim Barnett. "It was amazing how he could shoot with a guy pressuring him."

When it came to ballhandling, Robertson controlled the ball

as if he was dribbling a yo-yo. Though he wasn't lightning quick he had an array of clever moves, a change-of-pace dribble, and could fend off a defensive player with his off hand. "His greatest asset was when you take the ball from the top of the circle or halfcourt to the basket, you're always a little leery of somebody reaching in and stealing the ball," McMahon said. "I don't think it ever entered his mind that somebody was going to take it away from him. He could go from this point to this point and nobody was going to stop him from going from here to there. Never.

"And God forbid anybody ever did take it away from him. You can bet the next time down, [that defender's] going to get embarrassed. Oscar had great pride, but all the great players have that."

As a rebounder Robertson "was like a cunning cat, aware of what was going on around him and also keenly aware of his next moves," Hawkins said. He didn't recklessly crash the boards and let his man flee downcourt for a fastbreak basket if he missed the rebound, but often would lay back and anticipate where the ball would bounce. If Robertson got the rebound, that eliminated the need for an outlet pass to a ballhandler.

Lump together his size, skills, versatility, and commitment to every aspect of the game, and a defender was set up for a case of overload. "There have only been two of those—Michael Jordan and him," said Nate Thurmond. "Put them in another bag. There are always questions of who was the best. Those two stand alone. If there's another category against them I'll throw Magic Man in there, but Magic couldn't shoot like them."

"If Oscar, Jerry West, and Jordan were playing in the nineties," Barnett said, "they would be the best guards in the league."

Unfortunately for Robertson, after his second season his Cincinnati team was moved from the Western to the Eastern Division, which meant the Royals had to get past Boston to reach the NBA Finals. The Royals never completed the journey. They had a very talented team with Robertson, three frontcourt men—Twyman, Jerry Lucas, and Wayne Embry, who played in a total of thirteen All-Star Games while they were Robertson's teammates—and an accurate shooting guard in Adrian Smith, named an All-Star only once but winner of the MVP Award during that game in 1966. But in Robertson's first six years in the league the Royals lost the playoff series to Boston three times, two of those coming in the Eastern Division finals.

In his tenth season Robertson still dominated the NBA, but the Royals were going nowhere, having missed the playoffs for three straight seasons. By 1970 the former center at Cincinnati and Milwaukee's general manager, Wayne Embry, was trying to build a championship team around a tremendously talented young center named Lew Alcindor, and the Bucks needed a ballhandler to run the show. Embry traded for Robertson on April 21, 1970, and a year later the Milwaukee Bucks won their only championship in franchise history when Milwaukee swept the Baltimore Bullets in the Finals.

Robertson, although thirty-two years old, was still a force, averaging 19.4 points, 8.2 assists, and 5.7 rebounds, but for the first time in his NBA career he didn't have to carry the scoring load. Alcindor, who later changed his name to Kareem Abdul-Jabbar for religious reasons, handled that chore by averaging a league-high 31.7 points per game.

Robertson played three more seasons with Milwaukee, retiring in 1974. His contribution to the NBA extended far beyond the playing court when he succeeded Tom Heinsohn as president of the National Basketball Players Association (NBPA) in 1966. Under Robertson's leadership the "Oscar Robertson suit" was filed to block a merger with the American Basketball Association until favorable conditions could be agreed upon. Eventually the 1976 Oscar Robertson Settlement Agreement approved the college draft as the initial way of dispensing players. It also laid the foundation for the free agent system which has brought countless riches to players and resulted in the NBA's merger with the ABA in 1976 (a merger that put exceptional talents such as Julius Erving, George Gervin, and Connie Hawkins into the national spotlight). Ironically, Robertson retired two years before the settlement, so he never personally benefited from it.

Robertson fulfilled his role as labor leader using much the same style as when he played: not flashy but efficient, calculated, and stubbornly committed to his principles. "Once he became president [of the NBPA], he was very aggressive with getting the best deal for the players," Walker said. "He was very firm in his statements with the players. When he presented issues to players he would make sure you understood that this is what we needed at this time. Oscar is a great leader. I really thought at one time he would be a great commissioner of basketball. He took the time to explain things fully, and the fact was he had a tremendous amount of respect from everybody."

Robertson's success as the head of the Players Association reflects the quality of black athlete that entered college and professional basketball in the 1950s and early 1960s. "There weren't wholesale scholarships [for black athletes] at that time," Hawkins said. "I was the only black player at Notre Dame. They had Bob Boozer at Kansas State, Elgin at Seattle, Wayne Embry at Miami of Ohio. These were hand-chosen people who would lead major sports in terms of integration. There were no dummies there and no people who weren't interested in getting a basic education. And they weren't people who were going to flunk out. The players who are now being lauded for everything they've done—Elgin, Wayne Embry, Lenny Wilkens—these were all products of what I consider our era, and all were men who were capable of being proficient outside of basketball."

16

Black Coaches Extend Integration beyond the Sidelines

By 1966 black athletes had firmly established themselves in all three major professional sports. Every NBA team's roster had included at least one black player during each of the previous eight seasons. In major-league baseball and professional football the last bastions of segregation had fallen when the Boston Red Sox added Pumpsie Green to their roster in 1959, and the Washington Redskins acquired Bobby Mitchell three years later. All three sports were filled with black stars, and even the National Hockey League had its first black player by then—Willie O'Ree, who broke in with Boston during the 1957–58 season.

Nevertheless, by 1966 neither the NBA, the National Football League, nor any major-league baseball team had a head coach or manager of color. The professional coaching stints of Pop Gates and John McLendon were largely unknown since both had lasted less than one season and, in McLendon's case, it happened in an obscure league. Black people had proved they could perform (and often excel) as professional athletes, but the position of head coach—which presumably required extensive knowledge of the game as well as visible leadership qualities—had not as yet been offered. In a society that still largely recognized black people's brawn yet routinely ignored or underestimated their intellect, that was no surprise.

To change that perception a major professional sports league had to integrate its coaching ranks. Considering the NBA's more progressive racial history, it's no surprise that it made that breakthrough when Bill Russell replaced Red Auerbach as the Boston Celtics' head coach in 1966. Just as Boston's drafting of Chuck Cooper in 1950 had not been a social experiment in integration, neither was Russell's ascension to the position of player-coach. Instead, the move was rooted in the fact that after twenty years of coaching in the NBA, Auerbach was worn out. "I was doing too many things," Auerbach said. "I was general manager, the scout, on the Board of Governors. I had to replace myself as a coach. I was burned out. [Russell] called my wife and asked how to convince me not to retire because he didn't want to play for anyone else." When that proved unsuccessful, Russell asked if he could replace Auerbach, who granted the request. "It was like a common bond," Auerbach said. "I said to myself, 'Who could better motivate Bill Russell than Bill Russell?'"

Many years passed before professional baseball and football matched the NBA in integrating the coaching ranks. Baseball didn't have its first black manager until Cleveland hired Frank Robinson in 1975, and the NFL not until 1989, when the Oakland Raiders named Art Shell as the league's first black head coach in the modern era. (Fritz Pollard had coached several NFL teams in the 1920s, before blacks were banned from the league in 1934 for twelve years.)

In today's NBA Russell's double duty as player and coach would be eased by the presence of at least three assistant coaches. But then he coached when the NBA was still a streamlined, bare-bones operation; his support came from veteran teammates who helped him manage substitutions and timeouts. In three seasons as player-coach Russell continued to perform at an All-Star level as a player while also directing the Celtics to a 162-83 record and two NBA titles.

Perhaps his rookie coaching year, when the Celtics fell short of a championship, best reflects the respect he generated among black players. That year the Philadelphia 76ers, so often frustrated by playoff losses to Boston, finally knocked the Celtics out of the postseason by winning the Eastern Division finals. The Sixers had broken a string of eight Boston championships, yet in the Home Box Office documentary, *Bill Russell: My Life, My Way*, Philadelphia forward Chet Walker noted that black 76ers perceived their triumph with ambivalence. "It was kind of a joyous moment," Walker said. "We felt good about the fact that we won, but we were kind of sad that we had to beat Bill Russell."

He retired after the 1969 season, returned to coaching (with Seattle from 1973 to 1977 and for one season with Sacramento in 1987), then gave up coaching with a 341-290 record. After leaving Boston his teams twice reached the playoffs but never challenged for a title, perhaps because another Bill Russell wasn't around to play center for his team.

As Tom Hawkins mentioned about the early superstars, they

were extraordinary basketball talents with the skills needed to succeed in many professions. In light of that, it's no coincidence that four of the first five black NBA head coaches—Russell, Lenny Wilkens, Al Attles and K. C. Jones, in chronological order—had all entered the NBA as players in the first ten years of its integration, and as coaches had all won at least one NBA championship.

Lenny Wilkens (1969–2000)

Lenny Wilkens has traveled in fast company as a head coach. When Seattle named him player-coach in 1969, he followed Bill Russell as only the second black person to hold that position in NBA history. On January 6, 1994, Wilkens accomplished his greatest individual achievement by winning his 939th game as a coach, breaking Red Auerbach's record. In 1998 Wilkens joined John Wooden, former Purdue star and legendary UCLA coach, as only the second person inducted into the Basketball Hall of Fame at different times as both a player and a coach.

After struggling through a fretful, 28-54 1999–2000 season with Atlanta—only the fifth losing season of Wilkens's last twenty-two—he resigned and promptly was hired by the Toronto Raptors. By then he had participated in a record 3,460 NBA games as a player or coach; his coaching record was 1,179-981 over twenty-seven seasons. One way to appreciate that span of time is by knowing that when Atlanta's opening-game roster was announced for the 1999–2000 season, Wilkens had been coaching in the NBA longer than ten of his twelve players had been alive. Wilkens certainly hadn't set out to become the league's winningest coach. Yet he has been up to the challenge from the day he was born on October 28, 1937.

At a time when interracial marriages were banned in many states, the sight of his black father and Irish mother walking down the street must have caused some heads to turn. At the age of five, when his father died of a bleeding ulcer, Wilkens's mother became a twenty-five-year-old widow with four children to raise in Brooklyn's tough Bedford-Stuyvesant neighborhood. For sixty-three years Wilkens has faced many challenges just by living his life as a black person. Twenty-seven years as an NBA coach, as daunting as it sounds, has not been the pressure cooker one might expect.

"No, because we've been under pressure all of our lives that we had to be better," Wilkens said, repeating the age-old mantra black parents pass on to their children. "I was told that from day one—I couldn't be as good as [white people], I had to be better. I could see it in people's eyes, even in [Providence College]. Athletes, we were supposed to just be there, and in class I made it a point that I was prepared for every exam, that I got on that Dean's List. Because I wanted them to see that there was a black person on the Dean's List who was an athlete. I accepted the challenge, because I want you to know that we bleed just like you do. We have feelings just like you do. Let us read the same books and we'll understand it just like you do."

He has succeeded with a "no need to sweat" demeanor, one that caused the great *Los Angeles Times* columnist Jim Murray to describe Wilkens as "About as flamboyant as a spy." As a coach Wilkens's inner calm is manifested in his trademark pose on the sidelines: arms folded across his chest as the game seemingly goes racing by. But aren't his guts churning inside? "Sometimes, yeah, quiet rage," he said. "But perception is not reality. People who don't know me presume, 'Oh, he's laid back.' But players will tell you I'm not laid back. But this started early and it's a stereotype." The black coach, he contends, gets labeled "laid back," while a white coach like Larry Bird, who also doesn't castigate his players or referees, gets labeled "a genius."

In reality Wilkens is simply the product of the streets of Bedford-Stuyvesant and years of admiring his boyhood idol, Jackie Robinson. Both taught him that emotions are to be felt but not revealed. From Bedford-Stuy he learned, "I wasn't going to let you get into my head: 'I don't even worry about you. You're not going to affect me psychologically.' The first [reaction] if a guy nails you is to nail him back. I'm not going to nail you back because I've got the ball. I need to score. I won't forget, but I'll pick my spot and you're going to know it. Because if you don't remember, I'm going to tell you." And while sitting in the stands in Ebbetts Field watching Robinson revolutionize baseball, Wilkens observed: "He never got rattled, at least it seemed that way to me. And he suffered through name-calling and all the crap that he went through with dignity. And he came to play every night, never made excuses for himself. So I wasn't going to." Those lessons helped give Wilkens tensile strength, like a steel cable whose narrow width belies its resilience. It was just what he needed when he broke into professional ball in St. Louis, which was heavily racially segregated at the time.

St. Louis made Wilkens its 1960 first-round draft choice, but with his bachelor's degree in economics he was leaning toward getting his master's at Boston College instead of playing professional ball. One company that was recruiting him at the time, Technical Tape Corporation, got game tickets for its representative, for Wilkens, and for a college teammate to attend a Boston versus St. Louis game at Boston Garden during the NBA Finals. It was the first live NBA game Wilkens had ever seen. The crowd "was going crazy," and Wilkens observed that he was as good as the Hawks' guards. "It really got me going. I said, 'Wow, this may not be all that bad.' "

Wilkens signed with St. Louis for an $8,000 salary and a $1,500 bonus, the start of a fifteen-year playing career during which Wilkens produced 16.5 points and 6.7 assists per game, along with nine All-Star Game appearances. As a rookie he was the perfect addition to a team that already had the league's first trio of 20-point scorers: forwards Bob Pettit (26.1 points per game), Cliff Hagan (24.8), and center Clyde Lovellette (20.8). Pettit was the biggest star, which didn't escape Wilkens's notice. "I knew that if I wanted to stay around, then I was going to get the ball to Pettit," Wilkens said. He believes that by catering to Pettit, affectionately nicknamed "Big Blue," Wilkens lessened any animosity Hawks fans normally might have felt for a black playmaker. "They sort of welcomed me in. The fans never bothered me and I think maybe because they were in between as to what I was," Wilkens said (meaning that because he's light-skinned some fans probably weren't sure if he was black or white). "I heard from the black community that they weren't sure what I was, but then after a while they knew, because where was I going to go? They were my people, though."

Wilkens blossomed during his third season, his first as a full-time starter, finishing sixth in the league in assists and playing in his first All-Star Game. By the time his eight-year stint in St. Louis ended, Wilkens had been named an All-Star five times, had led the Hawks to seven playoff appearances, and had established himself as a coach's dream because he had "more of an understanding of the game than 90 percent of the guys who play," said Harry Gallatin, his coach from 1962 to 1965.

"He was in the right place at the right time, and that takes not only physical but mental ability," Gallatin added. Wilkens wasn't a fancy ballhandler. "He just got the ball where it belongs. If he ran a play and there were options involved in that play, Lenny was able to hold the ball and wait for the third option on the play, if that's what had to happen." A natural lefthander, Wilkens's uncanny passing ability meant that he also could slip into the cracks and crevices of a defense and put up a running hook or a scoop shot before it could be blocked. In addition, he was able to anticipate passing lanes to get steals. "Lenny was a better defensive player than offensive," Gallatin said. "Not even close. A lot of people don't know that."

Wilkens had an inner toughness that Gallatin described as "the fire burning in the belly." Gene Tormohlen, a St. Louis reserve from 1962 to 1968, noticed it, too. "I knew when I first met him that he was an amazing guy," Tormohlen said. "When you meet Lenny it doesn't take you three minutes to learn this guy is special. He's not jive. He's straight up. He's quick; he's tough when you're talking winning and losing. When you've got three minutes to go and it's tied and Lenny says, 'Give it to me and go to the hoop and I'll get something done,' that's when he showed his toughness."

As popular and effective as he was on the court, Wilkens still had to combat racism in St. Louis. It was difficult to find a white-owned restaurant that would serve black people, so Wilkens carefully tested a popular downtown cafeteria-style eatery decorated with photos of Hawks players. One day, "I was walking along and I saw all the Hawks pictures—I saw mine—so I decided to go in," Wilkens said. "People looked but no one said anything, so I went and got my food, paid for it, and sat down."

Wilkens encountered racism head-on when he and his wife, Marilyn, purchased their first home in the city in an all-white neighborhood named Moline Acres. Wilkens knew they might be inviting trouble, but he had grown up in an integrated environment and had served his country in the military like thousands of other black people, so he refused to be intimidated. "You're going to tell me we can't live certain places? I had a hard time with that," he said.

He and his wife bought the house in March but since their apartment lease hadn't expired, they continued living in the apartment for several months while Lenny and a friend of his, Hank Reed, remodeled the house. During that time there were no incidents, apparently because Wilkens's new neighbors presumed he and Reed were black workmen fixing up the house for new white owners. "Then when we moved in, 'For Sale' signs went up everywhere," Wilkens said. "We had a little collie puppy that got poisoned, but I felt as long as no one bothered me [things would be okay]. If they did I was going to protect myself, so I was ready. I had a gun in the house, and I made sure I didn't leave my family alone without my friend, Hank, coming by sometimes and checking on them . . . especially when I was out of town."

Wilkens was traded to Seattle in 1968 after a salary dispute, and was named player-coach after Al Bianchi resigned in 1969. Becoming a coach wasn't Wilkens's idea—after all, he had averaged a career-high 22.4 points and 8.2 assists, second only to Oscar Robertson, during the previous season. But general manager Dick Vertlieb said he insisted upon Wilkens becoming the coach because he wanted his team to mirror Wilkens's character and intelligence. "We talked a few days," Wilkens said. "I laughed. I told him, 'You're crazy.'" Vertlieb persisted. The general manager reminded Wilkens that he already was a coach on the floor. He pointed out that when Bill Russell was a player-coach he had been his own best player, and Wilkens would be the same for himself. Additionally, because Bianchi had resigned so close to the beginning of training camp, it would be hard to bring in someone from outside the organization. So finally he said he'd try it. Recalled Vertlieb: "I wouldn't have let him turn me down."

Vertlieb doesn't remember any discussion of the fact that Wilkens would become only the second black coach in NBA history (and the only one at the time). Had it been a problem for any of Seattle's white players? Tom Meschery, who was appointed player–assistant coach, wasn't aware that it had. "There were two key white guys on the team, me and Rod Thorn, and we had really strong leadership qualities, too," Meschery said. "We just thought that [Lenny as head coach] was a fine idea. All the other players were younger and I don't think any of them thought anything of it, and Rod and I were completely behind Lenny from the very beginning. They didn't see anything [negative] from older white guys, so they didn't think anything of it. If there were any problems, it was that he had to play on the court and try to run the team, and I had to play on the court. So actually Rod Thorn did a lot of bench coaching. In many ways Rod was more of Lenny's assistant." To this day Vertlieb regrets making Wilkens a player-coach instead of asking him to retire as a player. "I made a terrible mistake trying to save a half salary," Vertlieb said. "It's too big a job."

But Wilkens coped, and along the way developed the calm demeanor he's noted for (and sometimes criticized for) today. "When I was a player-coach, I used to yell and scream at guys sometimes because I would see the play developing and we wouldn't see the ball there or get it there," Wilkens said. That's not exactly how Meschery remembers it. "I don't remember him yelling at players," Meschery said. "I remember him being frustrated, and I remember him raising his voice. Guys that really raise their voice, he's not even in the ballpark." Then Meschery chuckled at the idea of Wilkens screaming at players. "He had a very quiet forcefulness," Meschery said. "I can't believe Lenny believes he yelled at people."

Nonetheless, Wilkens's mind was like a camera—it took a picture of what was happening on the court and never forgot it. University of Washington coach Marv Harshman, a close friend, reminded Wilkens of his unique ability to see the court after watching the Sonics practice. Wilkens said that Harshman told him, "You're screaming at them and they don't see it, and maybe you need to find a way to help them see it." So Wilkens began to observe practice more, and if a player didn't recognize a situation Wilkens would stop practice, explain the situation, and present a few options to exploit it. That method started working and the more success players had, the more receptive they were to his ideas.

Tyrone Corbin has a rare perspective on coaches, having played for nine different teams during a sixteen-year NBA career. He's had four different stints under Wilkens, covering seven seasons, and said Wilkens's patience and willingness to seek input from players are two reasons he has succeeded so long. "He doesn't try to control the entire game and the player," Corbin said. "He can have a game plan—push a guy to the left or to the right—and if you're following the game plan and the guy is killing you, Lenny's apt to change something. A player can say 'I don't feel comfortable pushing him that way or running a play.' It's a rare quality, especially in established coaches like him. Some feel 'this is the way to do it, and if it's not working, you're not doing it right.'"

As a journeyman player Corbin's role frequently has changed from reserve to starter and vice versa. That kind of shift can cause friction between a player and coach, especially if the move isn't fully explained. But communication is one of Wilkens's coaching strengths. "With me, in shootaround or practice he would come over and say 'for this reason we're going to make a change,' or 'the matchups are better this way,' or 'we need something coming off the bench,'" Corbin said. "He would always come to me beforehand and allow me to have input. After saying what he thinks about doing things, he would say 'how do you feel about it?' It was mutual respect, and that's why I enjoyed playing on any team he was coaching." Would he play for Wilkens again? "I'd love it," Corbin said.

Wilkens also adopted several philosophies of the coach he admired most, Red Auerbach. He liked Auerbach's ability to recognize each player's assets and maximize them, the fact that each of Auerbach's players was productive even if he played only five minutes per game, and Auerbach's use of a "sixth man" who could change the tempo of the game. On defense, however, the two coaches have an important philosophical difference. The Celtics funneled every opponent toward Bill Russell because he was such a quick shot blocker and could routinely shut off the foul lane. There's never been another Russell. Wilkens coaches his players to funnel ballhandlers to the sidelines and baseline, where their options are limited and defensive help can arrive. Combine that with Wilkens's vow to never publicly embarrass his players, and you have the winningest coach in NBA history.

Saddled with expansion teams and no coaching background, Wilkens didn't make the playoffs in his first five years at Seattle and Portland, four spent as player-coach. After being fired by Portland he returned to Seattle in 1976 as the Sonics' director of player personnel. When they stumbled to a 5-17 start under Bob Hopkins in 1977, Wilkens became their coach too. He utilized John Johnson as a "point forward" before the term was invented, made starters Downtown Freddy Brown and Paul Silas his top reserves, and coached the Sonics to a 42-18 record and into the NBA Finals, where they lost to Washington. The next season Seattle went 52-30 and won the NBA championship. Wilkins moved on to Cleveland in 1986, and in just three years upped their victory total from 31 to 57. Unfortunately, Michael Jordan and the Chicago Bulls, the scourge of the Eastern Conference, knocked Cleveland out of the playoffs four times in seven years.

Losing the series to the Bulls in 1989 on Jordan's famous jump shot in the closing seconds probably was Wilkens's most nightmarish defeat. Yet, in terms of maintaining his poise, it may have led to his greatest triumph. Craig Ehlo, who defended Jordan on that play, said he felt "devastated" after the game, as Wilkens must have. "But Lenny, he was so cool," Ehlo recalled. "He said, 'You guys gave everything. You played your hearts out. This guy is the best player in the league, maybe the best player ever, and it took him and 3 seconds and that shot to beat you. The greatest player maybe of all time beat you on a great shot. You did the best you could. Let it go.'

"I heard that and all the pain escapes me. Lenny just had this presence about him. He didn't come stomping in and throw a chair or cuss everyone out. He built something positive out of the whole situation, something positive that could carry us through a long, hard summer."[1]

Wilkins moved to Atlanta in 1993, winning his only Coach of the Year award that season (with a 57-25 record) and breaking Auerbach's record on January 6, 1995. Auerbach chided him for needing many more games to reach the 939-victory mark (Auerbach's record is 938-479; Wilkens's was 939-793), and Wilkens chided back that he never had the quality of players Auerbach enjoyed. Indeed, thirteen Hall of Famers at one time played for Auerbach; Wilkens has coached only two: Bill Walton at Portland and himself. None of the banter or comparisons really mattered. Wilkens's record spoke for itself, and the night he set it he was so happy that despite being a nonsmoker, he lit up a cigar, à la Auerbach, to celebrate. "Yeah, it was a huge achievement," Wilkens said five years later. "I think it just puts another nail there that we [black people] can do it, given the same opportunity. That's all we want, is the opportunity. And then I love it because I feel all the people who touched my life share in that—particularly family. But from the coaching ranks, Al Attles is my guy. Al and I broke in at the same time as rookies. We suffered through the same indignities, and when we would see each other we always kind of nodded, like we understood."

As a rookie Wilkens received unexpected encouragement from Philadelphia's black players, including Attles. Nineteen years later Wilkens's and Attles's careers again imitated each other when they both became rookie coaches; then Attles led Golden State to the NBA title in 1975. Even now, "I may not hear from Al for months, and all of a sudden from nowhere comes his deep voice, 'Keep it up,'" Wilkens said. "That's why I think our successes belong to a lot of people, not just you. Those are the people that keep me going."

Alvin Attles (1970–1983)

From 1960 to 1966 Al Attles had been Guy Rodgers's complementary backcourt mate with the Philadelphia and San Francisco

Warriors. While Rodgers ran the show—and often *was* the show because of his fancy ballhandling—Attles was a good passer but not someone who drew the "oohs" and "ahhhs" from the crowd. Any inclination he had toward that style of play was squeezed out of him by Dr. Randa Russell at North Carolina A&T.

One night A&T was winning easily and Attles started showing off during the game. "I'm doing all this nonsense," he said. "I was tricking guys and dribbling, not like they do between their legs now but just beating guys and making them look silly and smiling a little bit. . . . I was just having a good time." The next day Dr. Russell of the Physical Education department summoned "Mr. Attles" to her office. "Who was that I saw last night acting like a Globetrotter?" Attles recalled her asking. "So I sheepishly said, 'Well, it was me.' So she said, "I don't want to see that any more.' Just like that. She was really stern-faced, and I was kind of afraid of her. And I never did that again."

Attles wasn't a high scorer in the NBA, averaging only 9 points per game during an eleven-year career mostly by scoring on fast-breaks and capitalizing on turnovers. In fact, his timing was terrible in terms of having a stellar day as a shooter. Probably his best day occurred one night against the New York Knicks when Attles, a career 45 percent shooter, sank all eight of his shots from the field and his only free throw. Unfortunately that also happened to be the night that Wilt Chamberlain scored 100 points. The event left Attles with one of his favorite jokes: "Did you know that one night Wilt and I combined for 117 points?"

The six-foot-one, 180-pound Attles made his mark as an extremely strong, quick, fast, and aggressive defender. "Attles was probably as good a roving defensive player as anyone could ask for," former Warrior Tom Meschery said. "He was quick enough to get back to his man, so he could help out [against another offensive player]. He was pound-for-pound probably the strongest guy on our team, and that's saying a lot with Wilt Chamberlain on the team."

As polite as one could ask for off the court, Attles was nevertheless one of the NBA's best fighters when the need arose. Possibly a contradiction, but the description makes sense to Meschery, a very aggressive power forward himself: "I don't think Al ever started a fight in his life. If there was anybody more feisty it was me, but Al was like a pillar. He was there for everybody, so there were some people you could call enforcers; a guy like Al would be more like a protector. . . . He saved my butt a number of times."

Bill King, the Warriors' radio announcer, recalled a game in Philadelphia when Attles's fighting skills registered a near knockout, even though his foe was Bob Ferry, a six-eight center who outweighed Attles by 50 pounds. "There was a loose ball about at midcourt and there was a big scramble for it," King said. "Suddenly Ferry came up swinging at people and Alvin just dove right in, picked him up and literally threw him over his shoulders and started to pummel him. Wilt came over and was just shoving people out of the way and Wilt was shouting, 'Let him go, baby! Let him go!' Because Al wasn't short-tempered, but once it got triggered, look out." Alex Hannum, the veteran NBA player and coach, happened to be watching from the stands as Attles punched away. "Al just about decimated the guy in ninety seconds," Hannum said. "He must have landed fifty punches and as those fights usually do, they ended up in a wrestling match on the floor. Wilt had to break it up. He was the only guy big and strong enough to pick Al up and he pulled Attles off Ferry. If Wilt had not done that Al would have killed him, and I think from that he got the nickname 'The Destroyer.'" It definitely was not one of Attles's proud moments. King said that whenever Attles talks about it, he focuses on "the dressing down he got from his mother, because she was there. That's what Al talks about more than anything, that he had embarrassed his mother."

The 1969–70 Warriors were 22-30 under the coaching of George Lee when owner Franklin Mieuli replaced Lee with Attles on January 27, 1970. Mieuli, one of the NBA's most colorful characters with his trademark deerstalker's cap, was a good bet to name a black coach when it was a rarity because he was such an individualist. Naming Attles, however, who had doubled as a player and as Lee's assistant coach, was a strictly basketball decision at a time when the organization was undergoing great turmoil. The team had lost nine of its previous eleven games, and its star center, Nate Thurmond, had held a press conference the day before to announce that he was retiring at the premature age of twenty-eight because he was playing too many minutes and getting too many injuries. (Thurmond later changed his mind and played seven more seasons.)

Mieuli explained the coaching change by saying, "We need another pair of eyes to evaluate the team." Perhaps, as Lee had feared early in the season, the Warriors simply needed more team speed. "But I have the responsibility to evaluate whether we have the nucleus of a good team or whether we must build an entire new club," Mieuli said. "That's why I believe we needed another opinion."[2]

Mieuli originally offered the job to general manager Bob Feerick but was turned down, so he turned to Attles, who hadn't given any thought to making coaching a career. Technically he had been Lee's assistant, which Attles said mainly consisted of setting a hard-working example as a player during practices. Attles accepted the head job only because Mieuli agreed to let him coach the remaining thirty games as an "interim" coach and then would let him resume his playing career. Forward Dave Gambee was named Attles's assistant. In their second game as a coaching pair Attles passed to Gambee for a lay-up, prompting team publicist Harry Jupiter to declare, "That was a management decision."[3]

Attles finished that first season at 8-22, merely proving his belief that Lee hadn't been the cause of the Warriors' poor record. Instead of relinquishing his coaching duties, however, Attles decided to return for one more season as player-coach. "The only reason I came back was I really felt good about those thirty games," he said. "The team never, ever just gave up and quit. We prepared, went to practice, we worked hard, we went into every game thinking we were going to win." Obviously, having a black coach had been no problem for the eight white players on the team. "I would go to bat for any of those guys," Attles said. "I don't think anybody looked at it from a racial standpoint. I think it's a tribute to them because it was a bad season and they never stopped trying. And if they didn't want to play for a black coach, they could have really caved in."

With those many positives to encourage him, Attles returned as player-coach. "Franklin and I talked about it and said, 'let's take another year and see what happens,' and then we got lucky and made the playoffs," Attles said. "It wasn't any great revelation. I just really think the guys worked hard. We were only 41-41 but that wasn't a great step up." Those were coming, however. Attles's team went 51-31 the next year, his last as a player-coach and the first of his six consecutive winning seasons as the team's leader. He reached the ultimate in 1975 when his Warriors defied all preseason predictions by winning the Pacific Division with a 48-34 record; the team eventually swept the Washington Bullets in the NBA Finals, 4-0.

That team was distinguished by Attles's liberal use of reserves. It was an odd mix of a team: one superstar in Rick Barry, two outstanding rookies in Jamaal Wilkes and Phil Smith; nearly interchangeable shot-blocking centers Clifford Ray and George Johnson; a ballhawking corps of guards in Charles Dudley, Butch Beard, Charles Johnson, and Steve Bracey; an excellent rebounder-defender (for his size) in six-seven Derreck Dickey; and two over-thirty-three veterans Jeff Mullins and Bill Bridges. Attles sometimes substituted entire units because his starters and reserves were nearly equal in talent. The Warriors finished the season having nine players who played at least one thousand minutes each. Aided by assistant coach Joe Roberts, Attles had taken Red Auerbach's concept of the "sixth man" and stretched it to the "eleventh man."

Attles adopted that approach because his players were similar in ability and collectively had little ego. He believed that players do well in critical situations if they've experienced them before, and they remain motivated if they expect to get into a game. To demonstrate how important that is, he recalled the story of a teammate who was told to enter a game. The player began to pull off his sweatpants and suddenly realized he had forgotten to put on his basketball shorts. He may have been the ultimate unprepared athlete, and Attles wanted none of that on his team.

"There was a lot of evenness throughout that roster and I think that made it ideal for Al to deploy people the way he did," said King, the Warriors' broadcaster. "But the other thing people forget is that team was just a bitch on defense—a great defensive team."

The 1975 Finals were distinguished by the fact that for the first time the opposing head coaches were black. Attles's counterpart for the Bullets was K. C. Jones, the former Boston star, and each of them had black assistant coaches, Roberts with Golden State and Bernie Bickerstaff with Washington.

That was the year that Frank Robinson integrated baseball's managerial ranks and Lee Elder became the first black golfer to play in the Masters tournament. "What it means to me," Jones told the *San Francisco Chronicle* during the 1975 Finals, "is that [NBA owners] care only what a man can do. The NBA gave a black man a chance when Bill Russell became head coach of the Celtics. Since then they've looked at whether a guy can do the job. Basketball started acting when football and baseball were just talking." To NBA Commissioner Walter J. Kennedy, the presence of two black head coaches in the Finals was just an outgrowth of the league's development. "It's just a natural evolution," he said. "It wasn't any big precedent-shattering deal to us. We have black players. Some day there would be black coaches."[4]

The Bullets, whose 60-22 record had tied Boston for the best record in the NBA, were a 3 to 1 favorite to win the series against a team that had won just forty-eight games. Outside of the skills of the players, two things may have turned the tide of the series. If nothing else, they certainly lit a competitive fire under Attles.

The first occurred the night before Game 1, when Attles was sitting on his bed in his hotel room, killing time watching a newscast before going to dinner. Attles said that's when he heard a Washington television sportscaster predict that the Bullets would win in four or five games because, "Tomorrow the playoffs start and the Golden State Warriors are the worst team to ever play in the Finals."

Attles's reaction? "My temper starts to go and I want to throw something at the TV. So I go down and have dinner seething. I get back to the room and I'm watching a movie, and I'm figuring what in the world am I going to say? The next day is an afternoon game and my assistant puts some plays up on the board. He just gets ready to go over what the Bullets do and I say, 'Joe, hold it. Did anybody see the news last night?' Nobody saw it. 'Did anybody hear what the guy said?' No. 'I'm going to tell you what the guy said: The Golden State Warriors are the worst team ever to play in the Finals.' Let's go!

"Then the game starts and the first quarter we get behind by 16. I'm not telling anybody this but I'm sitting there thinking, 'You know, I wonder if this guy knew what he was talking about.'" But the Cardiac Kids, as the Warriors were called, pulled out the victory and swept Washington in four games. Just four minutes into the series-clinching game, the "Destroyer" part of Attles's personality appeared, resulting in one of the wildest scenes in NBA history.

Barry was the Warriors' only superstar, and Washington often guarded him with Mike Riordan, a roughhouse journeyman who once had played in the Eastern League. From the second the game started Attles believed the Bullets were trying to get Barry ejected from the game. Then 3:38 into the first quarter Barry tried to cut toward the foul lane, Riordan gave him what the *Chronicle* described as a karate chop, and Attles charged off the bench toward Riordan.

"When the ball went up for the first tip, Riordan just comes over and gives Rick an elbow in the jaw," Attles recalled. "Then we go down and take a shot and miss and they go down and take a shot and Rick's just running back on the sideline and Riordan's running alongside him and popped him again. When I saw that I went after him because I knew what was happening.

"The rule was the only guy who can go out there was the coach. [Somebody] tried to say I was going to fight. I told him I wasn't out there to fight; I was out there to protect Rick or to protect him from fighting. Let's be honest. Mike Riordan was a pretty good player, but if they lose Mike Riordan and we lose Rick, who wins that battle? So I didn't want Rick out of the game."

A photo shows an enraged Attles desperately trying to break free of the grasp of Bullets center Wes Unseld to get his hands on Riordan, who was being held back by teammate Elvin Hayes. Some punches were thrown and Attles was ejected from the game. Barry was not, so mission accomplished.

"People say 'do you think it was programmed?'" Attles said. "I know it was. Later on I talked to some of their players and their only concern was that somebody's got to get to me, because they knew I was coming. And Wes and Elvin were supposed to get me—not fight me but stop me."

The Warriors already were trailing 8–2 and had just lost their floor leader. But Roberts assumed control of the team and, though they eventually fell behind by 14 points, the Warriors rallied for a one-point victory that made Attles the second black man to coach an NBA champion—even if he wasn't on the court to see the finish.

The Warriors were 59-23 the next season, by far the best record in the league, but Phoenix upset them in the 1976 playoffs. That began a gradual slide in Golden State's fortunes caused by players' declining skills, the loss of several valuable free agents (mainly Wilkes, Gus Williams, and Bernard King), some poor personnel decisions, and plain bad luck. For instance, Attles's 1981–82 team went a highly credible 45-37 yet couldn't make the playoffs. After that, Mieuli's inability to match New York's high-priced offer to King doomed the team. Attles retired from coaching after one more season, finishing with a 557-518 lifetime record. He has stayed with the Warriors and serves in several executive capacities, most recently as vice president–assistant general manager when he completed his fortieth consecutive year with the franchise in 2000.

K. C. Jones (1973–92)

For K. C. Jones basketball wasn't just a game, it was a lifeline. He was born into the strict segregation found in Texas in the 1930s and raised in the 1940s in a loving family but with not much of a future. Jones parlayed his basketball skills into a college education, a nine-year NBA playing career as one of the best defenders the game has ever known, a ten-year NBA coaching career that left him ranked fourth in winning percentages in league history, and a place in the Basketball Hall of Fame.

There was nothing in Jones's early childhood that pointed toward any of those accomplishments. After his birth in Taylor, Texas, in 1932, his family lived in four different Texas cities before his mother took K. C. and his four siblings to San Francisco when he was about nine years old. In terms of racial dynamics and culture change Jones might as well have stepped from Texas onto the moon. "It was a revelation," Jones said. "It was like you had your self back. There in Texas you had to bow down to whites at the movie theater and in the back of the bus, and you had to stay out of white neighborhoods. That was the thing that did something for your mind. The anger is not there anymore, and you were not much of a person under those circumstances. So, you'd go hot and cold—anger, not much self-esteem, anger. I never had a conversation with a white person. Never sat next to them.

"We leave there in May and land in San Francisco because my mom took the five of us out there. I'm thrown into a school a couple days later and I'm sitting with Chinese and whites and Mexicans, and that's the first time I played on a basketball hoop. There was a soccer ball laying there, so I was shooting it. I only played softball in Texas."

San Francisco wasn't nirvana, however. His family was poor and lived in predominantly black projects in the Double Rock section of San Francisco. A recreation center provided a safe haven for kids like Jones who liked to play sports and attend Friday night dances, but it couldn't do much to broaden his perspective or raise his expectations.

"In San Francisco, you walked through the white neighborhood to school, and from school back to the black neighborhood," Jones said. "If you went downtown, you get on the bus to go to the movie theater or to shop and then back home. But there was never anything to do with going to the theater or museums, or visit businesses or walk through the stock market. There was none of that. It was never the museum or Golden Gate Park or cultural things. And tennis was something foreign. So was golf. . . . My thoughts were to get out of high school, get a job, get an apartment and a car. That was it. What I knew about college was there is college. That was as far as it went."

Jones didn't know it but fortunately one of his history teachers, Mildred Smith, who was white, was determined to convince the University of San Francisco (USF) to give a scholarship to Jones, who by then was a basketball star at Commerce High. She called USF coach Phil Woolpert several times about Jones, and ironically Woolpert offered Jones a scholarship on one of the saddest days of Jones's young life. "We're playing in a championship game against St. Ignatius High and I fouled out at halftime," Jones recalled. "There was some racism in that stuff. Bing, bing, bing, bing, bing, I'm out, and I was the star of the team. It was an almost all-black team. I'm crying like a baby in the dressing room instead of staying on the bench with the other guys. And then Phil Woolpert, the coach from University of San Francisco, came in and introduced himself, and through this waterfall of tears coming down he's saying I'd like to offer you a scholarship. That was the only scholarship or offer I got."

The summer before he entered USF in 1951, Jones suffered a player's worst nightmare when he inexplicably lost his shot after suddenly growing four inches. That horror changed his career forever. "To this day I can't understand what happened," Jones wrote in his autobiography, *Rebound*. "I went from being high scorer in the city league, one of the high scorers in Northern California, to an All-American brick thrower. Clang—off the rim. Whew—over the backboard. Ouch—Airball!"[5]

Jones tried all the adjustments he could think of to get his shot back and took plenty of shots as a freshman at USF as he tried to regain his accuracy. He made only 34 percent of them and averaged 5.6 points on a 7-14 team, so after the season Jones "had a long talk with myself" and decided to change his game. "I decided that I would be the director—the playmaker," he wrote. "The team would be the talent. From now on the points I would score wouldn't show up in the box score under my name but my teammates would score more and play better because of my efforts on the floor. Parts of the game that some more talented players paid less attention to—defense and passing—I would master." In addition, Jones made a promise to himself: "Nobody would ever out-hustle me. Not for one minute or part of a minute."[6]

At USF Jones roomed with a lanky center named Bill Russell, and they led the Dons to two NCAA championships while also developing several unique approaches to defense. In the 1956 draft the Boston Celtics traded with St. Louis to acquire Russell's draft rights, then on the next round Boston selected Jones. After spending two years in the army and trying out with the NFL's Los Angeles Rams, he joined the Celtics in 1958 but barely made the roster.

"He was a poor shooter and you figure you can't make the NBA just on defense alone, but there was an intangible in K. C.," Red Auerbach said. "Every time you put him in the game you increased your position. If you were 6 ahead, next thing you know you were 10 ahead. If you were 6 behind, next thing you're even. Whether he did it or somebody else did it, it happened. It happened in exhibition games. I said this is something I can't overlook." It also was a quality Auerbach didn't know about when he drafted Jones. "Absolutely not," Auerbach said. "I figured his defense was the primary factor. I figured he would become a better shooter, and he was so quick and we played fastbreak basketball. He concentrated totally and sacrificed offense to expend energy on defense. A lot of guards won't play strong defense because it tires them out and then on offense they won't shoot as well. He'd figure out how to play a guy. West and Oscar, just hound them. Make him work for his points. Nothing comes easy."

Jones backed up Bob Cousy for five years until 1963, when Jones became the Celtics' full-time starting playmaker and primary perimeter defender. He played defense with a studied, sophisticated approach. "There are things that don't come up in the book of fundamentals," Jones said. "The biggest thing is your ego in a man-on-man situation with a great player on offense. When you're on defense, your ego has to match the ego of that offensive player for you to be effective: 'I'm great at what I do on defense and he's great in what he does on offense, only he has an edge. He knows what he's going to do. [My job] is to have an idea of what he's going to do and still maintain position between him and the basket.' That's containment.

"If the egos don't match you don't have the mastery of the fundamentals, then what do you see in the defensive player? Fear. Then focus goes out the window. That's a dead giveaway to the guy with the ball. But if your ego matches his, then you know he's got somebody in front of him that he respects."

Preparation was just as important to Jones, whose defensive prowess made him a vital ingredient in the Celtics' success, though he averaged only 7.4 points per game and shot 39 percent for his career. Year after year Jones's greatest challenge was guarding the Lakers' Jerry West, who averaged 27 points per game during the regular season and upped that to 29.1 points per game during playoff games. To deal with West Jones needed to utilize every tiny advantage he could find. While trying to stay between West and the basket, Jones also was trying to anticipate West's next move. For instance, Jones knew that if he swiped at the ball and missed, West would use a crossover dribble and then go straight downcourt for a jump shot. Or he'd try to fake Jones into the air, then wait until Jones came down before rising for the jumper.

"I didn't know when he's going up for the shot or fake the shot, so I deduced that if he fakes it or shoots it, I'm going straight up in the air anyway," Jones said. "If he fakes it, then I come down with my hand over his shooting hand. He's still getting his 25 points a game, but he's not getting them in a cluster. During the course of guarding Jerry, he's going to scare the hell out of you." The key is, how long does the fear last? "Is it the rest of the ballgame or is it for a minute?" Jones asked. "It should not be for any more than a minute. You have to get back on track, so you say, 'I'll try this.' You have Plan A, and you have B, C, and D to get to."

Of course Jones had the luxury of knowing that Russell was behind him to cover any mistakes, but Jones didn't take that for granted. "If a guy got by you, Bill's there, but that didn't mean I could be reckless and open the gate," Jones said.

During the 1965–66 season, when he was thirty-three, Jones felt he had lost some of his quickness. Brandeis University had approached him about becoming its head coach so Jones considered retiring. Auerbach suggested he play one more season while recruiting players for Brandeis, and then step into the coaching job. That last season turned out to be Jones's only one as a Celtics player when they didn't win the NBA title; before that he had been 8-for-8. After three years at Brandeis, one also as an assistant at Harvard, another as Bill Sharman's assistant on the 1972 championship Los Angeles Lakers team that won a record thirty-three games in a row, and one as head coach of the San Diego Conquistadors in the American Basketball Association, the NBA's

Washington Capitals hired Jones as their head coach in 1973. He was an immediate success with the Capitals (who later changed their nickname to the Bullets and the current Wizards), leading Washington to records of 47-35, 60-22, and 48-34, along with two division titles. The pinnacle of his success was coaching the Bullets to the NBA Finals in 1975, where they were expected to trounce Al Attles's Warriors. Getting swept by them instead was bad enough, but worse yet, an incident during that series showed that despite the league's racial progress, even in the 1980s subtle discrimination could seriously harm a black person's NBA career.

Actually the incident was a fluke outgrowth of the television age that should have had no impact on Jones. During a long TV timeout, Jones told his players to run a certain play whenever action resumed. "It was a play we had been running all year," Jones said. "I told them what the play was and Bernie [Bickerstaff, his assistant coach] said, 'Do you want me to diagram it?' I said okay." In the meantime the commercial had ended and the TV cameras were focused on the Bullets on the sidelines. "But now what do you see in the huddle—assistants diagramming the play and the coach watching," Jones said. It should have meant nothing, but that scenario haunted Jones in years to come.

Jones believes that after losing the Finals, general manager Bob Ferry lost confidence in him. The next year the Bullets lost in the first round of the playoffs and Jones was fired for not leading them to a championship. Being fired was disappointing, certainly, though that's the risk any coach in professional sports takes and accepts. But because Jones had the third-best coaching record in NBA history at that time—155-91—he had every reason to expect that he quickly would be hired by another team. At worst, over the next two years he should have had the opportunity to accept or reject several job offers. Instead Jones went without a head-coaching job for seven years and in that span was interviewed for a head job only *once*—by Chicago in 1976.

If Jones had been white that would never have happened. For instance, during Jones's seven-year wait his white colleagues Larry Costello, Kevin Loughery, Gene Shue, and Doug Moe—all with inferior records to his—lost head-coaching jobs and were hired by other teams. But at the time the NBA was notoriously reluctant to give black coaches a second chance. In 1980, when this author wrote a series for the *San Francisco Chronicle* about the lack of black head coaches in professional sports, eleven of twenty white coaches had had two or more NBA head-coaching jobs; of the eight black coaches in NBA history at the time, only two, Russell and Wilkens, had been hired more than once.

In 1980 Jones didn't attribute his inability to get a coaching job to discrimination, saying, "I wonder [about not being rehired], but I never put time into researching reasons why not."[7] However, he did believe that infamous timeout in 1975 had generated questions about his competence. That was a huge hurdle to overcome during an era when sports owners and executives were still skeptical about blacks' ability to lead—as evidenced by the sprinkling of black quarterbacks and the lack of African-American head coaches in every major college and pro sport.

Mike Brown, a San Francisco diversity consultant, drew a parallel between Jones's plight and the frustrating experiences of black corporate executives. "In corporations, one thing blacks say pushes their rage button is over-scrutiny—the feeling that 'All you want to look at is what I didn't do right,'" Brown said. He characterized the NBA's feelings about Jones as: "I know you've won 63 percent of your games, but . . ."[8]

In 1978 Jones signed on with Boston as an assistant coach. Being passed over for head jobs tormented him for about three years more. "Then, [in about 1981] I said, 'Where am I? I've got a nice job. I'm in a business I love. I'm making money. I'm putting food on the table and have kids in college. Be thankful for what you have.' From there, I resigned to myself that head coaching is out and went on and had a better outlook when I woke up that day, it crossed my mind that there was nothing eating away at me any more."[9]

Fate fell Jones's way in 1983 after the Celtics had been swept by Milwaukee in the playoffs, ending a season filled with turmoil between coach Bill Fitch and his players. Red Auerbach, then the Celtics' president, chose the soft-spoken Jones to succeed hard-driving Fitch, and the Celtics responded beautifully to Jones's approach. Not only did they have the best record in the NBA at 62-20, but they also beat the Los Angeles Lakers in seven games in the NBA Finals, then won the title again in 1987 by beating Fitch's Houston Rockets.

Hall of Famer Bill Walton was the backup center on that 1987 team, and Jones's subtle style left an indelible impression on the former UCLA great: "He was a perfect coach—the most like John Wooden as any coach I played for," Walton said. "K. C. exemplified class, winning, and championships. Doing the little things. Doing your job and only being positive. Don't ever bring any of that [negative] trash around your team. And his ability to skillfully evoke Celtic pride was incredible. He would always talk about how all the old players called him up after an embarrassing performance and wanted to disassociate themselves from the Celtics. They wanted to mail in their championship rings, wanted their numbers removed from the rafters, and by this point there would be tears rolling down our cheeks and we'd want to kill. Hokey? The players have to buy it. If players don't buy what the coach says, it will never work. That's why a successful coach has to earn the respect of the players, because he has to ask players to do things that are not in their own self-interest. In professional basketball, you destroy your body doing this."

Jones was the perfect choice to follow the autocratic Fitch, himself a living contradiction. Although one of the wittiest coaches in the league who could deliver one-liners to reporters almost as well as Johnny Carson, Fitch also was a highly demanding disciplinarian. That quality was valuable when Auerbach hired him in 1979 after the Celtics had gone 29-53 the previous season. Fitch ran and badgered the Celtics into shape, re-energized center Robert Parish, and led them to a 61-21 record his first year—helped immensely by a rookie named Larry Bird. The next season Fitch made Boston a champion once again, but after two more years he had turned off many of his players.

When speculation arose that Jones, a quiet person who isn't comfortable talking in public, might replace Fitch, forward Cedric Maxwell was skeptical: "The reporters asked and I said I didn't know if K. C. [was authoritarian enough] to bark down orders," Maxwell said, "and I found K. C. didn't need to bark down orders. I was so embellished in Bill Fitch yelling and screaming, I thought that's the way it had to be done; that's the way we win championships. I was as much at fault as anybody. K. C. had a quiet, diplomatic way and it worked out great.

"You see a guy like Pat Riley strolling the sidelines and yelling out [instructions]. K. C. just sat there, sent players in and sometimes people took his silence and not being animated as the fact that he didn't know what he was doing. I think that was just the opposite. And K. C. had to deal with people thinking black coaches weren't intelligent, and K. C. had to battle that stereotype. Like it or not, that had to be done and K. C. was on the frontlines. He had to find a way to win."

As time went on Maxwell realized that Jones's greatest asset was his calming influence on the team. Jones merely stated what needed to be done and expected his players to execute it. Perhaps because he was a former player, the coach also loosened the reins somewhat, trusting that his players would not abuse their freedom. "He came after Bill Fitch, who was more a taskmaster and whipped the team into shape," Maxwell said. "The thing about Bill was he never relinquished that power. It was a championship team that he got from boys to men but never let grow beyond that."

For example, Maxwell said that Fitch had a rule that on the road all players had to ride on the team bus from their hotel to the arena and back. It doesn't sound irritating until looking at it from a player's standpoint. After playing in New York, "If you had friends waiting for you at Madison Square Garden, Bill had the rule that you had to ride back to the hotel with the team and then come back to the Garden," Maxwell said. "K. C. eliminated things like that—you guys are grown. Those rules may fit for a young team, but once you got [to championship level] you knew what it took."

Jones's diplomatic style also helped him prevent many problems that could have arisen despite the Celtics' immense talent. "K. C. helped guys find roles," Maxwell said. "It didn't hurt that K. C. had great players and great personnel. But teams pretty much self-destruct if they don't have that calming influence." Then he referred to the Dallas Mavericks of the mid-1990s, who supposedly were headed toward great success after they brought together three talented individuals in Jason Kidd, Jim Jackson, and Jamal Mashburn. That union won only thirty-six and twenty-six games before it was broken up by petty jealousies and trades. "Sometimes you need someone to right the ship," Maxwell said.

If a player wasn't performing up to his potential, Jones wouldn't embarrass him in front of teammates. Instead, "We always said K. C. would take you to his high chair, and that meant take you to his office and have a personal conversation," Maxwell said. He recalled one visit that occurred when Maxwell was in a scoring slump. "I'd coast along; I'd get 10 points a game and be satisfied. He would say, 'You're not a 10-point scorer. You can easily score 20 and we need your leadership.'" It was direct and to the point, without being harsh or a Knute Rockne–type, rah-rah speech. To Maxwell that was the kind of direction a veteran team like the Celtics needed.

However, one time Jones didn't adhere to his usual policy of critiquing players only in private resulting in a conflict between him and guard Dennis Johnson. Seeing how everyone involved handled that situation explains why the Boston teams were consistently high achievers under Jones.

In his autobiography Jones said that he criticized Johnson in front of his teammates for something Johnson had done wrong during practice, and the conversation escalated into a yelling match. "We wound up in a very heavy argument and I told Dennis that if I was wrong about this I would apologize and that we should both think things over," Jones wrote. "The next day before practice we had a quiet talk. He apologized and I apologized, and it all worked out for the best. The incident with Dennis taught me something—or re-taught me. I had done enough coaching to be aware of it and I shouldn't have had to be reminded forcefully: Don't strongly criticize a player in front of the others. . . . This is particularly important in the pros. Believe it or not, we're more sensitive than college or high school players."[10]

While Jones had been rethinking his role in the argument, something else important was taking place among the players. "K. C. didn't say a whole lot [after the argument]," Maxwell said, "but the players were self-disciplined and we were the guys who said, 'Dennis, you're wrong.' So K. C. had a support system. Because we respected him, we weren't going to put him in a situation like that. I don't think K. C. could browbeat a guy, and we were good enough as a team not to let something like that [destroy] us."

In five seasons in Boston Jones compiled a 308-102 record, his .751 winning percentage the best in franchise history. The Celtics reached the NBA Finals four times and won two championships under Jones. Despite all that, he never became the darling of the Boston media, which effusively praised his loyalty and relationships with players yet couldn't quite figure out why he was so successful. That was evident in a column written by the *Boston Globe*'s Bob Ryan after Jones announced during the 1988 playoffs that he was resigning as coach, effective as of the postseason, and would be succeeded by assistant coach Jimmy Rodgers.

In analyzing Jones's "rather remarkable accomplishments" as an NBA coach, Ryan wrote:

Yes, he has been blessed with two pretty good assignments. His Washington Bullets teams had Wesley Unseld, Elvin Hayes, and Phil Chenier. His Celtic teams have featured Larry Bird, Kevin McHale, Robert Parish, Dennis Johnson, Danny Ainge and, for one golden season, a fellow named Walton. As such, he has always been dismissed as strictly a button-pusher by people not familiar with the oft-quirky psyches of professional athletes.

K. C. is difficult to analyze because he has such a relaxed demeanor; it's difficult to believe he is on top of everything. And to some extent, he isn't. There couldn't possibly be another NBA coach in the past two decades less knowledgeable or less interested in pursuit of NBA minutiae. He doesn't know players' alma maters; he doesn't keep track of individual player perambulations; and he doesn't stay up until all hours awaiting the later scores from the West Coast. And he surely doesn't wear out his VCR with incessant viewing of game tapes.

All he does is show up for practices and games with more than thirty years of practical basketball experience, extracting good performances from players who would walk over hot coals for him. [11]

Jones's response to that opinion was: "Not only did I have Larry Bird and Kevin McHale, but so did Bill Fitch—and he didn't go to four Finals in five years. Besides," Jones said about his press coverage, "I was a quiet guy, would not have quips to hand to them, and I was not a yeller or screamer and I was a nice guy. They're not into that kind of thing. For the most part they're into the charismatic coach, the Pat Rileys, Rick Pitinos."

Pressure from the media and from within the Celtics' organization had been building for Jones to step aside since Boston had prevented the New York Knicks from hiring assistant coach Jimmy Rodgers the year before as their head coach. Facing that, Jones negotiated a contract extension with Auerbach that let him coach the 1987–88 season then promoted him to a front-office position. When the new position turned out to have little authority, Jones returned to head-coaching in 1990 with Seattle, going 59-59 in less than two seasons, then coached the women's New England Blizzard team in the American Basketball League until it folded in 1998. In the meantime, since the time when Jones was forced out as Boston's coach, the Celtics have had four head coaches, have never played in the NBA Finals, and had suffered through seven consecutive losing seasons going into the 2000–2001 season.

When that season began, Jones, who was inducted into the

Hall of Fame in 1989, still held the fourth-best winning percentage in NBA history. Yet, if the average fan was asked to name the league's great coaches, his name most likely would be left off the list. "I think K. C. will go down in the annals as one of the least-respected players and least-respected coaches in the history of the game," Maxwell said. "Playing with Russell, you won't get much credit there. Coaching Bird, McHale, Dennis Johnson, and Danny Ainge, you won't get credit for that, and that's just a freak of nature. That's just the nature of the game. Sometimes people are forgotten."

17

Today's NBA

_use this intro (somewhat)

- Four black players who intergrate the league??

much the NBA has
integrated the league
NBA of 1950 and the
s in the United States
of sports, whether
mporary NBA game
levision contracts,
ding the sport. Try
nt player in 1950,
ning a record label
O'Neal does. It is
comes into focus.

...ly, the status and stature of black players in the NBA has improved tremendously in fifty years. Chuck Cooper, Earl Lloyd, Sweetwater Clifton, and Hank DeZonie helped spawn a league in which roughly ten slots on every twelve-man roster are filled by a black player. The NBA's 2000–2001 season began with one black part-owner (Washington's Michael Jordan), four African-Americans heading up a team's basketball operations (Detroit's Joe Dumars, Philadelphia's Billy King, Vancouver's Billy Knight, and Jordan), and eight black head coaches (Lenny Wilkens, Paul Silas, Doc Rivers, Alvin Gentry, Isiah Thomas, Byron Scott, Sidney Lowe, and Leonard Hamilton). In addition, it's not unusual for the NBA office and teams to employ black men and women in their media relations, broadcasting, sales, marketing, and promotions departments. The links between the two eras sometimes are difficult to decipher, in part because current players often have little knowledge of their sport's past and partly because so little early NBA history has been written. The situation is exacerbated by the fact that athletes in general tend to be too "now" oriented and by the league's transformation from one almost exclusively comprised of college graduates to one with a significant number of high schoolers and college undergraduates entering every year.

Near the end of the 1999–2000 season, Minnesota Timber-wolves assistant coach Greg Ballard, Minnesota star Kevin Garnett, and Los Angeles Lakers centers Shaquille O'Neal and John Salley—all of whom are black—each took a guess at naming the first black player drafted by an NBA team. Their attempts show how little is known about the NBA's pioneers, regardless of color, but their interest in the topic also indicates that they understand its importance:

"I don't know who was the first to be drafted," Garnett said. "You'll have to school me."

"I started picking up basketball after I heard the name Dr. J. [Julius Erving]," O'Neal said, referring to the star of the 1970s and 1980s. "Anything before that, I'm slowly learning about—Dave DeBusschere and guys like that. But no, I don't know who the first black player is."

"Who the first one was, who the second one was," began Salley. "We really don't know about the first black players. I know a lot of guys don't. I saw Meadowlark Lemon [the famous former Harlem Globetrotter] the other day and one of the guys didn't know who he was, so that's scary."

Of them all, Ballard came closest. Who was the first black player drafted? "I want to say," Ballard replied. "I want to say. He played for the Celtics, didn't he? I want to say. I'm thinking Green. No. Wait, wait, wait, wait. Chuck something? Chuck . . . you'll have to give me the last name." Cooper. "That's it!" Ballard exclaimed.

They all agreed, however, about the significant role the black pioneers and their histories played in their sport. "It's always important to know history," Ballard said. "You've got to know where you come from and the struggles you went through to better yourself as a race and as an African-American."

Agent Aaron Goodwin, who has represented NBA stars Shareef Abdur-Rahim, Jason Kidd, and Gary Payton, believes some of his clients have read about basketball history, but the topic usually comes up only after being compared to a star from the past. "I think when they get compared to a player, they research the player a little bit," Goodwin said. He encourages players to delve into the NBA's past in a general way. "I don't say to Gary Payton, 'Go research Charlie Scott,' or someone with a similar, fiery game as Gary," Goodwin said. "I just told the guys years ago that what you should do is request some videotape from the NBA and look at all the players, and the NBA will provide it if you request it. I remember in 1995 Jason Kidd had all kinds of copies of Bob Cousy that he studied. He had been compared to Bob Cousy so much that he started studying Bob Cousy."

NBA Commissioner David Stern appreciates the first wave of black players, especially as groundbreakers. "Somebody had to wedge himself in so that we could begin to get access to an un-segregated talent pool, both as a country and as a sports league," he said. "Someone has to be first and I think we were very lucky that it began to flow as soon as it did. I think all of their stories are vital because what people don't focus on—because we tend to be so in the now—is how short a time ago it was. In the history of man, that's a blink of an eyelash. So to understand the forces that excluded them, opposition they overcame, and even the trials of their lives when they were in the league are vital for us to understand how recently our country was less than civilized."

The NBA, like the nation, didn't burst forth with a surge of integration. The entrance of black players began at a gradual pace, then sped up so that by the early 1960s the composition of rosters had changed significantly. By 1965, 51 percent of the league's players were black, which may be one of the reasons the league struggled for public acceptance for more than thirty years. From 1956 to 1969 the Boston Celtics owned an NBA dynasty unmatched by any franchise in any sport, yet they couldn't captivate their hometown fans. Even during the Bill Russell glory days the Celtics averaged only 8,406 fans in the 15,128-seat Boston Garden.

By the late 1970s the league was beset with serious problems. Incompetent ownership (particularly Cleveland Cavaliers owner Ted Stepien's penchant for foolish statements to the press and unwise trading of first-round draft picks for mediocre talent) began to produce apparently hopeless franchises. Drug and alcohol abuse by several star players hurt the league's image. The fact that until 1982 the NBA Finals were televised on a tape-delayed basis sent the message that it was a second-class event. Widespread suspicion that a largely white audience wouldn't embrace an increasingly black league didn't help. Together these facts led some members of the media to conclude that several teams would need to fold in order to help nurse the league back to health.

Stern, who replaced Lawrence O'Brien as commissioner in 1984, was cognizant of all the problems and all the rumors. He countered in the early 1980s by helping to arrange the sale of the Cavaliers to the Gund brothers, who retain ownership to this day. The league, along with the NBA Players Association under the leadership of Larry Fleisher, introduced professional sport's first league-run drug rehabilitation program, which raised credibility. A salary cap established a maximum and a minimum amount each team could spend on salaries and guaranteed players a certain percentage of the league's gross income. The changing color of the league, however, was a fait accompli.

"We decided there was nothing we could do about the color composition of our league," Stern said. "In fact, we knew it was going to get even higher in terms of African-Americans, and we were determined that America was going to accept this league. We understood it would be successful if we could just hold steady for the long term. We lived with [advertising] agencies saying to us that their clients decided to buy college basketball rather than the NBA because the NBA was too black. We said, 'we understand what your client said, but by the way, does your client know the racial composition of our fans is predominantly white?' They said, 'We don't care.'"

Then the NBA was blessed with a phenomenal streak of good luck and had the good sense to capitalize on it. By 1984, Jordan's rookie year, the league had a confluence of marketable players that launched a tremendous surge in popularity. The merger with the American Basketball Association had brought the NBA a galaxy of stars in Julius Erving, Artis Gilmore, George Gervin, Moses Malone, and Bobby Jones. Kareem Abdul-Jabbar, although thirty-seven years old that year, played five more seasons until he set an NBA record by playing 1,560 games. In 1979 the matchup between Indiana State and Michigan State in the NCAA championship game captivated the nation as Larry Bird and Magic Johnson went head to head. The rivalry only enriched the NBA during their 1979–80 rookie seasons, when Bird led Boston to the biggest one-year turnaround in league history (from 29 to 61 victories), and Johnson brought the Lakers the NBA championship (by registering 42 points, 15 rebounds, and 7 assists as an emergency *center*, replacing the injured Abdul-Jabbar against Philadelphia in the decisive game of the NBA Finals). The floundering Detroit franchise was rejuvenated by superstar guard Isiah Thomas. Secondary stars such as Kevin McHale, Robert Parish, Bernard King, and James Worthy contributed to the resurgence in popularity. The NBA did an exceptional job of promoting them all by encouraging accessibility to the media and fans alike.

Then came Jordan, who turned the sports world upside down from 1984 to 1998 by winning ten scoring championships, levitating the Chicago Bulls to six NBA titles, and becoming the advertising icon of the century.

Attendance kept climbing, increasing every year in the 1990s through the 1995–96 season, when it topped out at 17,252 fans per game. The league's popularity spread worldwide, and television ratings reached all-time highs—as did the percentage of black players on rosters. "It says more about America than the league," Stern said. "America's a pretty good country and the kids who were growing up as the league became increasingly dominated by African-Americans didn't care about the color of their athletes. Their parents had grown up with an essentially white league and saw it move to an essentially black league, and had a little more trouble with it. Familiarity does not breed contempt; familiarity breeds understanding. The young kid who wanted to dunk [emulated] Dominique Wilkins, whether Wilkins was black or white."

Then Jordan left after the 1997–98 season, followed by friction-filled collective bargaining negotiations that resulted in a lockout of players. By the time the contract was settled, the 1998–99 schedule had to be reduced to fifty games per team, attendance and television ratings had dropped, and talk of a troubled Jordan-less NBA began. The rumblings continued during the 1999–2000 season, while the television ratings for the first game of the NBA Finals between Los Angeles and Indiana got a 10.5 rating on NBC, the lowest-rated Game 1 in fourteen years.

"Think about it," Stern said. "You mean a black player retired and business is down? We're an equal opportunity adversity ratings." Then Stern discounted the drop in television ratings by noting the league's increasing following in foreign countries and through its Web site and video games. "The fans are still there; they're expressing affinity in different ways," he said.

Who will be the next Michael Jordan? Toronto's Vince Carter was anointed by the media after he won the 2000 All-Star Weekend slam-dunk contest, then followed it up with a flurry of game-winning shots in ensuing games. But Carter and his team faltered in the playoffs, leaving him and a bevy of young stars such as Garnett, Kobe Bryant, Allen Iverson, Stephon Marbury, and even season and playoffs MVP O'Neal still riding Jordan's vapor trail.

Today an ongoing argument persists about whether the league has had an overall drop-off of talent since the 1980s of Showtime in Los Angeles, the awesome frontline of Bird, Parish and McHale in Boston, Dr. J and Moses Malone in Philadelphia, and Jordan and Scottie Pippen in Chicago. A debate such as that should be addressed in three ways: from a team standpoint, an individual standpoint, and a maturity standpoint.

Undoubtedly, teams in the mid-1980s were stronger than those in 2000 because during those twenty years the talent pool has been diluted by expanding the league from twenty-three to twenty-nine franchises. In addition, the ever-increasing stream of high schoolers and undergraduates selected in the NBA draft means that, in general, today's young players have far less top-level experience under their belts than players of previous eras had. Stern argues that the infusion of players from foreign countries has given the league an injection of talent that wasn't available twenty years ago. Nevertheless, many of those players haven't played extensively in competition comparable to Division I college basketball; they cannot compensate for a league that's become so young that eighteen of the twenty-nine first-round draft picks in 2000 hadn't completed four years of college eligibility. It has only become more difficult to blend players into an efficient team.

On the other hand, in terms of individual athletic ability the talent level has never been higher. Billy McKinney, Seattle's executive vice president, has seen that evolution first-hand as an NBA executive for fifteen years (after completing a seven-year playing career in 1985): "These players are so good now, it's scary," he said. "Some of the players are doing things in high school I probably couldn't do until I was a second-year pro. Athletically, no question. Everybody can dunk now."

The style of NBA play has changed, too, and new fundamentals are being formed. "Guys are playing above the rim," McKinney said. "When you look at guys making passes, it used to be thread-the-needle bounce pass. Now you just throw it up somewhere near the backboard and somebody's going to get it. If I'm Dr. Spock [the famous Star Trek character], the game's no longer two-dimensional. You've got to look at that third dimension."

McKinney cites many reasons for the change: better off-season competition for high school and college players through the Amateur Athletic Union, the influx of conditioning coaches and improved physical training techniques on the college and professional level, state-of-the-art practice facilities, and even less stress on players' bodies (since instead of being stuffed into seats on commercial flights after a short night's sleep, they now usually ride in luxury on their own team's chartered plane directly after a game). Where the NBA definitely has slipped, however, is in the maturity level of its players. Many of them haven't completed four years of college eligibility and their salaries are high. When McKinney was a rookie in 1978 the average salary was $150,000, the minimum was $35,000. "I received a $10,000 bonus for making the roster because I was a walk-on," he said. "I thought I had hit the lottery." Contrast that to the 2000–2001 season, when the average salary was $3.9 million and the minimum was $316,969. "They're megastars with megamoney," agent Goodwin said, "and they're thrust out to have to deal with everyday issues of life. . . . Someone who's been in college for four years, you learn to deal with it; a lot of the high schoolers can't [handle relationships with] women, hangers-on. It's more social things, but the basketball, they're very, very advanced."

McKinney, an NBA executive for four different teams, said he has reminded every team owner and president he has worked for that they shouldn't assume that because a player is wealthy, it also means he's a responsible adult. "They're going through an incredible learning curve about handling money, handling fame, about making the best decision or even good decisions about things they aren't accustomed to dealing with," McKinney said. "So many players have come from challenged backgrounds, and they've gone from college or high school where they couldn't afford anything, and now they can buy a luxury car and pay cash for it, or buy a house and pay cash. I'm forty-five now, and I wonder how I would have handled it, and I'm a pretty responsible person."

Another concern of McKinney's is the endorsement and public-appearance opportunities that come to players—especially to black players. These situations make it is essential that players feel comfortable in public situations, speaking clearly and with correct grammar. "When I'm on TV or radio, I've always been sensitive to being able to articulate yourself the proper way because like it or not, people think you are a role model," McKinney said. "In so many instances, people judge a race by how you speak." However, he's found that players' ability to express themselves well has lessened over the years, even though their agents and the NBA make public speaking instruction available to them. "The hurdle is they have the resources to improve themselves, but many players have fallen into 'I have the money. It doesn't matter how I present myself.' But you have to think of what you might want to do ten years from now," McKinney said.

Since the racial pioneering days, the status of black players in the NBA has improved astronomically. They occupy such a high percentage of today's roster that the concept of a roster "quota" only comes to mind when one wonders whether some teams keep one or two token white players to mollify the league's predominantly white ticket buyers. Otherwise, said Salley, racial issues are almost non-existent. "The color in the league is green," he said. "Money covers a multitude of sins, man. We don't run into it. I mean, I can get a cab in New York City—sometimes. But as far as coaches and the way people treat you, I've never heard anyone in the stands yell out the "N" word. They treat us all as players." Salley recalled a scene in a Spike Lee movie in which a character mentions Magic Johnson and rock stars Prince and Michael Jackson, and then says, "Oh, they're not black." Salley believes that attitude also applies to current NBA players. "That's some people's mentality, so you kind of lose your color along with your anonymity," he said. "They don't come down and yell at you, or believe that to play basketball you have to be black. The funny thing is they call [Sacramento's white point guard] Jason Williams 'White Chocolate.' That's the change."

Goodwin, however, sees a bias in the different ways the media describe black and white players. "Too many times, African-American ballplayers are still referred to as just athletes, whereas a white ballplayer is usually [described as being] more intelligent," he said. "The African-American still uses a skill; the white player still uses his intelligence. When they blow [away] that myth to realize there are some extremely intelligent players regardless of color, that will be a lot better."

It is a problem Goodwin believes players can't and never will change because in his estimation, 90 percent of the media is white and prone to be fooled by racial stereotypes. "The bottom line is Jason Williams, who's the love of the league right now with his fancy passes, if he was an African-American he'd be [portrayed as] a hot dog. He'd be sitting on the bench. When Nick Van Exel [who is black] did those same things in Los Angeles years ago, the media fussed about how fancy he was and why doesn't he just tame it down. It's never going to change. It's fine; you just live with it."

Along racial lines, one is more apt to hear the NBA criticized for its disproportionately small numbers of black power brokers— head coaches, general managers, owners. "We're still trying to break down those barriers," said Kevin Johnson, former star of the Phoenix Suns.

Ballard, a former NBA player and assistant coach for eight years, aspires to be a head coach and believes chances of that occurring are much higher than they would have been when he broke into the league in 1977. "I think there's more awareness [of the need for black head coaches] and more African-Americans are playing basketball," Ballard said. Then, noting three black coaches who have won NBA championships, he added, "I think also we've demonstrated that we can coach at this level. Look at Lenny Wilkens. Look at Al Attles, K. C. Jones. I think all that helps."

Salley, who entered the league in 1986, agreed that many more opportunities exist now for aspiring black coaches, especially since owners are hiring more former NBA players as head coaches (such as Rivers, Thomas, and Scott). It's an approach that Salley approves. "Well, if I went on a tour of the Amazon, I wouldn't ask a lady from Long Island to show me the way to the Amazon," he said. "I would ask someone who's done it, who knows it, who's been through it. That's who you want to be your tour guide." Salley doesn't believe that black players should feel an extra sense of obligation to a black coach, however. "No, a black coach can be a bad coach, too," he said. "Let me tell you something. I found out a long time ago, and Martin Luther King said it, that you should always judge people according to their character. Reputation is what you fall for; character is what you stand for."

Stern believes that, ideally, the percentage of black coaches in the league should fall somewhere between the percentage of black people in the overall population and the current percentage of black NBA players. Of course, since blacks comprise only 12 percent of the nation's population and about 80 percent of NBA rosters, Stern has left himself a wide margin of satisfaction. The eight current black head coaches comprise 27.6 percent of the league's total. "Our owners want so badly to win, that I think they don't think about race," Stern said. He noted that the trend toward hiring former players will continue to bring more African-Americans into the head-coaching ranks; if there's a problem in the hiring process, it may be that not enough black candidates get interviews. The NBA has been trying to give black coaching aspirants more exposure by doing things such as letting Nate "Tiny" Archibald and Tony Campbell coach a team in Asia during the summer of 2000. "It may take a decade to take care of itself," Stern said.

Playing backup center on the Lakers' 1999–2000 championship team marked the end of the thirty-six-year-old Salley's playing career. Becoming a general manager is what fascinates him—"Helping guys, working out deals," he said. "The general manager puts guys together on the squad, and when you're able to put together a winning squad, there's a lot said about that. And hopefully, I'll be keeping guys happy, paying them righteously [that is, fairly]. We'll see how it all works out." If Salley seriously pursues his dream of becoming a general manager or eventually decides he wants to become a head coach, he may then encounter some frustrations based on race. "The NBA has been very progressive about it, but I'm sure there are coaches and [aspiring] general managers who feel they have been overlooked tons of times," McKinney said.

McKinney began his front-office career as an assistant coach-scout with Chicago in 1986, then rose to the position of vice president in charge of basketball operations. In 1989 he became the first director of player personnel for the expansion Minnesota franchise, then was appointed Detroit's general manager from 1992 to 1995 (when he drafted perennial All-Star Grant Hill, Allan Houston, and Lindsey Hunter as keys to Detroit's rebuilding process). McKinney has spent the last five years with Seattle as the Sonics' executive vice president for basketball operations. His goal is to become a general manager again, but McKinney finds that he and other blacks who aspire to head coaching and GM positions ponder one question again and again: "What's the criteria?"

McKinney sees white and sometimes black job candidates rise to top positions when black aspirants with more experience are passed over. It leaves him wondering what kind of experience, skills, personality, and contacts are needed to get those jobs. He would like to be a general manager again, and wonders why the opportunity hasn't come his way? "I've been in management sixteen years," he said. "I helped start an expansion team [Minnesota], helped build a championship team [Chicago], rebuilt a team [Detroit], and have been with a contender for five years [Seattle]," he said. "I don't even get an interview now. If you're with a team, another team has to call to get permission to interview you. But it seems a lot of times there was no interview process. Someone just gets the job. What do I have to do so I'm the No. 1 guy? Is it racial? I've been asked that thousands of times and it's difficult to answer." Difficult to answer because two black general managers, Jordan and Dumars, head up teams even though they had virtually no management experience. Jordan had none when he was appointed in 1999, and Dumars had one year as a vice president of player personnel before he was promoted in 2000. What did they have in common? They both had been NBA stars, which McKinney believes fits into the NBA's emphasis on marketing. "There's a perception now that if you have a name, you're qualified to do the job," McKinney said. "It's like the trend. Guys fortunate enough to be in those positions, I'm happy for them. But for guys like me and others who have been in those positions for years, guys like Wayne Cooper [Sacramento's assistant vice president of basketball operations] who worked hard to learn the trade, they deserve an opportunity."

McKinney, who was a six-foot guard averaging only 8 points during his NBA career, said he once asked a high-ranking league executive how he could improve his chances of getting a general manager's job and was told he needs to get to know more team owners. "And my question was, 'Where does someone who was not a superstar meet the owners?'" McKinney said. The league executive couldn't give him an answer. McKinney is encouraged, however, in seeing Seattle's general manager Wally Walker doing "a tremendous job" of touting McKinney's skills in conversations with other teams.

Finally, there is the giant step up to ownership. So far only Jordan has taken it, as part owner of the Washington Bullets. "I don't think there's as much interest [among current players] in being a general manager as there is in being an owner," Goodwin said. "There's a lot of interest in the younger players who are making a lot of money at an early age." Many entrepreneurial spirits start businesses during their basketball careers and consider owning an NBA team later. Basketball is such an integral part of Kevin Garnett's life—"It's in my blood. Cut me and I leak orange," he said—that he wouldn't rule out owning a team in the future.

Kevin Johnson believes an important step toward more ownership occurred during the 1998 labor talks when many black players were part of their union's negotiating team. "This collective bargaining agreement was critical because it involved a lot of black players with power and influence in some things that involved the politics of it and the economics," Johnson said. "That broadens horizons and lets people know we're more than guys dribbling a basketball. We're trying to be businessmen as well."

As time passes the players of today will become the legendary players, coaches, general managers, and owners of tomorrow. "We live a great life," Garnett said. "We make great money and I don't think you'll hear anybody bickering about the money or the opportunities that basketball has created. So, if anything, the Bill Russells, the Wilt Chamberlains, the Oscar Robertsons, the Magic Johnsons, the Kareems were the guys who laid the foundation for guys like myself, Iverson, Antawn Jamison, Stephon Marbury, or Shaq—the great players you see now. . . . We're stepping in the same footprints and are creating our own at the same time. That's just how history goes, and the opportunity we have now will be vastly greater for others down the line."

Appendix

The NBA's Black Pioneers, 1950–1965

A player's rookie year is indicated with an asterisk (*). If a player was on two teams during the same season, he is listed under the team he played for last.

1950–51 (4 of 135 NBA players, or 3%)

Boston:	*Chuck Cooper
New York:	*Sweetwater Clifton
Tri-Cities:	*Hank DeZonie
Washington:	*Earl Lloyd

1951–52 (5 of 116, or 4%)

Baltimore:	*Don Barksdale, *Davage Minor
Boston:	Cooper
Milwaukee:	*Bob Wilson
New York:	Clifton

1952–53 (5 of 125, or 4%)

Baltimore:	Barksdale
Boston:	Cooper
Milwaukee:	Minor
New York:	Clifton
Syracuse:	Lloyd

1953–54 (6 of 110, or 5%)

Baltimore:	*Ray Felix
Boston:	Barksdale, Cooper
Milwaukee:	*Isaac (Rabbit) Walthour
New York:	Clifton
Syracuse:	Lloyd

1954–55 (9 of 105, or 9%)

Boston:	Barksdale
Milwaukee:	Cooper, *Ken McBride
New York:	Clifton, Felix
Philadelphia:	*Jackie Moore
Syracuse:	Lloyd, *Jim Tucker

1955–56 (12 of 92, or 13%)

Fort Wayne:	*Jesse Arnelle, Cooper
Minneapolis:	*Robert Williams
New York:	Felix, Clifton, *Walter Dukes
Philadelphia:	Moore
Rochester:	*Ed Fleming, *Dick Ricketts, *Maurice Stokes
Syracuse:	Lloyd, Tucker

1956–57 (15 of 99, or 15%)

Boston:	*Bill Russell
Minneapolis:	Dukes, Williams
New York:	Clifton, Felix, *Willie Naulls
Philadelphia:	*Hal Lear, Moore
Rochester:	Fleming, *Sihugo Green, Ricketts, Stokes
Syracuse:	*Bob Hopkins, Lloyd, Tucker

1957–58 (13 of 99, or 13%)

Boston:	*Sam Jones, Russell
Cincinnati:	Ricketts, Stokes
Detroit:	Clifton, Dukes
Minneapolis:	Fleming, *McCoy Ingram
New York:	Felix, Naulls
Philadelphia:	*Woody Sauldsberry
Syracuse:	Hopkins, Lloyd

1958–59 (19 of 92, or 21%)

Boston:	*K. C. Jones, S. Jones, Russell, *Bennie Swain
Cincinnati:	*Wayne Embry
Detroit:	Dukes, Lloyd, *Shellie McMillon
Minneapolis:	*Elgin Baylor, *Boo Ellis, Fleming
New York:	Felix, Naulls
Philadelphia:	*Andy Johnson, *Guy Rodgers, Sauldsberry

St. Louis:	Green
Syracuse:	*Hal Greer, Hopkins

1959–60 (24 of 99, or 24%)

Boston:	Russell, K. C. Jones, S. Jones, *Maurice King
Cincinnati:	Embry
Detroit:	Dukes, Lloyd, McMillon
Minneapolis:	Baylor, Ellis, Felix, Fleming, *Tom Hawkins
New York:	*Johnny Green, Naulls, *Cal Ramsey
Philadelphia:	*Wilt Chamberlain, Johnson, Rodgers, Sauldsberry
St. Louis:	S. Green
Syracuse:	*Dick Barnett, Greer, Hopkins

1960–61 (27 of 93, or 29%)

Boston:	K. C. Jones, S. Jones, Russell, *Tom (Satch) Sanders
Cincinnati:	*Bob Boozer, Embry, *Oscar Robertson
Detroit:	Dukes, *Willie Jones, McMillon
Los Angeles:	Baylor, Felix, Hawkins
New York:	J. Green, Naulls
Philadelphia:	*Al Attles, Chamberlain, Johnson, Rodgers
St. Louis:	S. Green, *Fred LaCour, Sauldsberry, *Lenny Wilkens
Syracuse:	Barnett, Greer, Ramsey, *Joe Roberts

1961–62 (36 of 113, or 32%)

Boston:	K. C. Jones, S. Jones, Russell, Sanders
Chicago:	*Walt Bellamy, S. Green, Johnson, Sauldsberry, *Horace Walker
Cincinnati:	Boozer, *Joe Buckhalter, Embry, Robertson
Detroit:	Dukes, W. Jones, *Ray Scott
Los Angeles:	Baylor, Felix, Hawkins
New York:	*Cleveland Buckner, *Ed Burton, *Al Butler, J. Green, Naulls, *Sam Stith
Philadelphia:	Attles, Chamberlain, Rodgers
St. Louis:	*Stacey Arceneaux, *Cleo Hill, LaCour, McMillon, *Bob Sims, Wilkens
Syracuse:	Greer, Roberts

1962–63 (45 of 117, or 38%)

Boston:	K. C. Jones, S. Jones, Russell, Sanders

Chicago:	Bellamy, S. Green, *Charlie Hardnett, King, *Bill McGill
Cincinnati:	Boozer, Buckhalter, Embry, Hawkins, Robertson
Detroit:	Dukes, W. Jones, Scott
Los Angeles:	Barnett, Baylor, *LeRoy Ellis, *Gene Wiley
New York:	Buckner, Butler, J. Green, *Paul Hogue, *Tom Stith
San Francisco:	Attles, Chamberlain, *Wayne Hightower, LaCour, *Howie Montgomery, Naulls, Rodgers, *Hubie White
St. Louis:	*John Barnhill, *Zelmo Beaty, *Bill Bridges, Saulds-berry, *Chico Vaughn, Wilkens
Syracuse:	Greer, *Porter Meriwether, Roberts, *Chet Walker, *Ben Warley

1963–64 (42 of 111, or 38%)

Baltimore:	Bellamy, S. Green, Hardnett, *Paul Hogue, *Gus Johnson
Boston:	K. C. Jones, S. Jones, Naulls, Russell, Sanders
Cincinnati:	Embry, Hawkins, Robertson, *Tom Thacker
Detroit:	W. Jones, *Reggie Harding, *Eddie Miles, Scott
Los Angeles:	Barnett, Baylor, Ellis, Wiley
New York:	Boozer, Butler, J. Green, *Jerry Harkness, *Tom Hoover, McGill
Philadelphia:	Greer, Walker, Warley, White
San Francisco:	Attles, Chamberlain, Hightower, Rodgers, *Nate Thurmond
St. Louis:	Barnhill, Beaty, Bridges, Vaughn, Wilkens

1964–65 (56 of 115, or 49% [48.7%])

Baltimore:	Bellamy, Butler, S. Green, Hardnett, Hightower, *Les Hunter, G. Johnson, *Wali Jones
Boston:	K. C. Jones, S. Jones, Naulls, Russell, Sanders, *John Thompson
Cincinnati:	Embry, *Happy Hairston, Hawkins, Robertson, Thacker, *George Wilson
Detroit:	*Joe Caldwell, Harding, W. Jones, Miles, Scott
Los Angeles:	Barnett, Baylor, Ellis, *Walt Hazzard, McGill, Wiley
New York:	*Jim Barnes, Boozer, *Emmette Bryant, J. Green, Hoover, *Willie Reed

Philadelphia: Chamberlain, Greer, *Lucious Jackson, *Larry
Jones, Walker, Warley
San Francisco: Attles, McLemore, Rodgers, Thurmond
St. Louis: Barnhill, Beaty, Bridges, Burton, McGill, *Paul
Silas, *John Tresvant, Vaughn, Wilkens

Notes

*All quotations not otherwise cited are from interviews conducted by
the author between 1982 and 2000.*

1. One Step at a Time

1. George Beahon, "Prexy Podoloff, Royals Guest Here, Sees Basketball, Hockey Death Duel," *Rochester Democrat & Chronicle,* November 1, 1950, p. 26.
2. Al C. Weber, "Risen Paces Royals to Opening Victory," *Rochester Times-Union,* November 1, 1950, p. 50.
3. Gerry Finn, "Bucky Lew First Negro in Pro Basketball," *Springfield Union,* April 2, 1958.
4. Mike Funke, "The Chicago Studebakers," *Solidarity Magazine,* June 1992, p. 17.
5. Funke, "Chicago Studebakers," p. 19.
6. Robert W. Peterson, *Cages to Jump Shots* (New York: Oxford University Press, 1990), p. 131.
7. Edna Rust and Art Rust Jr., *Art Rust's Illustrated History of the Black Athlete* (Garden City NY: Doubleday, 1985), p. 301.

2. Jackie's Legacy

1. Jules Tygiel, *Baseball's Great Experiment* (New York: Oxford University Press, 1983), p. 195.

3. Just a Dab of Color

1. George Sullivan, "The Celtics, Chuck Cooper, and the Struggling NBA," *New York Times,* April 27, 1980, p. 2S.
2. Robert Cromie, "NBA Castoffs to Form Basket League," *Chicago Daily Tribune,* April 25, 1950, pt. 3, p. 1.
3. Joe Bostic, "The Scoreboard—It Wouldn't Surprise Me If," *New York Amsterdam News,* March 18, 1950, p. 27.
4. Sullivan, "Celtics, Cooper, and NBA."

5. Jerry Nason, "Globe Trotters' Boss, Riled by Cooper Deal, Bars Visits to Boston," *Boston Daily Globe*, April 27, 1950, p. 18.

6. George Sullivan, *The Picture History of the Boston Celtics* (Indianapolis: Bobbs-Merrill, 1982), p. 158.

7. Herb Ralby, "Auerbach, New Coach, Says All Celts on Block," *Boston Daily Globe*, April 28, 1950, p. 35.

8. "Stay Away from the Uline Arena May 14," editorial, *Washington Tribune*, March 8, 1943.

9. "Uline Arena Removes Ban on Negroes Effective at Once," *Washington Post*, January 22, 1948.

10. Jack Walsh, "Caps Draft Schnittker, Sharman, and O'Keefe," *Washington Post*, April 26, 1950.

11. Shirley Povich, "This Morning with Shirley Povich—To Whom It May Concern," *Washington Post*, April 30, 1950.

4. A Taste of Sweetwater

1. "Globetrotters Sail for Europe," *New York Amsterdam News*, April 29, 1950.

2. Original letter from Podesta to Ned Irish, May 3, 1950, reprinted in *The Legend*, 2.2 (October 1996).

3. Joe Bostic, "The Scoreboard—Monthly Meeting of the GMA," *New York Amsterdam News*, May 20, 1950.

4. Sid Friedlander, "Clifton Asks Share of $$$ Knicks Paid," *New York Post*, May 25, 1950.

5. Charles Salzberg, *From Set Shot to Slam Dunk* (New York: E. P. Dutton, 1987), p. 126.

6. Friedlander, "Clifton Asks Share."

7. "Hawks Purchase Negro Ace as Gayda Receives Release," *Moline Daily Dispatch*, December 1, 1950, p. 38.

5. "No" to the Trotters

1. Lee Gutkind, "Whatever Happened to Chuck Cooper," *Pittsburgh Magazine*, November 1976, p. 42.

2. Bill Nunn Jr., "Boston Celtics' Million $ Baby," *Pittsburgh Courier*, February 24, 1951, p. 7.

3. Nunn, "Million $ Baby."

4. Rust and Rust, *Rust's Illustrated History*, p. 312.

5. Telegram from Abe Saperstein to Chuck Cooper dated May 4, 1950.

6. Rust and Rust, *Rust's Illustrated History*, p. 313.

6. Frustrated Pioneer

1. Bill Nunn Jr., "Change of Pace," *Pittsburgh Courier*, October 7, 1950.
2. Wendell Smith, "The Grand Duke Likes Pro Basketball," *Pittsburgh Courier*, November 4, 1950.
3. Gutkind, "Whatever Happened to Chuck Cooper," p. 78.
4. Clif Keane, "Calm, Poised Donham and Cooper Dispel Tenseness of Pressing Vets," *Boston Daily Globe*, November 10, 1950, p. 26.
5. Joe Looney, "Celts Win Fifth in Row, 79–74," *Boston Herald*, November 16, 1950.
6. Bob Ajemian, "Celts Know Cooper Can Score," *Boston Evening American*, February 3, 1951, p. 18.
7. Gutkind, "Whatever Happened to Chuck Cooper," p. 78.
8. Sullivan, *Picture History of Celtics*, p. 161.
9. Jack Barry, "Cooper Shines as Celtics Trim Fort Wayne, 90–68," *Boston Daily Globe*, November 21, 1953.
10. Clif Keane, "Rochester Players Air Complaints After Celtics Score Decisive Win," *Boston Daily Globe*, December 28, 1953, p. 6.
11. Clif Keane, "Cousy's Knee Ominous Note in Celts Victory," *Boston Daily Globe*, March 17, 1954.
12. Sullivan, *Picture History of Celtics*, p. 159.
13. Gutkind, "Whatever Happened to Chuck Cooper," p. 79.
14. Gutkind, "Whatever Happened to Chuck Cooper," p. 42.
15. Gutkind, "Whatever Happened to Chuck Cooper," p. 79.
16. Gutkind, "Whatever Happened to Chuck Cooper," p. 79.

7. Moon Fixer Rises

1. Dave Heller, "Caps Lose to Knicks, 92 to 87, Plop into Cellar," *Washington Post*, November 15, 1950.

8. West Virginia State Pioneers

1. "State Quintet Leaves Tonight for California," *Charleston Gazette*, February 4, 1949.
2. "How Athletics Crash Color Line," *Color Magazine,* May 1950, p. 32.

9. The Gentlest Giant

1. "'Sweetwater' Clifton," *Ebony Magazine*, December 1948, p. 62.

2. Lyall Smith, "Clifton, Acker, Shoot It Out in Cage Finals," *Chicago Daily News,* January 3, 1942.
3. Sam Smith, "'Sweetwater' Clifton Keeps Rollin' Along," *Chicago Tribune,* June 9, 1985, p. 2.
4. Smith, "Clifton Keeps Rollin'."
5. Red Smith, "A Christmas Carol," *Chicago Sun-Times,* December 25, 1954.
6. Smith, "A Christmas Carol."
7. Salzberg, *Set Shot to Slam Dunk,* p. 136.
8. Salzberg, *Set Shot to Slam Dunk,* p. 136.
9. Associated Press, "'Sweetwater' Begins to Sour His Basket Foes," *Chicago Tribune,* December 9, 1951.
10. Smith, "Clifton Keeps Rollin'."

10. Barksdale, a Man of Many Firsts
1. Emmons Byrne, "The Bull Pen," *Oakland Tribune,* January 16, 1948, p. 31.
2. "Uncertain Weather Tonight Has Put Cage Fans on Edge," *Lexington Leader,* July 9, 1948, p. 6.

11. Barksdale's Long Haul
1. James Ellis, "Barksdale in Town," *Baltimore Sun,* October 16, 1951.
2. *Associated Press,* December 24, 1951.
3. *Associated Press,* December 26, 1951.
4. Walter Taylor, "Barksdale Ban Lifted; Double-Header Carded," *Baltimore Sun,* December 26, 1951.

12. Jealousy Kills Hill's Career
1. Bob Cole, "Cleo Hill Passes Roughness Test," *Winston-Salem Journal,* date unknown.
2. John J. Archibald, "Hill Hits Early for Hawks," *St. Louis Post-Dispatch,* October 22, 1961, p. 1G.
3. Special correspondent, "Dissension Not Hawks' No. 1 Problem, Seymour Says," *St. Louis Post-Dispatch,* October 26, 1961, p. 1E.
4. John J. Archibald, "Kerner Laughs Off Trade Offers, Not Coach's Trade Talk," *St. Louis Post-Dispatch,* November 16, 1961, p. 1E.
5. Bud Thies, "Ousted Seymour Blasts Players," *St. Louis Globe Democrat,* November 18–19, 1961, p. 1C.

6. Bob Cole, "Cleo Hill: Old Nest vs. New Hawks," *Winston-Salem Journal*, date unknown.

7. G. D. Clay, "Remembrances of Frustrations Past," *Sports View Magazine,* date unknown, p. 28.

8. Bob Broeg, "Sports Comment," *St. Louis Post-Dispatch*, November 19, 1961, p. 3E.

13. Eastern League Provides Haven

1. "Lear Too Small to Shoot from Corner, Must Change His Style for Pro League," *Philadelphia Inquirer*, October 14, 1956.

2. "Warriors Drop Hennessy, Lear," *Philadelphia Inquirer*, November 14, 1956.

3. Bob Vetrone, "Lear Is Averaging 37 in Eastern League; Side Job Could Cool His NBA Aspirations," *Philadelphia Inquirer*, January 27, 1957.

14. John McLendon, Naismith's Protégé

1. Chuck Heaton, ". . . as Piper Coach; Adams Is Traded," *Cleveland Plain Dealer*, January 30, 1962.

15. The Coming of the Superstars

1. Maurice Stokes, journal entry, September 30, 1967.

2. Clif Keane, "Russell's Rebounds Give Boston Edge," *Boston Globe*, April 9, 1959, p. 39.

3. Wells Twombly, "Basketball Immortal," *San Francisco Sunday Examiner & Chronicle*, November 7, 1971, p. C4.

4. Wilt Chamberlain, "In Wilt's Own Words," *Philadelphia Inquirer*, October 13, 1999, p. E13.

5. Ted Silary, "Standing Tall as a Teen-ager," *Philadelphia Daily News*, October 13, 1999, p. W-16.

6. Red Holzman and Leonard Lewin, *A View from the Bench* (New York: W. W. Norton, 1980), p. 69.

7. Wilt Chamberlain, *A View from Above* (New York: Villard Books, 1991), p. 20.

8. "Remembering Wilt," *Philadelphia Inquirer*, October 13, 1999, p. E12.

9. Chamberlain, *View from Above*, p. 152.

10. Phil Jasner, "Wilt Chamberlain Wants to Make His Positions Clear," *Philadelphia Daily News*, October 29, 1996.

11. Chamberlain, "Wilt's Own Words."

12. "Outstanding Performances Highlight Stokes Classic History," *35th Annual Maurice Stokes Memorial Basketball Program*, August 10, 1993.

13. Chamberlain, *View from Above*, dedication.

14. Frank Fitzpatrick, "Stars Come Out to Recall Wilt," *Philadelphia Inquirer*, October 22, 1999, p. A1.

15. Stephen A. Smith, "Chamberlain News Stuns Many Friends," *Philadelphia Inquirer*, October 13, 1999, p. E12.

16. Smith, "Chamberlain News."

17. Anne Byrne Hoffman, *Echoes From the Schoolyard* (New York: Hawthorn Books, 1977), p. 68.

16. Black Coaches Extend Integration

1. Michael Arace, "Who Better to Pass Red?" *Hartford Courant*, December 18, 1994, p. D1.

2. Dick Friendlich, "Al Attles Replaces Lee as Coach," *San Francisco Chronicle*, January 28, 1970, p. 47.

3. Dick Friendlich, "Well-Coached S.F. Beats Suns, 125–116," *San Francisco Chronicle*, January 31, 1970, p. 35.

4. Art Spander, "Quiet Coaches—Attles, Jones," *San Francisco Chronicle*, May 22, 1975, p. 59.

5. K. C. Jones with Jack Warner, *Rebound* (Boston: Quinlan Press, 1986), p. 49.

6. Jones, *Rebound*, p. 50.

7. Ron Thomas, "The Color Line in the NBA," *San Francisco Chronicle*, November 13, 1980, p. 75.

8. Thomas, "Color Line," p. 75.

9. Ron Thomas, "Celts Coach Overcomes NBA's Discrimination," *USA Today*, January 27, 1984, p. 5C.

10. Jones, *Rebound*, p. 27.

11. Bob Ryan, "Shouldn't Jones Have Pressed Bench to Action?" *Boston Globe*, June 5, 1988, p. 72.

Index

Barksdale, Don (*cont.*)
  and All-Star Game, xvi, 109, 110,
  130, 174; and army service, 114–15;
  with Baltimore Bullets, 109, 125–
  30; as a beer distributor, 125; with
  Boston Celtics, 130–31; and "bottle
  incident," 122–23, 124; as a club
  owner, 112; death threat against,
  117, 121; as disc jockey, 112, 125;
  discrimination against, 118–19,
  123; and friendship with Hutchins,
  129; in high school, 113; as host
  of "Sepia Revue," 109; in Marin
  Junior College, 113–14; memorial
  service for, 111; with Oakland
  Bittners, 115, 116; and Phillips 66
  team, 116, 117, 118, 122; and Save
  High School Sports, 112; at UCLA,
  109, 114–15; on U.S. Olympic
  basketball team, 109, 116–17, 119
Barnes, Jim, 255
Barnett, Dick, 164, 165, 166, 169, 253,
  254, 255
Barnett, Jim, 196, 207
Barnett, Shannie, 12
Barnhill, John, 149, 150, 166, 168, 172,
  254, 255
Barry, Rick, 224, 225–26
Bartlesville OK, 118; segregation in,
  119
Basie, Count, 7
Basketball Association of America
  (BAA), 10, 11, 14, 16, 21, 22, 26,
  27, 34, 115; formation of, xv, 39;
  merger with National Basketball
  League, xv
Basketball Hall of Fame, 7, 8
Baylor, Elgin, 67, 68, 159, 197, 210,
  252, 253, 254, 255; career with
  Los Angeles Lakers, xvi, 187–91;
  characterization of, as player,
  xvi, 187–91; racial discrimination
  against, 175
Baylor University, 117
Beahon, George, 2
Beard, Butch, 224
Beaty, Zelmo, 254, 255
Beck, Byron, 171
Beck, Ernie, 193
Bee, Claire, 14, 52, 93
Beeten, Scott, 192

Belafonte, Harry, 59
Bellamy, Walt, 253, 254
Belmont, Joe, 172, 173
Bennett, Carl, 23, 24, 25
Berger, Mike, ix
Berkeley High School, 113
Bethune, Mary, 57
Bianchi, Al, 157, 158, 217
Biasone, Daniel, xiv, 14, 21, 81, 135
Bickerstaff, Bernie, 224, 231
Big Cat. *See* Lloyd, Earl
Bird, Larry, xii, 214, 233, 236, 237, 243;
  and NCAA championship, 241
Birdland, 59
Bismarck Hotel (Chicago), 26
Blackbirds. *See* Long Island University
Black History Week, 87
Blake, Marty, 140, 141
Blattner, Buddy, 141
Blue and Gold American Athletic
  Union, 96
Blue and Gold beer, 125
Blue Devils, 28
Blue Goose, 9
Bolden, Frank, 50, 57
Boozer, Bob, 210, 253, 254, 255
Boryla, Vince, 102, 104; on U.S.
  Olympic basketball team, 117
Bostic, Joe, 26, 43
Boston Braves, 19
Boston Bruins, 27
Boston Celtics, ix, 2, 3, 26, 27–29, 30,
  31, 49, 51, 54, 55, 57, 58, 59, 60, 61,
  62, 64, 71, 90, 104, 150, 183, 212,
  233, 235, 240; exhibition game,
  vs. Baltimore Bullets, 126–27;
  exhibition game, vs. St. Louis
  Hawks, 176; vs. Houston Rockets,
  232; vs. Los Angeles Lakers, 232
Boston Daily Globe, 60, 65, 177, 235
Boston Evening American, 61
Boston Garden, 27, 28, 29, 240
Boston Herald Traveler, 61, 177
Boston Red Sox, 211
Boswell, Sonny, 10, 12, 13
Bowling Green State University, 26,
  29, 145
Bracey, Steve, 224
Bradley University, 95, 135
Bragan, Bobby, 19
Brandeis University, 230

New England Blizzard team, 236
New York Amsterdam News, 26
New York Giants, 20
New York Harlem Yankees, 45, 46
New York Herald Tribune, 20–21, 101,
    107
New York Knickerbockers, xi, xiii, xv,
    3, 16, 18, 21, 23, 27, 39, 42, 43, 44,
    45, 47, 56, 58, 66, 97, 101, 103, 104,
    105, 106, 107, 125, 134, 136, 149,
    155, 160, 164, 221, 236
New York Mirror, 40
New York Post, 40, 43, 101, 107
New York Renaissance, xv, 3, 6–9, 14,
    15, 16, 20, 36, 40, 45, 47, 58, 63,
    100, 106, 169. *See also* Dayton Rens
New York Times, 104
New York Tuck Tapers, 167
New York University, 21
New York Yankees NFL team, 128
NFL. *See* National Football League
NIBL. *See* National Industrial
    Basketball League
Nichols, Jack, 47
NIT. *See* National Invitational
    Tournament
Norlander, John, 34, 36
Norman, Jay, 152
North Carolina Agricultural and
    Technical State University, 137, 221
North Carolina Central University, 32
North Carolina College, 27, 32, 33, 35,
    37, 38, 76, 165, 166
North Carolina State University, 76
Northern California Junior College
    Conference, 114
Nostalgia Sports Research, 4
Notre Dame University, 49, 210
Novak, Mike, 12, 13
Novak, Stan, 152, 153
Nunn, Bill, Jr., 19, 51, 52, 57, 75

Oakland Athletics, 112
Oakland Bittners, 115, 116, 125
Oakland Raiders, 212
Oakland Tribune, 116
O'Brien, Lawrence, 240
Odom, Lamar, 175
Ohio State University, 37, 76, 89
O'Keefe, Dick, 33
O'Keefe, Tommy, 76

Oklahoma State University, 162
Olajuwon, Hakeem, 201
Olympic Basketball Committee, 117
O'Neal, Shaquille, xvii, 111, 238, 239,
    242, 249
O'Ree, Willie, 211
Original Celtics, xv, 7, 8, 106
Orr, Johnny, 12
O'Shea, Kevin, 49
Otis, Johnny, 113
Otten, Don, 40, 77, 78
Owens, Jesse, 17

Parish, Robert, 90, 233, 236, 241, 243
Parker-Gray High, 73, 80
Patterson, Okey L., 93
Pawtucketville Athletic Club, 4
Payton, Gary, 239
Peters, Joseph, 89, 90
Pettit, Robert (Bob), 66, 139, 141, 142,
    143, 146, 147, 215
Peyton, Tony, 12
Philadelphia Inquirer, 154
Philadelphia 76ers, 14, 150, 212. *See
    also* Syracuse Nationals
Philadelphia Tapers, 150
Philadelphia Warriors, xv, 22–23,
    26, 31, 63, 137, 153, 195; vs. St.
    Louis Hawks, 142; vs. Washington
    Bullets, 223. *See also* San Francisco
    Warriors
Phillips Oilers, 115
Phillips 66 Petroleum Company, 115,
    118, 167; basketball team of, 116,
    117, 118, 122
Phoenix Suns, 245
Pieri, Lou, 28
Pippen, Scottie, 111, 243
Pitino, Rick, 236
Pittsburgh Condors, 158
Pittsburgh Courier, 19, 50, 51, 54, 57,
    58, 66, 75
Pittsburgh Magazine, 49, 62, 68
Pittsburgh Pirates, 72
Pittsburgh Press, 54
Pittsburgh Steelers, 75
Pitts, R. C. "Butcher," 116, 119, 122,
    124
Pitts, William, 80
Podesta, Fred, xiii, 40, 41–43, 44, 100,
    103

MAKING YOUR APPLICATION RELEVANT

A typical problem for the mature jobseeker is that you will very often have a broader range of experience and skills than is required for the job. Sending a full work history will potentially rule you out because you will come across as having plenty of general skills but nothing specific to the role, or you will give the impression of having done it all before, leaving the employer wondering why you want the role.

When preparing an application, ask yourself: 'What are the top three to five attributes that I think the employer is looking for?' If it is an advertised role, these attributes will be listed. If not, some research among your network might be required. Focus on these attributes when selecting what to include from your repertoire of skills and experience. Make a table. In one column list the criteria the employer is looking for, and in the other your achievements, qualifications and experience – the things that demonstrate you have the skills and you meet the criteria.

Your application should be a complete chronological record, but what you say about each job and the skills and competencies you describe should be limited to those that are relevant. You are not trying to illustrate *all* the things that you are good at, but trying to show that you are *really* good at the specific skills required for the role you are applying for.

The top three to five reasons that make you suitable for the role should then appear:

- in your covering letter or e-mail;
- in the top third of your CV, usually in a 'profile' section;
- in any accompanying or supporting information.

The body of your CV should now back up the claims you make in the covering letter and profile. In your employment history, list the responsibilities and achievements that verify the statements you have made. Likewise, only add the educational and qualification information that is relevant.

When you read through your application for the job, it should be obvious that you have picked from your extensive background and experience only those elements that qualify you to do the job. Your capability should be evident. If it's not obvious to you, how do you expect a recruiter to spot it in 30 seconds? Typically, that is how long your application has to make an impression.

IMPORTANCE OF FOLLOWING UP

An employer or recruitment agent wants to know that job applicants are interested in the role on offer. All else being equal, the applicant who follows up with a phone call or e-mail a short time after sending their application, will stand out over those who just send it in and hope. Don't harass the employer or agent with calls, but do make sure that they know you are interested in the outcome of your applications. Is it 'yes', 'no' or 'we'll keep you on file'? And if it is 'no', is there any feedback on 'why'?

Many recruitment agencies and companies now openly declare: 'If you don't hear from us, assume that you were not successful.' This is in response to criticism from jobseekers that they never hear anything back. Even if this is the case, we would argue that if you are a good candidate for a role, it is always worth trying to get through by phone to demonstrate your real interest.

DEALING WITH REJECTION

Recruitment is a selection process. You are being assessed along with other candidates, who, like you, think they are suitable for the role. When rejections come in you have to see them as a natural part of the process, just as in a marathon race where there is one winner and many participants. The selection process is dependent on attracting many applicants, all of whom will be rejected except one. Rejection does not invalidate the skills and experience you have to offer.

It is important, however, to act on trends in the feedback you receive. Is there a common theme? Are you applying for the right roles? Does your CV need a makeover? Review the reasons for rejection, accept that it does not invalidate who you are, and then change your approach if you think it's appropriate.

MOVING FROM PUBLIC SECTOR TO PRIVATE SECTOR EMPLOYMENT

At a 'Beat the Credit Crunch' seminar in June 2009, the solution proposed for jobseekers was to seek government and public sector contracts – at the time their funding appeared unlimited and guaranteed. The public sector accounted for 20.9 per cent of UK employment[1]. Many roles were filled by ex-private sector employees.

The change was radical. In October 2010, the government announced that almost 500,000 public sector jobs would be lost in the next five years. Companies and consultancies serving the public sector were forced to radically scale back their business expectations. In 2011 and beyond, the pendulum will swing and ex-public sector workers will be seeking employment in the private sector. If you're one of them, how will you face the challenge?

WHAT'S THE DIFFERENCE BETWEEN THE TWO SECTORS?

By public sector we mean all jobs that are funded directly or indirectly by central, regional or local government. These include the NHS and the armed forces. By private sector, we mean the employer is a privately-owned company seeking to maximise profit for shareholders. Many jobs perceived to be in the public sector have already been outsourced to the private sector and so the lines are blurred. Some private companies provide services exclusively to, or on behalf of, the public sector. Service companies like Serco, Connaught, Siemens and Accenture provide services to government under long-term contracts.

Some private sector employers have a perception that employees in the public sector work in a sheltered environment and are therefore less professional. In fact, public sector employees are often equally committed and professional, but it's a different type of professionalism. To find employment, you'll need to challenge the stereotypes. Furthermore, you'll need to demonstrate how skills developed in the public sector can be applied in the private sector.

As an example, we recently learned that a small private company, a start-up specialising in the global export of IT equipment, had a recruitment problem. The ability to travel widely at short notice to developing countries, and work in small teams to manage complex local relationships were key requirements of the role. It proved difficult to find candidates in the private sector – but two public sector groups were sources of candidates: ex-UK Foreign Office and ex-UK armed forces personnel with engineering or signals expertise. These people have a well-developed ability to operate on their own initiative far from home – a highly-valued skill for this private company.

APPLYING FOR JOBS IN THE PRIVATE SECTOR

Research the opportunities where your transferable skills will be valued and use the tools and techniques described in this book. The table below identifies some of the specific differences to note when making the change from public sector to private sector, and how to tackle them.

APPLYING FOR JOBS IN SERVICE COMPANIES

The new environment is one that is highly scrutinised. Service companies may be private operations, but they are spending from the public purse. You'll need to demonstrate you can work to targets, operate in a fast-moving environment, and be able to change direction and bring stakeholders with you. Employers

Public sector	Private sector
Job titles will include terms such as 'officer' and may be strictly graded based on seniority.	Job titles tend to be made up as required. It's important that you investigate what your 'public sector' title would correspond to in the industry or company you are applying to. Use this terminology on your CV.
Typically direct recruitment via a website, newspaper adverts and internal HR department. Speculative applications will be discouraged.	Recruitment direct but also via agencies. Speculative applications may be successful if you contact the right person at the right time
Applications assessed after advertised closing dates and subject to strict internal processes.	Need to be much more proactive in seeking vacancies, not sending an application and waiting for an answer. Don't be afraid to circumvent the process.
Strict enforcement of equal opportunities policies with application processes designed to be fair to all applicants.	Application of policies at the discretion of the hiring manager. There can be opportuniuties to bypass the process through networking.
Applications usually submitted via a standard application form (SAF).	Application by CV and cover letter.
Formal assessment as to whether you meet the job specification.	Your ability to 'fit in', enthusiasm for the role and personal connections may override whether you have the proper qualifications for the job.
Salary will be pegged to national pay scales commensurate with your job title and responsibility, with little opportunity to negotiate.	Salary will be based on how much the company has budgeted for a position. If it is a senior role, total package may be entirely negotiable.
Continual monitoring of websites and public sector recruitment newspapers/ journals is the best way to find opportunities.	Networking and job sites are a more effective way to find opportunities.

Table 10.1

will be seeking people who are customer-focused: employees who can take on new expectations and responsibilities, work with partners and to very tight budgets. You'll need good IT, numeracy, written and communication skills. In leaner times, showing that you constantly seek service improvements and efficiencies will stand you in good stead. For more information, read Ben Makins' story on p.215.

PART 2: THE CV

We've been told that many recruiters spend no more than 30 seconds looking at a CV before coming to a decision. And most will only read the top third of your CV on a computer screen – that's all the opportunity you have to deliver a compelling message. This makes it even more of a challenge for the older jobseeker – how to impress in a short space and time when you have a long and impressive story to tell. There are countless specialist books that provide basic guidance on creating a CV. Our aim is to address the particular challenges faced by the mature jobseeker.

Your CV is your primary sales tool. It should present accurately and comprehensively what skills and capabilities you possess that make you the ideal candidate. It is not a life history or a career story. It has one purpose only – to make the reader want to meet you.

There are many different types of CV. If you're looking for employment you might use a 'functional', 'chronological' or 'hybrid' CV. Each has its own purpose. You might also need a 'summary' CV, as well as a full-length version. If you are applying for contract, consultancy or interim roles, you're likely to need a detailed CV that specifically describes the projects or assignments you have worked on. If you want to be self-employed you might need a 'bio' or 'profile' to send out when asked. All have a common purpose but are targeted at different audiences.

Whatever the format, your CV must be honest. Your skills and experience can be presented in the best possible light, but all the facts

– dates, responsibilities, job titles, company names – must be accurate. There are two reasons for this. The main one, of course, is that falsifying information on a CV is grounds for dismissal. In addition, you don't know where electronic copies of your CV might end up – it could be read by recruitment agencies, company HR departments, job boards and even your contacts. Nothing is guaranteed to lower your credibility more than someone coming across two CVs that make different claims for who you are and what you have done. Bear this in mind as you tailor your CV. Make sure the basic facts are accurate and honest.

CHECKLIST OF CV ESSENTIALS

If it's been some time since you wrote a CV, here's a reminder of the essential points to get right.

- Choose a 10pt to 12pt standard font that ensures your CV is readable on the majority of computers.
- Black text on a white background is still seen as the optimum combination for readability but also for printing and copying.
- Have each copy of your CV proofread by a partner, friend or coach. Check for spelling, grammar and punctuation.
- Where opinions differ on correct formatting, for example whether to capitalise the first letter in a bulleted list or not, decide what format you will follow and be consistent throughout.
- Write in the third person, not the first. Do not use 'I' in your CV.
- Your name and contact details should be on every page, in case the pages become separated after submission.
- Make sure your essential skills and experience are clearly visible to the reader, recognising that he or she may only spend seconds scanning your CV. The top third may be all that they read.
- Restrict yourself to two pages, or one if it is a summary or bio CV. Anything longer is highly unlikely to be read.

> • Unless asked to do otherwise, save and submit your CV as a pdf file, thereby preventing accidental editing, or formatting shifts. If you know that a recruiter will edit your CV, ask to see a copy of what has been submitted on your behalf.

THE RIGHT CV FOR YOU

The person reading a CV is trying to decide whether you are worth interviewing. With this in mind, the presentational challenge for the older worker is twofold:

1. A career spanning decades is simply too much to describe in two pages.
2. There may be periods which are best 'glossed over': gaps that include a period of unemployment, or work in an industry that is not relevant to the position. Simply put, anything that encourages the perception that you are right candidate for the job should be included. Anything that detracts from that perception should be excluded.

A 'functional' CV places your skills and competencies on the first page, with employers and dates relegated to the second page if mentioned at all. This type of CV focuses on your skills and is most useful when these are more appropriate than a list of the jobs you have held. For example, if you are making a career change to a new industry, a functional CV will highlight the transferable skills you can offer, and it will give concrete examples.

A 'chronological' CV is the traditional format. All your previous jobs are listed in date order, starting with the most recent. This type of CV is most appropriate for someone seeking the next logical step on a career ladder. For example, a project manager who is looking to step up to a programme director position, or a sales director wanting a move to a board level position.

A mix of these two types is called a 'hybrid' CV. Your profile, skills and achievements are highlighted at the top of the CV, and then a chronological list of employers and jobs is provided further down. This is the best way to highlight your relevant skills, while not detracting from the fact that those skills are backed up by a considerable amount of experience with different companies. Of the three main CV types, the hybrid version is the most useful type for the mature jobseeker in our opinion and the one we recommend most often.

The sections of a typical hybrid CV are:

Page 1
  Profile
  Skills summary
  Employment history (summary)
Page 2
  Detailed employment history
  Education, professional development and memberships

A sample layout of a hybrid CV is shown at the end of this chapter. There will be occasions when a chronological or functional CV is required. Many recruiters still prefer chronological CVs so that they can see your career progression and compare your CV with others. You'll also find sample layouts of functional and chronological CVs at the end of the chapter.

You'll need as many CVs as jobs you are applying for. Every job application you make should be accompanied by a CV that is specifically tailored for that role. Given the ease of document editing, there is no reason to submit a 'stock' CV for an advertised position where you know what the recruiter wants.

CREATING THE CONTENTS OF YOUR HYBRID CV

Refer to your self-assessment for a comprehensive review of your skills, competencies, experiences and achievements. You will use this to create all of the parts of your CV.

Profile

This is a short summary that describes you, what you offer and what you are looking for. For example:

A sales director with a track record of 17 years of successful sales and business development activities in the IT outsourcing sector in the Middle East. Now seeking a board level position in the UK with a growing IT outsourcing consultancy.

Your profile should be as attention-grabbing as possible but also clearly justified by the content in subsequent sections. It may take days or weeks to get right, but it's worth the effort because often it is the only part of your CV that the recruiter reads. The profile should be tailored to the job.

Skills summary

This section should provide a concise overview of your skills, competencies and achievements. It allows you to highlight those that are relevant to the role, regardless of when you acquired them. From your self-assessment in Chapter 4, combine your skills and experience into factual statements such as:

Planning and Organising: A PRINCE2 Practitioner with 15 years of programme management experience in the financial services arena with [bank 1, bank 2]. Managed programmes up to £100m in annual value.

In this section you should also identify relevant vocational and technical qualifications (e.g. MCSP, CCIE, Lean Six Sigma Green Belt) that might be essential attributes for the role. If the recruiter is seeking someone with qualification XYZ and you have that, then include it in this section and not at the bottom of page two.

The skills section is where you put any keywords that employers or recruiters will be looking for, such as *leadership, staff, SAP, PRINCE 2, IBM, director, planning, implementation, board-level, entrepreneur, business development, sales.* It's important because CVs can now be scanned electronically for keywords.

Employment history

The person reading your CV will expect to see a chronological list of the jobs you have done, with the most recent appearing first. List the job title, the employer's name and from/to dates. In a hybrid CV we recommend doing this in two parts:

- on the first page, include a summary list of employers, showing just the company name, job title and dates of employment;
- on page two, include a more detailed listing showing the responsibilities you held and any achievements. This will probably fill most of the second page.

When describing each role, ask yourself: 'What is specifically relevant to the job I am applying for now?' Concentrate on describing only the pertinent aspects. Be as factual as possible. In general, the more recent the job, the greater the detail should be. When describing the role, focus on what you did, using action words rather than describing the role itself. For example, *Responsible for improving product quality by 25 per cent over a two-year period by leading a comprehensive company-wide overhaul of the quality assurance process* is much more impressive than stating: *Senior member of quality control function, was responsible for defining processes and procedures as well as implementation thereof.*

In most cases, detailed descriptions of positions you held more than 10 years ago are unlikely to be relevant. Some jobseekers will summarise these experiences under a separate heading, 'Earlier career', and simply list the employers. This illustrates the breadth of career experience you bring while acknowledging that a junior sales role in retail 15 years ago is not hugely relevant to your employment today.

Education, professional development and memberships

Relevance is doubly important here. Typically you would include details of university degrees but not O and A level results. Include any technical training you undertook that led to a vocational qualification (Cisco CCIE) but not all the management training courses (presentation skills, time management, etc.). List membership of professional institutions (accountancy, law, engineering, IOD) but not your membership of a model railway club (unless you know the recruiter is also a member).

Other information

You may include other information that is important for the recruiter to know. This may include: technical and/or business publications; papers or books; professional or personal interests that are relevant, e.g. president of the local chamber of commerce or rugby club; a language ability or sporting achievement, e.g. Olympic gold-medal winner, or national representative.

Don't be overly forthcoming with your interests outside work, unless they illustrate a relevant skill. For example, if you are applying for a management role in a leisure centre, the fact you are chairman of the local rugby club in your spare time is relevant: it demonstrates your community spirit and skills in sports management. But if you are applying for an IT consultant role that requires lots of international travel, it is not.

What NOT to include in a CV?

Remove all details that reveal your age – there is no need for this information. This doesn't just refer to your date of birth. Don't put dates against your qualifications. Likewise there is no need to reveal any details about your ethnic origin, religion, sexuality, political affiliation or marital status.

FREQUENTLY ASKED CV QUESTIONS

Our experience at the Job Club is that older workers are faced with certain challenges that require a more specific approach.

How do I deal with career gaps?

Don't hide them – be honest about why they occurred, but don't draw attention to them. By a career gap we mean a period on your CV when you were not in employment. A typical example might be a person who, after redundancy, made childcare or parental duties his or her prime focus for a period of time. On balance it's best to state this honestly but also to highlight any voluntary or part-time responsibilities you took on at this time, if it's relevant to the work you are applying for. Recognise also that, whatever the reason for your career gap, an employer who is looking for a specialist in a certain field, when faced with two candidates – one who has worked full-time in their chosen field for the last ten years and the other who has considerable experience but has been a stay-a-home parent for the last four years – will most likely choose the former as their skills will be more up to date. This is not discrimination but just common sense. However, there will be employers who recognise the advantages of taking on employees who have been through the parenting or childcare career gap and will see that as a positive.

How do I convince an employer I can make a career change?

The mature jobseeker may have a number of career changes on his or her CV or be hoping to make one. There are two challenges to consider – how to present past changes in a coherent way on your CV and, if you're planning a change, how to justify why you should be considered for a role in your new career field. In both cases, career specialists point to the concept of transferable skills. What skills did you use across different careers that are an indication of your strengths and capabilities in any role? What skills did you use in past roles that will be an asset in a new career? When creating your CV, highlight those skills in the top third of the first page. The functional CV wins out over the chronological and hybrid CVs in this case as it allows the career-changer to point clearly to transferable skills. Once the reader understands you have the skills to do the job, then you can go on to describe your employment history and achievements.

How do I list qualifications: academic, vocational, etc?

It's important to recognise that all qualifications have a limited time of relevance. Clearly they have a longer shelf life if they directly relate to the job offered. A long list of management or technical training courses attended more than ten years ago is best left off your CV. At this stage in your career, your recent training or a skills upgrade is more relevant. Be ruthless when pruning old qualifications from your CV.

How far back in time do I go with my employment history?

A good compromise is to include fewer details the further you go back chronologically on your CV. For jobs held over ten years ago, simply state the role title and employer. For jobs more than 15 years old, add the title 'Early Career' and list the industry or the employer if it's a household name.

How long should I make my CV?

Accepted wisdom is that two pages is the maximum length. A one-pager is sometimes useful when sending a speculative application. In some sectors and situations it might be appropriate to use a longer format. For example, a consultant or an IT contractor might list all the assignments they have had, and a research scientist might include a list of scientific papers they have authored. However, for most management and professional positions, recruiters and employers would see an overly long CV as evidence of poor writing skills and an inability to present information concisely. You can always include extra information as an appendix. Examples of your work, case studies of situations you have managed, lists of published papers, an account of project success could all be included as appendices. Ask whether the recipient is interested in seeing them before sending.

SUMMARY

The outcome of a successful application is not a job – it's an interview. If your application has been successful you will have left your potential employer with the impression that you may be the perfect candidate. They have a document that describes what you can do and how you meet the requirements of the role. They are excited that their problem (the vacancy) is about to be solved. In the next chapter we tell you how to continue to build this impression through the interview.

PAGE ONE

Name
Occupation or Profession

Address
Telephone
E-mail

Profile

Summary profile statement that describes you, your key achievements, what you bring to the workplace, how you work and mentions your career objective.

Skills summary

List the skills that you bring in relation to the role you are applying for, mentioning under each skill specific achievements or notable occasions when you used those skills.

Summary employment history (in reverse chronological order)

<from>	<to>	<employer>	<job title>
<from>	<to>	<employer>	<job title>
<from>	<to>	<employer>	<job title>
<from>	<to>	<employer>	<job title>
<from>	<to>	<employer>	<job title>

PAGE TWO

Detailed employment history (in reverse chronological order)

<from>   **<to>**   **<employer>**   **<job title>**

Short description of each employer's business.

List your responsibilities and achievements at each employer.

<from>   **<to>**   **<employer>**   **<job title>**
<from>   **<to>**   **<employer>**   **<job title>**
<from>   **<to>**   **<employer>**   **<job title>**
<from>   **<to>**   **<employer>**   **<job title>**

Earlier career

For employment more than 10–15 years ago, summarise positions and employers.

Education, qualifications and memberships

<qualification>   <institution or college>
<qualification>   <institution or college>

Name   Telephone   E-mail

Table 10.2 Hybrid CV Format

PAGE ONE

Name
Occupation or Profession

Address
Telephone
E-mail

Profile

Summary profile statement that describes you, your key achievements, what you bring to the workplace, how you work and mentions your career objective.

Skills summary

Describe the transferable skills that you bring in relation to the role you are applying for, mentioning under each skill specific achievements or notable occasions when you used this skill.

Skill 1

Skill 2

Skill 3

Skill 4

PAGE TWO

Detailed employment history (in reverse chronological order)

<from>   <to>   <employer>   <job title>

Short description of each employer's business.

List your responsibilities and achievements at each employer.

<from>	**<to>**	**<employer>**	**<job title>**
<from>	**<to>**	**<employer>**	**<job title>**
<from>	**<to>**	**<employer>**	**<job title>**
<from>	**<to>**	**<employer>**	**<job title>**

Earlier career

For employment more than 10–15 years ago, summarise positions and employers

Education, qualifications and memberships

<qualification>   <institution or college>
<qualification>   <institution or college>

Name   Telephone   E-mail

Table 10.3 Functional CV Format

PAGE ONE

Name

Occupation or Profession

Address
Telephone
E-mail

Profile

Summary profile statement that describes you, your key achievements, what you bring to the workplace, how you work and mentions your career objective.

Employment history (in reverse chronological order)

<from>   **<to>**   **<employer>**   **<job title>**

Short description of employer's business.

List your responsibilities and achievements at this employer.

<from>   **<to>**   **<employer>**   **<job title>**

Short description of employer's business.
List your responsibilities and achievements at this employer.

PAGE TWO

Employment history (cont'd)

<from>   **<to>**   **<employer>**   **<job title>**

Short description of employer's business.

List your responsibilities and achievements at this employer.

<from>   **<to>**   **<employer>**   **<job title>**

Continue to cover at least 10 years of employment.

<from>   **<to>**   **<employer>**   **<job title>**
<from>   **<to>**   **<employer>**   **<job title>**
<from>   **<to>**   **<employer>**   **<job title>**

Earlier career

For employment more than 10–15 years ago, summarise positions and employers.

Education, qualifications and memberships

<qualification>   <institution or college>
<qualification>   <institution or college>

Name   Telephone   E-mail

Table 10.4 Chronological CV Format

THE INTERVIEW

There is no such thing as a bad interview, only a badly-prepared candidate. An interview is a key milestone in the job-search process. It's an opportunity for the employer and prospective employee to evaluate each other. The employer wants to determine if the candidate will be able to perform the role and fit into the existing office culture. The candidate wants to know if the workplace is congenial and if the job will provide satisfaction. So an interview can only have a positive outcome in that both parties have the chance to gather more information before coming to a more informed decision. If an employer decides not to proceed, it does not mean the candidate has failed, only that the employer has decided that person is not right for the role. The candidate may also decide, after the interview, that this is not the job for him or her.

The employer's decision is based on the impression the candidate makes at the interview, which should complement what is written on the CV. The strength of this impression will depend on how well-prepared the candidate is and how well they perform on the day. In some ways the interview is an act: the candidate turns up to put on a 'show' for his prospective employer. Any actor will tell you that a good performance is dependent on thorough preparation, and it's the same for an interview. Of course, the employer also has to prepare to run the interview, although sometimes there is little evidence of this. In this chapter we discuss preparation and execution from the candidate's perspective.

You may not have had a proper interview in years. It's quite possible to move from job to job via internal interviews and finding work through network contacts. Suddenly having to re-enter the job market via a formal interview process can come as a shock, so we will try to cover all the bases.

By 'interview' we mean the *entire* employer-to-candidate assessment-related process that takes place after the application. It follows the decision to meet the candidate, and precedes the moment when an offer is received. The interview process is not a one-off meeting. It happens over a period of time, during which one of more of the following will occur: telephone interviews and conversations; online assessment; a case study; selection panels; informal chats or meetings; first or 'screening' interview; follow-up interviews; and the final interview. Some of these may not take place directly with the employer but with a third party, a recruiter or consultant operating on the employer's behalf. With the company, an interview may be conducted by HR, by the hiring manager, a colleague or a senior executive.

If you are in the interview process this means the employer likes something about you, thinks you are a potential fit and would be happy if you turned out to be the ideal candidate. Remember, the whole selection process starts with a business problem: a vacancy that needs filling. The employer has shortlisted you because they consider it a possibility that you are the solution to the problem. You begin from a position of strength.

A well-run selection process is designed to find the best candidate, but even the best process is sometimes run by non-expert interviewers and recruiters. As a candidate, you will have to manage your way around poorly-asked questions, disorganised company departments, reluctant recruiters and uninspired executives. Remember that you are not there to judge the interview process; you are there to impress.

Take one step at a time. The objective of a CV is to get an interview, and the objective of each interview stage is simply to move to the next step. If it's a screening interview, you must concentrate your efforts and perform well enough to get on to the final shortlist. If you are asked to meet a potential colleague for an 'informal chat', treat it as just one more step and prepare accordingly. Do your research and know what type of candidate they want. Never assume that it's in the bag until you have a job offer in your hands, and always concentrate your efforts on getting past the next hurdle.

TYPES OF INTERVIEW

There is more than one kind because over time, employers have refined, and continue to refine, the interviewing process to make it more effective. The number of stages in the process will depend on the size of organisation and the seniority of the role being filled. When interviewing for a senior role in an SME, the interview process will likely consist of a series of meetings with functional directors and perhaps a final chat with the MD, after which a collective decision is made whether or not to make an offer. The interview process for a middle-management role in a large corporate may follow a rigid, well-defined series of steps: 1. Initial interview 2. Personality profile and numerical reasoning tests 3. Competency interview 4. Senior manager interview. After each step you are informed if you have passed.

The initial screening interview

The purpose of this is to meet you and determine whether it is worth investing any more time in you. The desired outcome is that you move forward to the next stage of the process. The interviewer is checking that the view they formed of you from your CV is correct, as well as other aspects that don't come through on the CV: your ability to speak clearly and articulate a point of discussion, the impression you give, and your level of confidence in your abilities. The goal in this interview is to deliver on the promise of your CV. By this time you'll have a clear idea how well your skills match the brief. Don't introduce complications like salary or place of work into the discussion. Do rehearse the stories of your achievements so that you speak credibly and confidently, demonstrating your capabilities and ensuring that these are related to, and confirm, what is on your CV.

Competency interview

This method of interviewing is based on the principle that the best predictor of how a person will apply their skills in future work situations is their behaviour in similar situations in the past. Rather than ask about your experiences and achievements, the competency interview focuses on situations you were placed in and how you used your skills to make progress. The situations don't have to be related to the greatest achievements in your career – often the best examples of how effectively you used your skills come from times of adversity rather than triumph. So interviewers will ask questions like:

'Can you tell me about a time when you felt you were the only one in your department or management team who had the "right" answer to a problem. How did you go about enrolling others in your approach?'

'Can you give me an example of a time when you had to make a very unpopular decision? How did you arrive at the decision? How did you communicate it?'

You could be asked some very challenging questions. The interviewer is trying to determine how you apply your skills in the situation and is not particularly interested in the business outcome. When answering, focus on your own skills and actions rather than the company or team. The interviewer is interested in your competencies, not the team's achievement or the company's progression. Think in terms of *I did...I decided...I thought...I told...I argued that...I persuaded... I presented...I asked...I bought...I sold...*

The best way to prepare for competency-based interviews is to make sure you understand the key skills required and then practise answering questions around those skills. Note that a competency-based interview may be a specific part of the interview process, or the interviewer might use some competency-based questions in a more general interview. The technique is now widely used, and it's best to always prepare for competency-based questions.

Functional interview

The purpose is very simple: Can you do the job? The employer seeks to understand whether you have the technical and/or management skills to do what is required in the role. They are checking you have done what it says on your CV.

It's important to be clear about what you did and how you did it, to show how you applied your skills and to demonstrate a thorough knowledge of those areas in which you claim to be an expert. Prepare by studying your subject matter. Practise by speaking to other experts on the topic and update yourself on the latest technical trends. You should be able to speak confidently about any technical subject areas on your CV.

Panel interview

Here you are interviewed by more than one person simultaneously. There are several reasons for this: it may be company policy, or a number of departments may have to reach a collective decision on a candidate. Your challenge is to prepare to meet more than one person and build rapport with the group. If a panel interview is run well there should only be one person asking questions at any one time. You need to concentrate your efforts on answering that question. If two or more people ask questions at once, it's perfectly acceptable to ask which one you should answer first, or state that you will answer first one then the other. It may be that the company wants to find out how you cope with being the centre of attention in a board meeting, and they are testing your ability to manage communication with a challenging group. If you are invited to a panel interview, ask what the nature of the interview will be (e.g. questions from separate people with different functional expertise, or a challenging board style interview as described above) and request the names of the individuals who will be on the panel and their job titles. Be prepared to be exhaustively examined on all aspects of your CV, as one questioner will pick up from another.

The telephone interview

This is a great way for a recruiter or employer to save travel time for all concerned. In some cases, if the interviewee and interviewer are in different countries it may be the only possible way to conduct an interview in a reasonable time frame or at reasonable cost. There are a number of simple principles to bear in mind for telephone interviews because all the non-verbal communication that normally takes places in a conversation cannot happen. The interviewer will form an impression about you through your tone of voice, clarity of enunciation, your accent, and how you order and structure your answers. It's important to speak slowly and coherently and make an effort to match the pace of the interviewer. Keep your responses short where possible and always check for understanding. In a face-to-face interview you receive messages from body language and facial expressions as to whether your answers are hitting the right buttons; in a telephone interview you must be alert for changes in tone and pace that indicate whether or not you have answered a question correctly.

Treat it like a business meeting. Make sure you are alone in a setting or location where you can concentrate on the interview and where you won't be disturbed. A telephone interview requires a high level of concentration. You will need to have the same documents to hand that the interviewer does, including CV, job specification and any other information about the role. This will minimise any misunderstandings about you and the role being discussed. These could be easily cleared up when meeting face-to-face but could get quite complicated on the phone.

At the end of the call, it's worth being explicit regarding subsequent steps. Ask what will happen next, and by when. You might probe the interviewer for a brief summation of their conclusions. It's acceptable to ask: 'How do you think that went? Will you want to see me or speak to me again?'

Final interview

This is the last hurdle before that elusive job offer. Sometimes you will have a clear set of instructions to follow. You might be asked to present your case to the board or a senior manager. It's usually established that a decision will be made immediately after the meeting.

At other times the final interview is called something else. For example, you might be told: 'We just want you to have a chat with the managing director before we make you an offer.' Beware – this is not 'just a chat', it's a final check as to whether or not they think you will fit in.

By the time you get to a final interview you will have researched the company and the role and you will know why they think you're a suitable candidate. In a final interview, reiterate your strengths and demonstrate again how you will bring value to the role, building on what you have already said at previous interviews. At this stage it's yours to lose. Bear in mind this is also your last opportunity to interview them. Do you have all the information you need to make a decision? If not, now is the time to ask.

OTHER ELEMENTS OF THE INTERVIEW PROCESS

Personality and aptitude tests

These are designed to create a profile of how you operate in life and work, so you can be compared to the profiles of other people applying for the role. There are no right or wrong answers, and it is very difficult, even if you suspect you know what sort of personality traits the role requires, to fool the tests. They come from reputable suppliers. Tests include embedded questions to check for honesty and integrity in the responses. You'll jeopardise your chances by attempts to second-guess your responses.

If you have not done these tests before or for some time, it is a good idea to do a few test papers (available on line from SHL: **www.shl. com**) to get into the right mindset. The tests may be administered in person by an interviewer, in your own office or online. For online tests you will be sent a logon to the test provider's site by the company. When it is time to take the actual test you need to be in a work frame of mind. Be calm and focused so the results are a picture of you at your best. Results may be e-mailed to you but it's more likely that the company will receive a copy and discuss them with you at an interview.

Verbal and numerical reasoning tests

These examine your problem-solving and decision-making capabilities. Based on statistical data, optimum results for specific roles are compiled and your scores will be compared to them. This helps the employer to judge how well you are likely to perform in the role. In contrast to personality tests, there are definitely right and wrong answers, and we recommend you do some trial tests in advance. Your recruiter may be able to supply sample tests or you can find some online. Doing cryptic crosswords, sudoku and mental arithmetic are other ways to prepare for these tests.

Case studies

A case study is a common way for employers to test the clarity of your thinking, your analytical skills, and your ability to present a case for action. Typically you will be given a scenario to evaluate. It could be presented on a written document, a DVD or a website, and you might receive a verbal briefing. You will be given a fixed time to analyse the situation and present your findings and recommendations to the interviewer. It may require a short presentation or involve cooperating with other interviewees. There is no specific online resource for practising for case studies. A well-established company may have an archive of case studies that you can research, but otherwise, be yourself and respond as you would if you were in the job.

PREPARATION FOR INTERVIEWS

As a mature worker, you have the advantage of being well-versed in the rules of business and the importance of preparation for any meeting. Companies and interviewers often report how surprised they are at the lack of preparation by interviewees. So learn as much as you can about the company, their services and reputation, why they're adding staff, and what challenges they face. If this information is not available online, use your network to contact people who know about the company. At the interview you want to be to able to speak coherently about what the company does. Use social and business networking sites to research the people you will meet. What are their interests and backgrounds? Where did they last work? How long have they been with the company? This could be valuable information when you make small talk initially, and it may offer clues about the employer's ideal candidate.

You cannot afford for your early interviews to be practice sessions, because you might miss a great opportunity, so make sure you practise well beforehand. Either find a willing partner or colleague, or seek professional help – many career guidance and career coaching companies will offer a test interview service, where you attend a mock interview based on the real job description and give the interviewer a copy of your application. Top services will provide you with a video recording of the interview and a summary with feedback on how you came across, identify your strengths and your weaknesses, and how well you match the impression given by your CV.

In the book *What Color Is Your Parachute?*[1], Richard N. Bolles notes that all the interview questions in the world can be summarised in just five questions you have to be able to answer when going to any interview. As two of them are similar we have listed just four 'big questions' below. All the other questions you will be asked will relate in some way to these four: 1. Why do you want this job? 2. Can you do the job? 3. Why are you the best candidate? 4. Will you fit in here? Be prepared to answer them at any stage in the interview process – some might come up at an initial interview and then be repeated in more depth as you go through the process. You need to have a 30-second 'elevator pitch' response to these questions, with a more detailed answer prepared as well, one that includes evidence and will back up your brief answer. In other words, the elevator pitch functions as a kind of executive summary for a much longer answer.

1. Why do you want this job?

No company wants to employ someone who is only doing the job because there was nothing else on offer or because the package sounded good. This is a recipe for disaster. Once the novelty of being employed in the new role or having a higher income has worn off, what will keep the employee motivated and engaged? Extensive research points to job satisfaction, opportunities for development and good management as the top reasons why people remain in a role. Salary and benefits are always way down the list. At the interview, the company is looking for evidence that you have good reasons for wanting this job and that these will match what they can offer you in the medium to long term. Think through what it is about the role and the company that means this would be a good move for you. You want to be able to express this as a win-win, not just in terms of what you can get out of it. Here's an example of a short, elevator-pitch answer:

'I want this job because my experience in this sector means I can focus my efforts from day one on developing new revenue streams for this business unit. I'm also excited that senior roles might exist in future, because the company is growing fast and has a good reputation as a place to work.'

2. Can you do the job?

If you convince the employer that you want the job, the next consideration is whether you can do it. To find the answer to this question, the interviewer will focus on exploring the relevant experience from your CV and also the 'soft' skills that may not be apparent from the CV but are just as important. Technical skills can be judged by tests (e.g. verbal and numerical reasoning tests) or case studies. Soft skills are explored with competency questions as well as personality and aptitude tests.

The skills you need for the job are found in the job description. Prepare for this question by making a list of relevant experience and qualifications that demonstrate that you can perform above expectations. Where you have an obvious gap, acknowledge it and describe how you will address it.

This question is often the first one an interviewer will use to create a shortlist of candidates based on CV analysis. By the time you get to the interview, the recruiter already considers you can do the job. The interviewer is now looking for further evidence to make a stronger case for you. Your answers to questions relating to this point should therefore back up what is already on your CV. Be well-rehearsed.

3. Why are you the best candidate?

Another way to phrase this is: '*You want the job and I see you can do it but so can 20 other people, so why should I choose you?*' This is difficult to answer, because you can't compare yourself to your competition. You can only make your strongest case based on what you know about the role and the company. This is where your maturity and experience as an older jobseeker come into play. If you can show that you are fully aware of what the job entails and you are able to demonstrate insights into the challenges you might face, you will stand out from the crowd. Describe similar roles you have done in the past and what the critical success factors were in the first hundred days of employment and also in the first year. Seek to demonstrate your value proposition. Ask intelligent questions that demonstrate your expertise.

If the interview is for a senior role, the interviewer has half an eye on where you might move within the organisation – for example, have you the potential to be the next CFO or COO? The more potential value you can offer, the more likely you are to stand out from others. On the other hand, you may be interviewed for a junior role – a step down from your previous status – so you'll need a convincing rationale. You'll have to explain why it makes career sense for you to take this role now. Valid reasons are: a move into a new industry, career change, a desire to improve your work/life balance, or a specific objective. See Michael's story (p.184) for an example of how this can be done.

You can prepare for the 'best candidate' question and the 'why do you want this job?' question simultaneously by listing 10 strengths you have that are relevant to the role. Decide which of these allow you to do the job well, and which offer future opportunities to the employer. Emphasise the latter at the interview.

4. Will you fit in here?

This is potentially the hardest question for the older worker. As we mentioned in the first chapter, if success in the job depends on fitting in with a young team, your chances are not very good. If this is a role where the need for your technical expertise outweighs any concerns the employer has about age, then you stand a chance. You cannot rely on government legislation to protect you from exclusion on the grounds that you do not fit in.

Don't bang your head against a brick wall. Find employers who value what you can bring to the organisation. When being interviewed, don't be afraid to ask the direct question: '*Do you think I will fit in here?*' Listen for the answers. You have a chance to sell yourself if you engage in a dialogue about the issue. There is no longer an 'elephant in the room' because the age issue is out in the open. There will be situations where age is genuinely not an issue. In this case you can only answer honestly to questions about your working style and how you like to be managed. The personality tests you have undertaken will have given the employer clues as to your fit with the role. How you perform at interview complements this view.

Be aware there are other ways to determine fit. Some employers will ask off-the-wall questions designed to see what sort of person you are outside of work: '*If money was no object, what car would you drive? If you had an extra day a week for the rest of your life what would you do with the time? Which three famous people, alive or dead, would you choose to join you for your fiftieth birthday party?*' These questions are designed to form a better picture of the person you really are and how that might affect your ability to work with other people in the team. For example, if you answered the car question with '*a Ford Focus Estate because it's practical for my current lifestyle*', and the rest of the management team pride themselves on their luxury four-wheel drives, then however well you could do the job, you just might not fit in!

The secondary element to the 'fit' question relates to salary. Your fit in terms of salary is just as important as your personality fit. '*Are you too expensive for us?*' is a real concern for a small company hiring someone with a corporate background. Be honest and up front about what your negotiating range is; it's best for both parties to find out early whether this is going to be a waste of time if the company is unable to match your salary expectations.

THE SEVEN KILLER QUESTIONS

In addition to the four big questions, there are seven killer questions that you must be ready for. We can't offer answers as they will be particular to your situation. Think through them and practise your responses.

1. Why have you been looking for work for so long?
2. Why were you made redundant?
3. How long will you want to work here?
4. What have you been doing while out of work?
5. What are your aspirations for the next five or ten years?
6. Why does your CV look like it does (one employer in 25 years or 20 employers in 25 years)?
7. What makes you think you can make the change from self-employment back into corporate employment again?

MANAGING THE INTERVIEW

It's worth reiterating some of the essential points that are easy to overlook if you have not been to an interview for some time.

Time

Allow plenty of time in order to arrive early at the interview. If you cannot attend or decide not to, in the interests of networking make your reasons clear and inform the company or the agent.

CV

The interviewer may not have seen your CV until you arrive. You might think your CV has been pored over and analysed in great detail, but it is quite possible for the interviewer to either be reading your CV while interviewing you, or never to have seen it at all. So always take two copies with you and be prepared to draw attention to the points relevant to your application.

Dress code

The rule here is simple – always dress to impress as if you were doing the job. If you are applying for a job in a company where casual clothing is the norm, then very smart casual or even a suit might be appropriate. If it's a company where suits are still the order of the day, then a new shirt and clean tie are definitely recommended. Always remember: if you were working at this place, what would you wear to impress? If it's not clear, than ask the recruitment agent or the employer directly.

Rapport

The initial part of the interview, like any meeting between strangers, is where rapport is established. Rapport means that you are connecting with the other person. It's important to remember when meeting a person for an interview that you are a guest in their world. You can build rapport by conforming easily to the rules they have set up for the interview: *You sit there and I sit here. I ask the questions initially and then you ask some later. I want to tell you about my company before you start talking. I want to hear you speak about your journey here while I get comfortable.* You can break rapport early on by deliberately flouting the rules the interviewer is trying to impose, or by seeking to take control of the conversation.

Other simple rules for establishing good rapport are to use the interviewer's language or jargon where possible, and to mirror their posture without being obvious. If they are sitting upright, forward and with both hands on the table, then you should too. If they start using technical terms to describe an aspect of the role, then include those terms in your answer. Reply to short succinct questions with a brief answer.

Speaking and listening

It's very easy to half-listen, especially when being interviewed for a job for which you are highly qualified. You might find yourself mentally preparing to answer the question you think should have been asked rather than the one you actually were asked. Listening carefully is doubly important if you think the interviewer knows less about the topic than you. Answer the question as asked, showing your experience where possible, and focusing on the thought that you are here to pass the interview and not to intimidate the interviewer.

When speaking, try to avoid giving a longer answer than the interviewer is expecting. Again, with your experience, it might be possible for you to give a competent 15-minute answer to an open question about how you would approach the role. However, unless asked to give a presentation, you should limit the length of your answers to what would be appropriate in a conversation.

Answering difficult or unexpected questions

Despite all your preparation, you will sometimes face an unexpected or difficult question. Some interviewers will deliberately plan these questions to see how you react, others will simply be obvious to the interviewer but ones you didn't expect. Either way, rather than stammer or rush in with an ill thought-out answer, the best approach is to:

Pause – don't feel you have to answer immediately; you might even say: 'I'll need a couple of seconds to think about that.'

Breathe – take a breath while you gather your thoughts.

Think – ask yourself what the interviewer is trying to achieve with this question. What examples or knowledge can you call on to find an answer that best fits with what they want to hear?

Speak – confidently and assertively, looking out for clues in the interviewer's body language as to whether or not you are on the right track.

Material to leave

It is sometimes appropriate to take examples of your previous work to the interview and to show or leave this as evidence of your capabilities. If so, make sure that you have checked with someone else first that the items are of good quality and convey the right impression. A market research report that you wrote might have been fit for purpose by the standards of the small family-run company you worked for, but could appear amateurish when judged by the standards of a multinational. The reverse could also be true – examples of your work with a large corporate could appear overly complex and theoretical if you are interviewing for a role with a three-person start-up company.

Asking questions

Any interview process should allow you the opportunity to ask questions. You are also conducting your own interview – *'Is this company one I want to work for? Will I fit in? Will I get the opportunities I want?'* It's best to prepare your questions in advance to ensure that all the points important to your decision will be covered.

HOW LONG SHOULD I WAIT FOR A RESPONSE AFTER AN INTERVIEW?

Ask this question *before* you leave the interview. A professional approach means establishing the next steps before you leave. Will they contact you? Directly or through an agent? By when?

It's good practice to send a thank-you e-mail after the interview and within 24 hours. You might follow up on any outstanding points and reiterate your interest in the role. If you haven't been told when you'll hear of the outcome, we recommend following up with the agent within a day, or directly with the employer within three days.

POST-INTERVIEW REVIEW

After every interview you attend, you should make notes about how you performed. Each interview is another opportunity to learn about how you come across when applying for work. A bad interview will teach you more about yourself than a good one. As soon as possible after the interview, note down answers to the following questions:

- How did I do?
- Which questions did I answer particularly well?

- Which questions did I answer particularly badly?
- What did I learn about how I present myself?
- What did I learn about the company?
- In summary, what did I learn about my interviewing skills that I can take forward to the next one?

If it's possible to get feedback from the company or the recruiter who put you forward, take the opportunity to do so. By analysing the feedback you receive, you will be better prepared for the next one. When reviewing feedback, remember that most people tend to be cautious about what feedback they offer, for fear of giving offence. So it's important to note the trends and unspoken messages in the feedback you're getting. For example, if all the responses are positive but most interviewers hint at your slightly 'direct' nature, then consider whether you are coming across as too aggressive in the interviews. Act on any consistent trends in the feedback you receive.

NEXT STEPS

After every interview there are three possible outcomes:

1. You've passed and you move on to next step in the interview process. Excellent! It's now time start your preparation for what is to come.
2. Rejection. It's always disappointing to be rejected. Treat every rejection as one more learning step in the process towards finding the ideal role.
3. You got a job offer. Great! Fantastic, well done!

Before you celebrate, wait to see the offer in writing. Now is the time to think about what you want from the role and whether there is scope for negotiation. The point at which you are made an offer is the point at which your negotiating power is highest. The company has decided that they want you. There is a more than reasonable chance that you are motivated to do well and will fit in. Now is the time for you to be clear about your salary, benefits, reporting lines, job title and so on.

A full review of all the aspects of negotiating your terms of employment is beyond the scope of this book. However, it's worth mentioning that you also have to gauge how open the company is to negotiation. What alternatives do they have if you are insisting on a higher salary or certain conditions? If you really are the only person that can do the role, then hold out for what you want. If other potential candidates are still available, be careful about how you position your requirements. Make clear that you are not threatening to withdraw; you only want to secure the right offer for the role.

SUMMARY

An interview can be daunting, especially if you have not been interviewed for some time. There are several steps in a process which you and the potential employer will go through to assess your suitability for the role. Through adequate preparation and practice you can give yourself the best possible chance of success. Aim to walk out of every interview having left the best possible impression. The final decision is always with the interviewer, but you'll want to be able to say: 'I did my best. Now it's up to them.'

SUCCESS STORY: MICHAEL

One of the hardest things to do is sell yourself *down*. Most employers won't hire an experienced person to do a job that has lower status and pay than in their previous role. The assumption is that someone who is overqualified will get bored and leave quickly; that their motive for seeking the position is simply to get working again in order to have an income while they look for a better job. And yet many older workers would be happy to step down a level and do a job they enjoy, working in congenial surroundings for a company they respect. Michael's story is an example of how it can be done. It's also a heart-rending tale of a man who overcame one of the worst results of unemployment:

clinical depression. He asked us to conceal his identity, and that of his employers.

With a blue-chip education starting at public school, followed by an Oxbridge degree and an MBA, Michael was set for a promising career in corporate finance. Following a stint with a private equity firm in the City, he was taken on as a financial analyst by an industrial conglomerate. He was spotted as a future finance director, but the 1991 recession meant that there was no opportunity for progression within the company. After answering an advert in the *Financial Times*, he was recruited by a major telecoms firm, where he spent a decade in their corporate finance operation. He faced his first redundancy in 2002 in the media/telecoms recession that followed the bursting of the dotcom bubble in 2001. Michael was out of work for a mere six weeks, and then another advert in the FT helped him secure a senior role in project finance for another conglomerate. It was essentially the same job that he'd done previously. The company was sold in 2008 and so, at age 49, Michael faced his second, life-changing redundancy.

There was conflict with his former employer over his redundancy package. Anxiety about his situation led to constant sleepless nights, loss of appetite and dark moods. After four months he went to his doctor. The diagnosis was depression. He was sent away with recommendations for herbal remedies, over-the-counter soporifics, and self-help books. His depression was so severe that none of the remedies, or the advice, was of any use. He says four things helped him through this difficult period:

- Having no serious financial worries. His partner has a good salary and he had money saved.
- Caring for his young son, who has special needs. This gave him a powerful reason to get out of bed and face the day.
- Proper medication in the form of sleeping pills and antidepressants (they were finally prescribed).

- Therapy provided by the NHS, available through a programme for the unemployed.

Michael was out of work for 18 months. During that time he was always looking for a job. There was no 'lightbulb' moment of inspiration; it was sheer perseverance that got him through. And each time he faced an interview or networking meeting he 'pretended confidence'. 'We all do that, don't we?' he says.

Michael's new job didn't come through an advert in FT; it came from networking. A former colleague told him about a job that was being offered by a big multinational that had been refused by the applicant, so he knew they were recruiting. Through his network he got the name of the department head, spoke to him directly, and then went in for an informal chat. This was for a junior position, one with a much lower salary than what Michael had been accustomed to. His challenge was not to convince his future employer of his talent, but of his sincerity. He did it by being honest about his rationale, so that his employer could understand why he would be willing to take a step down. He had two convincing reasons:

- His son needed special care during the working day, something he was unable to provide adequately by himself. This family situation was believable to his employer.
- He was impressed by the company and has always wanted to work for them.

The employer was sold on the benefits of having Michael on board and he got the job. He likes the people he works with; he's proud that he sold himself down – it is a real achievement. And he agrees with his partner who told him, 'This job just might suit you.' Over time, he might try for a higher position in the company but the role will have to be right for him, his family and his lifestyle.

SECTION

5

Move Forward:
Self-Employment

INTERIM MANAGEMENT

THE WORK FUNNEL

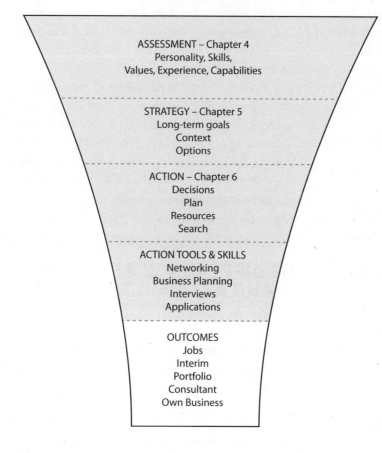

ASSESSMENT – Chapter 4
Personality, Skills,
Values, Experience, Capabilities

STRATEGY – Chapter 5
Long-term goals
Context
Options

ACTION – Chapter 6
Decisions
Plan
Resources
Search

ACTION TOOLS & SKILLS
Networking
Business Planning
Interviews
Applications

OUTCOMES
Jobs
Interim
Portfolio
Consultant
Own Business

WHAT IS AN INTERIM?

Interims are experienced senior managers and directors who are appointed temporarily, either in a functional role or to manage a short-term project. An interim will usually have board-level experience, be part of the management team and committed to its objectives, and then leave the company with an action plan in place, having completed a pre-agreed set of objectives.

This is one occupation where age is seen as an advantage. When an interim is required, most employers will seek an older person who is sensibly overqualified, someone with skills and knowledge that can be put to use immediately. All of the invisible age barriers to permanent employment now work in your favour.

If you succeed as an interim, you could find yourself getting regular work contracts without ever having a permanent position. It's also a good way to stay working at a senior level so that your CV remains current and viable, should a permanent role become available. Being an interim means that you're in line with trends in the economy. Employers are managing a more agile workforce, with an increasing number of part-time and temporary jobs. Similarly, at a senior level more work is being contracted out, so the need for interims is growing.

WHAT IS THE DIFFERENCE BETWEEN AN INTERIM AND A CONSULTANT?

There can be some confusion about the role of an interim manager and that of a consultant. To be clear: a consultant is someone who is hired (either individually or as part of a team) to diagnose and resolve a problem (which might, on examination, appear to be many problems), works to a timescale that could be expanded, resulting in a report that presents recommendations for someone else to implement. An interim is a doer, not an adviser, and an implementer, not a report writer. Interims will manage the solution to a problem or they will be the temporary replacement for a permanent manager. Interims work in the company office on a daily basis, whereas consultants are always external people. Consultants may be free to come and go, and to work from home – sometimes on several projects at once. Diagnostic skills are required in both roles, but the major difference is that interims are hands-on, whereas consultants typically examine and then offer advice, plans and proposals. Sometimes there are grey areas and overlap between the two roles.

WHY HIRE AN INTERIM?

Interims are employed for a variety of reasons: to implement the solution to an outstanding problem; manage a board-level project; or to fill a gap during recruitment. Crisis management is often a motive for hiring an interim: there may be a reorganisation or insolvency. An interim could also be used to assist with starting or closing a division, or to implement a new system. In essence, a company will hire an interim because they have a situation that requires immediate attention and they need a competent person who can step in and take charge. Interims will typically work from four to nine months; this may be full-time or three to four days per week. Longer assignments are possible. Some employers offer flexible contracts, such as 90 days in six months, which allow for periods of leave and the ebb and flow of workload in the role.

ARE YOU SUITED TO INTERIM MANAGEMENT?

Here's a short list of some characteristics that an interim should have:

- instant credibility;
- able to lead from the front;
- recent experience in the sector, typically at board or director level;
- up-to-date knowledge;
- experience with project management concepts – managing a set of activities that have a start and an end;
- impartiality;
- comes with no agenda (does not want a permanent job).

You must be a person who enjoys diversity and a challenge, someone who is able to get things going rapidly. And you must also be able to sell yourself in order to get contracts.

Interim management is not for everyone. If you value security and regularity more than the excitement of a new task, then it won't be suitable. Some other things to consider: starting out is not easy; gaps between jobs may be long (especially at the beginning); and you're responsible for your own continuing professional development. You'll be freelance, so you'll need to set up a personal services company that will carry an admin overhead. Pension and health insurance will be your responsibility.

Mike Taylor has worked as an interim and he has set up public sector interim divisions within two major agencies: Tribal and Boydens. Mike and his partners are currently running their own agency, Your Choice Interims. He offers excellent advice for anyone considering work as an interim, either in the public or the private sector. He says you should consider four questions:

1. Can you afford to be out of work for any period of time? Do you have a cushion? How long will it last?
2. Can you handle not living and working from home? Many assignments mean living in a hotel room for several months or travelling abroad, or there could be travel at the beginning and end of the working week so you can return home at weekends.
3. Can you think of yourself as a different entity and redefine yourself? Are you able to rewrite your CV to include transferable skills that work in your market?
4. Can you move flexibly into organisations? Are you outcome driven?

If you've answered yes to all these questions, we recommend that you discuss it with your family, or anyone who is reliant on you for income. Seek an objective perspective. Talk it over with a neutral third party, perhaps a career counsellor. Interim agencies such as Veredus run free seminars; you may want to take one to find out if this type of work will suit you. Mike recommends a one-day workshop offered by the IMA Institute. Details are found on their website: **www.ima-institute. com.**

HOW TO SET UP AS AN INTERIM

As with any new business, you'll need to define exactly what product or service you're selling. In this case, *you* are the product and your services are for sale. What is it that you do best? In which area of management have you been most successful? Write down your capabilities. Next, follow Mike Taylor's advice: 'Write your CV as if an ill-informed person were reading it. An interim CV is about abilities more than experience – concentrate on the outcomes of the roles you have completed.'

- Express your core skills in plain language.
- Specify your skills and give evidence.
- Don't diminish the talents you take for granted.
- Don't assume that others will understand what your experience means.

As an example of the final point above, all accountants have audit experience; therefore, all accountants assume that everyone knows that. But it may not be the case. HR can be uneven and your CV may be seen by a lower-level person. If that person doesn't know that all accountants have audit experience, they won't know that you possess an essential skill required for the role. If you haven't included it in your CV, you might be passed over in favour of someone who has.

When you've finished a draft CV, it's time to approach an agency. The interim sector is well established and there are many good ones. Once you've expressed your interest, there will be a follow-up phone call or a meeting, giving you a chance to establish a relationship and find out what openings there might be for you in the market. This will also provide you with an opportunity to get feedback on your CV, so that it can be revised as necessary. Mike suggests that you don't register with too many agencies; five or six will do for a start. We've listed some in the Resources section at the back of the book.

Next ask yourself: 'Where would my boss go if he was looking for me?' If it's an agency, then contact that agency. When companies want someone they frequently ask this question internally: 'Does anyone know someone?' That's why it's important to use your network and inform everyone that you're available. If you know an interim, or if you have a friend who can connect you with one, by all means have a meeting. First-hand knowledge is of great value when you're starting a new venture.

For most people, landing the first interim assignment is the biggest hurdle. Some agencies will only take people who have experience as an interim. Be tenacious and keep networking. If you've developed your list of contacts by working through the networking chapter, you may find someone who can help you with your first assignment; they can either hire you or recommend you (three or four enthusiastic referees are a must). Once you've done your first assignment you'll have an interim reference and then the agencies will take you seriously. In other words, your network could land you your first contract, which gets you the necessary interim experience so that an agency will take you on; after working on some agency assignments you may no longer need an agency because you are likely to get your contracts through your own network. Or you may find that you never use an agent (see Graham Stephens' story on p.197). In any case, you will trade on your reputation: every job builds your credibility for the next interim role.

If you haven't yet been made redundant, consider approaching your boss and offering to complete an outstanding project on a freelance basis; convert yourself into a private contractor before you leave. You could ask for it as part of your outsourcing package. If you succeed, it would be your first statement of independent activity.

WHAT DO YOU CHARGE?

Interim fees are determined by the market and most people charge themselves out on a day rate, and invoice monthly. There is a considerable variance of rates, depending on your functional area and the geographic region where you work. There are no hard and fast rules; the only guideline is to be good value for the money. To get your first assignment, you might undercut the competition on price, and attach a performance-related bonus to the contract.

IS A CONTRACT NECESSARY?

It's important to get a formal agreement, either a contract or a simple letter of agreement. Mike says that you must define ten key objectives when arriving as an interim. Get them in writing or have your agent include them in a contract before you start. That way you'll avoid any misunderstandings that could arise with regard to what's expected of you in the assignment. Mike describes this as the 'millstone in the middle of the table' syndrome: you're having meetings where some unresolved issue just lies there and it's not your responsibility, although other people may think it is. An agreement sorts that out beforehand.

MORE EXPERT ADVICE

Mike suggests that before you complete an assignment, ask for a testimonial and send it with your updated CV to all your agencies and contacts. Every contract adds 'interim value' and enhances your presentation of skills and abilities. Your next assignment could come a lot faster as a result.

Finally, never break a contract by leaving early. You will damage your reputation.

THE PAPERWORK

Paperwork is something to be reckoned with, but rest assured you're in good company; every self-employed, freelance person has to deal with admin. These are the essentials:

- set up as a limited company;
- opt out of Employment Agency Act (EAA) regulations;
- get professional indemnity insurance (as required);
- hire an accountant with IR35 one-man-company experience;
- register for VAT if necessary.

Companies only hire other companies for contract work. If an individual's tax status is challenged, the company is liable for any tax and National Insurance contributions (NICs) that are due. That's the first reason you need to set up as a limited company; the second is that interim managers are classified as temporary workers under employment regulations introduced in 2004, called the Employment Agency Act (EAA). The act was set up to protect temporary workers and give them some of the rights of permanent employees. With your company acting as contractor, you do not require those rights and so you will need to sign a letter or form whereby you opt out of EAA. Agents should provide the form for this as part of the contract material for an assignment. If not, ask for it. Opting out has the additional benefit of reinforcing your protection against IR35, another piece of legislation that impacts on the activities of free-lancers. IR35 was introduced in 2000 as an attempt by Inland Revenue to tax what is deemed to be 'disguised employment' at a rate similar to employment. There's no need to be frightened of these regulations; interims operate in a completely legal way. Interim managers are contractors, not employees. What you are doing is protecting yourself from legislation that was not designed for the interim and freelance sector as it effectively operates. At the time of writing, the government was reconsidering legislation affecting freelancers (including IR35), presumably with the intent to simplify matters. If you have questions, discuss them with an agent or seek advice from your accountant.

Professional indemnity insurance protects you against any suit that could be brought against you because of the actions you have taken as an interim. Some agencies recommend that you take out insurance in the amount of £250,000 and upwards; again, you may want to discuss this with an accountant, or seek legal advice.

VAT registration can be done by yourself at no cost or through your accountant.

An excellent free guide to freelancing is available from the Professional Contractors Group (PCG) website. Go to **www.pcg.org. uk/cms** and you'll find everything you need to decide how to set your-self up and get started with the necessary admin for a freelance career.

SUMMARY

Consider the pros and cons of interim management by discussing them with someone who is working as an interim, or with an agent, or both. A course or seminar will help you decide. Then devise a CV that you think will sell your skills in the sector. Get feedback from an agent to determine if your CV will be effective.

When you start your first assignment, make sure that you have a contract and you have sorted out your admin requirements. When you're near completion, obtain a reference, update your CV, and look for your next assignment.

SUCCESS STORY:
GRAHAM STEPHENS

In 2000, following a long and successful career as Director of Customer Services in the IT sector, Graham Stephens saw a redundancy looming. He was able to negotiate a 'soft landing'; a good package that allowed him, at 50 years of age, to take a break and consider his options.

After a few months, a former employer called and asked him to take on a project as an interim manager. He enjoyed it so much that he decided not to accept a permanent role when it was offered. Instead he carried on working as an interim and, after three further assignments, he realised that what he liked best was setting things up and getting them running. With the permanent jobs he'd done, once clear goals had been established and a plan put into operation, his time was spent making sure things were ticking over – something that Graham found less stimulating. Interim roles meant that he faced a new challenge with every assignment. And it hasn't always been in IT; he's also worked for an oil and gas company and an image library.

After nine years, he decided that the long hours necessary in an interim role were not what he wanted in the next phase of his career. His interim experience has given him the opportunity to work in many different organisations, and he's now operating as a senior management consultant focused on leadership and management development. This is delivered through executive coaching and training. He often works in partnership with Southampton Solent University, where he was recently appointed to Visiting Fellow in the Faculty of Business, Sport and Enterprise. He is also starting to build his SME client base, which is all part of his plan to carry on working well into his 60s.

Graham has some sound advice for those getting started as an interim.

- Know what you're good at. You cannot be a jack of all trades.
- Understand the value that you can offer to companies.
- Make sure you are able to sell yourself as a *product*.
- Network like crazy and use LinkedIn. (All of Graham's interim work came through his own connections. In his case, he didn't find interim agencies very productive.)
- Get on the telephone and call people; there's no substitute for personal contact.

When you have the job, be prepared for surprises. Graham says that, even though a problem has been previously identified, you may find that the current management is part of the problem. Treasured systems that are still deemed to be effective by a company's founders might be the things that need to change. Political nous and diplomatic skills are very important in the role. Graham was once called in for an assignment by the chairman of a company, only to find that the MD did not want him there. Graham also cautions that being an interim is hard work and the hours are long; it's not for those who want an easy ride.

In his opinion, there is a gradual increase in the need for interims, with many businesses slow to recognise the benefits they can bring. He thinks that SMEs, in particular, could use interims and their expertise to catapult themselves to the next stage of growth.

CONSULTANCY

It sounds like an appealing situation: be your own boss, work as often as you like, sell your expertise for a high price and be recognised as an expert in your field. Others have been successful at it, so why not you?

The starting point is a rigorous assessment of your skills to determine that you have the essentials. Then you'll need to research your market, understand how to position yourself competitively and decide how to target customers and sell to them. If your skill set matches the profile of a consultant, you'll engage with two important questions: *'What is your proposition (what value do you bring your clients)?'* and *'Why should your clients buy your services when someone else might offer them cheaper and better?'*

THE BASIC REQUIREMENTS

There are two broad categories of essential skills: content and process. 'Content' skills include your specific technical knowledge. Do you have expertise that is rare or unusual, or which people and companies normally buy as required? For example: companies don't hire office managers as consultants but they might require a relocation expert to make recommendations on an office move. Lots of IT disciplines lend themselves to consulting because in-depth experience is needed for a short time. Business and management consultants are hired because they have specialist skills. The need for consultants can also be event-driven: the 2010 deep-sea oil rig leak in the Gulf of Mexico required people with highly specialised knowledge.

It isn't necessary to be unique or have an exotic specialism but it is important to:

- be credible with the depth of experience and knowledge in your field;
- be able to define specifically what you are offering;
- have something that companies or individuals want to buy.

To discover what 'content' skills you have, go back over your academic and work history and list the areas of knowledge that you know are highly developed. Make your list as thorough as possible. Look for situations where you analysed a problem and took action that resulted in measurable outcomes. Because you've had many years of experience in your field, you may have forgotten something that you haven't used recently but could be updated and made relevant. Try to be as inclusive and as specific as possible.

After that exercise, consider your 'process' skills. They fall into five categories:

1. *Problemsolving.* Also known in business schools as 'decision analysis', this is an essential skill for a consultant. You'll be expected to define the problem (or problems) and then work with your client to find solutions. It's important to be able to prove your problem-solving abilities to a potential client by using examples to show how you've influenced real-life situations. Be able to quantify the value: '*We saved £10 million*' or '*We grew the business by £150,000.*'
2. *Communication.* Many consultants consider this to be at least as important as their problem-solving skills. You'll have to be a good listener, be able to present well and write clear reports. If you're lacking in some of these abilities it may not be fatal; this is an area that can be improved by taking courses.
3. *Interpersonal.* Building relationships with clients, agents and other consultants is essential in order to obtain the contract and retain the client. Much of your future business will come from referrals. Your personality plays a key role here. Are you a person who gets on easily with others? Are you perceived to be someone who is credible and trustworthy?

4. *Marketing.* The ability to sell yourself and your business are key attributes. If you can't get customers you won't have a business. You will need to package and present yourself in a way that impresses clients.
5. *Business.* Even if you're gifted with technical and communication skills, you may not know how to run a business. A self-employed consultant needs to understand the basics of starting and operating a small business, which can be learned. Start with your local university or find seminars that are appropriate. See if you can meet with some consultants who are successful. Find someone with first-hand knowledge who will tell you what they have done to make their business run smoothly. Alternatively, you could form a partnership with someone who has that skill.

THE COMPETITION

As an occupation, consultancy has been around for a long time. There are many people who have been with large consultancy firms (such as KPMG and Deloitte), training and working for years and honing their craft. You'll be entering a highly competitive field, one that has been developed and cultivated by other experts. How will you position yourself?

You compete on the basis of your 'value proposition' in addition to your skills. If you take a good look at yourself and your market, you can determine if there are many other consultants out there in the same field. In terms of your speciality, if one person in ten has your knowledge, then you are less valuable than you would be if the ratio were one in a hundred or one in a thousand. Take some time to honestly assess your position with regard to others who are working as consultants in your field. Seek opinions from colleagues and friends. It's important to have a realistic view.

One way to overcome competition is to bring better value to clients. If you can convince them that you can do the same thing as a high-priced firm, then you could gain a contract. Being able to further illustrate the savings you will bring to the company will also aid your case. Will your work enable the client to make cost savings by improving systems or by increasing sales? Can you improve performance by bringing clarity to a contentious situation?

As you would in a job interview, you'll need to be prepared to show evidence based on your previous track record. You will be interviewed at some point in order acquire the contract, so if you find the process daunting it would be a good idea to get some professional coaching with someone who can assist you in preparing your pitch to clients. Your pitch will include several stories about your successful projects.

DEVELOPING YOUR PROPOSITION

Consider reasons that clients use consultants and then structure your offering to fit their needs. Consultants are hired in order to:

- provide expertise not available from within a company;
- supply objective advice from an outsider's perspective, someone removed from corporate politics;
- solve a problem that has no obvious solution; and
- improve performance in a specific area.

You may already have ideas to present to a company or a set of clients. In the course of your previous employment, have you identified inadequate systems that you know you can improve? Is there a sales channel that isn't being exploited? Are there personnel or recruitment problems in a firm? Can you present solutions?

This is an invitation to engage with entrepreneurial, outside-the-box thinking. Being able to imagine a solution is part of the consultant's remit. As an exercise, think of a company you've done business with (or worked for) and write down a solution to a problem that you've seen. Then think of a way to get in touch with a decision-maker at that company. Use your network and make a sketch of your route to that person. You may find that they're only one or two degrees of separation from you. If so, then there isn't much distance between you and your first client.

Contacting potential clients and sounding them out with your proposition will aid you in your decision to proceed as a consultant.

Your first clients will likely be people that you know in your industry. Read the success stories included in this chapter and you'll notice each consultant found clients in their network, and they continue to do so.

SUCCESS STORY: **JANE EVANS**

A career in HR led Jane Evans straight towards her own consultancy, with a move that was carefully planned and executed at the age of 45.

After taking a degree in Psychology at the University of Lancaster, Jane's first job was with Millward's Shoes, as a trainee in retail management. Then she joined the HR department at Mr Harry Frame Clothing, a move that she says was natural because of her psychology background and her interest in people. She left when one of their suppliers, Blue Arrow Personnel Services, offered her a job as a recruitment consultant. She was there for two years before she joined Vodafone to set up a recruitment function in the early days of the company's development. She stayed there for 18 years, always in HR, changing roles every two years and supporting a multitude of HR projects and activities, including mergers and acquisitions. In the year 2000, the company underwent a major restructuring, giving Jane an opportunity to develop her skills and expertise in organisation design, development and change, which subsequently became her speciality.

Jane left Vodafone in 2008, having progressed to a European organisational development role. She'd achieved the goals she had set herself within Vodafone and was looking for new challenges. Jane wanted to be master of her own destiny, with a better work-life balance, so she formed a consultancy partnership with a colleague from Vodafone. Jane says, 'We have a Venn diagram of skills that are complimentary and overlapping.' Their values are also in synch, something that is very important in their partnership. Integrity isn't compromised and clients know that they can be trusted; it's part of their brand.

Unlike other start-ups, these two found their clients relatively easily. Here's how they did it: first, they spent a lot of time on their value proposition. What exactly were they offering and why was it better? They developed a full understanding of what they were about before they made themselves available. Next, they developed a simple, attractive website. On the day the site went live, they contacted all of their colleagues and friends, directing them to the website by using a friendly tone that informed everyone they were ready to launch their business. That same day they got a response and an assignment. It sounds easy, but it should be noted that in their careers they had developed a fan base; not consciously, but simply through becoming known for the quality of their work and the effectiveness of their working relationships. Both of them had established sterling reputations and excellent connections in their field before they launched their business. They were very credible.

Here is Jane's advice for new consultants:

- **Work out what makes you unique – most of the time it's simply the fact that you are you!**
- **Understand and be able to explain your value proposition, but be flexible to accommodate the client's real needs.**
- **Know who your proposition will appeal to, in what circumstances, and market to them appropriately.**
- **Have the right mental attitude about consulting.**

Of course, there were many lessons learned along the way. Shortly after they started, and by way of testing out their offering, they presented their proposition to a 'friend of a friend' who was a well-known HR consultant. They were challenged hard about their presentation, with the recommendation that they find a way to explain why their offering was unique. After a rethink, they came up with an elevator pitch that captured what they were all about, without having to make a 10-slide presentation. Jane says it's important that your pitch is something you can use at any professional or social function, as well as with clients.

They don't try to compete with the larger consultancies, but seek clients whose culture and stage of development are more suited to their consultancy style. While at Vodafone, they had been regarded as 'internal consultants' who had to persuade their directors to work with them as an alternative to bringing in external consultants to do the work. This gave them an understanding of what clients are looking for, and what irks them about consultants too.

When asked what she would have done differently with the benefit of hindsight, Jane says, 'a lot more networking in my last year at Vodafone'. She readily admits that all of their clients come through their network. Jane has a few more words of advice.

- It is often more realistic to charge a day rate, rather than a project rate, as projects change and expand over time in unpredictable ways.
- Keep clients up to speed with changes that affect the budget. That way, there aren't any surprises.
- Sometimes it can be useful to showcase your work by offering some support to a client without expecting a fee – what goes around comes around.
- Maintain your portfolio of clients by keeping in touch and checking in on how things are going after you've left.

Finally, Jane says, 'Don't undersell yourself. Be confident that you're worth what you say you are worth.'

ROUTES TO CONSULTANCY

There are three ways to get started in consultancy.

1. *Join a consulting company as a full-time employee.* If you have specific expertise in an industry sector and lots of contacts, you may be an asset because you can develop new business for them. This approach builds career capital in the field. Freelance work remains an option for the future.
2. *Become an associate.* In this situation, you work on an as-and-when basis, taking projects that are assigned to you. This could be a good way to jump-start a consultant career because the selling and marketing are done by someone on your behalf. You get to be your own boss from day one, and still build up career capital as a consultant.
3. *Become an independent/freelance.* You're on your own: finding clients, getting contracts and delivering your services. This approach has the highest risk. When you're working on a project, you also need to be looking for your next client.

SUCCESS STORY: NATALIE MCLELLAN

Natalie became a consultant with a career change that she made in her early 30s. She went freelance at the age of 40. It was a struggle at first, but she persevered and is now in a position to say that she thoroughly enjoys her work.

Natalie graduated in 1986 with a 2:1 in Modern Languages. She was hired by Cummins Engine Company in a corporate drive to recruit more women and, in her case, someone who had language experience to help them market to a variety of territories. She was assistant to the head of communications, doing publicity for OEM (Original Equipment Manufacturer) accounts. Then she had her first involvement with change, working as part of a director-level team, leading an initiative to deploy a customer satisfaction measurement programme and customer-led improvement process across the EMEA (Europe, Middle East and Africa) region. During her time at Cummins, she took an MBA, which was sponsored by the company. After ten years, a change in management at Cummins and a desire to broaden her experience meant that it was time to leave.

As a result of her MBA studies, Natalie was attracted by the idea of consultancy. She was able to join Ernst & Young as part of a mature hire scheme, and she spent two-and-a-half years there. Then she went to PricewaterhouseCoopers (PWC) as a principal consultant, leaving three years later as a director, after taking a voluntary redundancy. With children now on the scene, Natalie wanted to be self-employed and change her work-life balance. That was her primary motive for going freelance.

Her first attempt at a business start-up was not a success. The lessons she learned are worth noting. First, she spent 12 months working with a new partner who, like Natalie, didn't enjoy selling. So they spent 12 months polishing their proposition, instead of getting new business. Their offering was confusing to their customers: they were attempting to integrate branding, marketing and customer management. The proposition was difficult to sell to a client organisation. After much frustration – and a few contracts – she decided to go out on her own.

That wasn't as easy as she'd hoped: she spent ten months developing her relationships with agencies before she got her first contract in June 2005. And it was a step down in terms of the status she'd held previously, because it wasn't a full consultancy role. She worked for 11 months as a project manager (so she combined an interim role with consultancy) for an insurance company, helping them to define a new customer value proposition and associated operating model. Her next role was as strategic project manager with an international optician, where she put her strategy and business architecture knowledge (the core skills she acquired at PWC) to better use. As a consultant, she worked with the international director and the chief executive in evaluating the potential of a new business proposition. The insurance company brought her back in a customer relationship management role for a brief spell, and then she was hired by a private health insurer, consulting at board and senior management level. She was there for over two years, leading a variety of initiatives which included the establishment of a new business architecture capability and the definition of a new target operating model.

After five years operating as an independent consultant, she's come full circle and is undertaking the type of work she did with Ernst & Young and PWC. It hasn't been easy, but she is now able to land the kind of stimulating roles she enjoys and, at the same time, have the flexibility and control she needs as a working mother of three.

Natalie has a lot of useful advice for those who want to get started.

- Be patient. It was 10 months before Natalie got her first contract.
- Establish and maintain agency relationships. Her work at both insurance companies came through an agency.
- Pick one thing that you're really strong at and develop it further.
- Invest in yourself. Take courses (such as Project/Programme Management, Lean/Six Sigma) that enhance your skills and look good on your CV.
- Develop a massive network. Consultants need to know a lot of people, including interims and contract workers. Natalie has had work come to her though interims she has hired previously.
- Use LinkedIn.

Natalie says it's difficult to compete with a trained consultant such as herself, especially in a slow market, but people are doing it successfully. Developing a broad network of clients and agencies is key, as well as clearly defining the specialist expertise you offer to the market.

HOW NOT TO BE A CONSULTANT

Peter left his full-time job with the idea that his knowledge was valuable in his sector. In his opinion, finding clients wouldn't be a problem. He kept in touch with former colleagues, resulting in some consultancy work with his previous employer. He was happy to lose himself in a project for nine months, secure in the knowledge that he was being well-paid for his expertise. When the contract ended, Peter started looking for a new assignment. Time passed and the months rolled by until he realised he had to do something different because his business was failing.

What went wrong? First, he went straight to freelance without planning or preparation. Peter didn't develop a client base by networking and marketing himself. Next, he didn't consider how to develop himself as a product. Finally, he made the biggest error a business can make: he relied on one customer.

THERE IS A BETTER WAY

Start with a short-term contract with an ex-employer, but be sure to invest some of your earnings in workshops, seminars, and other activities that teach you to be an effective consultant. Build relationships with agencies that understand you and your field and hone your personal proposition. Develop your network and widen your contracts. Implement a system to generate a stream of leads. Consider becoming an associate with a consultancy firm. Create a marketing plan to sell your skills. Have plenty of leads to follow when your contract ends; one of them will get you your next client.

DEVELOPING YOUR BUSINESS FURTHER

Following a succession of contracts, you may be able to enter the second stage of a consultancy: taking on associates who will sell their time to companies, allowing you to earn a mark-up for yourself. To do that, you'll need to invest in your methods and systems, and also in marketing in order to attract associates as well as clients.

Good businesses develop long-term strategies. A formal business plan is a requirement, not only for your business, but also for your personal offering. A consultant needs to be up to date or their services will soon be obsolete.

MORE ABOUT THE BUSINESS

'Running your own business has three parts: fee earning, development and admin. The constant challenge is finding the right balance between the three.'
Paul Lower

If you've skipped the interim chapter and come straight here, be sure to go back and look at what we say about setting up as a limited company and the other admin requirements for a freelance business. As with interim work, a contract is essential. You can gain advice from an agency or from visiting the websites we recommend for freelancers. If your clients are individuals rather than companies, you may be able to initially operate as a sole trader, thus avoiding some of the paperwork that a company entails. Remember that companies do business with other companies, so you may not be able to attract corporate clients as a sole trader.

Try to charge a day rate for your services. Clients may want a fixed price for projects, but projects can change and expand (see Jane Evans' story on p.204). Price yourself competitively and know that you're worth what you're charging.

Nearly every sector has an association for consultants. Find the website for one that is relevant to you. Most of them have information about those working in the field, which agencies are active and recruiting, plus news and tips on how to get started and stay active. As well as helping you keep informed, joining an association will assist you in expanding your network.

SUMMARY

Analyse your 'content' and 'process' skills to determine if you have something to sell and if you will be able to operate effectively as a consultant. Research the market and see if there are customers for your offering. Develop your value proposition: be very clear about what you offer and the ways you can help your clients save money by improving sales, operations, or services. Be able to explain why you're worth what you charge. Test your proposition with an agency.

Once you're in business, invest time and money in personal development so that you stay current in your field. Always look for your next client while you're working on a project and, as we've said so many times before, network like crazy.

SUCCESS STORY: PAUL LOWER

Self-employment is a journey as well as a destination. Although Paul Lower set out to be a consultant – and he's had success as one – he discovered that what he really enjoys is an educator's role, training and coaching businesses of all shapes and sizes in his area of expertise: business finance. He came to this realisation when he discovered that his greatest satisfaction is in helping people understand what the numbers really mean, because numbers are the language of business. The message here is that you may not know what your best self-employed business will be until you get out and try something. Your efforts may lead you to unexpected places.

Paul has had an exciting career working in several different sectors. After leaving school in the early 70s, he started work as an accountant trainee at ASDA and left after three years as a partially qualified accountant. He landed a role at Heinz as a cost analyst while continuing his studies at night school for a full accreditation. His next job was at Coty (later bought by Colgate Palmolive) where he was Senior Management Accountant at the age of 24. In the late 70s he was recruited by Geosource, a US company, as

Regional Financial Controller. Their business was much different from the manufacturing background he was used to, in that they were involved in land-based geophysical exploration, primarily for oil. Paul was made Financial Controller for Africa, and his territory included Sudan, Nigeria, Somalia, Tanzania and what is now the Democratic Republic of the Congo. He left in 1983, with a full accountancy qualification and a desire to escape from an outbreak of cerebral malaria that was plaguing Africa at the time. A recruitment agency sent him to Polygram (now Universal Music) where he was made Senior Management Accountant at Phonogram, one of their subsidiaries. Those were high-growth times for the recorded music industry, as the 1980s saw most people replacing their vinyl records with high-priced CDs. Paul was asked to join Roger Ames in the creation of a new label: London Records. Ames was Managing Director and Paul was subsequently made Finance Director, a role he held from 1985–99, when London Records was sold to Warner in a deal that saw Ames become head of the worldwide interests of Warner Music. This meant a big change in corporate structure and, to an even greater extent, in corporate culture, so Paul took a redundancy package. David Hockman invited him to join Edel (a German record company) as Finance Director for a new music publishing division. Edel is famous for its rapid expansion and swift decline. An attempted management buyout did not succeed, his friend David left, and Paul continued to commute between the UK and Hamburg until he exited the company in 2002 – his second redundancy.

He decided to set himself up as a consultant in the music business. With his expertise and his contacts (two absolute prerequisites for a consultancy) he was soon working as a virtual finance director (two or three days a month, paid on invoice) for a music DVD company. He also developed an accounting software tool for Olswang, the media law firm, and a programme for the record business that incorporates advances, royalty rates and recording costs in one convenient package.

Music Sales, an international book and music publishing company, offered him a full-time job in 2004. He saw it as a challenge, taking a company that was organised on a federal basis and bringing it under central control. As Finance Director, a role he held for about four years, he replaced their accounting and reporting system and hired new staff to fit with the restructure. But the travel and long hours were taking their toll. In 2008, Paul had a rethink and decided to negotiate a withdrawal so he could be self-employed again. He didn't need a six-figure salary and he wanted to do work that was fun and engaging.

Now he offers business finance training and coaching. Drawing on his cross-sector experience, he can advise any type of business, from Angel Trains (a rolling-stock company) to Primark. His African connections have proved useful, and he's done work for the Nigerian public sector, helping their Civil Aviation Authority and Securities and Exchange Commission. He has also developed a course for one of the major Nigerian banks, teaching them to make improvements to their anti-fraud systems.

He knows that business training and coaching is a saturated market. How does he differentiate his business? He trains with the benefit of experience and he can research and develop bespoke courses. His one regret is that he named his company Paul Lower Consulting, because consulting is only a small part of his business.

SUCCESS STORY: **BEN MAKINS**

Once you have taken the decision to become self-employed you don't know where it will lead and things may not always turn out as planned. After many years as an employee in the public sector, Ben Makins became a consultant, started a new business with a colleague, was head-hunted to develop a consultancy within an established business and then joined a partnership. His story is an example of how to seize opportunities when they arise. And he has some advice for those public sector workers who might hope to emulate what he has done in the current market.

Ben graduated in the 1970s with a degree in Politics from York University. He acquired a professional qualification in social work and a Master of Social Work degree from York, followed by a Diploma in Management Studies from Coventry University.

He spent three years as a social worker with a rural team, working in the areas of mental health, child protection and older people's services. Then he moved 'from the dales of North Yorkshire to the wilds of Notting Hill', as he describes his relocation to London in the 1980s. Ben started as a senior practitioner in Kensington and Chelsea, before moving on to become a team manager and then area manager in Hounslow – a middle management position. In 1990, he faced his first redundancy at the age of 37 due to a restructure. Before the redundancy could occur, he successfully applied for a job at Ealing Council (effectively a promotion) and subsequently spent ten years there, first as an area manager and then in a number of roles – his final one as Assistant Director. In 1999, with a restructuring underway, Ben thought he would like to be self-employed. He used his previous experience of redundancy to negotiate an exit package that allowed him to stay in control and take some time to consider his options..

At the age of 46, he had a broad range of experience and a solid reputation. He got his first consultancy offer from his network That led to a second contract where Ben collaborated with a former colleague who had also gone freelance. They decided to team up and form their own service company, AQSC, which they managed for five years. They could have carried on, but his partner had different aspirations and didn't want to continue. Being head-hunted to develop and run a consultancy within Care and Health (a company with several interests) gave him the opportunity to refresh his networks. It was also a rich learning experience. However, after two years in the role he could see that, in spite of his own efforts, the company was going to fail. It was time to bail out. What to do?

Ben is an excellent networker, and so his problem was soon solved when he was approached by two former colleagues who invited him to join their limited liability partnership. Together they run SCP Consult, a service company that provides senior interim managers as well as consultancy and project management services to local authorities and primary care trusts. They work with over 100 associate freelances and have grown turnover five-fold in three years.

When asked if his approach could be replicated, Ben says it can't be done in the same way. The market is very different today than it was under 13 years of a Labour government, when there was growth in the number of service companies under contract to local and national governments. But while there is a backlash against big profits being earned from public services, there are still opportunities for small and medium firms with reasonable prices, which means smaller margins and low overheads. Some individuals will continue to work as consultants and interims but it won't suit everyone in the new environment.

Ben's advice to those wanting to be self-employed in the public sector is:

- get ahead of the game early;
- stay on top of a rapidly-changing landscape;
- don't rely on your title or station;
- analyse your skill sets and be able to show how you can think outside of your experience and comfort zone;
- be proactive and seek opportunities; focus on your experience and skills that would help organisations to innovate, make service efficiencies, cost savings, and performance improvements.

Ben says that in very lean times, smarter local authorities will take on people with strong skills to help them deal with making savings. For example: they'll be looking at procurement specialists who deliver results. He suggests having a good look at social enterprises such as mutuals or cooperatives as a way of providing services to councils, either by setting one up or acting as a consultant and advising clients as to how it should be done.

Ben has never regretted his decision to go out on his own. He admits that he could not have foreseen where it would lead, but the result has been a rewarding career.

CHAPTER 14

START YOUR OWN BUSINESS

There's a new term that has been coined by the media, one that is also appearing on age-related websites: 'olderpreneur'. It's a play on the word entrepreneur, which is derived from the French *entreprendre*, meaning 'to undertake'. In most business cultures an entrepreneur is defined as someone who sets up a business that involves financial risk, and does so with the aim of making a profit. Typically, an entrepreneur will own and manage the business, either alone or in association with others, depending on the nature and size of the operation.

Our contacts at London Business Angels, a leading UK angel investment network, have told us that they are seeing an increase in the numbers of older entrepreneurs seeking funding. Age is a factor in reducing risk in a new venture and it is valued by some investors. Studies show that businesses started by olderpreneurs have a higher-than-average survival rate[1]. If the proposition and the team are sound, then business angels may be interested in investing. Angels are private individuals who invest in high-growth businesses in exchange for an equity share in a company. The fact that a company is managed by an older person can be a selling point, since trust is essential with angels. Evidence of capability builds trust.

The image of the entrepreneur as a flashy Richard Branson type is not wholly accurate. It takes courage to start a new business, and entrepreneurs are charismatic individuals, but success is achieved with a good idea and a great team. The lone entrepreneur is a myth. He or she depends on a partner or a small group that is central to the success of the operation. You may be one of those people: a valuable team member who, by working in combination with the right partners, will be part of a successful start-up. Alan Saxon (see p.228) is an example of someone who discovered that he was a valuable team member, someone essential to the success of a new venture.

TYPES OF ENTREPRENEURIAL VENTURES

Ownership, management, risk and profit are the basic components of an entrepreneurial venture. Corner shops, franchises and consultancies fit the definition, but they usually have one characteristic that differentiates them from companies that grow into big money-makers: they are 'lifestyle businesses'. If successful, they provide the owners with a good income that meets their needs and perhaps leaves something behind for the kids. You may decide that you want to start a lifestyle business. Matt Williams did, and he's happy with his choice (see p.220). There's plenty of information in this chapter for you to consider if you choose to create a lifestyle business – although we don't discuss franchises or buying a pre-existing business. Our expertise is with starting new businesses from scratch.

Funding for a lifestyle business often comes from the owner's resources, perhaps combined with a bank loan, credit line, or investment from relatives or friends. However, to attract funding from a third party, or a group outside of the owner's circle, a business must be 'scalable', which means it should have the potential for rapid growth and for generating future profit for the investors. In this chapter, we refer to a 'fundable business' as one that is scalable. That sets it apart from a lifestyle business that is entrepreneurial, but doesn't have the potential to grow to a size that can generate a big return on investment.

We'll look at the basic requirements of a business start-up in the light of what will attract investors – and business angels in particular – because if someone smart wants to own a share of your business, then you know you've got a better chance of success, whether you take the money or not. But if a lifestyle business is what you want, please read on as the tools and techniques described are equally relevant to any start-up.

SUCCESS STORY: **MATT WILLIAMS**

After being made redundant, Matt Williams decided that he would convert his experience into a business he could call his own. His pragmatic approach is a lesson in how to take the right steps in getting started.

Matt's first job was as an apprentice, working for his father's printing company. He left at age 29 as a deputy manager and spent 12 years with Field Packaging. He joined as a printer and worked his way up, first as a shift manager and then reaching the position of production planner. The company closed in 2000 and, after a brief stint in sales with Carter Litho, he was re-employed by his father's company in 2001 as production manager. When his father passed away in 2008, the corporate culture changed and Matt took voluntary redundancy and moved to a large firm in East London as production manager. He left after four months because the long commute from Maidenhead took all the pleasure out of his work. He found a position closer to home but that was soon ended by the recession. In 2009, Matt was 48 years old, unemployed and uncertain about his prospects as an employee in the printing business.

He considered that his options were as follows:

- get a job outside the industry;
- buy a printing company;
- buy a franchise;
- start a new business from scratch.

He quickly discounted the first choice. Printing had been his whole life; finding work in another sector was too daunting a task. As well as looking at the franchise option, he researched businesses that were for sale. His conclusion? Mortgaging his house to buy a standalone business, or perhaps a franchise for

£54,000, cost too much and had a lot of risk attached. Why not go it alone with a new venture?

Realising that he had a limited knowledge of how to run a small business, Matt enrolled in a course at Thames Valley University called Start Your Own Business. He learned the fundamentals and fleshed out his knowledge with a Business Link course: Foundation to Success. With new confidence and £8,000 of his own money, he set himself up in a digital printing business that he runs from home.

What's his unique selling point (USP)? Matt says he doesn't have one, but on further questioning he reveals that his customers come to him because he offers a friendly, personal service, unlike the online businesses that he is currently competing with. He's easy to deal with and he offers a very fast turnaround at a good price.

How does he get customers? Following instructions from his course instructors, Matt found that over 50 per cent of his business came through networking; he recommends 4Networking and Refer-on as two groups that are practical and useful.

He says that his biggest obstacle was overcoming the doubts and critical comments that were thrown at him by friends and other well-meaning people. He was strong and positive in his mind that this was what he really wanted to do.

At the moment Matt has a lifestyle business. He's doing something he enjoys, and he has a five-year-plan that may see him converting it into a scalable business by creating a franchise or developing a chain of printing shops. For Matt, this is just the beginning.

WHAT DOES IT TAKE?

You'll need six things to get started:

- a good idea;
- a great team;

- a market opportunity;
- growth potential;
- a sound business plan that describes all of the above;
- a business mentor.

It has to be said that energy, dedication and a love of business (or at least a love of the business you are starting) are essential. Without those qualities, you should be looking for another way to earn money. The road to success is long and arduous; passion for the enterprise is a basic requirement. It's better to start something you love doing, rather than creating a business you don't enjoy simply because you suspect it will make money. Utilise your talents and connections, and start locally – that's where your largest network is. Our two success stories in this chapter illustrate this point. Both Matt and Alan had lots of previous experience in their respective fields, and they genuinely like what they're doing.

1. The big idea

If you struggled in your former job with a product or service that wasn't fit for purpose and you think you can improve it, then you have an idea. If your nephew is a software programmer who's been bugging you to take a look at his latest program – one that makes something run faster and better – then you know someone who has an idea that you can develop into a business. In order to start a new venture it isn't necessary to invent something radical or earth-shattering; many successful businesses are built on improvements to existing products and services, or they take advantage of a 'dislocation' in the market, meaning a change in the way people do things. Mobile phones morphing into handheld computers is an example of a dislocation (think of the number of apps that Apple now has for its iPhone) or e-readers replacing books (whole new businesses have sprung up, such as digital warehouses for adapting and storing content and online bookstores that compete with Amazon by only selling downloadable books). As a general rule, it is easier to start a service business than it is to launch a product. That's because initial customers – an essential requirement – can be acquired through a simple and cost-effective manner by networking.

The best question to ask when evaluating a new business idea is: *Where's the pain?* Followed by: *How does my idea make the pain go away?* This strategy examines problems and solutions. The more painful the problem, the greater the value of the solution: your product or service. A cure for cancer would be extremely valuable, while a new way to get fresh vegetables to market would be lower down in a problem/solution hierarchy.

How do you know if it's a good idea? If it survives a night at the pub with your friends and it appears to be sound in the cold light of day, that's a first step. But then you'll need to take it further by doing a lot of research to determine if your service idea is already in the market, or if someone is making and selling your gadget that beats all gadgets. Having convinced yourself that you might be on to something, the next thing is to run the idea past other people with expertise in your chosen field, preferably those whom you trust to be honest with you. Your idea must be credible beyond your circle of family and friends.

The best way to prove that an idea has merit is to find a customer. Your first sale, an order or a promise to buy, will confirm that you're on to something. So will an endorsement, either from your first customer or a respected person in your sector.

Earlier in the book, we mentioned the TMAY, or elevator pitch: a brief summary of who you are and what you're seeking. With an idea, a customer and an endorsement you can create a two-sentence elevator pitch that describes your business. The first sentence is the concept (the solution to a problem) and the second is the endorsement. So an example might be:

We've got a (insert product/service description) *for* (insert customer/market description). *We've already sold to* (first customer), OR (name of notable person) *is supporting our concept.*

You can vary this according to your needs. It's a useful tool to help you describe your business without getting bogged down in technical language.

2. The core team

An idea isn't worth much unless it's well executed. Many investors believe that the team is the most important thing because, without excellent people managing a business, it has little chance of success. Your core team has to have what it takes to succeed, because in order to get funding you're going to have to sell your concept and your team to investors. They have to buy into what you're doing and, crucially, so do you. Team members don't have to know everything at first; willingness to learn and adapt are necessary attributes for everyone in a start-up. What's important is that key roles are filled by credible people.

The first person to consider is the 'lead entrepreneur': the man or woman who may have had the idea in the first place (but not necessarily). They will be the face of the company and the nominal boss. All of the core team will be equal but there must be a leader, someone to take the role of managing director. Without that person you will not appear credible in the market. Lead entrepreneurs have vision; they are confident, ambitious, energetic and driven. They're certain that the business is destined for massive success, and they're able to convince others that this could be true; they're brimming with energy and ideas about how to make it work. This is the person that investors examine closely. They need to see two qualities above all others: enthusiasm and trustworthiness. And when it comes to trust, older entrepreneurs can have an advantage.

There is sometimes a dark side to the lead entrepreneur: they can be arrogant and manipulative, and prone to dishonesty when stressed. When building a team, look for those who can temper the worst traits, and always include process-oriented people to manage the details – an area where most lead entrepreneurs are often woefully inadequate.

Your core team must include a member with sales experience. A start-up without a sales person has no hope of success. That's because every business is all about cash flow. Someone has to make the deals and close them; no sales means no cash, which means no business. This is the team member who gets your all-important first customer (if the lead entrepreneur hasn't already), the one who can make cold calls, the one who has a list of contacts and a multitude of potential leads, or at least the talent and enthusiasm to get them. Some would argue that a marketing professional is what's required; that's only a good idea if your marketing person can also sell. Selling means closing and marketers aren't always very good at that. You can outsource marketing services and bring on a full-time person later. What you need is sales.

There will be a technical person on the team, the brains behind the product or service. In a creative business, this could be the designer, author or filmmaker; in IT the programmer fits the bill; pharmaceuticals will have a scientist. Many businesses have engineers in this role. A delivery specialist is also required: someone to make sure the thing gets made and into the shops, or that the techies show up and repair the equipment as specified.

A start-up is more credible to investors when there is a finance director (FD) on board. Funders want to know that their money is in safe hands and it's being used properly. They will expect timely and accurate reporting. Regular cash-flow forecasts are required and they should be created by a dispassionate team member, one who won't overestimate a potential income stream. This is the person who can sort out the admin. Even without any initial outside investors, all the other team members will be much happier if they don't have to deal with the bank or the tax inspector. Accountants are required for this role, not bookkeepers, who can be hired by the finance person on a part-time basis. You can have a part-time finance director. A small business doesn't require a full-time person in this role, especially at the outset. If your idea is good enough, you can attract a qualified accountant to act as FD by offering shares for their labour. Between five and ten per cent is usual, and with no salary on offer until a pre-agreed point. This type of FD is trading skills for equity and, for small operations, this is an excellent arrangement.

A core team could be structured like this:

Fig. 14.1 Core Team

The team represented above is an example. There is no absolute requirement in having five people. However, the *roles* described need to be filled. It's possible for team members to combine roles, as long as there is an MD and three basic functions are covered: sales, finance and production/delivery.

A smaller core team might look like this:

Fig. 14.2 Smaller Core Team

It's best for a start-up to have an odd number of principals. Even numbers don't work as effectively because start-ups need to be light on their feet, able to seize opportunities and act on them quickly; majority decisions are required. Getting bogged down in a two-against-two deadlock is counterproductive and very common in a company of four.

Will a start-up work with two people? Many successful companies had only two core members at the beginning: Apple and Google, for example. However, an FD should be added to the mix (as above) and then you're back to the number three if you've given the FD voting power, which they must have on decisions of a financial nature.

It's best if everyone in the core team is an equal shareholder (except your part-time FD, if that is your arrangement). The team must be incentivised, free to work hard without feeling that they're helping someone else get rich, especially since most of the members will not be drawing a realistic salary at first. The lead entrepreneur/MD might object if it was their idea, but they should be persuaded that a company of equals is a company that's much more likely to succeed. Everyone's equity will be diluted if the business can attract investment – that's the nature of the game. However, by retaining equal status with each other before and after funding, all of the principals will keep their dignity and passion for the long journey to success. Consider that everyone in the core team will be a future board member and successful companies have strong boards.

Choose reliable people for your team, those whom you trust and respect, with talents that are complementary to yours. You'll have to like them too, because you'll be spending a lot of time together. Family members and close friends are usually not a good idea if you value the long-term relationship. Businesses do fail, even those that are strong at the outset, and you won't want to lose a marriage or a friend if it all goes wrong.

SUCCESS STORY: **ALAN SAXON**

One way of staying active and credible in your sector is by taking short-term contracts. Instead of waiting for the perfect job, Alan Saxon decided to create opportunities that might pay off in future. The result was an offer to join a new venture as a valued team member; now he's an entrepreneur.

Alan's experience in packaging is extensive. He left his first job with a printing company after eight years, having risen to the position of senior designer, with clients that included Boots and Marks & Spencer. He was hired by a major toy company, Kenner Parker Tonka, where he was European Package Development Manager for ten years. (Those who remember the original *Star Wars* merchandise will have seen samples of Alan's work.) He was happy there, and would have stayed had the company not entered Chapter 11 bankruptcy protection in the US, resulting in a corporate sale to Hasbro in 1989. The new operation had no packaging development department, they used different working methods and so Alan found himself sidelined. He left for a position at Woolworth's where he stayed for 17 years, until the demise of the company in 2008. Deloitte was the receiver. They rang Alan because he knew where many of the brand assets were located. That got him a three-month contract with Argos, helping them with one of the brands they had purchased, and he began his search for a full-time position.

Alan discovered that ageism would play a big part in his struggle for re-employment. He was 58 years old, something that was easy to detect from his CV because he put down the dates of his education (not necessary) and he listed his first job, which confirmed that he was older. He says that he didn't know how to write a tactical CV, i.e. one that's written to target a job ad (rather than a full chronological history) and he's certain that meant lost opportunities. After a couple of sessions at the Job Club, he rectified the situation but continued to have trouble finding a permanent role. Alan applied for jobs that were tailor-made; some of them matched his job description at Woolworth's. He knows he was passed by in favour of younger workers and he doesn't understand why employers wouldn't hire him.

His solution was to take contracts for a limited term and work for much less than his former rate, in the hope that a better job would emerge through the contacts he made. He was approached by a small design studio in London and worked there for three months, developing pitches for some big brands. His only remuneration was his expenses. Following that, he used his network to land another short (but paid) contract with a company that wanted to expand into multilingual packaging, one of his areas of expertise. He proved his worth and, even though the company didn't survive, the owner asked Alan to join him in a new venture: a start-up.

The company is a language service provider, supplying translations and branding. They believe they can take on the big agencies by offering a high-quality, lower-cost alternative in a market where price is an issue. They're a small outfit with eight employees, and Alan was offered a senior role as Head of Operations, with equity shares in the company. He accepted the offer. Prior to this, he'd never considered himself an entrepreneur, but he is now a member of the core team – he's their delivery expert. The MD considers him to be his right-hand man. Alan believes in the other team members; together they're set to grab a share of the market.

Alan's looking forward to taking this as far as he can. 'It's invigorating to try new things,' he says, 'and it's a chance to see what you're made of.' He's 59 and he sees a bright future for himself and his new company.

3. The market opportunity

Your product or service must have an obvious differentiation in the marketplace, or there is no opportunity. What makes it special? What makes it stand out from your competitors? What is the USP? The strength of your USP will determine your position in the market and the size of the opportunity.

Answer the questions below to better understand your USP and your business:

- Who will buy this product/service?
- Why will they buy it?
- How many/how often will they buy?
- Why would they buy more over time?
- Why would they buy it from your company?
- What value are you actually delivering to your customers?

To attract funding, you'll have to demonstrate that there is a genuine opportunity and then be prepared to explain why your product or service will succeed in the market. It is essential to answer these questions for lifestyle businesses, as well.

4. Growth potential

Stand outside of your business and look at it like an investor. Focus your mind on the scale of your enterprise and imagine you are selling the business in five to seven years. What will it be worth? A person who invests £100,000 for 20 per cent of the company expects to get a return of a million pounds – ten times their original investment – on their share of the company at the time of sale. That's the rate of return angel investors are seeking. They may not get it, but they need to believe that it's realistic and possible.

So what will the business be worth in order to return a million pounds to someone with a 20 per cent share? The company value, at sale, would be five million pounds. What will turnover be at the time of sale? How can you grow your business to that size? What steps will you take to reach that goal? These are all questions that relate to scalability. You will need plausible answers before you seek investment.

Keep in mind that funders don't invest in lifestyle businesses – it's one of the biggest turn-offs. So if your chip shop can't become a best-selling chain of chip shops, then you should be content with a small operation. And there is nothing wrong with that, if it is your goal.

5. The business plan

You can start your business without a business plan, but that would be like hiking in new terrain with no map. Your plan won't be etched in stone; it will change over time, as you identify and face new challenges and opportunities, but it is essential to have one right from the start. You will have written project and business plans as a manager or professional, so this won't be the onerous task that frightens some younger entrepreneurs.

Think of your business plan as a story: one that explains where you are now, where you want to go, the people you're travelling with, and why those people are the best ones to take on your voyage. Tell investors why they should help to fund the ship and the crew. They need to know about the wonderful lands of profit that are your destination. You'll also have to tell them about the reefs and shoals you will encounter, how you plan to sail around them, and how you're rigged for stormy weather.

The sections of a business plan are typically as follows.

- Executive Summary (1–2 pages).
- Management Team: qualifications and experience.
- Product or Services: description and necessity (2 pages).
- The Market: detailed research, customers and competitors (3–4 pages).
- Operational Details: facilities, premises and suppliers.
- Strategic Planning: sales and marketing (2–3 pages).
- Financial: equity distribution, cash-flow projections (2–3 pages).
- Appendices: as required, and include a diagram of milestones.

The plan needn't be 50 pages long; something between 15 and 20 pages will be sufficient at the outset. You're writing for the average person, so use plain English and make it as free from technical jargon as possible. The Executive Summary must be at the front, with appendices at the back, but otherwise the order as outlined above can be varied.

If you're seeking funding, include an exit strategy for your investors in the financial section. Don't worry about how that will come about – it will either be a trade sale or an IPO (initial public offering of shares); the nature of your business will determine which one. It's the company valuation at sale that's difficult to predict, but your FD or a valuation expert can help you make an educated guess.

Once you have written your complete plan, go back and spend time on the Executive Summary, the first document that someone will ask for before they read the rest of your plan – rather like the covering letter that stimulates interest in a CV. The summary will clearly state the opportunity and the product, where you are now, what your vision is for the future, who is in the company, how you plan to achieve your vision and how long it will take to get there. The body of the plan is where you provide evidence to support the statements that you've made in your Executive Summary.

There are plenty of good books to help you write your plan and one, in particular, is mentioned in the Resources section which starts on page 253.

6. Mentors

Even with experience in your field, there will be holes in your knowledge: unforeseen hazards, potential customers and additional sources of revenue you may not be aware of, or competitors who might finish you off before you get started. Contacts outside of your team with experience of your business can provide invaluable guidance through the troubled waters of your start-up. You might find a mentor at your professional association, or perhaps through your network. Try to get one (or more) as soon as you can. A mentor can be of enormous help to a new venture.

MORE BASICS

Concurrent with the six things you need to get started (as above) there are several other tasks that need to be completed:

- choose an appropriate name;
- acquire a web domain (URL);
- incorporate as a limited company;
- draft and sign a shareholders' agreement;
- register your trademark;
- get patents for formulas and designs;
- find premises.

Some companies have websites that make name searches and incorporation very simple. They also provide information on the different responsibilities that companies and company directors undertake. You should make yourself familiar with those responsibilities before you incorporate as a limited company. Having a web domain is essential and it's easy to get one. See the Resources section for a short list of websites that will help you get started with the basics, including trademark and patent registration.

A word on registering your trademark: try to register the company name (or trading name) as your trademark. It can be done, and that way you won't have to worry about registering your logo as a trademark. Your logo may change over time, and this way you retain rights to incorporate your name into any logo as you see fit. Also register your company in as many categories of trade as possible, thus allowing for future business possibilities.

Premises are necessary for your start-up. That's because there is a perception that sole traders work from home. It's also best for your budding enterprise to have a base where the core team can meet regularly, as well as for conducting business in professional surroundings. A word of caution: make it as simple and cheap as you can. There's no need for an expensive office at first, unless you're starting a luxury brand and your customers need to see you residing in splendour. A few desks, a phone line, and Internet access are usually sufficient.

A shareholders' agreement is often overlooked by many start-ups, and that can cause problems later. On incorporation, your company will have drawn up articles of association that describe the relationships between shareholders and directors. Together with the memorandum of association, these documents comprise the constitution of the company, which sets out the internal legal framework. However, there a number things that are often not covered. What if a shareholder dies? What if one of the directors fails to perform as agreed? Should that person retain all of their shares while the other directors do the work? These matters can be covered by a shareholders' agreement: a private, legal letter that can specify any number of things including provisions for dispute resolution, agreements regarding the sale and disposal of shares, disbursement of salaries and dividends; and the appointment and removal of directors. Think of it as a prenuptial agreement that you make before you marry your business partners. Having one in place will not only put your mind at ease, it will also enable potential investors to understand your corporate governance. Upon investment, your investors will become new shareholders, and they will insist on drafting a new shareholders' agreement, subject to negotiation. Be sure to seek professional advice on all legal matters pertaining to your company.

FUNDING

The best way to run a business is by using the 'lemonade-stand' method. You purchase the ingredients with your own money, sell the lemonade at a price that covers costs (including wages) and earns a profit, and then you retain some of the profit and use the rest of it to invest in more lemonade stands until you've got dominance in the local lemonade-stand market, and so forth. It's also called the 'organic' method, which refers to the absence of funding, not the lemons. If you and your team can do this you'll be happier in the long run. Your net returns to the initial shareholders will be higher because you won't be sharing equity with investors, and you won't have a bank loan to worry about. If you never need outside investors and your business grows to a massive size, you'll have accomplished a truly great thing. It's an ideal that many businesses can't achieve, especially if capital costs are high at start-up, or the company requires development funding at any stage. There will come a time, hopefully later rather than sooner, when you will need outside investment to grow the business. Funding sources are listed below.

1. 'Soft' money: yours, family and friends. Money that doesn't come with hard terms of repayment, or require an exchange for equity.
2. Grants.
3. Bank loans, including those under the Enterprise Finance Guarantee scheme (formerly known as the Small Firms Loan Guarantee scheme, or SFLG for short).
4. A line of credit.
5. Strategic money.
6. Business angels.
7. Venture capital funds (VCs).

Loans or overdrafts are only good if you know you can repay them. They are favoured by some because it means you don't have to give up equity. However, if your cash flow is uncertain, or you are asked to put your house up against the loan or credit line (which is likely) then angel investment can be a better choice.

Strategic money is acquired when a customer pays in advance in exchange for an option on future rights. That means that a small share of equity is sold to the customer at an agreed date. It's smarter to get your customer to pay in advance without giving up equity, if you can.

As mentioned previously, business angels are private individuals who typically invest from £100,000 to £1 million in a new venture. They do this in exchange for a negotiable equity share in the company. Angels are a good solution for most new businesses that aren't well-funded at the outset, or when there is an increased capital requirement for growth at an early stage. Why? Because unlike a bank loan, you don't have to pay them back and, if you are fortunate or choose wisely, they will bring valuable business expertise to your operation. In exchange for which you will relinquish a percentage of equity in your company.

There are an estimated 18,000 angel investors in the UK, investing between £800 million and £1 billion in SMEs per year[2]. Approximately nine in ten are male and over the age of 50. Many will have an entrepreneurial background; some will be semi-retired or have retired from a successful business career (for an example of a business angel, see William Priest's story p.243). An angel will typically invest between 10 and 20 per cent of their wealth in a number of different ventures. In order to be part of an angel network they will have to certify as a high net worth individual, earning over £100,000 per year or having net assets of over £250,000, those assets *not* being a primary residence *or* including insurance contracts and pension benefits. They can also join a network if they meet the requirements of a self-certified sophisticated angel investor.

Your Uncle Robert can act as an angel to your business if you can persuade him to part with his hard-earned cash. However, as a family member, there could be hard feelings if things go wrong. An angel from a network will dust himself off and move on to the next exciting venture.

Angels invest for a number of reasons. It's often a way of staying involved in a sector they understand. There is tax relief under the Enterprise Investment Scheme (EIS) and your company will need to qualify[3]. Angels put in high-risk money, so it's a form of gambling – but a sensible angel will never bet more than he can lose. He will often invest in a company as part of a syndicate with a lead investor; many angels will put in amounts from £10,000 to £25,000 in several different ventures. As we mentioned above, angels expect a return of ten times their initial investment, generally after a three to five-year period. The expected rate of return is high because they anticipate losing money on four in five of their investments. If a single one earns as predicted, it pays for the losses *and* puts the angel in a profit position.

You can find angels by looking at the website for the angel network trade body, the British Business Angels Association. There you will find a list of angel organisations in your region. Angels invest close to home: about one hour's travel or within 100km from their place of residence. They want to be able to visit you at the office, but usually not to pester you. You should choose your angels carefully, and do as much diligence with them as they will with you. Every angel organisation has regular presentation evenings, where companies pitch to qualified investors. You'll receive the information you need to prepare yourself when you make your enquiry.

Given that most angels are over 50 and they like to invest in a sector they understand, you will usually encounter angels who know what you are doing. Remember that evidence of credibility builds trust, and as an older person your business experience can mean that you and your proposition are more plausible. Trust is very important to an angel, so if you can convey your enthusiasm and present a sound plan, you're more than halfway there.

Venture capitalists (VCs) are last on our list of funding sources because they do not usually invest amounts under £2 million, their equity demands are onerous, and they always insist on a fast-growth strategy that puts huge pressure on companies. Unless your business has a very large capital requirement at start-up and no foreseeable revenue stream until later in development, there is no need to share your business with VCs at an early stage.

CHALLENGES FOR 'OLDERPRENEURS'

We would be remiss if we didn't point out some of the difficulties, aside from risk, that are faced by olderpreneurs. The following list is based on one issued by the Silver Academy[4], a partnership between South East Chambers and the University of Surrey.

1. *Personal sacrifice.* It is hard work and the hours are long. There will be an impact on your family. Some new businesses (see Ben Makins' story, page 215) are less demanding in that the owners can create income without a large capital investment and adapt their hours to suit the demands of the business. Not all businesses are like that.

2. *Financial insecurity*. This can be stressful for many people. An uncertain income won't suit everyone.
3. *Loss of company perks.* Start-ups can't afford benefits like pensions and paid holidays.
4. *Isolation.* Being your own boss, or part of a very small team, can be lonely. A network of helpful contacts will ameliorate the situation.

BUSINESS ADVICE

Try to fill in the holes in your knowledge before you get started. Visit the Business Link website for general information: **www.businesslink.gov.uk**. PRIME is an initiative started by the Prince of Wales to assist over-50s in starting their own business. They have an excellent website: **www.primeinitiative.co.uk**. Your local council, college or university may offer courses or know where they are located.

SUMMARY

If you have a good idea – one that you're passionate about – you know you have customers for your product or service, you fit the description of a team member, and you can build a team to drive your business forward, then you may be ready to start your own business.

Most of the attributes that funders seek are the same ones that every business needs. If you're happy to stay small and have a lifestyle business, be aware that outside investors won't be interested. You'll need a scalable business to attract funding.

Seek as much advice as you can beforehand and be sure to find a mentor. As well as customers, your success will depend on having as many positive supporters as you can muster.

PORTFOLIO CAREER

Over time, you've developed a variety of interests and talents. Arriving at a crossroads in middle age can be an opportunity to utilise them and create income streams from several sources. If you do that, you'll have a portfolio career. It might consist of two or more part-time jobs, or it could be a combination of work activities that includes regular wages combined with self-employed earnings from freelance and consulting work, a small business you've set up, or teaching. Any combination would qualify you as a portfolio worker; the key point is that you are doing more than one job simultaneously (in any given week or month), rather than sequentially (one contract following another).

There was a time when this type of career lacked respectability and someone who practised it was called a jack of all trades, perhaps with a tone of derision. That has changed in the past two decades as jobs for life have disappeared and the concept of permanent employment has been replaced with more flexible attitudes towards work. If you decide that this is the route to take, you may also have to adjust your personal thoughts about employment.

'To have a portfolio life you need to think beyond simply having or not having a job.'[1]
Dr Barrie Hopson

The term 'portfolio career' was coined in 1989 by management guru Charles Handy. In his book *The Age of Unreason*[2], he describes a 'portfolio worker' as someone who holds a number of jobs, clients and types of work all at the same time. Handy's five portfolio categories were defined as:

1. wage work: earned as an employee;
2. fee work: payment for results delivered;
3. study work;
4. gift work: for charities, friends or in the community;
5. home work: care of the home and family.

Adrian Bourne, co-author of *Building a Portfolio Career*[3], adds another category: 'Time for you', meaning holidays and non-work pastimes. He says the portfolio concept involves ring-fencing time for all of life's activities.

You may already have an unpaid work portfolio that includes numbers 3, 4 and 5 above. We'll discuss creating a paid work portfolio, combining items 1 and 2, perhaps with additional earnings from a small business you might have. The exciting thing about a portfolio career is that you decide what the balance will be; your work life will not be controlled by a single employer.

Charles Handy practises what he has preached. He resigned his full-time professorship at London Business School to create a 'portfolio life'[4]. For him that means an annual work-life balance where 100 days are spent earning money, 100 days are set aside for writing, 50 days for what he considers 'good works', and 100 days are for spending time with his wife, photographer Elizabeth Handy, with whom he has co-authored several illustrated books.

FOUR TYPES OF CAREER PATHS

To understand the portfolio concept better, it helps to have a look at different career types and compare them with what you have done in your working life. Four categories are defined by Barrie Hopson and Katie Ledger in their book *And What Do You Do?: 10 Steps to Creating a Portfolio Career*[5].

1. Single track: one career

By this, we mean a career as a doctor, lawyer, engineer, or teacher (as examples). This is considered a traditional career, where the end point is retirement at the end of a long climb upwards on the career ladder.

It used to mean job security (which isn't necessarily so any more), a pension and the identity that comes with a job title. In one or two words you can describe yourself to another person. This path is the one that most mature workers have been following. Vocational counsellors told us what we were best suited for, we got qualifications and then we specialised in a particular sector, looking for opportunities to move upwards.

If you've been in a single-track career, it may be difficult to imagine yourself doing anything else or having the time to develop a new work interest. But it's a bit like having a one-track mind: if you see only one thing as possible, then other options don't become apparent.

2. Serial career

Here you can move up, down, or sideways as on a chequerboard, changing sectors – or areas within a sector – every few years. Essentially, it means following your interests. People who do this are motivated by a desire to develop new skills and acquire fresh knowledge; they seek challenges that aren't available in a single-track career. The downside to this approach is that a serial CV may be hard for employers to understand, and people who do this can be regarded as flighty, even though they dedicate themselves completely to any work they undertake.

For an example of a person who followed a serial career path, read William Priest's story on p.243. William has worked as a civil engineer, a management consultant and as a senior vice president in telecoms. Each time he made a change he was pursuing an opportunity that was personally challenging.

3. Lifestyle career

People who do this are adapting their work to the way they like to live, instead of the other way around. If you know someone who works part-time in order to bring up children, or takes an undemanding job so that they can pursue a hobby that doesn't offer financial reward, you've met someone with a lifestyle career. They may not be rich, but it's quite possible they're happy.

4. Portfolio career

The simplest definition is 'someone who has two or more jobs with different employers, one of whom may be yourself'[6]. The jobs may be unrelated, or they may be similar, as in William Priest's portfolio. This is not a substitute for the first three career paths, nor is it having a group of unsatisfactory part-time jobs. It's a strategic way to achieve financial and personal goals.

MOVING TOWARDS A FLEXIBLE WORKFORCE

We've included the definitions above to illustrate that there are options besides the single-track career that many older workers will have pursued. In postwar Britain – as in the rest of the Western world – a single-track career has been the cultural norm. Schools educated future workers to find a single occupation at an early age; agencies, recruiters and coaches guided and encouraged the practice (they still do) because corporate hiring policies demanded it. There hasn't been much room for the Renaissance man, a multi-talented character resigned to history (although nowadays we might call such a person a polymath). Our economy demanded specialisation. It still does, but there is good evidence that things are changing. Corporations are now asking for a flexible workforce; they're looking for people who can bring special skills to short-term projects. Portfolio workers can do that.

It's possible to move between career types. Starting a portfolio career doesn't necessarily exclude you from returning to a single-track or serial career, but it has become a respectable option. The trend began with older workers and is now growing throughout all generations. Bourne says, 'The decline of the old contracts of certainty between employer and employee has led people of all ages to seek a life of careers, not a career for life.'[7]

SUCCESS STORY: **WILLIAM PRIEST**

A portfolio career offers freedom and variety, something that isn't usually available in mainstream, full-time employment. William Priest decided it was his most appealing career choice, because it means he can pursue several interests simultaneously and stay involved with business ventures he is passionate about. William has worked at a senior level in several sectors, gaining experience and developing a personal business strategy that has served him well. He's now applying that strategy to his portfolio career.

His BSc in Civil Engineering, followed by an MSc in Water Engineering, led him to work on agricultural development projects in Africa, at the age of 22. He says he was given the opportunity to manage big projects as a young man (some were funded by the World Bank) because he was prepared to take a risk and work in Africa. He had eight years' experience as a civil engineer when he decided to make a major career change. With a young family to support, overseas assignments were no longer suitable and he wanted to earn more. He chose management consultancy and then spent eight years in the sector, working for PA Consulting Group, Ernst & Young, Unisource NV and Price Waterhouse, where he left as a senior manager when he was offered a job by a client in the telecoms sector. It was a sideways move and one that he made because he was more interested in tackling a new challenge than climbing the career ladder.

William spent three years working for IBM Global Services, growing their European telecoms business. His next move was to take a small step down on the career ladder, a strategic decision that saw him getting promoted much faster than his contemporaries. He started as UK Director of Professional Services at Equant (the global B2B network service provider majority-owned by France Telecom) and finished as Senior Vice President at Orange Business Services (wholly owned by France

Telecom from mid-2005) where he was Head of Global Strategy, Marketing and Communications. How did he do it? During his first year at Equant, he exceeded his performance targets. That got him noticed by an influential board member, someone who was able to help him attain a board position by 2004. He stayed for a further three years and then decided to manage his way out; that gave him the time and money to consider a change.

William chose to spend six months considering his next career move. He spoke to many different search firms and companies – from consultancies to corporates – before joining Airwaves Solutions as Executive Director for Strategy & Marketing. The company was going through a transition and change that led to a major restructuring to focus on core offers and markets. This led to a smaller company and less potential for William to achieve what he wanted, so he saw that it was a good time to re-evaluate his options.

Was a CEO role the next best career move or a more varied and plural career after nearly 30 years of corporate life? Having built up a number of non-executive board roles over the previous couple of years, William felt it was a good time to become more involved with these smaller, entrepreneurial companies. He decided to leave Airwave and embark on a portfolio-based career. He now spreads his time between five organisations – four in the private sector and one large public sector board role. This enables him to bring the experience he has gained in the past to add value to these businesses and it allows him to continue to learn and develop. At the age of 52, he still believes in personal development and growth.

Here's a list of what his portfolio contains:

- **Non-executive Director at WorldSkills London 2011. He advises on marketing, branding and strategy.**

- Board Advisor, investor and Non-executive Director at Intergence Systems Ltd.
- Angel investor in two companies. As well as investing, he is a Non-executive Director.
- Executive Board Director at IP Innovation Partnerships Ltd. The partnership raises funds and invests in start-up businesses and assists them in accelerating sales growth.

It's easy to see from this brief précis that William is an ambitious and self-motivated person (he is someone who moves towards a goal, rather than away from a consequence – see Chapter 2). His drivers have always been challenge combined with opportunity. Staying in the same organisation or sector for a lifetime wasn't as important to him as taking a risk and being rewarded by success in a new endeavour. His career strategy was to keep learning, find new opportunities and embrace risk when it's balanced with common sense. He saw his situation as a mid-life opportunity. Instead of seeking a return to corporate life and the daily grind it entails, he chose to pursue a portfolio career, and he planned for it while he was in his last full-time position. Note that there is an obvious synergy in his activities, given that much of his time is spent in helping new enterprises get up and running.

For those who are considering a portfolio folio career he has the following advice:

- plan for your portfolio while you are in full-time employment;
- use your networks;
- join executive network forums;
- look for opportunities that interest you;
- try things outside of your comfort zone.

Now that William has embarked on a portfolio career his business life is under his control – and it is more creative – something that wouldn't be possible if he was director of a large company. It also gives him the option of returning to South Africa in the coming, years. After all this time, William still has a heart for the region, and he'd like to return in some capacity to work or to support development activities.

IS IT FOR YOU?

Those with multiple skill sets and a wide range of interests and who have little trouble 'changing hats' in the middle of the day or week are suited to a portfolio career. If you're in doubt, answer the following questions:

- Are you self-directed and self-disciplined?
- Are you prepared to take risks?
- Does the idea of working on several different projects excite you?
- Can you handle pressure?
- Are you flexible in your thinking *and* in your work routines?
- Do you like new challenges?
- Would you rather take a low-paying job you enjoy rather than one you dislike, but which pays more?
- Have you got the financial flexibility to manage your life with a variable income?

You don't have to answer 'yes' to each one, but if most of your responses are affirmative, you can move forward with some confidence.

WHEN TO START PLANNING

Ideally, you start to plan your portfolio while you are in employment. But if you have been made redundant and this is the first time you've considered this option, don't worry. In the case of older workers, most portfolio careers come about as a result of a redundancy. For many, a portfolio career is what happens, not what is planned. A part-time job could lead to a private contract, a voluntary role becomes a paid one, then another job is bolted on, until it's obvious that a portfolio exists.

GETTING STARTED

It's best to be proactive and plan your portfolio career. Once again, it's time to get out paper and pen. You're going to imagine a new life for yourself. Note that this is similar to the exercises that you did in Chapter 5, which were aimed at creating a singular goal and a strategy to support it. In this case, there is a plurality of options for you to consider.

Use your self-assessment from Chapter 4 to find your list of motivated skills. These are the abilities you get up in the morning to use – your life would be boring if you didn't. They are your key to creating a successful portfolio. The concept here is to play to your strengths; there's no point in starting new work based on skills that you've had to develop later in life to overcome a deficiency. You may have to use those skills when you undertake a job in your portfolio, but the important thing is to base your portfolio career on motivated skills: the ones you use with enthusiasm, the ones that feed your passion.

Stand back from your list and consider jobs where those skills are used, jobs that may be done on a part-time basis – not one permanent full-time job. You're thinking about teaching a swimming class, not running the pool. Or perhaps you could offer accountancy services to small businesses rather than a major corporation. If top-level management is your passion, you could follow William's example and take on several non-executive director roles.

Now make another list: one that is dedicated to your private passions. Name your hobbies and special interests outside of commercial work. Are you a golfer, a tennis player or a musician? Could you teach any of those skills on a part-time basis? Or is there a product or service that you might create to service a need that you've seen when you pursued your hobby?

This is a creative exercise. You need the time and space to imagine revenue streams that could come from the potential jobs that you've listed. It's useful to consider where you'd like to be in five or ten years time (as you did in Chapter 5), and what your financial needs might be. What work would bring you fulfilment? How would you do it?

GO FOR THE SURE THING – THEN EXPAND

Having made your decision, put your plan into action by securing one job that you know you can do well. You might ask for a part-time position with your current employer. Or perhaps there are clients you can approach who don't need a full-time consultant. In any event, try to have one tent-pole job that you're certain will bring consistent revenue. That's the confidence-builder that will enable you to start your portfolio. You can grow it from there.

YES, IT'S A RISKY BUSINESS

As with self-employment in general, there is risk attached. You may lose an important client at the last minute, or the local authority that employs you in a part-time job decides to make cutbacks. There are no guarantees that you will have the same income every month. But just as wise investors have a broad investment portfolio – never putting all their eggs in one basket – you will have the advantage of spreading your risk across your job portfolio. That's something that a self-employed interim or consultant is less able to do.

There's risk in permanent, mainstream employment as well. We've seen several people come through the Job Club, find re-employment and then return to the club a year or more later when they've been made redundant – yet again. Our economy is changing and there is less certainty all around. Having a variety of income streams can protect you against uncertainty, because it is a flexible approach that allows you to pick up another part-time job should one fall out of your portfolio.

RISK HAS ITS REWARDS

Here's a short list of the benefits of a portfolio career.

- Freedom: you're in charge of your own work life.
- Enjoyment in doing what you like best.
- Flexible security: if one job goes away, you can replace it with another.
- Improvement of your motivated skills: you get better at what you do best.
- Expanded networking opportunities: more jobs means meeting more people.
- Your income is self-generating.

PRACTICAL ASPECTS

There are other things to consider in this type of career.

1. The complexities of PAYE jobs combined with contract and self-employed work are best handled by someone with expertise so you'll need an understanding accountant.
2. You will be creating multiple personas, and so you may need separate business cards and websites for each occupation in your portfolio.
3. Time management is an issue.
4. Is there synergy within your portfolio? Is the whole greater than the sum of the parts?
5. How will your clients perceive you, if they know that you do everything part-time?
6. Consider your long-term career goals. How will this look on your CV if you plan on returning to a single-track or serial career?

YOU'LL HAVE LOTS OF COMPANY

There isn't a great deal of research on the topic, but a recent estimate[8] puts the number of portfolio workers in the UK at well over 1 million, and growing. Anecdotal evidence would indicate that the number is much larger. The Office of National Statistics doesn't measure this type of employment: jobs are full- or part-time, employed or self-employed. But if we consider that there are 6.6 million part-time workers in employment, and 1 million self-employed part-time, then numbers that combine these two categories could total much more than a million.

SUMMARY

A portfolio career has now become a respectable option, one that suits many older workers. Those who enjoy multitasking and have a variety of interests are best-suited to this type of career.

Start by building on your strengths; use a cornerstone occupation – one that you enjoy doing and you know will bring revenue – as the foundation of your portfolio. Expand further and be sure to include your hobbies and special interests. What you may sacrifice in terms of security can be balanced by the satisfaction that you get from using all of your talents. Whether you set out to create a portfolio before leaving employment, or if you have it thrust upon you due to circumstance, approach it with the same care and enthusiasm that you would have devoted to your previous, single-track career. This time, you'll be in charge.

SUCCESS STORY: JUDITH WATTS

If someone had told Judith Watts at the age of 43 that she was going to be a teacher – and still enjoying it at 48 – she would have laughed at the idea. And yet that's what she's doing now. Her career journey led her to a vacancy at a university where she discovered that she had the right background and skills for a position that suits her perfectly. Judith says it didn't happen overnight; it took five years from the time she took her first tentative steps on a creative writing course. But now she says she's really looking forward to the next 20 years of her working life, with further development of her portfolio career.

Judith got her degree in English Literature at York University. Her first job after graduation was managing a bar in Manchester but she soon moved on to starting a business, using enterprise grants. It was 1982, and the company supplied healthy snacks to theatres and cinemas in London. The business didn't last, but this early initiative illustrates that Judith has an entre-preneurial streak – something of benefit to those who develop a portfolio.

She next took a job selling books at Blackwell's in Oxford and then she applied for a job in Blackwell Publishing. Judith enjoyed her first role as publicity controller, and she decided to set out on a career in publishing. Two years later, she had a job in London with Routledge. She started as a marketing assistant, worked her way up, and over the course of ten years rose to a senior marketing manager position, leading a team of 30. She says she really enjoyed the work as it put her at the leading edge in publishing: helping to develop new products and introducing them to the international market – especially the US and Asia.

Her first child was born in 1994 and Judith's job in central London became difficult to manage, so she left. In 1999, she embarked on a two-year stint with a business start-up, offering marketing and training services to the publishing industry. By the time her third child arrived in 2001, she found that a traditional approach to work was becoming impossible. She took a break, one that lasted two years. That was when panic set in: she would need income in the future and she wanted a career plan but she was indecisive about what action to take. She couldn't decide if she should develop her interest in interior design, or take up writing – something she had explored previously by studying journalism. To aid in her decision, she took a self-development course where 'I learned to stop panicking and be positive about the future,' she says. Judith decided to do something she believed in, rather than worry about money. She signed up to a local education poetry course, and enjoyed it so much that she went on to apply for an MA in Creative Writing at Kingston University. Two years later, she had her degree.

While she was studying, Kingston University was growing its publishing degree. One of Judith's instructors suggested she apply for a lectureship. She got the position because she was able to demonstrate a high level of talent, passion and commitment and she was recognised for her previous experience in the publishing industry. Those with experience in the commercial world are valued by universities if they have practical knowledge that can attract students (see Pippa's story on p.122).

Now she occupies a niche where all of her previous experience and skills are valuable. Her advice to those who might be at a similar career crossroads:

- choose something that you're really interested in and passionate about;
- be prepared to work hard at being a beginner;
- don't overthink and bring in doubts – take the plunge;
- consider that your choice is not an indulgence;
- invest in yourself;
- persevere (because it won't be easy).

The teaching role is part-time, which gives her the opportunity to do other things. She's carrying on with an MFA (she may go further and get a PhD) and she is able to perform and promote poetry at local events. It's possible that she'll start a small press.

As a summary, we can say that her years in publishing gave her the career capital that she needed to acquire the teaching role, and she's been able to combine that with her natural creativity to begin a fulfilling portfolio career.

RESOURCES

Some books referenced below may appear in more recent editions than those cited.

INTRODUCTION

The Foundation for Jobseekers (formerly the Thames Valley Executive Job Club Network) is a network of five executive job clubs in the Thames Valley. The clubs assist experienced managers who want to remain economically active, often following redundancy. Each of the executive job clubs is run by volunteers with experience of both management and redundancy.
www.tvexecutivejobclubs.org.uk

The Job Clubs
Aylesbury Careers Springboard
www.careersspringboardaylesbury.org.uk
Sivatech Ltd
Gatehouse Close
Aylesbury
Bucks HP19 8DJ
Meets on a Thursday evening (see website for details).

Gerrards Cross Careers Springboard
www.careersspringboard.info
United Reform Church Hall
Packhorse Road
Gerrards Cross SL9 7QE
Meets on a Monday evening (see website for details).

Bracknell Careers Springboard
www.careersspringboardbracknell.org.uk
Open Learning Centre
Brakenhale School
Rectory Lane
Bracknell RG12 7GR
Meets on a Friday afternoon (see website for details).

West Berkshire Careers Springboard
www.careerswestberks.org.uk
Town Hall
Mansion Street
Newbury RG14 5AA
Meets on a Tuesday afternoon (see website for details).

Windsor and Maidenhead Executive Job Club
www.executivejobclub.org.uk
The Old Vic
St Mary's Church
St Mary's Close
14 High Street
Maidenhead SL6 1YY
and
The Parish and Garrison Church of the Holy Trinity
Trinity Place
Windsor SL4 3BB
Meets on a Thursday morning in either Windsor or Maidenhead
(see website for details).

Chapter 1: The Age Factor

The Centre for Research into the Older Workforce (CROW) carries out research into the nature of the older workforce. It examines older peoples' attitudes to and experience of work, employers' responses to ageing, and policy issues that arise as the government seeks to encourage people to stay in work later in life.
www.niace.org.uk/crow

The National Institute of Adult Continuing Education (NIACE) aims to encourage all adults to engage in learning of every sort.
www.niace.org.uk

TAEN (The Age and Employment Network) works to promote an effective labour market that serves the needs of people in mid- and later life, employers and the economy.
www.taen.org.uk

Books
Hallpike, Helen. *Career Crunch!* 1st ed. London: Lulu Enterprises Inc., 2010.
www.career-crunch.com

Chapter 2: Coping with Redundancy

Jobcentre Plus, part of the UK Department for Work and Pensions, provides an online facility for searching for jobs, career information, voluntary work and childcare providers. The jobseekers web page has a wealth of information on careers, preparing for interviews, CV writing, career change etc.
www.jobseekers.direct.gov.uk

GB Job Clubs is a charity that provides training, resources and a network for job clubs.
www.gbjobclubs.org

Career consultants

There are many companies offering personalised career and job search advice for a fee. These are some we know of personally. By listing them here we do not vouch for them or recommend their services for everyone – their suitability will depend on your needs and personal circumstances.

PCS Executives: **www.pcsexecutive.com**
Proteus Career Consultancy: **www.proteusconsultancy.com**
Connaught Executive: **www.connaughtexec.com**
HDA: **www.hda.co.uk**

Volunteering

The following organisations match volunteers with open positions for volunteers.

www.do-it.org.uk
www.volunteering.org.uk
www.reachskills.org.uk

Books

Kübler-Ross, Elizabeth, and David Kessler. *On Grief and Grieving: Finding the Meaning of Grief Through the Five Stages of Loss.* London: Simon & Schuster, 2005. Kübler-Ross first presented her theory on the five stages of grief in her book *On Death and Dying* (1969).

Chapter 3: Motivate Yourself

Neuro-Linguistic Programming (NLP)

Many of the tools and techniques in this chapter are NLP based. Liam undertook his NLP training with Pegasus NLP (www.nlp-now.co.uk) and they have some useful NLP resources.

www.nlp-now.co.uk/tips-n-tech.htm

Books

Maslow, Abraham H. *Motivation and Personality.* 3rd revised ed. Hong Kong: Longman Asia Ltd, 1989.

Burton, Kate and Brinley Platts. *Building Self-Confidence for Dummies.* London: John Wiley and Sons, 2005.

Ingham, Christine. *101 Ways To Motivate Yourself*. London: Kogan Page, 2007.

Chapter 4: Self-Assessment

Alison Fair contributed the content for the section on 'skills and abilities'. She is a careers counsellor based in Maidenhead, Berkshire. You can see her profile on LinkedIn if you are a member. You can also contact Alison by e-mail: **alisonfairconsulting@yahoo.co.uk**

The Myers & Briggs Foundation is a useful first port of call if you are considering taking an online personality indicator. The website has links to accredited providers and information on results.
www.myersbriggs.org

Thomas International provides behavioural and personality tests based on the DISC model.
www.thomasinternational.net

Books
Schein, Edgar H. *Career Anchors: Discovering Your Real Values*. Revised ed. New Jersey: Jossey-Bass, 1985.
Tieger, Paul D., and Barbara Barron-Tieger. *Do What You are: Discover the Perfect Career for You Through the Secrets of Personality Type*. 3rd ed. London: Little, Brown & Company, 2001.

Chapter 5: Create a Winning Strategy

Adult Directions, from Cascaid, Loughborough University, is a unique online resource which helps adults to make decisions about their career direction. It uses your work-related interests, skills and desired occupation level to identify suitable careers.
www.cascaid.co.uk

Next Step is a publicly funded service that helps adults find the advice they need for future skills, careers, work and life choices.
https://nextstep.direct.gov.uk

Books

Covey, Stephen R. *The Seven Habits of Highly Effective People: Powerful Lessons in Personal Change.* Revised ed. London: Simon & Schuster UK Ltd, 1999.

Chapter 7: Networking or Not Working

LinkedIn is the networking site for managers and professionals with over 80 million registered users, over 11 million of which are in Europe (source: Wikipedia). If you are new to LinkedIn be sure to read the guide (http://learn.linkedin.com) or get someone at a job club to show you how it's done.
www.linkedin.com

Facebook is now the world's most popular social networking site.
www.facebook.com

Twitter is used for instant communication via short 'tweets', which are like mini-blogs. Useful if you can find the right 'streams' and, if you contribute your own tweets, it's a way of networking in social and business circles.
http://twitter.com

Ecademy is a membership organisation for entrepreneurs and business owners.
www.ecademy.com

Toastmasters is a useful club to develop your networking and communications skills while improving your ability to speak in public. Find and join a club near you at:
www.toastmasters.org

Local networking

In the UK, the following organisations run business networking groups on a local basis. They will allow you to visit and try before joining. In some cases you will need an invitation from an existing

member. We do not recommend any particular event or group but list
them here for you to contact.

4Networking:	**www.4networking.biz**
BNI:	**www.bni-europe.com/uk**
Refer-On:	**www.refer-on.com**
NRG:	**www.nrg-networks.com**
Business Biscotti:	**www.businessbiscotti.co.uk**
Ladies who Latte:	**www.ladieswholatte.com**
Local Chambers of Commerce:	**www.britishchambers.org.uk**
Federation of Small Business:	**www.fsb.org.uk**

Business cards

From simple to bespoke designs, effective business cards to use at
your networking meetings are available at:

www.goodprint.co.uk

www.moo.com

Chapter 8: Upgrade Your Skills

UK government adult-learning gateway.

**www.direct.gov.uk/en/EducationAndLearning/AdultLearning/
index.htm**

The Open University: **www3.open.ac.uk**

APMG: the UK accrediting body for project management and IT
service management training organisations.

www.apmg-international.com

Chapter 9: How to Find a Job

Companies House is the foundation of company information
exchange in the UK. You can use their website to research companies
you would like to approach.

www.companieshouse.gov.uk

Below is a selection of job sites that we have used or have had recommended to us:

Executive Grapevine: originally a database of head-hunters, this is now also a jobs board.
www.askgrapevine.com

Exec-Appointment.com: The Financial Times jobs board, 'the global job board for executives in all sectors'.
www.exec-appointments.com

The Ladders: job board for £50k+ jobs.
www.theladders.co.uk

Jobsite: **www.jobsite.co.uk**

CV Library: **www.cv-library.co.uk**

Career Site Advisor: aggregator of job sites by category and career advice.
www.careersiteadvisor.com

Indeed: job site search engine.
www.indeed.co.uk

Executives on the Web: the No. 1 UK executive jobs and career site offering free access to pre-screened senior management jobs across all industry sectors in the UK/EMEA.
www.executivesontheweb.com

Telegraph jobs board: **www.jobs.telegraph.co.uk**

Top-Consultant.com: for consultancy jobs.
www.top-consultant.com/UK/career/appointments.asp

LinkedIn jobs board: **www.linkedin.com/jobs**

Chapter 11: The Interview

GlassHouse Technologies: provides free information on salaries in industries, companies and by profession. Useful when negotiating a salary.
www.glasshouse.com

SHL: provides workplace talent assessment solutions – including ability and personality tests, and psychometric assessments.
www.shl.com

Books

Bolles , Richard N. *What Color Is Your Parachute?: A Practical Manual for Job-Hunters and Career-Changers.* Revised ed. New York: Ten Speed Press, 2010.
Fisher, Roger, and William Ury. *Getting to Yes: Negotiating an Agreement Without Giving In.* Revised 2nd ed. London: Random House Business, 2003. The classic book on negotiation.

Chapter 12: Interim Management

The Interim Management Association has lots of advice about becoming an interim, what makes a good interim, etc.
www.interimmanagement.uk.com

More advice, and information about a one-day workshop, is found on the IMA Institute website.
www.ima-institute.com

PCG (Professional Contractors Group) is an independent not-for-profit professional association that represents, supports and promotes the freelance community, with specific attention to the needs of freelancers who are members of PCG. The website also has information on setting yourself up as a freelancer.
www.pcg.org.uk

Interim agencies

The following agencies have been recommended to us by reliable sources. We do not vouch for them or recommend their services for everyone – their suitability will depend on your needs and personal circumstances. You'll find that some of them serve the public sector exclusively, while others offer services to both the private and the public sector.

Boyden	**www.boyden.com**
Gatenby Sanderson	**www.gatenbysanderson.com**
Odgers Berndtson	**www.odgersberndtson.co.uk**
Penna	**www.penna.com**
Solace	**www.solaceenterprises.com**
Tribal	**www.tribalgroup.com**
Veredus	**www.veredus.co.uk**
Your Choice Interims	**www.yourchoiceinterims.com**

Chapter 13: Consultancy

Top-Consultant.com is the leading management consultancy recruitment website in the world.
www.top-consultant.com

Skillfair is an independent online resource and network that specialises in matching small businesses and freelance consultants to projects.
www.skillfair.co.uk

Chapter 14: Start Your Own Business
Information and advice
The PRIME Initiative provides free information, events and training to help older people (over 50) get back into work by starting their own business.
www.primeinitiative.co.uk

PRIME has another website with practical information for older entrepreneurs. **www.primebusinessclub.com**

Business Link is a free nationwide (UK) business advice and support service, available online and through local advisers. **www.businesslink.gov.uk**

Startups is the UK's leading website for information and advice on starting or running a small business. **www.startups.co.uk**

Growing Business is a magazine for entrepreneurs with a useful website. **www.growingbusiness.co.uk**

Yoodoo takes you through steps in developing a business idea by using online video instruction and interactive exercises. It's free. **www.yoodoo.biz**

Company, trademark, and domain registration
Complete Formations provides information and enables company registration. **www.completeformations.co.uk**

The Company Merchant offers a similar service. **www.thecompanymerchant.co.uk**

Patent Office/Trade Marks Registry: **www.ipo.gov.uk**
Registering a domain name: **www.easily.co.uk**
Another service is: **www.123-reg.co.uk**

Angel investment
British Business Angels Association (BBAA) website is a good source of general information and a way to find an angel network near you. **www.bbaa.org.uk**

London Business Angels: **www.lbangels.co.uk**

Other funding sources
J4B is a comprehensive grants information database.
www.j4b.co.uk

The National Endowment for Science, Technology and the Arts
(NESTA) provides funding and mentoring.
www.nesta.org.uk

Oxford Innovation Ltd supports the exploitation and development of
science and technology, and runs investment networks.
www.oxin.co.uk

Books
Khedair, Jane and Michael Anderson. *Successful Business Plans: Get
Brilliant Results Fast.* Richmond, Surrey: Crimson Publishing, 2009.
Highly recommended. Michael Anderson writes from the perspective
of someone who has been a successful business angel and an
entrepreneur. He is a Director of Business Plan Services, a leading
resource for business planning in the UK.
Southon, Mike and Chris West. *The Beermat Entrepreneur: Turn Your
Good Idea into a Great Business.* 2nd ed. London: Prentice Hall, 2005.
The Beermat series also includes excellent books on sales, marketing
and finance. All of them are useful guides for entrepreneurs.
Gerber, Michael E. *The E-myth Revisited: Why Most Small Businesses Don't
Work and What to Do About It.* 3rd revised ed. New York: HarperCollins,
2001. This is worth reading as a precautionary measure.

Chapter 15: Portfolio Career
Portfolio Professionals offers more information on the topic.
www.portfolioprofessionals.org

Portfolio Careers has a regular blog on the subject.
http://portfoliocareers.net

Books

Bourne, Adrian, Colin McCrudden and Christopher Lyons. *Building a Portfolio Career: How to Create a Portfolio of Roles to Suit Your Work and Life.* 2nd ed. Kemble: Management Books, 2009.

Hopson, Barrie, and Katie Ledger. *And What do You Do?: 10 Steps to Creating a Portfolio Career.* London: A & C Black, 2009.

NOTES

Chapter 1

1 *SERFA Conference: Summary of Skills and Employment Workshop*, 10 March 2009.

2 *ONS Labour Market Statistics*, November 2009.

3 Interview with Isabella Kerr, 16 July, 2010.

4 Cattell, R. B. *Intelligence: Its structure, growth, and action.* New York: Elsevier Science, 1987.

5 Cavanaugh, J. C., and F. Blanchard-Fields. *Adult Development and Aging.* 5th ed. Belmont, CA: Wadsworth Publishing/Thomson Learning, 2006.

6 Department for Business Innovation and Skills, *Statistical Press Release,* corrected July 2010, http://stats.bis.gov.uk/ed/sme/Stats

7 In July 2010, the government announced that it was phasing out the Default Retirement Age, beginning in April 2011.

8 Interview with Chris Ball, TAEN, 8 September, 2010.

9 Hallpike, Helen. *Career Crunch!* 1st ed. p.41. London: Lulu Enterprises Inc., 2010.

10 *The Silver Tsunami,* The Economist, 4 February, 2010.

11 Source: TAEN (The Age and Employment Network).

12 Interview with Professor Stephen McNair, 13 September 2010. At the time of writing, McNair was formally retired, but he retains his positions as Senior Research Associate at NIACE, President of the National Association of Adult Guidance, and he is a member of the UK Advisory Forum on Age.

Chapter 2

1 Kübler-Ross, Elizabeth, and David Kessler. *On Grief and Grieving: Finding the Meaning of Grief Through the Five Stages of Loss.* London: Simon & Schuster, 2005. Kübler-Ross first presented her theory on the five stages of grief in her book *On Death and Dying* (1969).

2 http://en.wikipedia.org/wiki/Elizabeth_Kübler-Ross

Chapter 3

1 *The Concise Oxford Dictionary*, 7th ed. Oxford: Clarendon Press.

2 Maslow, Abraham H. *Motivation and Personality*. New York: Harper, 1954.

3 Carroll, Lewis. *Alice's Adventures in Wonderland.*

Chapter 4

1 http://uk.linkedin.com/pub/alison-fair/4/69/386

2 Schein, Edgar H, *Career Anchors: Discovering Your Real Values*, Jossey-Bass: Revised edition, 1985

3 Isabel Briggs Myers introduced the concept of four dimensions to assess personality: I (Introverted) or E(Extroverted), S(Sensing) or N (Intuitive), T (Thinking) or F (Feeling), P (Perceptive) or J (Judging) and devised a test to determine a person's preference. This is now known widely as the Myers-Briggs Personality Indicator (MBTI). A person who 'is ISTJ' tends to have preferences for Introvert Sensing Thinking Judging.

4 Proteus Consultancy, www.proteusconsultancy.com

5 http://www.cascaid.co.uk/home/main.do?section_id=373)

6 Tieger, Paul D., and Barbara Barron-Tieger. *Do What You are: Discover the Perfect Career for You Through the Secrets of Personality Type*. 3rd ed. Little, Brown & Company, 2001.

Chapter 5

1 Covey, Stephen R., *The Seven Habits of Highly Effective People: Powerful Lessons in Personal Change*. Revised ed. London: Simon & Schuster UK Ltd, 1999.

Chapter 7

1   Based on a method of categorising business contacts according to usefulness in personal effectiveness courses run by Leadership Management International (LMI).

Chapter 10

1   ONS Statistical Bulletin, Public Sector Employment, 16 September 2009.

Chapter 11

1   Bolles, Richard N. *What is Your Parachute?: A Practical Manual for Job-Hunters and Career Changers*. Revised ed. New York: Ten Speed Press, 2010.

Chapter 14

1   *South East 40-70 Tomorrows Workforce Programme, Interim Report:* June 25, 2009.
2   Source: *Business Angel Investing: A Guide to the Legal, Technical & Regulatory Issues*. Found online at: www.bbaa.org.uk/library/file/BBAA_Legal_FAQs_Single_Page_Format.pdf
3   To determine if your company is eligible for EIS tax relief, visit: www.hmrc.gov.uk/eis
4   The Silver Academy was a project designed and implemented in 2010/11 to help unemployed people over 50 to start their own business. It was a partnership between the University of Surrey and South East England Chambers of Commerce, in conjunction with the southern Spanish region of Andalusia and the Malopolska region in Poland.

Chapter 15

1   Hopson, Dr Barrie. *From Vocational Guidance to Portfolio Careers: A Critical Reflection*. 12th Annual Lecture, University of Derby, 10th December 2009.
   www.derby.ac.uk/files/icegs_from_vocational_guidance_to_portfolio_careers.pdf

2   Handy, Charles. *The Age of Unreason*. London: Hutchinson, 1989.
3   Bourne, Adrian, Colin McCrudden and Christopher Lyons, *Building a Portfolio Career*. p.38 Cirencester: Management Books 2000 Ltd, 2009.
4   *www.globalideasbank.org/site/bank/idea.php?ideaId=1100*
5   Hopson, Barrie, and Katie Ledger. *And What Do You Do?: 10 Steps to Creating a Portfolio Career*. London: A & C Black, 2009.
6   Hopson, Dr Barrie, vocational guidance speech as above.
7   Bourne, et al. p. 180.
8   These are the 1.13 million workers described by the Office of National Statistics (August, 2010) as: 'workers with second jobs'.

INDEX